LOOKING FOR DOUG

Doug Walters:
An Australian
Cricketing Legend

LOOKING FOR DOUG

Doug Walters: An Australian Cricketing Legend

NIMAL R. CHANDRASENA

Dedicated to my father, mother and Dilsiri
— for tolerating an obsession with bat and ball
and encouraging the pen

Published in Australia by the Fine Leg Press
17 Billings Way, Winthrop, WA 6150

First published in Australia 2024
This edition published 2024
Copyright © Nimal R. Chandrasena 2024
Cover design, typesetting: WorkingType (www.workingtype.com.au)

The right of Nimal R. Chandrasena to be identified as the
Author of the Work has been asserted in accordance with the
Copyright, Designs and Patents Act 1988.

All rights reserved. No part of this publication may be reproduced, stored in a retrieval system, or transmitted, in any form or by any means without the prior written permission of the publisher, nor be otherwise circulated in any form of binding or cover other than that in which it is published and without a similar condition being imposed on the subsequent purchaser.

ISBN: 978-1-7636564-3-7

 A catalogue record for this book is available from the National Library of Australia

ACKNOWLEDGEMENTS

Cricket has been a consuming passion and obsession for me. It all started around eight to ten years of age, and my interest in cricket has not dimmed much. I must thank my father and mother for letting me indulge in cricket for a long time, from my teen years to adulthood. They could have discouraged the obsession, but they didn't.

I thank my wife, Dilsiri, for coming along the life's journey with me and listening to cricket stories since we met in 1973. Often, she was the sounding board for my excited ramblings when the side I barracked for won a Test match or a favourite player did something remarkable. She also heard my frustrations about a team that I supported losing a game, a nasty on-field or off-field incident involving players, or even an atrocious fielding or umpiring blunder. My family tolerated my freakish obsession with cricket. Listening to my endless stories, they appreciated the fine individuals who graced our beloved sport. They also saw me vent my anger when some cricketers used racial abuse and other disgusting tactics to mentally destabilise the opponents.

Most importantly, I thank Kevin Douglas Walters, *my cricketing idol*, for being that. As I describe in the book, Doug's life intertwined with mine through our shared love of cricket, although he didn't quite know that until we finally met in 2009. We differ on the account that his life was that of a *brilliant batter, an Australian legend*, in the true sense of the word, while mine has been one of a passionate cricket fan and an *armchair cricket tragic*.

Nevertheless, as a researcher, a bit of a cricket historian, avid reader and enthusiast, I've brought our lives together by developing a friendship with Doug and telling this *Doug Walters Story*, describing how it entwined with my personal cricket journey.

I was also fortunate to have an interview with the former Australian Test captain, Ian Chappell, who knows Doug better than most people. I am grateful to Ian for his enthusiastic insights on Doug, which enriched the book. I am also indebted to several friends who reviewed drafts of the book and provided feedback. They include Maithri Panagoda, a Sri Lankan-born Lawyer; Neil Fox, my neighbour and a die-hard cricket fan; David McGilvray (Alan McGilvray's nephew); and Janet Mackay, a librarian friend. I also thank Doug's family and a friend for providing some pictures of Doug from private collections.

CONTENTS

Preface		vii
Chapter 1	The Dairy Farmer's Son Goes the Milky Way	1
Chapter 2	Enter The Champ	13
Chapter 3	A Cricket Freak	30
Chapter 4	Seeing Cricket 'Beyond A Boundary'	43
Chapter 5	An Uncontrollable Passion	58
Chapter 6	Comeback	87
Chapter 7	Looking for Runs and Enjoying It	101
Chapter 8	Plundering Runs	132
Chapter 9	Making Runs – Ups and Downs	154
Chapter 10	Runs Win Matches	178
Chapter 11	Agonies and Ecstasies	202
Chapter 12	Triumph, Defeat, Mateship: All Part of the Game	217
Chapter 13	The Last Stand	241
Chapter 14	Once a Champion, Always a Champion	255
Chapter 15	Different Countries, Different People, The Pleasure is The Same	275
Chapter 16	The Game Has Changed	301
Chapter 17	An 'Artist' to the Core	313
Appendix	Doug Walters – Playing Records	328
	Bibliography and References	330
Index		341

PREFACE

I wrote this book because of my admiration for Doug Walters, a genuinely unique Australian cricketer and my cricketing idol since 1965. When I chose the book's title, it was the literal truth: I had been *'Looking'* for Doug since I arrived in Australia in July 1993.

In early 1994, living in Sydney, one of our family's earliest journeys out of the city was to '*look*' for the township – Dungog – in the Hunter Valley of New South Wales (NSW), where Doug was born and raised. It sounds a bit crazy! At Dungog's Tourist Information Centre, a lady advised me that Doug moved out of the town years ago but was a frequent visitor. She directed me to the local Returned & Services League of Australia (RSL) club, where I could admire a display dedicated to the great cricketer and town hero.

Years later, *I found Doug* serendipitously in 2009. By a stroke of luck, in 2009, I ran into Brynley, Doug's eldest son, to whom I was introduced by a friend (Trish Chadwick) who worked on ecology and environmental science matters just like I did. She had heard that I was a cricket fanatic. Brynley was astounded by my knowledge of Doug and called his father immediately to introduce me. On invitation, I then visited Doug at home in Carlingford, NSW.

Once we met, Doug and I quickly became friends, fulfilling my dream. A few years later, I indicated that I would like to write a book about him to better understand Doug's cricketing history, the social milieu in which he played, and his perspectives on cricket. I clarified that instead of being his biography, I would weave my personal experiences as a cricket fan into the book. *It is the humanity of cricket as a whole*, more than anything else, that my book will attempt to highlight.

Doug is a truly enduring Australian cricketing legend, a fantastic cricketer and a warm human being. Doug epitomises the best 'spirit' of Australian cricket and the best elements of any sport: the passions, skills, joys and the highs and lows that affect sports people. As a 'team player' and 'match-winner', he was second to none, as his former captain – another Australian legend – Ian Chappell attests.

Doug is well remembered by tens of thousands of cricket fans of the 1960s, '70s and '80s for his adventurous, competitive and inventive cricket, sportsmanship and fair play. These are the principal elements of any sport. Doug was always a brilliant 'performer' and an 'artist'. He both played and entertained at the same time. Thus, he commands respect and is much-admired in his community and cricket circles.

Describing Doug as a *Master of Cricket*, Reg Edwards (1977) wrote that at the Sydney Cricket Ground (SCG) if Doug did anything – even something as humble as fielding a slow-moving ball – a tremendous roar of approval rolled down from The Hill from his admirers in the unofficial 'Doug Walters Stand' near the scoreboard. It showed the incredible popularity of the *Dungog Dasher* (Gibbs 1979). But time is passing. We are also getting older by the day. Memories are beginning to fade. Time does not stop for anyone.

Generations of fans born after the 1990s may not know much about Doug Walters' impact on cricket in the 1960s, 70s and into the early 80s. He was, undoubtedly, one of Australia's most loved cricketers. The mere mention of his name often brings a smile to the faces of his ardent fans. He has frequently been described as the 'best-of-the-best' of batters in his era by other cricketers like Ian Chappell and his teammates, including Ashley Mallett (2008: xvi):

> *Doug Walters is a constant in Australia: a national treasure like the Opera House or the Sydney Harbour Bridge. Cricket fans embraced him as one of their own, for here was a national batting hero who did the sort of stuff they did: he drank, smoked, and had a bet and a laugh...*

Doug's legendary stories have been told a few times. His triumphs are also on record and widely acknowledged. Therefore, I am not making an attempt to evaluate him in statistical terms. I aim to tell his enjoyable and enriching story in the way I understand it because it was, and still is, somewhat intertwined with mine.

He has been described as a '*droll*' – a humorous person, perhaps even a jester. But that's only one of his distinctive sides. Doug has a more serious side, too, evident when you get to know him, as I did. He is as astute as any great cricketer, a cricketing gentleman and a humble, extremely generous human being.

But this book is not just a *re-telling* of yarns about Doug. It is unique because it was born out of memories and passions that I *wallowed in* and incubated in my mind for six decades, primarily as a follower of Doug's outstanding career and, secondly, as a cricket fan.

Over many decades, as I wallowed in my collection of newspaper articles, books and magazines, I learned a lot about cricket's history and parochial nature. Its 'Englishness' (Pollard 1992: 1-19; Wagg 2008: 1: 22), power constellations, and how the game changed over 150 years didn't surprise me.

I also learned that cricket is a great leveller. Even the greatest cricketers have ups and downs, just like in life. One has to learn how to accept the good times with the bad. Cricket also helped me cultivate other virtuous life elements, such as respect for opponents, obedience to rules, teamwork and fair play.

Although I found my *métier* – true profession – that of a scientist in the mid-1970s – it was nothing but cricket that allowed me to expand my social network. I won the respect of colleagues, especially in the UK and Australia, and these friendships quickly became enduring because of my knowledge of cricket's history and cricket-related conversations. Therefore, I am thankful for cricket.

People have told me that I am 'freakish' for idolising an Australian cricketer. If fervent admirers are 'freaks' – indeed I am! But isn't Doug Walters worthy of idolising? His sporting prowess, boundless self-belief, and humble persona enriched my life. Since meeting Doug for the first time in 2009, getting to know him has been a pleasure and a privilege. It is not often that a fan is united with their celebrated idol.

More than simply filling pages, *I kept my eyes on the ball*. I made my choices in a way that illustrated Doug's achievements and those of the teams he played in. My motivation included chronologically analysing the games Doug featured in and highlighting his contributions within the context of those games. I also teased various perspectives on current topics in cricket that matter to cricket freaks worldwide.

Burrowing through the ocean of cricket literature was tremendously rewarding as *I lived those experiences*. Although I wasn't there in the flesh to witness the matches, the next best thing was to follow cricket by listening to the evocative ball-by-ball descriptions by the world's best commentators or watching cricket on TV, which is what I did. In *re-enacting* some great moments, I delighted in meticulous research and re-interpreting these events while putting my own spin on them.

From a personal viewpoint, while growing up, cricket was not just a joyful adventure but a *spiritual essence* for me – a life energy that moulded my character. The book is, therefore, the outcome of a *joyful experience*. Although the book is about a person I idolised, I strived not to put Doug on a pedestal. I hope readers will see it that way and enjoy reading this story as much as I enjoyed writing it. I dedicate the book to all cricket lovers, especially the *Doug Walters Fanclub*.

May our great love – brilliantly and appropriately played cricket – prosper for future generations to enjoy as much as we did.

Nimal R. Chandrasena
Perth, August 2024

CHAPTER 1

The Dairy Farmer's Son Goes the Milky Way

I was a kid when I became a fan of Doug Walters in December 1965. What attracted me to Doug was his young age when he made his Test debut. Doug was only 19 years and 354 days old when he debuted. Perhaps in my mind, I dreamt that I could be a young batter like him. That dream did not eventuate, as I had to choose a different path in life. But one thing is sure: I became one of that period's greatest Sri Lankan cricket tragics.

I followed everything Doug did, listening to the cricket commentaries on the radio, collecting pictures from newspapers and magazines, and reading articles and books that had even the vaguest mention of his exploits. I regularly walked about three km to my hometown's Public Library (Panadura, Ceylon), each way from home, sometimes on consecutive days, to read about Doug and cricket in general in newspapers and magazines.

For people to appreciate Doug Walters as a cricketer and his brilliance, it is important to place him in the context of the era in which he emerged and blossomed. Like many great cricketers, his journey had a dream beginning. Doug rose rapidly through the ranks and made an incredible impact throughout most of his career, but he also had many ups and downs on the way. He was the youngest player, and only the tenth of any age, to hit a Test century on debut, even dwarfing Don Bradman.

Born and Raised in Dungog

In this book, dedicated to *re-telling* the Doug Walters story from a fan's viewpoint, I must first introduce the reader to the great cricketer. To do this, I must briefly look into Doug's early life, which is well documented elsewhere. Doug's first book –*Looking for Runs* – was written in 1971 with Richie Benaud's assistance. Doug told me how Richie read every page and made corrections.

In 1999, Doug wrote his second book, *The Entertainers*, which was co-authored by another famous cricketer, Mark Waugh (Walters and Waugh 1999). Both books contain accounts of Doug's childhood, growing up in the Australian bush, breaking into competitive cricket via NSW Colts, the NSW State team and his Test debut. In *Looking for Runs*, Doug also described the cricketers he admired, ending with his views on Ray Illingworth's highly skilled outfit, which beat Australia at home. Doug still greatly respects Illingworth, Derek Underwood, John Snow, Geoff Boycott and Alan Knott, who were the key architects of England regaining the Ashes in that fiercely fought series.

Before I met Doug, I knew of his childhood. Doug grew up in Dungog, a small township in New South Wales. He first learned how to bat and bowl on a rolled antbed and then a concreted tennis court before being selected to play for NSW Colts, the State and National teams. In this journey, and winning many international cricketing honours, Doug became Dungog's most famous son.

Thirty-seven years passed before the much-loved, tall off-spinner and story-teller – Ashley Mallett – wrote a book on Doug. His 2008 book – *The Story of Doug Walters*, is titled *One Of A Kind*. With the title, Mallett was absolutely spot-on. Doug was indeed one of a kind!

Mallett gives an insightful account of Doug's career and personality, which he saw first-hand as a comrade who played many Test matches alongside Doug and one who toured with him several times. No one can touch the admiration with which Mallett described Doug. In my book, I can only recount, with respect, the significant events of Doug's past and achievements, which I watched from a distance[1].

Looking for Runs was also an apt title for Doug's 1971 book because that's what he did – when he came to bat. He wasn't one to be tied down for too long. He *looked for runs* from the first ball he faced – as Fred Titmus, the English off-spinner, found out in the first few balls that he bowled to the 19-year-old on his Test debut in 1965. Doug described this occasion well to Mallett (2008: 9):

---

[1] Ashley Mallett, a West Australian, was a key member of Ian Chappell's team in the 1970s. Along with Terry Jenner, another West Australian, Mallett moved from Perth to Adelaide in 1967 to seek more spin friendly conditions to develop their art (Brettig 2021; Chappell 2021). The move was prompted by two Western Australia's spinners – Tony Lock (captain) and Tony Mann – being ahead of Mallett in the pecking order. The switch to South Australia was a masterstroke. Mallett flourished in a first-class career spanning 183 matches. Mallett played 38 Tests from his debut against England in 1968 and took 132 wickets at 29.8. He finished his Test career against England in 1980.

My second ball from Titmus was flighted a bit higher than the first. I latched on to the length early and jumped down the track to hit it wide of mid-on for four. I guess when you're playing your first Test match at 19, nerves don't really come into it...And if I had any nerves at all, they disappeared with that boundary to get off the mark. Nerves usually do disappear when you get off the mark.

Doug Walters was born on 21 December 1945 in Dusodie, a small town 15 km north of Dungog, in NSW. Born to Ted and May Walters, Doug was the third child: he has two elder siblings, Warren and Colleen and a younger brother, Terry. Ted Walters was a timber cutter who worked in the local timber mill. Doug helped his father drag out fallen logs from the bush when he was about six or seven. Doug was also good at milking the cows, playing cricket and tennis, and hunting rabbits, which was good pocket money.

Mallett (2008: 17) noted that trapping rabbits brought good money for Doug, selling them to the local butcher for two shillings and sixpence a pair. Doug made more money on a good weekend than his dad earned at the mill. Doug recalled that he convinced his father to come rabbiting with him to earn some extra pocket money.

Another well-known story is that *there were no rabbits left in the area*. Doug became an exceptional fielder. Building on his rock 'throwing' skills with rabbits, Doug built a reputation for razor-sharp returns or throwing the stumps down with direct hits from mid-on or mid-off.

Cricket was in the Walters family's blood. Ted Walters was a club cricketer who played regularly for the local Telligra Bs. May Walters kept wickets for a local ladies' team. The four children spent hours playing cricket and engaging in fierce combat. Sometimes, Ted and May joined them in three-a-side contests. Doug also played in the school teams and Under-12 tournaments in the Hunter Valley.

While under 10 years old, he was recognized for his skills by many adults who played in the area with Ted. At around 12, Doug turned up for Under-15 teams, playing with his older brother Warren. In the 'Newcastle' competition, he played for Ted's team, Telligra (in the Hunter Valley of NSW). In those days, Doug loved bowling fast and shattering opponents' wickets. Doug clarified that bowling fast was his first love in cricket, not batting (Mallett 2008: 21-22).

When Ted Walters moved from the declining timber industry to managing a dairy farm set up by the timber company in Raglan, the family moved to a homestead. Doug attended the Dungog High School and became one of the best athletes – in the school. Studies were a bit of a distraction for him; he wasn't born to be a scholar, but he became very good at cricket and tennis.

In a chapter titled *'Cows, Cricket and Cigarettes'*, Doug described getting up at 3:30 a.m. and helping the family to milk about 150-180 cows in the summer. He didn't like milking very much. He found it boring (Walters and Waugh 1999: 23-29). Although the number of cows was reduced to about half in the winter, life at the farm was tough. Nonetheless, Doug never dodged his duties. As a kid, Doug much preferred driving the tractor and ploughing the soil along with other taxing tasks at the farm, which included loading the filled, heavy milk cans when the milk truck arrived (Mallett 2008: 23-24).

* * *

Doug grew up as a sturdy and resourceful kid with strong arms and wrists due to the heavy work on the farm and running around in the bush. Using anthill soil pounded to the ground, Ted made a backyard cricket pitch for the family to play on. This improved Doug's batting technique. One had to be pretty good at defence to survive on the variable bounce when the pitch cracked and opened.

At around 14, Doug attended some coaching classes and net practices at the SCG in Sydney, arranged for promising young cricketers from country towns. It was Doug's first visit to the hallowed SCG, the stage where he would later perform well. At the SCG, he saw some cricketing greats from NSW State's side for the first time and learnt a great deal from them. However, he missed the NSW Schools Under-14 tournament selection because his birth date fell a few days outside the required date. Nonetheless, in 1961, the 15-year-old Doug was given the chance to tour Tasmania with a NSW country team. He made an immediate impact and impressed the seniors.

The young man, still a boy, thrashed a Northern Tablelands team, making 123*, followed by 79 and 72 against Tasmanian Colts and University Seconds, respectively (Mallett 2008: 26). At such a tender age, these feats ensured that Doug got selected for a NSW Country XI and played at the SCG for the first time in 1961. Although he scored only 22 and 38, he impressed everyone. He was seriously spoken about among NSW's highest cricket circles, including Benaud.

Jack Chegwyn and Benaud have a special place in Doug's life. Between 1939 and 1969, Chegwyn, a former Randwick and NSW player, led and managed numerous tours by teams of leading Sydney players to NSW country districts. The teams, known as *Cheggy's Champions*, and the tours to country towns enabled people outside the major cities to see some of the leading State players of the day. They allowed talented country players to be known more widely.

Chegwyn was a respected NSW cricketer and a State selector. One of his favourite jobs was to spend time and effort 'scouting' the countryside for talented cricketers. He is credited with 'discovering' Doug as a potential future Test star from Dungog, a part of the NSW country below the Chichester Dam in the Upper Hunter River region. Chegwyn also discovered the 'mystery spinner', Johnny Gleeson, who played with Doug for several years, from Tamworth, another country town in Western NSW. To name just two, Sir Donald Bradman and Bill 'Tiger' O'Reilly, legendary Australian cricketers, were not *city boys* either. They, too, emerged from the NSW country.

In a match against Cheggy's Champions in 1962–63, Doug hit 51* in the second inning. Chegwyn was actively scouting for talent from the bush and was delighted. As a State selector for NSW, Chegwyn saw that Doug's future lay in him moving to Sydney and playing in a well-known club under State seniors. He persuaded Doug to move from the bush to the city (Sydney), which Doug did.

* * *

Following the success against Chegwyn's team, Doug was picked to play for NSW Colts against Queensland Colts. At 16 years of age, Doug had already become a much-talked-about talented *kid from Dungog*. In the match at the SCG, Doug thrashed the visitors, making 140*. The inning included a huge six, which has also been talked about often. The ball ended up in Kippax Lake, a small water body between the SCG and Anzac Parade (Sydney).

As Doug clarified to Mallett (2008: 30), the distance between the SCG pitch and the lake (about 270 metres at the nearest point) is too far for a huge ball carry to land in the lake. Most likely, the ball bounced a few times across Driver Avenue and the bitumen paths and then rolled into the lake, ending up wet. But the masterful knock cemented his credentials as an up-and-coming star.

Richie Benaud explained in his *Foreword* to Doug's book – *The Entertainers* – that Chegwyn first introduced Doug to him in 1961. Chegwyn told Benaud that the 16-year-old was impressive on the Tasmanian tour and asked Benaud to take Doug under his wing. At that time, Benaud was the captain of the Central Cumberland Cricket Club in NSW, which was, in those days, the Parramatta District Cricket Club, the second oldest cricket club in Australia, formed in 1843.

Benaud was also the captain of the NSW State team, and he obliged. No wonder Doug considers Benaud a father figure in his cricket life because of

Richie's colossal influence. In those days, senior players were always looking for youngsters who could one day play for their state or national teams. Benaud found the youngster to be 'a quick learner, an outstanding talent and a charming personality'.

Doug was only 17 when the NSW selectors named him to play in the Sheffield Shield match against Queensland. Norman Tasker, the sports journalist who co-authored two books with Alan McGilvray (1985; 1987), was the first to tell the Walters family in a phone call. Doug's family was elated at this success (Mallett 2008: 30).

Doug made his Shield debut at the SCG on 31 December 1962. The NSW side was bowled out for 82. In this entry to first-class cricket, Doug was bowled for just a single run by a swing bowler, Barry Fisher, who took 5/18 on the day. But in the second inning, Doug made a solid 50 before being bowled by Col Westaway, a leg-spinner.

At that time, Wesley Hall, the powerfully built West Indian paceman, was playing for Queensland. Still, he didn't bounce Doug in the second inning. When Doug made polite inquiries later from the great man, Hall responded, 'Hey, m-a-an, you were just a kid; I wasn't going to bounce a kid!'. What a generous man the great Barbadian was!

Wesley Winfield Hall, a greatly respected figure in Australia, was knighted in 2012 for his services to cricket and Barbados politics. Doug's recollections of Hall then were that he came off a long and beautiful run-up and was lightning fast on pitches that suited him.

Doug's second Sheffield Shield match was against Victoria, also at the SCG. He was lucky that six members of the NSW team – Benaud, O'Neill, Harvey, Booth, Simpson and Davidson – were all still on Test duty. So Doug got the opportunity and top-scored with 60.

* * *

Doug's career was formed in the summer of 1963-64, his first season with the Cumberland Club. Having left the dairy in Dungog, Doug lived at Wentworthville, a Western Sydney suburb. His first job was as a storeman at David's Wholesale grocery chain at Homebush. Packing grocery trolleys and loading them onto trucks became tedious after a short time. Within three months, Doug moved to work for Grimleys on Sydney's Broadway, a company that sold sports goods. The company gave Doug time off to play for both NSW and Australia. The sale of sports goods picked up with Doug's success in cricket.

After two years with Grimleys, Rothmans employed Doug as a cigarette salesman. This job came with a company car and time off for cricket. One condition of his employment was that, although Doug was a non-smoker those days, he had to carry cigarettes in his pocket and offer them to others. He stayed with Rothmans for 15 years (Walters and Waugh 1999: 27).

Success as a young all-rounder continued for Doug in the summer of 1964-65, a purple patch in his early career. The second string to his bow was his medium-fast bowling that broke partnerships. His record also indicates capturing some prized wickets at critical times in important matches (Edwards 1977a).

Against South Australia, the 19-year-old Doug scored 253 (his highest in first-class cricket). He shared a partnership of 378 in 307 minutes with a 22-year-old left-hander, Lyn Marks. Until their massive partnership, NSW was thought to have little chance in the game, while South Australia was poised for a win. Thus, at 19, Doug became the youngest Australian to score a double-century in first-class cricket. This was a remarkable achievement at that time, given that the country had had so many brilliant past legends and prolific accumulators of runs.

Doug's best bowling figures in first-class cricket (7/63) also came in the same game against South Australia, which NSW won. In the Shield final against Western Australia in the 1964-65 season, Doug made a massive impact by taking 5/92 and scoring 57 and 34*. NSW won the shield in February 1965. Doug scored over 600 runs in the season and took 32 wickets. Thus, at 19, Doug became the NSW State's most impressive performer and the State's leading wicket-taker.

Before the Test debut later in the year, the touring English team under Mike Smith saw him in action. Doug made a century against the English in a match for NSW at the SCG (26-30 November 1965). The MCC scored 6/527, and NSW, led by Brian Booth in the absence of an injured Simpson, replied with 288. The total was anchored by Doug's brilliant 129. NSW only managed 240 in the second inning, and MCC won by nine wickets. It was the first time the NSW State team had been beaten by a touring MCC since 1932.

Notably, Doug *experienced* how the MCC bowlers bowled, especially the off-spinner – Fred Titmus, who would, two weeks later, become the first bowler Doug faced in Test cricket. In that match, Titmus spun most of the NSW batters out, picking up a bag of 8/99.

* * *

Alan McGilvray (1987) stated that although he was raw, Doug Walters had a few years of high-class, competitive Shield cricket behind him when he was selected for National honours. Pundits regard Doug's story as a lesson to all young cricketers on how to have a common-sense approach to life and cricket. Like a father figure, Benaud profoundly influenced the young Walters. 'My father died during my first Test series, and he was only 50. So Richie became a second father. I miss him, and I'm sure everybody misses Richie', he once told the *Sunshine Coast Daily* after Benaud died in 2015.

In his books, Doug admitted how lucky he was to have played under Benaud in the early 1960s. Roland Perry's *Captain Australia* (2000: 212-224) praises Benaud as Australia's best captain in the post-Bradman era. In Benaud's obituary, Frith (2015) described Richie's tremendous impact on Australian cricket for over four decades.

Just like the former Australian captain, Ian Craig and the dashing batter O'Neill before him, early in his career, Doug was likened to Don Bradman and Stan McCabe, legendary heroes. Many saw similarities in the early careers of these run-machines in the way they batted, piled runs and emerged as future stars. However, Doug wasn't perturbed at being heralded as *'Another Bradman'* or *'McCabe Reincarnated'*.

I believe Doug was a blend of the classical attacking batter with a short back-lift and the typical 'compact' style of an Australian batter. This blend allowed him to play freely and make plenty of runs. He was well-balanced at the crease with a classical stance. Film footage shows how still and watchful Doug was at the crease as the bowler ran in. Doug was also relaxed between deliveries, radiating confidence.

He wasn't prone to fidgeting, endless strutting around the crease, box-adjusting, shirt-tugging and bat-twirling that we see these days at the crease. Doug's muscular forearms developed as a teenager, working on the Dungog farm and in the timber mill when he had to support the family's daily activities and income. With this upbringing, it was 'no wonder Doug Walters became so tough and wiry' (Edwards 1977a).

Doug was essentially an on-side player who was very good at using his feet to get to the ball – either going forward or back. But his natural talents were to rely on hand and eye coordination and the strengths of his arms and wrists, like all naturally gifted stroke-makers. Like Bradman and many other prolific scorers, Doug favoured batting primarily off the back foot, which gave him a wider variety of shots. Because his wrists were strong, Doug could also hit decisively off the front foot, even though his initial movement could often be back.

In my reckoning, Doug wasn't too conscious of records and personal kudos. His attitude to run-scoring would have been somewhat different if he had. He was not into philosophical pondering much but far too relaxed as an individual. Long hours of net practice were not for him, but match practice and physical fitness were. He was also not a selfish cricketer and often put his team's position ahead of his interests. Also, unlike many others, he trusted his natural talent and technique to succeed and played with those strengths.

The Emergence of a Batting Prodigy

Doug was born at a time when the world had been turned upside down by World War II, and cricket fans all over the world eagerly awaited the resumption of Test cricket. In that sense, 1945, his birth year, was significant. World War II ended in May 1945.

As many pre-war legends (such as Bradman, Miller, Lindsay Hassett and Ian Johnson) ended their careers, another generation of Test players emerged in the 1950s. It included Neil Harvey, Richie Benaud, Colin McDonald, Jim Burke, Wally Grout, Norm O'Neill and Alan Davidson. They also faded away in the late '50s and early '60s. It set the scene for Doug to burst into Test cricket brilliantly as he did under the age of 20, in the summer of 1965-66.

Barry Gibbs, a former Chief Executive of cricket in two Australian States (South Australia and Queensland), paid high tribute to Doug. In an article for the *Cricketer* (Australia) in 1979, Gibbs (1979) described how he first met Doug in November 1962, when he first arrived in Brisbane as 12th Man in an all-conquering NSW side led by Benaud. Gibbs had heard that the 'cool and confident 16-year-old country boy from Dungog' might soon become Australia's next batting superstar.

Gibbs found it hard to believe that the 'slim, little bloke' had already been marked down for greatness. He observed that Doug's was a case of a young man 'stepping out of the rural paddocks straight into first-class cricket'. Doug's being on the NSW side spoke volumes for him.

The State had successively won the Sheffield Shield nine. Breaking into such a powerful team wasn't easy. But Doug learned quickly as the 12th Man in the company of Benaud and others. A few weeks later, playing for NSW Colts, Doug carved up the Queensland Colts, hitting 140*. From very early days, Alan McGilvray (1987: 61-62), the famous Australian cricket commentator, saw something exceptional in Doug:

> Doug had 'the same individuality about his cricket that Bradman had', and neither ever lost it. They both regarded the best defence as an attack, but sensibly. 'The way he strode to the wicket was something special. He (Doug) had the same country toughness as Bradman when he first came to the city.
> He has the speed of eye and feet that is the hallmark of the good player

and the steely forearms that could whip the bat through the ball like a scythe, cutting hay on a farm.

The *Bradman Tag* stuck for some time. McGilvray compared the introduction of Doug with that of Ian Craig, a former Australian captain, who was also tagged in the early 50s as a 'wonder boy' and the 'new Bradman' but whose career was short. McGilvray (1987: 58) wrote that Ian Craig was a casualty of being rushed into the Test arena too soon. Craig first won Test status at 17 in 1953, as the Australians didn't have young batters to follow *Bradman's Invincibles* of 1948.

Looking to the future, the selectors overlooked the more experienced Harvey and Benaud when they made Craig the captain for the tour to South Africa in 1957-58 and New Zealand in 1959-60. Although the tours were successful, Craig's poor form with the bat and a bout of hepatitis cut his tenure short. It paved the way for Benaud to become captain in the 1958-59 season. The choice of Benaud over Harvey was also a surprise because Harvey had been Craig's deputy on the tours to South Africa and New Zealand (Simpson 1966: 39).

Unlike Harvey and Craig, Benaud had a reputation for being aloof. However, Simpson said that once he became captain, Benaud changed himself to become one of the most admired captains Australia has ever had. In contrast to Craig, before Test cricket, Doug benefitted greatly from the exposure to the senior players in the NSW State team. Doug was already a 'comparative veteran' of four Shield cricket seasons before he was 20, which stood in good stead for him. McGilvray (1987: 61) said, 'The results were instantaneous: a century in his first Test; another century in the second. And by the end of it, what a career!'

* * *

Doug was on the cover of the May 1968 issue of *The Cricketer* (U.K.), batting in the nets. The magazine described Doug under the cation: *'Man of the Moment – Doug Walters'*, as 'The most gifted cricketer Australia has produced for years'. In the same magazine, Richie Benaud (1968) cautioned England to be wary of 'two young ones':

> *Walters hails from the dairy farming district of Dungog, 100 miles from Sydney; he is just as elegant [as Sheahan] in his stroke play, but the power is not nearly as obvious as when Sheahan plays his strokes. I first saw Walters when he came from Dungog one Saturday afternoon to play for my own club, Cumberland, in the Sydney Grade competition.*

> He made 29 that day on a soft pitch, batting against some fine spin bowling from Johnny Martin, and the thing that impressed me most about him was his magnificent footwork. He was a quiet, shy lad then, still a quiet youngster but much more mature.
>
> Over the years, Australia has often produced a fine young batter for a tour of England. Still, it is not often that <u>two</u> such gifted players as Walters and Sheahan come on the one tour. Back in 1930, Australia produced Bradman, Jackson and McCabe for the England tour and without trying to draw pointless comparisons, it is fair to say that Lawry now has with him the best pair of 'new boys' since that earlier trio did so well in England.

Benaud also noted, 'At 22 years of age, Walters had nine centuries in first-class cricket before he came of age; already he captains NSW in the Sheffield Shield and must be one of the youngest cricketers ever to lead a first-class side'. The modest and humble *droll* was also not the first young player to be labelled a *Second Bradman*.

In the same article in *The Cricketer Magazine* (May 1968), the caption under Doug, bowling at a practice session, said: 'Some are already considering him as a future Australian Captain'. This, of course, didn't happen. Nevertheless, Doug was only 23 when he was pressed to become NSW Captain in January 1968 when Simpson gave up the State captaincy. Senior NSW players, such as O'Neill, Philpott, Booth and Grahame Thomas, were also close to retiring. Doug was a reluctant captain at this tender age.

At least for a short time, the burden of captaincy affected Doug, as he returned to first-class cricket after two years of being in the army for National Service and, for a large part, missing competitive cricket. That year, NSW had one of its worst Sheffield Shield seasons as Doug struggled to find form (Edwards 1977a).

In his memoir, Doug said that although he had played under two colossal NSW captains (Benaud and Simpson) and had observed how they operated, he was probably not mature enough to be a captain at that stage. Captaincy was a position Doug had never sought, and he found himself not quite suitable for the burdens a state captain was required to carry. Nevertheless, Doug became the NSW captain again in 1973-74 when John Benaud retired (Walters 1971; Edwards 1977a).

On reflection and comparing with the personalities of successful Australian captains, Doug's somewhat introverted personality also may not have been suited for being Australia's captain. As Simpson (1966) explained, an Australian captaincy was a highly demanding job. One had to be good at captaining the team and holding one's place. One also had to manage many other burdens, including the needs of individual players, cricket officialdom and the pressure from the media.

*   *   *

Doug was a bit lucky in that he had a fast rise through the lower grades of cricket, playing for NSW Colts at 16 plus. Getting called up to the NSW State side to replace one of the six Test players who were unavailable because of Test duties was also a lucky break. In the early-to-mid 1960s, many key players were getting older; they also needed steady jobs to support their families.

Overseas travel, or even travel within Australia, wasn't easy in the 1940s, 50s, and 60s, and this contributed to players retiring early and younger players being sought. Somehow, Doug was fortunate. With his obvious talents, he was unstoppable as he became a regular member of the star-studded NWS State team.

Doug's first test cricket experience was also in that summer of 1963-64 when he watched the touring South Africans play Australia at the SCG (third Test, 10-15 January 1964). Doug saw someone his age – the 19-year-old Graeme Pollock – hit a masterful hundred (122) that day. Australians were led by Simpson against the visitors led by Trevor Goddard (Walters 1971: 65-69). The Australian bowling attack was strong, comprising Graham McKenzie, who combined with Neil Hawke, Alan Connolly and Benaud. None deterred the young left-hander, who emerged as a true batting great.

Following the century in Sydney, young Graeme Pollock reeled off another century in the next Test, in Adelaide (24-29 January 1964), a monumental 175, which Lindsay Hassett described as 'an inning of unusual brilliance and a truly great exhibition of batting', on par with Garry Sobers's century in the first Test in Brisbane in 1960-61 (Hutchinson and Ross 1997: 349).

Richie Benaud had indicated to the selectors that he wouldn't be available for the 1964 tour of England. He was only 34 when he decided to retire. Thus, Simpson became Australia's next captain in the second Test against South Africa at the Melbourne Cricket Grounds (MCG, 1-6 January 1964). Simpson had a dream start to his captaincy, winning that Test with eight wickets. The hard-fought 1964 Australia vs. SA series ended 1:1 with three drawn Tests.

The captaincy change to Simpson went smoothly. After missing the second Test due to an injury, Benaud played under Simpson in the last three Tests before retiring at the end of the series (Perry 2000: 222). Benaud also set a pattern, which Simpson followed in 1968 when he handed the reins to Lawry. Years later, Ian Chappell followed the same way when he handed over the captaincy to his brother Greg.

CHAPTER 2

Enter The Champ

Entry into Test Cricket

Bill Lawry's account of Doug's entry into Test cricket is in Chapter 15 of his autobiography. Lawry named the chapter: *'Enter The Champ'* and paid a high tribute to the emerging talents of the 'willowy, immaculate teenager' (Lawry 1966: 113-126).

The first Ashes Test in the 1965-66 series was played from 10-15 December 1965. One exceptionally significant event occurred during this first test, which will live with me forever. Australia was without their regular captain – Simpson. The selectors (Don Bradman, Jack Ryder and Dudley Seddon) introduced the newcomer- a strongly-built 19-year-old from the bush – *Kevin Douglas Walters* – to Test cricket.

Doug was eleven days shy of his 20th birthday. Instantly, upon introduction to Test cricket, Doug became a batting sensation and my *Idol* as I listened to his performances as a 10-year-old in faraway Ceylon, 5000 miles away. From reading newspapers, books and magazines and watching footage of Doug's batting, I know he was brilliant yet mercurial, laid-back, and a delight to watch.

Unfortunately, I never saw him bat, except on TV and film footage of past Test matches, now available on YouTube. In my interview with Ian Chappell (6th May 2023), he repeatedly confirmed what a 'great player' Doug was. Ian described Doug as a 'great batter, fielder' and 'match-winner' who contributed immensely to Australian cricket.

Doug's emergence as Australia's newest Test star in this 1965-66 series was expedited by the injury to Bob Simpson (a broken hand). Simpson was hit by the Queensland paceman Peter Allan in a Sheffield Shield match a few weeks before the first Test (Simpson 1966: 83-84).

Simpson's misfortune was a lucky break for Doug as a vacant spot suddenly appeared in the Australian line-up. He had been scoring heavily in the Shield matches for NSW, and his hundred for NSW against the touring MCC cemented the selectors' decision. It was a purple patch that Doug went through in the 1963-64 season that got him seriously noticed as 'something special' (Mallett 2008: 41).

Lawry (1966: 114) also explained how lucky Doug was as the selectors had seriously pondered whether Alan Connolly should play as a third seamer in the match. In their wisdom, they had finally decided that the pitch was nothing more than a sparsely-grassed, typical Brisbane pitch and chose to play Doug as a batting all-rounder.

As the events transpired, in his debut Test, Doug became the first change bowler to the two pacemen – Peter Allan and Neil Hawke. On the eve of the match, Graham McKenzie had been pronounced unfit to play, which was a blow to Australia (Simpson 1966: 84). The absence of Simpson meant Ian Redpath would open the batting with Lawry, followed by Bob Cowper, Peter Burge and Brian Booth. Doug was also expected to strengthen the middle-order batting.

The selection of Doug as an all-rounder was a close call and typical of the *fortunes and breaks* players experience. In the end, Doug bowled as the first change. He took a wicket in each of the two England innings (10 overs, 1/25 and 5 overs, 1/22), proving to be a valuable all-round asset. Lawry (1966: 113) wrote in praise of Doug:

> *Supposing he had missed the first and second Tests and then came in for the third Test on that difficult Sydney "turner". Or, perhaps, the fourth Test, where he was out for a duck! No matter. Nothing could have more than temporarily held back the ascent of young Walters to the forefront of the world's most exciting batter...A new star was climbing into the cricketing firmament.*

Lawry also said, 'Doug Waters was Australia's most talented young batter since Neil Harvey'. Lawry noted: 'Doug's eyes were scarcely adjusted to the light before he despatched a Titmus off-spinner flashing to the boundary. Thus was launched an amazing young cricketer on what could well become an amazing career'. Doug's career blossomed from that eventful week in December 1965. His travails are well documented in his and Mallett's (2008) books. They show the agonies and ecstasies of a developing cricketer who later became a great but poorly paid professional.

But to this date, as a supreme entertainer, Doug remains an antithesis to some of the overly aggressive Australian cricketers of the late 1980s, '90s and the millennial decades who disrespected their opponents. Even the hard-nosed Australian cricketers freely admit that Doug is much loved by the public for being a classical cricketer. Many of his peers have also said that Doug is admired and will not be forgotten because he is such an easy-going, *cool guy* and a *good bloke*.

* * *

In Simpson's absence, Brian Booth captained Australia on that day in the first Test of the series (10-15 December 1965). But rain spoilt the Test, permitting only 36 overs on day one and washing out the second day. When the match began, the pitch had sweated under the covers. Simpson said (1966: 84) that batting wasn't an easy pitch.

However, after winning the toss, Booth elected Australia to bat first, possibly because of the likelihood that rain would affect the match later on. Even with the stops and starts, Lawry started the series well, defying the English pace attack of David Brown and Ken Higgs, who moved the ball under the overcast conditions. Only two and a half hours of play was possible on day one, and with rain breaks during the day, Australia reached 1-79, losing only Ian Redpath (17).

The second day, a Saturday, was washed out, and rain continued on Sunday, the rest day. However, Monday 13th December was clear with no rain when Australia resumed their innings. David Brown was lively, and a few wickets fell quickly at the beginning of day three (Cowper, 22; Burge, a duck and Booth, 18) while the dour Lawry dug in. Australia was in a tight spot at 4 for 125 when the debutant – Doug – walked in for his first Test innings.

The state of the game might have strained the nerves of even the most seasoned of players. The off-spinner, Titmus, had just caught and bowled Booth for 18. He was bowling with a good rhythm and gaining considerable turn. However, the 20-year-old Doug settled in quickly. As Simpson recalled (1966: 86), 'Doug showed no nerves but with poise and confidence, set about the bowling with power and aplomb'.

In describing the scene accurately with Doug's help in recalling the first few minutes, Mallett (2008: 8) wrote:

> *Doug met the first good-length delivery in the middle of his bat. Although he only pushed the ball back to the bowler, Doug's face lit up and his smile got bigger and bigger as he watched the rocking motion of the bowler.*
>
> *Titmus cradled the ball in both hands as he moved in. He had a classical sideways action, spending lots of time on his front foot. He rocked back and forth, spun the ball appreciably at times and was unerringly accurate...*
>
> *But Doug had 'seen' it all before. He had watched Titmus' action for years: the family would gather around a roaring fire in their lounge room, and they would all listen intently to the wireless as the Tests in England were fought out.*

Doug was superb on his feet, finding the gaps, cutting and driving the two experienced off-spinners Fred Titmus and David Allan, which forced Mike Smith to change his field many times. Still, he beat the deep-set field with precise placement. 'He relished the pace bowling even more than the spin and made the formidable Brown look easy to hit all over the field' (Simpson 1966: 86). The English bowlers surely misjudged the young man's maturity, courage and talents.

As I listened to the Australian Broadcasting Corporation's (ABC) cricket commentaries of the unfolding events in the Test in Ceylon, my ears strained to get every description the commentators gave. I recall how Doug batted calmly, sharing a 187-run stand with the experienced Lawry for the fifth wicket, thus stabilizing the Australian inning. Lawry compiled 166, while Doug made 155, hitting 11 fours and two sixers.

His innings lasted a little over five and a half hours. When Doug approached his debut hundred, a small dog ran onto the pitch twice. The dog first ran in when Doug was 89 and reappeared when he was 93. The dog held up the play on both occasions. A horde of small boys hopped over the fence and chased the dog. The English fielders sat on the turf for several minutes while Doug leaned on his bat and waited.

Commentators wondered – *Did it break Doug's concentration?* Doug said it didn't, but it had the opposite effect: calming his nerves. Also, the stoppages gave him a bit of a breather. But when the officials bundled the dog away, Doug resumed his innings calmly as if nothing eventful had happened. Taking his time, run by run, he crept up to 98 and hit a perfect on-drive through mid-wicket for a four to reach his debut hundred. It took him fifty minutes to creep through the nineties.

* * *

Entering the Test cricket arena, like a seasoned gladiator, the impish youngster had batted his way into Ashes history. He was the youngest player, and only the tenth of any age, to hit a Test century on debut, even dwarfing Sir Don. In so doing, Doug surpassed the Test debut of Don Bradman, the acclaimed greatest batter in cricket [2].

Praising the young Walters, on the following day, a leading newspaper, *The Australian* screamed: *Toast of the Test*. Other accolades flowed, invoking the Don. In the *Wisden* report, Wellings (1967) said:

---

2   Bradman only made 18 and 1 on his Test debut (first Test of the 1928-29 'Ashes series; 1-5 November 1928), at the Exhibition Ground, Brisbane). Bradman was then made 12th man for the second Test. Recalled for the third Test (MCG, 1-5 January 1929), he made 79 and 112, thus becoming the youngest man to score a Test century at that time, launching an incredible career in which he scored 6996 runs at 99.9 in only 52 Tests.

Walters, who became the ninth Australian to score a century in his first Test, in particularly testing circumstances, confirmed his class by his mature batting in an inning lasting five hours twenty-two minutes. With his quick footwork, he played Barber's leg breaks particularly well. In one over, he hit Barber for four fours and later hooked him for six. He also drove Titmus over mid-off for 6 and, in addition, hit eleven 4's.

Doug became a national hero overnight (Haigh 2006: 281). The famous English journalist Ian Wooldridge, writing in the London Evening Standard on 13 December 1965, while the match was going on, said it was *'Young Bradman All Over Again'* (Mallett 2008: 43):

From the moment he met Titmus' second ball a yard out of his crease and struck it cleanly into the long-off fence, it became impossible to avoid the comparison with Bradman. Walters is straight, correct, deceptively strong, unashamed to loft the ball into the air, unimpressed by any reputation and totally run-hungry.

The great leg-spinner Bill O'Reilly, whom Bradman considered the best-ever bowler of any type he ever played with or against, writing in his *Sydney Morning Herald* column, said as follows:

England's captain Mike Smith crowded two short legs and a silly point into the close positions for Titmus to give Walters a searching personality test. The youngster came through it like a veteran.

In fact, he shaped up aggressively. Throughout his long innings, it was obvious that Walters was holding many of his aggressive shots in check. The lofted on-drive, for instance, seldom came into play.

'Dairy Farmer's Son Goes the Milky Way' was a Newspaper headline I saw in Colombo. The article also published a photo of Doug seated, chatting with Don Bradman. The newspapers in Australia screamed – *Doug Walters – a Huge Talent* – and the Reuters reports in Ceylon echoed the same sentiments.

Simpson (ABC 1976: 102) said that he doubted any player had made such a dramatic impact in a first appearance since the days of Norm O'Neill. As a kid, I was thrilled by listening to Doug's assured batting display, so vividly described by the commentators as the crowd went into raptures with loud cheering that went on for several minutes.

Photographs show that Ken Barrington was the first to congratulate Doug, followed by Geoff Boycott. It was a crucial debut for a youngster, launching a Test career – the moment deeply appreciated by those two great English batters. They knew what it was all about, to emerge as a new 'batting star'.

When Doug returned to the pavilion, 119*. Bradman was sitting on the first chair near the Australian dressing room. Doug recalled: 'He stood with his hands out to congratulate me...he shook my hand and said, 'If you need my advice, come and see me'...I guess Bradman said that to a lot of people'. However, Doug said he had never sought Bradman's advice during the next 15 years of his career. However, Doug recalled having many pleasant exchanges with The Don over the years, as the great man served as chairman of the panel of selectors from 1948 to 1971 (Mallett 2008: 242).

* * *

After the second day was rained off, and when play resumed on day three, Lawry batted carefully and was finally dismissed for 166 (in seven hours), caught behind by Parks off Higgs. Lawry's stubborn inning included 20 fours. After his memorable 155, showing 'deft footwork and a range of strokes' (Frith 1997), Doug, too, went the same way, caught behind by Parks off the bowling of Higgs.

The English press criticised Lawry as having 'declared war' by staying at the wicket unmoved after an appeal for a catch behind off Brown. Lawry always said it is the umpire's job to give a batter out if he thought so, an opinion echoed by Simpson (1966: 90) and Ian Chappell. They believe that a batter should be entitled to any benefit of the doubt where there is doubt about dismissal in an umpire's mind.

Australia declared at 6/443, holding an advantage. But they had batted nearly nine and a half hours in making these runs. As the first inning ran into the fourth day, a result was unlikely. England replied with 280. Jim Parks (52), Ken Barrington (53), Geoff Boycott (45) and Fred Titmus (60) batted defensively and carefully on day four. Peter Philpott, the right-arm leg-spinner from NSW, took 5/90.

England was 163 behind, and Booth forced the follow-on, knowing well that a result may not eventuate as the Australian attack wasn't at its best, mainly due to McKenzie's absence. It was just a psychological move on the last day. England again batted well to reach 3-186, playing some bright cricket and saving the match simultaneously.

Boycott (63*) batted throughout the three and three-quarter hours, supplying solidity. His batting, combined with Edrich (37), Barrington (38) and a swashbuckling knock by Bob Barber (34 in 37 balls in 45 minutes), showed that England could also play entertaining cricket. The series would be a close contest between the evenly matched teams.

Doug's performance delighted the whole of Australia, which saw his emergence as a great hope for the future. England saw him as a real threat in the series. Star batters – Harvey and O'Neill – had retired by this time. O'Neill's premature retirement, at only 28, was a massive loss for Australia because he was a peerless stroke-maker who made batting an art form. To fill the gap left by them, Australia needed a top-class batter and seemed to have found one in Doug. His brilliant fielding and medium-fast bowling were added bonuses.

Seeing Lawry's stubborn application at the other end helped Doug steady his nerves initially. Appreciating Lawry's impact, Simpson (1966: 85-87) doubted whether Doug would have played his innings the way he did without the reassuring figure of Lawry at the other end.

Lawry batted on after Doug was dismissed with the score at 5-312 and had another century partnership with Tom Vievers (56*) before Australia declared at 6-443. When Australia bowled, Doug was also the first change bowler after the pacemen Peter Allan (who played only this Test in his career) and Neil Hawke. Doug took a wicket each in the two innings, which proved his all-round value.

* * *

Bob Simpson returned to the side in the second Test played at the MCG in Melbourne (30 December 1965-4 January 1966). Illness and injury kept Brown and Higgs out of the England side, and they were replaced by Jeff Jones and Barry Knight. The match was drawn mainly due to England's slow batting.

Australia's 358 on a two-paced, greenish wicket was built around the runs of Simpson (59), Lawry (88) and Cowper (99). Doug made 22 before being caught behind again, this time off Barry Knight, who took 4/84. When England batted, they made a large total of 558. They took the upper hand with some daring top-order batting and solid batting in the middle (Simpson 1966: 94). England's score included centuries from Edrich (109) and Cowdrey (104) and half-centuries by Boycott (51), Barrington (63), Parks (71) and Titmus (56*).

Graham McKenzie, back in the side after missing the first Test due to a back ailment, bowled tirelessly, taking 5/134 off 36 overs. Doug bowled 10 overs for 32 runs and took Boycott's crucial wicket. Australia began their second inning 200 runs behind and needed to bat well. Another 100-odd Simpson-Lawry opening stand gave Australia's second reply a good start. Simpson made 67 and Lawry 78, but at one stage, they were 4-176, still 24 runs short of England's lead when Doug joined Peter Burge, the burly Queenslander.

Burge wasn't in top form and was scratching around with 30-odd. Doug then proceeded to make his second consecutive century of 115. It showed everyone that the debut hundred in the first Test was not just a flash in the pan. Simpson (1966: 96) said Doug's was a *'gem of an inning'*, which helped the more senior man, Burge, find form, set about the English bowlers, and crack 120. Burge did not finally yield his wicket until he and Doug had assured their side of a draw. They put on 198 in just over three hours, and both played supremely well.

Doug was finally caught and bowled by Barrington, bowling leg-breaks. The press noted that England missed Brown and Higgs in this Test. The two opening bowlers, Jeff Jones and Barry Knight, were ineffective. The two specialist spinners – Titmus and Allen, backed up by the part-timers – Barrington, Boycott, Barber and Smith himself- could also not dislodge Burge and Doug as they sought to attack.

Simpson (ABC 1976: 103) said that while Doug batted superbly, he was again fortunate to have an experienced batter at the other end as Australia (426) forged a 236 lead. England had only two overs to bat out, resulting in a drawn match. But it was an excellent match for Doug. Once again, he entered the annals of cricket history. After Bill Ponsford, the great left-handed opener of the 1920s and '30s, Doug became the second Australian batter to notch a century in his first two Tests. Commentators quickly pointed out that a tremendous cricketing talent had arrived, much like Don Bradman had done forty years earlier.

* * *

I also remember the third Test in Sydney (at the SCG, 7-12 January 1966) well. I was seriously infected with the *cricket bug* by this time. Brian Booth captained again as Simpson was struck down by chicken pox. England won the toss, batted first, and was well past 200 without losing a wicket. When Boycott was out for 84, the opening stand with the left-handed Bob Barber was 234.

Barber's inning (185) ensured that England won within four days. His inning and Edrich's 103 set up England's total of 488. Simpson (ABC 1976: 103) described Barber's innings as one of the best played in Australia. Hardly known in Australia then, Barber 'became the fuse, which ignited the English batting on tour' [3].

I remember how infuriating it was for me, listening in Ceylon as the

---

3   Incredibly, this was Barber's only century in his 28 Test career between 1960 and 1968 in which he averaged 35.6 and hit nine other fifties. The 1965-66 tour was a purple patch in his career. In 13 matches (22 innings), in Australia, he was the only player to pass 1000 runs at an average of 50 (Wellings 1967).

opening stand went on past 200 to a score of 234. This was followed by a second partnership of 69 with Edrich. In both, Barber scored most of the runs, and England scored 2-303 when he got out. Neil Hawke's lion-hearted effort (7/105 in 33.7 overs) contained England.

Wellings (1967) noted, 'When Barber succeeded, runs gushed like oil from a new strike'. Barber played exclusively attacking cricket from start to finish, and his 185 off only 255 balls in the innings took just under five hours and included 19 fours. It was described as an innings of magnificent aggression and 'the most superlative achievement of the whole tour' from an English viewpoint.

In reply to England's 488, Australia managed only 221. Cowper batted slowly for four hours, making 60, and the newcomer Grahame Thomas[4] made a half-century of fighting (51). Doug failed in the first innings for 23. David Brown took 5/63; Jeff Jones and David Allen took two wickets each. Supporting the Australians, I wasn't impressed with their show, as their batters collapsed again in the second inning, as the two off-spinners took advantage of the turning pitch.

Fred Titmus and David Allen took 4/41 and 4/47, respectively, as they bowled Australia out for only 174 in the second inning. Doug batted for over two hours for 35* and ran out of partners to save the match. Writing in *Wisden*, Wellings (1967) heaped more praise on Doug for batting so well on a turning wicket:

> *In the follow-on, the off-spin of Allen and Titmus was decisive on a broken pitch. The longest stand was 46 for the first wicket by Thomas and Lawry, but Walters was again responsible for the best batting. For two hours, he played the turning ball with rare skill. So, he came off splendidly for the third time running when his side was in difficulties.*

England deservedly won by innings and 93 runs, which ignited the series. The English press praised Smith's captaincy for inventive field settings, supporting the two off-spinners. It was England's first win by an innings in Australia since the 1936-37 series, when Bradman became Australia's captain for the first time and 'Gubby' Allen captained England. Wellings (1967) reported that England's success in Sydney was determined by winning the

---

4   Grahame Thomas was a player with mixed parentage (a part-Aboriginal, part-American Indian by birth). He was a hard-hitting batter from Sydney who debuted in the Sydney Test, partnering with Lawry, in Simpson's absence. I was too young to understand the implications of 'coloured' players in those days.

toss and first use of the pitch, which became more and more favourable to spin bowlers.

Lawry was blamed by the English press for his selfishness and for running out his partner Peter Burge in the second dig. London's *Daily Mirror* reported, 'Twelve men have won the third Test match. Eleven were Englishmen. The twelfth is an Australian, William Morris Lawry. By his selfishness, no less, he hastened his country's defeat'.

* * *

Simpson was fit and resumed as captain in the fourth Test (Adelaide Oval, 28 January-1 February 1966). Australia dropped Booth, Cowper, Philpott and Sincock, making way for Simpson, Veivers and two young bowling all-rounders – Ian Chappell and Keith Stackpole.

Cowper was dropped for slow scoring in the previous Test. A fifth change also discarded McKenzie, but a late injury to Peter Allan caused a recall of the fast bowler. Wellings (1967) wrote that the 'changes cleared away the cobwebs and stirred the survivors to keener effort'.

England batted first and was bowled out for 241 despite several batters getting starts (Cowdrey 38; Smith 29; Parks 49 and Titmus 33). Barrington made a half-century (60) before running himself out. McKenzie was at his best, capturing 6/48. A record 244-run opening partnership by Simpson (225) and Lawry (119) led Australia's fight back to square the series. They bettered the 234-run partnership of Barber and Boycott in the previous Test at the SCG. It was also Australia's highest partnership for the first wicket in Tests.

Simpson's imposing performance, still recovering from chicken pox and hardly fully fit, and then a nine-hour long inning was praised by everyone. Scoring his 225 out of 480, Simpson hit one six and eighteen fours. Countering England's go-slow tactics, Simpson and Lawry scored fast, running 95 singles in their 244-run partnership. This tactic ran England's fielders ragged, and Mike Smith didn't know how to stop the run flow. England's first change bowler was Boycott. It showed a lack of bowling depth. At No. 3, Grahame Thomas attacked (52 in 75 minutes) in an 85-run stand with Simpson, helping the captain build the Australian total.

On debut, Keith Stackpole, at No. 8, made a solid 43. As Doug said, his 'bubble burst' and his 'feet came down to earth pretty quickly' when Parks caught him again, off Brown, for a duck. Jeff Jones, the left-arm fast bowler, finished with 6/118.

Replying to the Australian total (516), England collapsed to accurate bowling, again from Hawke (5/54 in 21 overs). Doug was Simpson's first change bowler. He took a wicket in the first inning (1/50 in 14 overs) but went wicketless in the second (0/47 in nine overs). Chappell and Stackpole added variety to the bowling and also made valuable late-order runs.

As I listened intently, England resisted with resolute batting from Ken Barrington (102, his 15th century and fourth against Australia) and late-order resistance of Fred Titmus (53), which only delayed England's defeat by innings and nine runs. Barrington stayed five and a half hours for his century, which contained only four fours. Australia squared the series, and I remember being delighted. With the loss looming, Titmus hit Doug for four boundaries in an over at one stage to reach his fifty.

The press said Australia's batting in the match was 'light years ahead' of England's – Barrington and Titmus excepted. I knew Australia would win when the Simpson-Lawry stand blossomed into a double century and passed England's first-inning score. Simpson's return gave extra strength to the team, which lost so badly in the third Test. Wellings (1967) said McKenzie and Hawke formed a match-winning pair for Australia.

* * *

The fifth and final Test at the MCG in Melbourne (11-16 February 1966) was also rain-affected but dominated by Bob Cowper's triple hundred (307), ensuring Australia did not lose the series. I remember hurrying home from school to check the scores on the radio.

As soon as I walked into my home, my grandfather, listening to the broadcasts that day, informed me with all smiles that 'Cowper made a triple hundred'. I was elated. Cowper, a Victorian left-hander, had been a solid performer for many years in the team. However, he was dropped for the Adelaide Test for slow scoring in the third Test.

With the series locked at 1:1, England pressed to claim the Ashes. They won the toss and batted. Barrington hit a second consecutive hundred, scoring 115 in only 122 balls faced, bringing his 100 up with a six, thus becoming the first person to do so twice in Ashes Tests. Adopting a buccaneering style, he thrashed two sixes and eight fours in under three hours. The score was 3-219 when he fell, and the pace slowed. Edrich made 85; Cowdrey, 79; Parks, 89; and finally, Titmus needed over two hours for his 42*. Finally, England declared at 9/488.

In reply, Australia batted for over two days and declared 8/543. Making 307, Bob Cowper batted for over 12 hours, hitting only 20 fours, before Barry Knight bowled him. It was one of the longest innings in Test history. Cowper surpassed Don's 299*, the highest individual score in Australia then. Doug struggled a little in making 60 in four hours, facing 201 balls. A strike rate of about 30 runs per 100 balls faced was unusual for Doug.

Lawry made 108, his fifth century against England. Still, it took over six hours, contrasting with Barrington's, which took under three hours. When Lawry and Cowper added 212 for the third wicket and batted for five and a half hours, the match was already half-dead. Cowper's stand with Doug was 172 runs. The score was 4-420 when Doug departed. By batting for more than two days full, Simpson shut the match down and drew the series 1:1. England had no choice but to bat out time, finishing on 3/69.

The fear of losing frustrated the good intentions with which both sides entered this quickly-to-be-forgotten Test match. It was a sour ending to an appetising tour in Australia (Wellings 1967). Listening in Ceylon, I didn't see it like that. As a kid, I thought *this was normal 'Test' cricket*. The slow grind didn't matter, as I enjoyed the commentaries. I still dreamt each day about these epic batting feats of my heroes. I paid no attention to the 'dull' cricket I read about in the newspapers.

During the season, Lawry batted over 41 hours and averaged under 24 runs an hour, a *snail's pace* by today's standards. Wellings (1967) noted that Lawry was a tedious accumulator of runs, 979 in 11 innings. This was also Wally Grout's last Test as Australia's wicket-keeper.

* * *

Mike Smith's men flew by air to Australia in 1965-66 for the tour with a brief stop-over in Ceylon. Flying to Australia *spooked the team*, while it shortened the time away from home (Wellings 1967). The main disadvantage of flying was the sudden switch from a cold English autumn to a hot Australian summer. The time for acclimation was too short. The taller players also didn't enjoy the discomfort of economy class, and several suffered from stomach ailments and viral 'flu-like' symptoms before landing in Perth.

As the manager Billy Griffith later wrote, 'the sudden, rather than a gradual change in climate and playing conditions, denied the squad a chance to acclimatize properly, and there was less time for team spirit to be forged' (Tuberville 2021). Aware of Mike Smith's natural caution, the MCC had given Billy Griffith extra powers above a regular tour manager, allowing him overall control of cricket on tour. He was to force players to play entertaining cricket to draw the public and win more respect for England's cricket, which had been branded dull and boring. But Griffith hardly used those powers and preferred the diplomatic route. Nevertheless, he urged attacking cricket in the tour (Wellings 1967).

It was a 1-1 drawn series. However, it has remained indelible in my mind because of Doug's emergence. I didn't know then that the previous Ashes series (1958/59 and 1962/63) had been regarded by cricket fans as so dull that the English arrived in Australia determined *to entertain*. This was not the case, as the team was jaded and tired at the end of the hot Australian summer and the drawn series.

Alan McGilvray (1985: 107) explained that Simpson and Lawry comprised one of the finest opening pairs in Australian cricket and took the same stubborn approach to their captaincy. Despite unimaginative captaincy, they made Australian cricket secure by not being beaten. While they scored big, winning a game became laborious and not a priority in those days.

Between the more adventurous captains (Benaud and Ian Chappell), in 20 Ashes Tests, only six had a result, three wins each. Fourteen draws were testimony to an attitude on both sides that kept Ashes Test cricket on a low simmer as far as excitement went. Thankfully, this 'dull' form of Test cricket did not last long, as the 1970s brought an era of intense and thrilling contests under Ian Chappell's leadership.

Wellings (1967) criticised M.J.K. Smith for allowing his bowlers to waste time. The required rate was 15 eight-ball overs per hour. In the final test, England's bowlers averaged only 96 balls per hour (12 overs). Wellings (1967) also said: 'However amiable Smith was in the way he captained the team, the slow tempo of this England side was a serious failure on his part as captain. This was one of the reasons why Cowper, Lawry and Walters were unusually slow in their run-scoring in the fifth Test'.

* * *

Doug's first Test series performances (a tally of 410 runs at 68, plus nine wickets for 283 at 31) were good news for Australia as it was looking for all-rounders. These performances established Doug as a regular in the team. The country knew another 'gem' had been 'found' from the bush, and it wasn't the first time. Doug was named *Australia's Cricketer of the Year in 1966*. Doug quickly became a 'mature' cricketer, not because of years but because of a positive outlook.

Reporting in *Wisden*, E. M. Wellings (1967) heaped praise on Doug:

> *At nineteen, Walters was a remarkably mature cricketer. He made a century in his first Test in Brisbane when four wickets had gone for 125, another in the second when he and Burge saved the match. In the third, he alone was able to fight long against Allen and Titmus on a turning pitch.*

His bowling also was useful enough for the selectors to dispense with a specialist third seamer.

Returning to Dungog, Doug received a hero's welcome after these successes. Almost 'the whole town of Dungog' paid tribute (Simpson 1966: 88). More than 2000 people attended a civic reception. The town band marched ahead of an open sports car where Doug proudly stood, parading through Dungog's main streets. This, in itself, must have been a very unique event in Australian cricket.

Doug recalls this occasion well and said in a nervous speech how incredibly proud he was to hail from Dungog, attend the local school, and learn to play cricket as he did. He also thanked his parents for their support when he was growing up and playing cricket and other sports.

In the same season (1965-66), Doug played a leading part in NSW winning the Sheffield Shield in consecutive years. He headed the batting averages with 651 runs at 72. With the two Test centuries, Doug passed 1,000 runs in first-class cricket in only his second season (1,332 runs at 70 with six centuries), a truly fantastic performance. As Australia rejoiced, Reg Edwards (1977a) noted that 'comparisons made with Bradman were as unfair to Walters as they had been to O'Neill a decade earlier. Every player is an individual, and no one should ever be regarded as another edition of an earlier star'.

Call for National Duty in 1966

Just after the completion of that successful debut series, the call for National Servicemen Duty in 1966 interrupted Doug's early career, much to my personal disappointment. Private Doug Walters was in the army on National Duty from April 1966 to March 1968.

As the globally unpopular Vietnam War raged, and Australia was reluctantly dragged into it, Mallett (2008: 45) said it was a grossly unfair call for Army conscription by lottery. In that year, all young Australians in their 20th year faced the prospect of being conscripted into the army. It was a National Service Lottery, and Doug's number had come up regrettably. I recall reading this 'news' about my cricketing idol' but was too young to understand the gravity of the outcome.

Richie Benaud advised Doug to go straight into the army without complaint and be available for the 1968 tour to England. Mallett (2008: 45-46) recorded that the decision to join the army was a hard one for Doug; it cost him an all-expenses paid trip to England in 1966 by way of an invitation from MCC (by Trevor Bailey) to play for a World Xi against an England XI.

Doug also missed the 1966-67 tour to South Africa, for which he had been selected. Throughout 1966-67, he missed high-level cricket and part of the series against India in the summer of 1967-68. Still, he was back in the side for the last two of the four Tests, replacing Simpson, who was unavailable for the third Test.

Resuming his career, Doug scored 93 and 62* in the Brisbane Test (19-24 January 1968) against India. Simpson (1966: 87) said that Doug's absence made Australian cricket poorer for two years. Simpson had indicated that he was retiring. It was a young age for a cricketer to retire, as he was only 32 and 'at the height of his great powers' (Edwards 1977b). This news surprised Australia. Simpson scored a century each in the first two Tests, which helped Australia beat India. Doug, however, benefited from Simpson's retirement and was also made captain of NSW in 1968, which didn't last long.

Doug wasn't keen on joining the army but won the nation's hearts by accepting his fate. However, he thought his conscription was a 'government plan', and the Australian authorities made him an example for everyone else (Mallett 2008: 58). It was well-known in Australia that World War II interfered with the careers of many former greats, such as Keith Miller, Ray Lindwall, Arthur Morris, Ian Johnson and Lindsay Hassett. Their careers were short because of the military call-ups.

Doug withdrew from the South African tour when called for National Service. Although he reluctantly joined, Doug's decision to take up the army challenge was applauded by veteran cricketers like Benaud and Johnson and, more broadly, by the cricket fraternity. It was widely discussed in Australia then as 'a leading cricketer setting a splendid example to others in 'facing up to his responsibilities'.

Mallett (2008: 47) noted the contents of a letter dated 4 March 1966 from Ian Johnson, former Australian captain, who was then the Secretary of the Melbourne Cricket Club. Johnson praised Doug for 'doing the right thing'. Johnson had also served in World War II as a Royal Australian Air Force (RAAF) flight lieutenant in the West Pacific during 1941-45. Mallett (2008: 69, 81-82) also recorded that Doug's commanding officer (Major A.W. Hammet) pressured him to stay in the army and go to Vietnam instead of England on the Ashes tour.

Hammet thought visiting his company 'on duty and seeing some action in North Vietnam' would give Doug a 'world of good'. Luckily, Doug didn't go to Vietnam to fight someone else's war. Later, after Doug did well in his first Test in England, in Manchester, scoring two half-centuries, Major Hammet congratulated him in a personal letter.

Only a few years later, in India, it caused an angry public reaction as people accused Doug and the Australians of being complicit in the Vietnam War. However, although his battalion did, Doug never left Australia's shores to participate in the war. Doug was among the 63,740 men in Australia who had enlisted in the army. Some 19,000 served in Vietnam, of which 511 servicemen and one servicewoman were killed in active service in Vietnam (Mallett 2008: 49-50).

During his second year with the army, on 26 August 1967, Doug married Caroline Joy Redman, whom he knew from school in Dungog. Caroline, a schoolteacher at Wentworthville, in NSW, at that time, helped Doug see out the army training. Doug recorded his gratitude to her several times in his books. He was also thankful for not being sent to Vietnam for action. During his two years in the army, Doug played a fair amount of cricket against the Navy and the RAAF. He returned to civilian life just in time to make the 1968 tour of England and bore no grudges for missing out on cricket due to the Army commitments.

Doug Walters featured in Cricket – 'The Australian Way' (1968)

In 1968, Doug was the key batter featured along with others in the Fourth Printing of a book titled *Cricket – The Australian Way* (Pollard 1968). Jack Pollard, a famous journalist, edited the book. The foreword carried words of wisdom from Bradman. A beautiful photograph of Doug illustrated the book's dust jacket. Other pictures from the personal albums of famous players enriched the book, which was described as not just a 'comprehensive instruction course in all cricket's skill' but an 'exclusively Australian expression of how to approach the game'. It was later serialised by the Indian magazine *Sport & Pastime*.

Doug was the main star featured in the book, posing to show a perfectly balanced stance, various defensive and attacking strokes, and fielding. Obviously, the editors wanted to use this emerging 'star' to influence youngsters to the maximum. As Pollard explained, the book intended to teach kids how to enjoy the 'true flavour of Australian cricket'. The book became a standard instruction manual in Australia. The articles from many legendary players said that 'only those men who have played Test cricket can really tell what it is like to play in a Test match'. It also showed the world the 'unceasing flow of great players from a scantily-populated country'.

I was delighted to see *Cricket The Australian Way* in a bookshop in Colombo in 1972. Mesmerized, I stood silently gazing at its cover when I saw the upstanding Doug Walters straight-driving photo. My mother, who was with me then, didn't miss this moment and kindly let me buy the book. The date I've scribbled on it says 28th June 1972, quite a few years after the book was first published and sold in other cricket-playing countries.

The National Service interruption was a setback as Doug peaked early in his career. Some said Doug wasn't the same player after his army service. But Doug's batting after resuming his career against the Indians and the West Indies proves this is false, despite losing form for a short time in 1968. He is also on record saying: 'As for my conscription into the army, I don't think it had any great effect on me — I was playing some of my best cricket as soon as I came out'.

Doug had a carefree but dignified approach to the game, much like the *gentlemen* of the past. I don't think Doug ever had a ruthless desire to 'win at any cost'; it simply wasn't his style. For me, these attributes made him such an endearing hero. In his approach to cricket, he was like Garry Sobers, playing to enjoy a game. Quick reactions, hand-eye coordination, natural ability and attacking instinct make them great strokemakers. Like Bradman, both saw an attack as the best defence. They broke the hearts of even the best bowlers. Their habit of taking bowling apart with counter-attacks shows that these 'showmen' enriched cricket.

Among those who played against Doug, Sobers, Graeme Pollock, Geoff Boycott, Barry Richards, Vivian Richards and Clive Lloyd must also come into this category of cricketing royalty. In more modern times, peerless stroke makers – Brain Lara, Sachin Tendulkar and Virat Kohli – may also come into such royalty. However, the latter players I named carried more team responsibilities at their peaks.

These modern-day *Kings of Cricket* also had ups and downs, but they never doubted their abilities. All of them, including Doug, scoffed at excessive coaching and enjoyed the camaraderie of people brought together by cricket. For them, everything else in life was secondary. 'Coaching is a curse – no other phrase can express the evil' – that was Cardus when he took exception to how professional instructors of batting in England numbed the natural talents of school kids and younger club players. Cardus' words were (1935: 46):

> *Don't do this; Don't do that; Don't drive when the ball is new, and when it is old, remember there's a man at long-on...Watch for the wrong 'un...Who coached Trumper....Bradman and Jessop? Experience taught them to get close to the ball; their genius did the rest.*

CHAPTER 3

A Cricket Freak

Cricket: A 'Window to the World"

Having introduced Doug Walters to the reader, let me blend my story with that of Doug through our shared experiences in cricket. From about eight or nine, I became devoted to cricket. Over the past five decades, that devotion allowed me to acquire considerable knowledge about the game and its personalities.

My devotion might surprise strangers but not those who have some awareness of the glorious game. Its influence on me has been overwhelming. I am unashamedly a cricket-tragic who succumbed to the devilish lure of cricket. Getting my education in the 1960s and 70s interfered so much that I never got a chance to play any competitive cricket. But I believe *living a wholesome life without cricket would be impossible*!

My family used to call me *'Cricket Pissa'* (a lunatic!!). I still wear that nickname as a badge of honour. In English, it means a 'Cricket-Buff', a bit more than a freakish fan. But a 'knowing connoisseur' would be a better description. Cricket was a passion, a healthy obsession, second to none as an influential factor in growing up on a cricket-crazy island.

After I began idolising Doug, I became a voracious reader of anything on cricket – newspapers, magazines, books, posters – the lot. In 1966, my father bought me the Indian magazine *Sport & Pastime* when Garry Sobers's West Indies was touring India. I still have those cherished, old copies. I took delight in conserving the magazines, now nearly six decades old, which made the 5000 km journey from Sri Lanka to Australia. In later life, when I read the timeless classic of cricket writing – *Beyond A Boundary* by the West Indian Cyril Lionel Robert James (1963), it became clear to me that just like it was for him, *cricket was my window also to the world*!

James (1963: 41)⁵ showed how cricket shaped not only the West Indies cricketers but also the social life in the Caribbean islands as they yearned for independence and self-governance. As in the Caribbean, cricket was also a significant social force in Ceylon during the struggle to break away from the colonial rulers. Cricket was also a tool for smashing down class, race and status boundaries.

Early in my life, my father realised his youngest son was mad about cricket. When he returned from work at the Survey Department (at Narahenpitiya), he had to catch a bus to the Colombo Central Railway Station and then a train home to Panadura, where we lived. Panadura was a delightful township 17 miles south of the capital city. On his return journey, my father would have spent a few rupees at the Tamil shops near the station, which sold magazines from India. I still remember the beaming smile on his face as he took the magazine out of his briefcase and handed it to me, who would wait in anticipation.

The Indian magazines in Ceylon, in those days, included the famous *Filmfare* and *Sport & Pastime*, stocked by the Tamil importers. For several years, my father bought me the *Sport & Pastime*, this precious gift to a kid, every Wednesday. I recall reading every word in the magazines and learning about cricket, life in India and Pakistan, and how they played the sport. Having my own collection, which other kids my age didn't have, made a big difference.

* * *

Soon, as I wallowed in cricket magazines, I understood how great cricketers like the Nawab of Pataudi (Mansur Ali Khan, India's captain) and Hanif Mohammad (Pakistan's captain) developed their teams in the sub-continent after independence. The magazines gave me details of those cricketers' careers and social lives. They also recorded the boundless hospitality these countries showered upon visiting teams.

I was unsurprised that visiting teams were greatly respected as part of the innate sub-continental hospitality culture. However, I realised that visiting teams to the sub-continent often didn't reciprocate the host's generosities. Tours to the subcontinent were unpopular among other Test-playing nations,

---

5   To this date C.L.R. James' *Beyond A Boundary* remains one of the most-admired books ever written on cricket. Writing on *Wisden Almanack*'s Centenary Edition (19 April 1965), John Arlott, the great English broadcaster, wrote that 'it is the finest book written about the game of cricket'.
    Arlott cautioned that 'A reviewer should check his adjectives several times before he described it and, since he is likely to be dealing with superlatives, to measure them carefully to avoid over praise – which the book does not need' (Selma James 2013).

particularly England and Australia, as hot conditions and food stifled their cricket. I've read many accounts of visiting teams complaining about bad pitches, large crowds, lousy umpiring, and awful food, transport, and hotels in India.

Nevertheless, some touring teams looked forward to these 'whistlestop' tours as the ships from England to Australia stopped for a breather in the reverse direction. Travel was quite difficult in the early half of the 20th century, and most players enjoyed a break during the long sea voyages and seeing the *other world* on these tours.

In one account, Percy Chapman (1935), a former England captain, expressed what a delightful experience it was to stop in Ceylon in October 1928 because 'You were royally entertained by the locals'. But he did say that the heat and humidity were 'Usually like a Turkish Bath' and 'A stiff collar and a boiled (starched) shirt were an impossibility'.

Chapman's team, known as Marylebone Cricket Club (MCC) in those days, were on their way to Australia, a long voyage in a paddle steamer for the Ashes battles (1928-29), which they won 4-1. Chapman (1935: 129-131) said that 'the tours were good for both the visitors and visited; educationally, socially and politically; individually and collectively'. He also wrote that apart from financial benefits, the tours 'taught comparative values and created interest in the game, not only among the thousands of spectators but also among the English-speaking people in all parts of the world'.

* * *

As I literally 'consumed' every conceivable material on cricket, I learned that *organised cricket* was an ancient pastime in England. An English journalist, Thomas Moult, compiled some important early 20th-century cricket articles in an edited volume, *Bat and Ball* (1935), which revealed that the game could be considered dating back to the times of Henry VIII. However, with the emergence of rules to govern the 'elegant and scientific' game, modern cricket's origin had to be around 1743-44. Hence, it would be fair to say that the game we love so much has been around for 250-plus years, closer to 300 years.

It was first played with 11 players on each side around London (Middlesex) and Kent and then expanded into Sussex. The first recorded match with a scoresheet was between an All-England team vs. Kent, played in 1944. There was also heavy betting linked with the early matches. Before round-arm bowling came about in 1790-91, it was all under-arm 'lobbing' (Moult 1935: 17-40).

There were no leg guards, batting gloves, forward or backfoot play, round-arm, slow or fast bowling even in the latter part of the 18th Century (1792-93). All those cricket 'phenomena' came about later in the 19th Century. By this time, the British had conquered Australia (1788) and arrived in Ceylon (1796). The timeline provides relevant context to cricket fans, especially in these countries.

* * *

Through the rich literature I read, I learned much about life and its joys through the *social phenomena* related to cricket in cricket-playing countries. At the same time, I discovered a great deal about the cricketers and the cities in which the famous cricket grounds were built. I also studied the material about cricket's institutions, including player profiles, tours, and countries. As a result of studying cricket, my cricket knowledge far exceeded that of other kids my age.

In later years, cricket provided a lens through which I examined various social issues related to British rule. These included the struggle for independence, nationalism, emigration and the behaviour of diasporic cricket fans worldwide. All such phenomena linked to cricket influence the lives of thousands of people.

Cricket was established in some nations with painful memories related to colonialism, slavery and brutal British rule. Although it didn't take long for cricket to become a global sport, it was initially played by all kinds of people in former British colonies, by all major religious groups (mainly Hindus, Muslims, Buddhists and Christians), some of whom could be bitter rivals and enemies (such as India and Pakistan).

Looking through the *window of cricket*, I realised that there were always intense inter-island rivalries in the Caribbean, and the 'West Indies' existed only for cricket! In the early days, the easy-going Caribbean people also didn't have much impact on Test cricket until after World War II. As Viv Richards said (1991: 73), 'They are very calm, cheery, very peaceful people'. However, they are also renowned for their volatile temperament and impetuousness.

The Caribbean way of life is reflected in all the inherent doubts the players reveal under pressure in cricket. The Windies were often erratic despite brilliant individuals like George Headley, Learie Constantine, Frank Worrell, Everton Weeks, Clyde Walcott, Garry Sobers, Rohan Kanhai, Conrad Hunte, Basil Butcher, Seymour Nurse, Lance Gibbs, Clive Lloyd and Wesley Hall. The West Indian cricketers have always been full of spontaneity, character and individuality.

As great entertainers, they handed down the *cavalier* style of playing cricket to the present generation, giving the game so much joy. The Windies have the genius to turn a Test match their way in a few astonishing overs. Yet it could go the other way, too. Sometimes, a rush of hot blood could see them lose wickets in a heap, drop catches and get run out with silly calls. They could easily fall from seemingly dominant positions by taking things too easy. *Unpredictability* characterizes the Caribbean cricketers and their cricket to this date.

Cricket's greatest all-rounder, Garry Sobers, mesmerized me as a kid. Starting cricket tentatively, Sobers developed quickly, due to natural talent, to be the peerless legend that he was (Arlott 1979: 97-103). Sir Garry epitomized everything glorious and endearing about cricket and the Caribbean people.

* * *

There is a severe intensity in how Australians play their cricket, which reveals the stubborn attitude of their cricketers. It is a product of how Australian society developed as a colony, trying to break away from the British and form its own identity. Cricket and all other sports allowed Australia to show the world that her sportsmen and women were as good as, or better than, others. *Pommie-bashing* is pervasive among the public. It rears up its ugly head whenever an England-Australia clash (an Ashes series) looms [6]. In 2007, Peter Roebuck, as astute an observer as any on both cricket and society, said:

Australian cricket reflects the origins of the country. 'Class' was never a factor, and the game was not regarded as a means of instilling manners. Cricket has simply offered an opportunity to express talent and enjoy ferocious competition.

As a new and remote country, Australia yearned for sporting achievement and the recognition that came with it. As a country forged by the unwanted, it yearned for success. Therefore, sport took a prominent role in the forging of the national identity, and every victory boosted confidence.

Australian people of European descent are descendants of early settlers (colonisers). They faced tough conditions in the harsh environment of the world's driest continent when they first arrived in 1788. The vast landscape, hostile fire, and drought-ridden environment challenged the

---

[6] The *Oxford Dictionary* says that the word *Poms* came to use in 1912 as slang for British immigrants, with a reference to sunburn turning their pinkish skin to pomegranate red. Pomegranate (*Punica granatum*), a famous fruit, has seeds with a deep red, pulpy seed coat. The term '*Whingeing Poms*' is used to deride a person of British origin who constantly complains about things.

new arrivals, who had been primarily penalized for petty crimes (such as stealing a loaf of bread in London streets).

The convicts, their guards, and a few sailors comprised the first waves of settlers. The new arrivals found it challenging to survive in an unfriendly, distant continent, which was already occupied by tens of thousands of Indigenous people. Cricket, as a sport, began in the 1850s as pastoralists gradually expanded their territories, among brutal conflicts with the indigenous groups. While the disputes were going on, the setters had to battle the vagaries of a dry and harsh continent.

Nothing was easy for the early settlers. It bred a certain kind of extra hardness and strength in people. Australian cricket, in general, perhaps, reflects this toughness and stubbornness. The dislike for the British can be ascribed to the anger of those associated with waves of convicts sent away 'as far away from Britain as possible' for petty crimes, some as ridiculous as stealing a loaf of bread.

It hasn't been easy for Australia to forget how the 'Colony' was initially formed. The intense rivalry between Britain and Australia manifested in cricket is due to this bitterness. The typical Australian thinks of the British as full of snobbery, unable to jettison the tendency to differentiate 'classes' of people depending on wealth and inherited social status (such as landlords, peasants and the working class).

* * *

In the early decades, cricket dominated my young life and my dreams. It was the first thing I thought of upon waking up and the last thing I went to bed. Much to the amusement of my family, I used to mutter *Soto voce* descriptions of the games in commentary form, emulating some of the great broadcasters. Such was my passion.

Exploring photographs, I used to imagine what the settings were like. Although I hadn't travelled out of Ceylon as a kid, I knew quite a bit about the famous cricket grounds in the world. For instance, I knew what to expect if I ever got to the SCG with the beautiful Sydney Harbour and the Opera House near the Adelaide Oval, presided over by its splendid cathedral and many other churches.

In Australia, the first Test of a series was customarily played in Brisbane. The city of Brisbane, in those days, wasn't as well developed as Sydney or Melbourne. But its famous cricket ground, the *Woolloongabba* (the Gabba'), was the venue of the most memorable Test – the Tie between Benaud's Australia and Worrell's West Indies in the 1960-61 series. I also knew that Perth, in Western Australia, had the fastest pitch, which was bouncy, and cricket played there is often affected by *Freemantle Doctor*, a sea breeze from the southwest.

I knew that Lord's, the world-famous cricket ground, was created by Thomas Lord, who set it up at its present location, St. John's Wood, in North-West London, in 1814. Another sponsor, William Ward, bought the lease from Lord in 1825 and ensured its permanence.

Sir Pelham Warner reminded everyone, 'He who plays at Lord's today treads on the same turf as the cricketers of one hundred and fifty years ago' (Moult 1935: 31). However, Lord's was not where the first Test match was played – that distinction went to *The Oval* in Surrey, South-East London. It was in 1884 that the Australians played the first international match at Lord's, which England won by an innings (MCC 1987). The first match recorded on the present-day Lord's turf was between the MCC and Hertfordshire in 1813.

Wallowing in Cricket

In the 1960s, my hometown's Public Library (Panadura, Ceylon) had *The Cricketer* (U.K.), *Sport & Pastime* (India), the *Wisden Annual* and the *Wisden Cricketer's Almanack*[7] on its shelves. I benefitted greatly by reading them along with the English newspapers. I quickly realised nothing else gave me as much joy as Test cricket, the fiercest of fights for cricket supremacy. Test cricket madness was the same in England and Australia. On *Test* cricket, Sir Jack Hobbs (1935) once wrote:

> *Here in England, the eager throng pours into Nottingham, Leeds or London and packs around the arenas as it seldom does at an inter-county match. Rich men, poor men, everyone is cricket mad; mad for an English victory…And yonder in Australia, the sheep farmers, merchants, and stockmen pour into Sydney, Melbourne, Adelaide and Brisbane – rich men, poor men – cricket-mad for an Australian victory. Many travel a thousand miles under the blazing southern skies just to see their team beat ours!*

With my mother's support, for a few years (1966-69), I bought *The Cricketer* magazines at the end-of-year auctions by the Public Library at Panadura. My mother used to wait in the car while I sneaked to where the auction was held. People stood around a desk, and the librarian (auctioneer) sat with piles of books and magazines. Little me was supposed to bravely

---

7 John *Wisden*, a '*very fast and ripping*' bowler in the mid-19th Century (Moult 1935: 35) founded the *Wisden Cricketer's Almanack* in 1864, a lasting legacy.

make a bid (I think my mother was embarrassed to bid for a bundle of magazines for just three rupees!)[8].

After acquiring bundles of magazines, I then became a passionate 'collector' of pictures, gathering them from everywhere. I also spent much more energy than my school friends collecting facts about the players I liked. I still have newspaper and magazine clippings collected over five decades, some of which are now jaded.

By spending countless hours reading about the great cricketers of the past – Grace, Trumper, Ranjitsinhji, Jessop, Bradman, Headley, Constantine, Miller, Worrell and others- I *found them out* through reading and dreaming! Child though I was, in the 1960s, I imagined what these brilliant cricketers must have been like in their prime.

Some, like Hanif Mohammad (Pakistan) and The Nawab of Pataudi (India), were already national heroes in their respective countries. I also wondered what made them so great as cricketers. Apart from being masterful in batting, some were brilliant cricket ambassadors.

Reading about the lives of cricketers, I learned about the cricketing nations, counties, states, and the teams they played for. I also learned about the backgrounds in which cricket developed in the lives of cricketers. I was also aware of the tradition in countries of the British Empire of families sending their children to England for education. This trend created a kind of *unnatural selection* in which the most successful left their native land and the least successful stayed behind.

When I began understanding social phenomena related to cricket, several Ceylonese cricketers had already migrated to England to develop their cricket careers. Among them, some notable players who played County Cricket were Laddie Outschoorn (Worcestershire), Gamini Goonasena (Nottinghamshire and Cambridge University), Stanley Jayasinghe and Clive Inman (both of Leicestershire).

* * *

I also became well-versed in cricket's rich colonial heritage. The game's values, rules and language evolved as an essential English activity in the Georgian period (1714-1837). According to Allison (1980) and Sandiford (1982), 'The long evolution allowed cricket to absorb all the noblest elements

---

8   The dummy bidder at the auction, whom I recall well, was a labourer at the library. When my three-rupee bid failed, he used to come around say *'Bubba, you can have the magazine bundle for rupees three-fifty'*, to which I would willingly oblige. Once I got the bundle, I would return to the car with a beaming smile with cherished my booty. At home, I would read them, word-to-word, many times, over the years.

of the Anglo-Saxon character and culture....Cricket was a tool to make pre-Victorian society healthier'.[9]

Although cricket was a *white man's* pastime, *natives* in many British colonies saw cricket as a way to get ahead in a society divided by race, status and class. As James (1963: 160-180) traced, cricket developed at least two generations before the Victorian era (1837-1901) and became a national sport during the Victorian period. This outcome was largely due to one man's efforts – the incomparable W.G. Grace:

> *All essentials of the modern game were formed between 1778 and 1830...It was created by the yeoman farmer, the game-keeper, the potter, the tinker, the Nottingham coal miner, and the Yorkshire factory hand. These artisans made it, men of hand and eye. Rich and idle young noblemen and some substantial city people contributed money, organization and prestige.*
>
> *By 1837, they had evolved a highly complicated game with all the typical qualities of a genuinely national art form. There was nothing in the slightest degree Victorian about it. At their matches, cricketers ate and drank with gusto of the time, sang songs and played for large sums of money.*

* * *

I grew up when my fellow citizens learned to play in a disciplined and energetic way but in a gentler game. Despite the noisy crowds, drumbeats, cheering, flag-waving, singing, and revelry, for which the Sri Lankan spectators are globally famous, gentle combat was always expected in the middle. From school days, cricketers were expected to maintain a high standard of decorum and good relationships with their opponents. These were initially *moral virtues endorsed by Christian schools*.

While alcohol *was* consumed at the cricket venues by adult revellers, in the inter-school *big matches*, it was generally well-controlled by the same adults, who did not wish to demean themselves in the eyes of their children. This is in contrast to unruly, rowdy and boozed-up sections of the crowds in countries like England, Australia, New Zealand and, of course, the West Indies, where 'grog' flows openly.

In Sri Lanka and India, the cricket-watching public also *dressed up* for the occasion, creating a carnival-like atmosphere. Dressing up to mimic someone is prevalent in Australia. The trend has now spread to other Test-playing countries as well. Unfortunately, going against the norms and borderline anti-social behaviour are common in Australia.

---

9   Cricket, introduced by the British to Caribbean islands in the early 19th Century, was intertwined with slavery for a long time, a theme well explored in James' book (1963) and Michael Manley's *History of West Indies Cricket* (1988).

Raucous, animated and boisterous large crowds attending Test matches at the SCG or MCG are an Australian *summer phenomenon*. Often, relentless chanting in unison and noise from these crowds create a gladiatorial-like atmosphere like that of Ancient Rome. It is sufficient to awaken touring teams from any cricketing slumber!

* * *

I couldn't forget how I first got hooked on cricket. It was by listening to a Test match broadcast from India. Although my father was slightly interested in the game, he occasionally listened to the commentaries, and I used to join him. Our parents realised that both my brother and I were very keen on cricket in the 1960s and tolerated our passion for cricket. They knew we were good enough to stay within boundaries and not let cricket interfere with our studies. They might have occasionally reminded us not to get too distracted.

At the age of around 10-12, they also allowed me to go and watch some club games played at the Panadura Public Grounds (Panadura Esplanade) in our hometown. The Panadura Sports Club had been playing first-grade cricket since 1924. The games they played in the 1960s were during weekends and were either short-format games, which lasted six hours, or two-day matches. Sometimes, I was *the only kid* who sat in the pavilion's old terraces to watch the game played by the adults as visiting teams clashed with the Panadura team.

Some people might think that sitting near the radio and listening to Test match broadcasts for hours on end is a boring way of spending time. Actually, *listening* demanded considerable concentration and imagination. The subtleties of the game ensured that real lovers of the game could *live the experience*. To understand the depth and complexity of cricket, one needs to span its history, politics, and characters, which requires dedicated effort.

As my cricket knowledge grew, I understood the beauty of words used in cricket. I knew what the commentators meant when they said Derek Underwood bowling on a sticky wicket 'could make the ball do anything but talk'. Jeff Thomson and Dennis Lillee were 'Sending down missiles'. The 'shell-shocked' English players were 'mentally shattered' but bore the pain of getting hit 'with a stiff upper lip'.

I invoked images of the 'fighting qualities' of Barrington or Lawry, batting doggedly, which 'made the score-board go to sleep' (this was vintage John Arlott). This Orwellian 'double-speak' made perfect sense to me. I also knew what Cardus (1968) meant when he wrote, 'Jessop would have cut them to ribbons'. Cardus was commenting on Lawry's Australians bowling too many bumpers in the 1968 Ashes series.

Learning to Bat and Bowl with a Tennis (Soft) Ball

Sir Garfield St. Auburn Sobers, the greatest all-rounder the world has seen, wrote his autobiography in 2002. On p. 18, I was chuffed to read that many West Indian greats, including the *'Three Ws'* (Frank Worrell, Everton Weeks, Clyde Walcott), Conrad Hunte, Basil Butcher and Seymour Nurse, learned cricket first by playing tennis-ball cricket in their native islands, on the beaches and roads.

Sobers also noted that 'the West Indies play so well off the back foot and on the up because one cannot drive a tennis ball off the front foot – the bounce is too high'. The Windies also learned how to 'hook well and play across the line because there was no other way to play the bouncy tennis ball' (Sobers 2002: 18).

I was thrilled when I read in an old *Sportstar Magazine* that the English all-rounder Trevor Bailey (1978) suggested a softball knockout tournament be introduced in England among primary schools. Having observed how much softball cricket was played in the Caribbean, he said the islands were: 'A sunny breeding ground for cricketing greats'.

Bailey wrote that in the longer term, it would 'raise the standard and increase interest in an area the game has often ignored. It would also be fun to play, cheaper to run, and produce good players' [10]. There is hardly any softball cricket in Australia. Sadly, kids as young as seven or eight years are rallied into teams in the suburbia and exposed to the hard leather ball. Many get hurt and give up cricket too early.

I played softball cricket for several years, almost daily, in school or at home. Like the West Indians and sub-continental India, it was all softball cricket for the kids. We seldom played with a proper leather ball and were fortunate to have access to tennis balls. However, when batting in our backyards, we learned to keep the ball down and not hit it upwards for fear of losing it if it went into other properties.

Most kids on the island didn't have tennis balls. Still, they played cricket passionately, using a dried, round, and firm fruit from a tree called *'Kaduru'*, dipped in rubber latex for strength. These *'Kaduru Bola'* as they were called (*Bola* is Sinhalese for a ball) were commonly used for cricket in the island's coastal areas until the 1970s.

Several kinds of *Kaduru* exist in the flora of a tropical island like Sri Lanka. The fruits for cricket balls came from *goda-kaduru*, best known

---

10   Bailey (1978) noted that the tiny island of Barbados produced more great cricketers per square mile than any other place on earth. The galaxy of stars includes The *Three Ws*, Sobers, Wesley Hall, Charlie Griffith, and also Conrad Hunte, one of the most accomplished West Indian openers.

as the 'Strychnine tree' (*Strychnos nux-vomica*), a source of the highly poisonous alkaloid strychnine. The round fruits of *goda-kaduru* were the right size as substitute balls and behaved well when bounced. We used to wrap the *Kaduru* ball in scraps of rubber latex from drippings on a rubber tree (called *ottapalu*). The wrapping made the round objects bouncy on hard surfaces, but they hurt too much if one got hit.

* * *

In those younger days, at our school in Panadura, it was only on very few occasions that we had access to proper equipment – pads, bats, gloves, stumps and a hard leather ball. The ball we were given was often a scuffed-up leftover from senior cricket, which had already split. It was an awkward missile to face. But that didn't always deter us as we played on the coconut matting on a hard clay bed in the school playground. Often, we played with a single pad on the front leg and shared the pads. We never had any 'boxes' even to share.

Even so, we enjoyed the games. At times, as we got hit on our shins or thighs, we went home in pain, tending to our bruises. I think we dreamt of becoming better at cricket someday. Somehow, my brother (a medical doctor in the U.K.) and I were both pretty good at softball cricket in all aspects, batting, bowling and fielding. More than any other sport, cricket allowed kids to get along, be friends with each other, and learn discipline. While focusing on enjoying the time out in the playgrounds and fun, we played competitively, excitingly, but fairly.

Some games were serious encounters, played over several days, continuing each morning on the playground. Our class team was a motley outfit of good and bad players. We cheered in excitement as our team did well. We also booed our opponents, using an insulting term – *parippuvas*. The term meant *lentil-eaters*, meaning peasants or 'country-people' who were not good enough to beat us because they didn't have well-developed cricketing skills [11].

Incredibly, this jocular term is widely used by the cheering Sri Lankan crowds even today when backing the national team or their favourite school. In some ways, it expresses a class divide, a legacy of the British colonists. The *yeomanry* that James (1963: 160) refers to, playing cricket in pre-Victorian Britain, was as raucous as we were.

That unruly behaviour in Britain was fuelled by beer and spirits,

---

11   Lentil (*Lens esculenta*) is the famous sub-continental curry called *dhal*. Lentil dhal (*parippu*, in Sinhalese) is *the* most popular of Sri Lankan curries. The reference to dhal alludes to the poor nutrition of *commoners* relative to the urban *elitists*. The presumption is that the *urbanites* would be unbeatable in cricket because they have abundant food, money, and prestige.

which flowed abundantly in those times at village greens. In contrast, as kids, we were *drunk only with the excitement and thrills of cricket* and the extraordinary clashes we witnessed between the bat and the ball.

* * *

While doing all this, we realised that cricket was such a fantastic game of skill and artistry, offering endless opportunities for fun. Cricket also taught essential life lessons, such as self-discipline, loyalty to your team, restraint and respect for opponents' skills.

The bitter lessons of defeat in a school cricket match also taught us the 'glorious uncertainties of cricket'. Living the cricket experience, we got psychologically involved in the skirmishes between batters, bowlers and fielders. As kids, I recall how we picked our favourite eleven from different countries and grappled with getting the balance right.

We learnt that one has to accept defeat with good grace. Our schoolmasters emphasized that cricket, after all, is only a game to be played and enjoyed. However, we also knew that 'It's only a game; it doesn't matter who wins or loses' does not always cut the muster. *Of course, it did matter*! We were also told there was no reason to feel inferior if one lost and not to jeer the defeated. We had to express ourselves, 'try hard', apply our 'hands, feet, and minds to our work, and take pride in our skills'. These were great lessons in life.

The cricket played at our schools demanded tackling the game with discipline, confidence, self-belief, and having tactics and strategies to win any game. In many ways, it was parallel to learning problem-solving early in life. Winning in cricket was a prestige and honour to enjoy. Like food and shelter, cricket was an essential item in life in those days! It was a form of joyful, *lived experience* and an uplifting madness in a way. At the same time, it was a good learning experience.

As Bradman said in his *Farewell To Cricket* (1950), 'Cricket was supposed to stand for everything decent and upstanding'. In my world, people were also supposed to be disciplined, play the game fairly, and be generous towards the defeated. Cricket continues to be an enriching reservoir of joy for me, with all its good, bad, ugly, and funny qualities.

It was the *sport of gentlemen*. As Sir Neville Cardus so aptly said: *The very poetry of Life*! In this glorious game, 'Scores and results don't always matter; how you play the game matters' (Cardus 1949a;b). As I explore in the book, my idol – Doug Walters – allowed me to hold on to the cherished values in cricket that can be extended to society despite the scandals and controversies that have plagued the game's history.

CHAPTER 4

Seeing Cricket 'Beyond A Boundary'

If ever a book changes your thinking or opens doors and windows to reveal a better world, it is C.L.R. James' 'Beyond A Boundary'. If one reads it, one will never forget it. Nor would one ever forget the author or the 'actors' and the great individuals (Grace, Headley and Constantine, in particular), who were so well described as to make people fall in love with them!

James said one of his primary motivations for the book was to correct the 'wrongs' done to these remarkable cricketers. Using cricket as the central theme, James encouraged people to break the social boundaries that separate them and visualize a society with its diverse interconnections.

The Glory and Pride of English Cricket – 'W.G.'

In his book, James argued that these great past cricketers had not been adequately appreciated for their roles in the evolution of the modern game. James went to extraordinary lengths to describe how Dr. William Gilbert (W.G.) Grace (1848-1915) 'transformed' cricket into an *'Art'* during the Victorian era. W.G., a medical doctor, played for England (MCC), Gloucestershire and 'Gentlemen' and was crucially important in developing the modern game.

Grace was the primary force behind introducing the techniques of batting, bowling, and fielding positions. He is, therefore, entitled to be classed as one of the greatest all-time cricketers and even be called 'the father of cricket'. In praising Grace, Thomas Moult (1935: 36) wrote:

'It needs to be put on record that although the game was played between the counties in the first part of the last century (19th Century), there was no serious cricket before Grace'.

Pelham Warner (1935: 177) said Grace was 'The champion of champions and the glory and pride of England who epitomised the nation's devotion to the game'. With his beard, height of six feet two inches and 17 stone weight,

W.G. was a formidable sight. Wherever he played, Grace dominated cricket with his presence and deeds.

C.L.R. James (1963: 170-185) detailed W.G.'s career, appealing to everyone to recognize the great man's enormous contribution to cricket. However, while acknowledging that Grace was 'A genius who invented modern batting and batsmanship' in one of his early books – *Days In The Sun* (1924: 68-69), Cardus didn't quite go that far with praise for Grace as James did. Not everyone liked the great doctor all the time.

One story said that in a friendly match watched by hundreds of admirers, W.G. was bowled for not much. Then, he gently straightened the stumps, put the bails back on them, smiled at the bowler, and said, 'Carry on, the crowd is here, expecting me to bat and not you bowling me out! The match continued. Such was his stature.

As Moorehouse (1998) noted, an angry James berated the history books of the period for the *great wrong* and *omission* of not admitting the great man's contributions and rightful place in cricket:

> *This man, for heaven's sake, opened for England at the age of 50 – and at the age of 18, he had scored 224 not out for England against Surrey, in a match which he left halfway through in order to win a quarter-mile hurdles championship at the Crystal Palace!*
>
> *No wonder he was the best-known Englishman, apart from Mr Gladstone, so much so that Evelyn Waugh's friend, Monsignor Ronnie Knox, waggishly suggested that Gladstone and Grace were really one and the same celebrity.*

James (1963) wanted everyone to look *beyond the boundary* at cricket's societal role. A Marxist at heart, he described how colonialism affected the sport that the locals loved so much. James was critical of the Caribbean team being led by a white captain for decades, ignoring the abundant 'coloured' talent that was available, including Headley and Constantine. Calling this an unforgivable travesty, he argued:

> *The more brilliantly the black men played, the more it would emphasise to millions of English people: 'Yes, they are fine players, but funny, isn't it, they cannot be responsible for themselves? They must always have a white man to lead them.* [12]

---

12   It was Keith Miller who first raised the issue of West Indies captaincy in his 1959 book, *Cricket from the Grandstand*: 'A problem in West Indies cricket is that the captain has usually been chosen from among the European stock. Just think of the most famous cricketers, Constantine, Headley, Worrell, Weeks and Walcott; all are coloured, but none have led his country. Yet Worrell was often skipper of

James's book, written 60 years ago, shows how success in cricket represented a victory for the islands over the colonial rulers. That success, then, he said, 'enabled the man and woman in the street to walk taller, to conceive that they have a right to regard themselves as "equals" of their social superiors'. Success in cricket allowed the Caribbean people to show that: *They are no better than we*'. Using cricket as the theme, James encouraged people to break the social boundaries that separate them (Brearley, 2013a;b; James 2013). The same beliefs were prevalent in the defiant society in post-independent Ceylon when the island was rebuilding a new social fabric.

Borrowing from the English poet Rudyard Kipling, James invented the epigram: *What do they know of cricket who only cricket knows?*. Cricket's brilliant players were 'not an accident', he wrote. 'They were part of a social phenomenon'. A psychoanalyst, Mike Brearley (2013a, b), explained: 'For C. L. R. James, the cricket field was a stage on which individuals played representative roles charged with social significance'.

Kipling popularized the notion that *natives* in the Empire were always looking to cheat the rulers. In 1899, he created a false idea of British compassion, stating that the British had a responsibility to 'civilize' the Indian population: 'The untrustworthy native was 'the white man's burden' and had to be 'taught the higher British values.

Kipling may have deceptively crafted a white supremacist narrative to mislead people. His famous phrase was: *What do they know of England who only England know?* It was published in *The English Flag* (1891). It was part of his attack on what he saw as the blindness of the English to their Empire (mainly sub-continental India, Ceylon, Singapore, Burma, Egypt and Sudan) and the men who defended those colonies [13].

Waking Up to Alan McGilvray's Golden Voice

As a kid, I spent hundreds of hours glued to the radio, listening to cricket broadcasts. The voices of the Australian Broadcasting Commission (ABC) commentator Alan McGilvray and the English broadcasters John Arlott, Brian Johnson and Henry Blofeld of the British Broadcasting Corporation (BBC) were pure joy to listen to.

Commonwealth teams in India, and he did a fine job. Politics interfere with cricket more in the West Indies than in any other place'.

13   Kipling emphasized the neglect most Englishmen showed towards the Empire, 'the other world' that was critical in maintaining Britain. Kipling's other world-famous phrase: *'East is the East, West is the West, Never the twain shall meet'*, was written in *The Ballad of the East and West*, a poem published in 1889. Kipling vacillated between showing empathy for the sufferings of the native populations and advising his own breed to be strict disciplinarians.

I also liked Pearson Surita's sophisticated and poetic voice, which I heard on All India Radio for many years. One thing I remember well, learnt in those hours of listening to these broadcasting giants, was how a game can change within a few minutes by the fall of a few wickets. It only takes a few loose shots or good balls to turn a match around.

McGilvray was the *voice of cricket* in Australia for over 50 years, starting his career while playing for NSW in 1935 and retiring in 1985. He broadcast 225 Tests in those 50 years. Mark Browning, a journalist (1968), noted what Norman Tasker, who co-wrote two books with Alan, said:

> *Alan was not just the voice of cricket but the 'voice of summer'. He was also a 'constant symbol of a more relaxed era when sport played for sport's sake was indeed a part of the Australian way of life, and the standards of sportsmanship, fairness, and right and wrong were identified through sport as our ethos.*

Such a set of ethics, virtues and morals, nurtured by McGilvray, with his command at the microphone, made me a cricket freak through the joys of living cricket by listening. I thank Alan for that.

Doug knew Alan well as a cricketer, friend and broadcaster and confirmed that Alan had this same effect on him. A story that Doug told me has already been reported by Ashley Mallett (2008: 8-9):

> *You could say I was taught the game of cricket by the commentators. Alan McGilvray, John Arlott and Brian Johnston were terrific. They described my heroes—Hutton, Edrich, Peter May, Colin Cowdrey, Ted Dexter, Fred Trueman, Tony Lock, Jim Laker, Alec Bedser, Richie Benaud, Alan Davidson, Neil Harvey, Garry Sobers, Wes Hall, Lance Gibbs and Rohan Kanhai.*
>
> *If Davidson came on to bowl, you bowled as Davo bowled, left-handed. Edrich was a left-hand batter, so you bat the way he batted as the England opener. Lindwall was a fast bowler, so you raced in and bowled as fast as possible as he did ... when Richie Benaud was bowling, you bowled leg breaks. I could 'see' through the radio the blokes who hitched their pads or fiddled with their box.*

Both Doug and I conjured images of cricket by listening. In the sanctity of my home, with the Grundig radio, I was mostly alone when I listened to cricket over long hours. The solitude allowed me to wallow in the atmosphere of Test cricket that the commentators created. It really was pure magic. These gentlemen of the highest calibre were responsible for my cricket madness. Alan McGilvray, my favourite, was involved in broadcasting cricket for over 50 years at ABC (Bennett et al. 1982) and was the most loved commentator in Australia.

My knowledge of the game rapidly expanded as I collected cricket pictures, newspaper articles, magazines and books. My collection was nothing fancy. Nevertheless, I enjoyed my collection. While I dreamt of cricket, becoming a cricketer instead of pursuing higher education was never on. Although I was good at arguing cricket's technical points, its history, and cricketers, I wasn't very good at the game.

Cricket is a physically demanding game that requires excellent hand-eye coordination for batting, a lot of running for bowling and fielding and good hands for catching. Although I had a few of those attributes, I was nowhere near physically fit to succeed. Besides, cricket was considered a sport, an enjoyable pastime for people in Ceylon to engage in, but not a way to earn a living.

The Influence of a certain Mr. Miller

Continuing my story, in the 1960s and well into the '70s, finding another youngster in my age group who could match what I knew about cricket was hard. Fascinated by the game, I used to write down all the major cricketing events on a country-by-country basis in a diary.

The passion ensured that the information stuck in my mind. I rarely missed anything as there were not so many Tests per year in those days. It wouldn't be unfair to say that cricket became a bit of a religion for me! Not everyone understood why I was so obsessed with cricket. But cricket was my window to a new world, especially outside Ceylon.

My father, who worked in the Survey Department at Narahenpitiya (Colombo), also had a friend, a fellow cartographer – Fitzroy De Mel – a pioneering local cricket umpire in the 1960s. He officiated at several 'unofficial' Tests and in some international matches when visiting teams played in Ceylon. Fitzroy served as Vice President of the Association of Cricket Umpires and Scorers in Sri Lanka (ACUSL). He was also a member of the Association of Cricket Umpires (ACU) in England. At the time of his death, he was an Assignment Secretary to the Board of Control for Cricket in Sri Lanka (Sunday Times 2002).

My father told me Fitzroy De Mel talked a lot about cricketers, especially the brilliant Australian – Keith Miller – who mesmerised the world with his all-round talents and good looks. Fitzroy lived at Moratuwa, a township not far from our home, and my father used to visit him. Later in life, I realised that perhaps my father was interested in cricket because of his friendship with Fitzroy.

I still remember the twinkle in my father's eyes when he spoke about Keith Miller, The Golden Nugget (*Wisden* 2019b; Hayter 2019). He earned the nickname 'Nugget' from the English Press, who called him 'The Golden Boy' from Australia. An incredible 'devil-may-care' personality, the Victorian all-rounder and fighter pilot who served in World War II was held in the highest regard by all Ceylonese, West Indians, Australians and even the English.

It was wonderful to learn that Doug also had a friendship with Miller until his demise in 2004 at 84 years of age. Doug still talks with a deep respect for the legendary cricketer, an influential figure. Doug said that Miller never forgot a face and would instantly recall someone he might have met decades earlier.

A tall man with broad shoulders, Miller bowled fast and hair-raising deliveries and sometimes mixed them cunningly with medium-pacers, off-spinners or leg-breaks. Len Hutton said he would rather face the pace of Lindwall than Miller because he knew what was coming. Blessed with a magnificently proportioned physique, as Arlott said (1979: 66-67):

> *Miller didn't even bother to mark out his run, but he was an extremely dangerous bowler. He just tore in, with varying paces, with the ball in his left hand and long black hair blowing all over the place.*
>
> *Some of his fastest balls of the 1948 summer were bowled with a half-length run…Keith Miller reminds people that "great" is a great word, and as one facet of living, he was a great cricketer.*

Never afraid to express his views, Flying Officer and Seargent Miller was often critical of Board officials and the selectors and how the Australians sometimes played the game. Although he was a key player in 'Bradman's Invincibles' in 1948, Miller's relationship with The Don wasn't amicable. It possibly led to Miller's omission from a tour to South Africa in 1956 and why he never became Australia's captain.

As a kid, stories about Keith Miller's legendary exploits captivated me. In 1945, it was Miller's presence in the combined cricketers' team in the 'Victory Tests' that rekindled cricket's spark after the horrors of World War II. The 'Victory Tests' were played immediately after the war ended, in May 1945 (Holland 2020). Afterwards, Miller was asked by a journalist, a young

Michael Parkinson, about the pressure of playing Test cricket. 'I'll tell you what pressure is', Miller famously quipped. 'Pressure is a Messerschmitt up your arse. Cricket is Not' [14].

Miller lost five years of his career to war. Still, he flew hundreds of missions with RAAF mosquitoes and survived many close encounters with death. In the war, Miller saw some of his friends lose their lives and decided to live his own after that 'as if living for them'. He knew he had been lucky. For the 'swashbuckling flight lieutenant', cricket was 'all about entertainment, sportsmanship and fun; no cricketer should ever forget these important tenets' (Frith 2010; Mallett 2014; Hayter, 2019). 'Enjoyment' was precisely the same sentiment with which Doug played his cricket. Both believed 'if one wasn't enjoying cricket, one couldn't entertain the crowds'.

The consensus is that while these records were impressive, they didn't do justice to the great all-rounder's talent and impact with his mere presence in a team. Neville Cardus called him 'The Australian in excelsis' ('of the highest quality and calibre'). In the priceless bible – 200 Seasons of Australian Cricket, Hutchinson and Ross (1997: 254) noted the tribute to Miller that Arlott had written in 1948:

> *Miller was an immense spectator attraction throughout England. He could infuriate a crowd in a matter of seconds by tossing his long hair forward over his face and sweeping it back with an elaborate gesture or by bowling a bouncer, or he could charm them with a wave, a brilliant catch, or an expansive stroke... If I had to choose a player to win a match off the last ball, whether it required a catch, a six or a wicket, I would pick one player – Keith Ross Miller...*

Thousands of cricket fans worldwide admired the 'imperious and unpredictable' Australian. Miller's opinions were widely respected. He was adamant that 'Bradman was 'The greatest batter ever in the world of cricket, but Sobers was the greatest cricketer'. Greatly admired for the delight he gave millions of people, Keith Miller was among the first 'athletes' to be inducted into the Sports Australia Hall of Fame in 1986. Later, he was recognized further in the Cricket Hall of Fame in 1996 (Sports Australia 2024) [15].

---

14   Miller made 2,958 Test runs at 37 and took 170 wickets at 23 from 55 Tests. He made seven centuries and one 10-wicket match haul. His highest score (147) was one of the three centuries he made in the Caribbean in 1955.

15   Richie Benaud explained in an interview for the ABC that 'speech-making' was one of the reasons why Miller was overlooked by the Australian selectors for the country's captaincy, which was handed over to Ian Johnson (ABC 2006). Miller wasn't very good at public speaking. But *Was Richie joking?*

Building a Life - *Listening and Learning Cricket*

Apart from Miller, I recall asking my father about the Three Ws – West Indian legendary cricketers of the past – Worrell, Weeks and Walcott. With his rudimentary cricket knowledge, I realised he didn't know much about them. All Three Ws were sporting heroes in the Caribbean colonies that the British ruled for centuries.

The English press called these cricketing giants the Terrible Ws for tormenting England in the famous 1950 series in which the Windies recorded their first 'away' from home series win (3-1) against England. Preston (1951) noted that the Windies firmly established themselves among the top Test-playing nations on their seventh tour to England.

It was 22 years since they were given Test status in 1928. Not so long after that, one of the greatest days in the history of West Indies cricket dawned. On 26 February 1930, they won their first Test, beating England at Georgetown by 289 runs. George Headley hit a century in each inning [16].

Headley, Worrell, Weeks and Walcott were not just stylish batters. They were also gentlemen of the highest calibre who brought honour to Caribbean people as they struggled to gain independence. Success in cricket and beating England was a landmark event in their cricket history. The 1950 series was also the first time five-day Tests were given to the Windies, a privilege only Australia enjoyed up to that time.

C.L.R. James's *Beyond A Boundary* (1963) gives a fascinating account of the era in which Headley, Constantine and the Three Ws played a liberating role in the 'de-colonization' of the Caribbean islands. The book was part of the black power struggle, breaking the shackles of the colonial rulers. It shows that persistent clashes between the 'haves' and the 'have-nots' of race, caste and class stimulated cricket instead of retarding it. Selma James (2013) clarified how her husband schemed and finally succeeded in promoting Frank Worrell as the first 'coloured' cricket captain (James 1963: 59). Worrell went on to distinguish himself as an outstanding servant of the cricket world.

* * *

Just like in the Caribbean islands, cricket was introduced to Ceylon by the British, who first arrived in 1796 and entirely conquered the island by 1815. Cricket was then played as a pastime around Colombo even before the island fully surrendered. History shows that cricket was first introduced to the sub-continent in the early 1700s by the East India Company and

---

16   George Headley was 'saved for cricket because he was born in Panama and lived in Jamaica, although his parents were in the USA'. After batting so successfully again the visiting English team, Headley chose to give up on the idea of going to the USA (Manley 1988; James 1963: 12).

was played by British Mariners at various places in 1721 (ESPN Cricinfo, 1967). One of the oldest clubs formed in India was The Calcutta Cricket and Football Club, established in 1792, followed by a club in Bombay in 1797.

The Indians paid scant regard in the early days for what the rulers were doing with small, wooden sticks and a red, round 'projectile'. They also noted that the three sticks were placed side by side, and people were disposed of at various points on the ground in relation to the three sticks. Many thousands of Indians would have passed by, wondering what these people were up to.

Nevertheless, despite the gradual subjugation of the sub-continent, cricket prospered. Within a few decades, 1840 to be exact, some Indians were playing alongside the Europeans. The East India Company built the Indian cities, including Madras, which had its first cricket club in 1846 (ESPN Cricinfo 1967). The game also began to be played in Karachi and Lahore (after partition, Pakistan) before 1850.

The British ruled Ceylon with an iron fist, quashing many rebellions through the 19th Century. They introduced cricket as a pastime for tea planters in Ceylon and the elite. Ceylon gained its independence in 1948 after decades of struggle, during which tea and cricket have long been closely intertwined. Hatred towards the rulers shaped the society that evolved in independent Ceylon in the 1950s and '60s. The same hatred was, however, not extended to cricket as I was growing up.

Michael Roberts (2008), a Social Scientist, observed that despite belonging to various ethnicities, the cricketing fraternity in Ceylon quickly became a 'community' that was 'united by its interest in the game and its genteel amiability'. The talented locals didn't take long to produce teams that defeated the better-known touring teams (Roberts 2008; Brookes 2022). It was a case of 'let's show them what we can do'. Like in the Caribbean islands, the bitter sentiment towards the British in Ceylon was they were no better than we were.

Once cricket began to be shown on TV in the late 1970s, it became a transcendental influence that unified people in Sri Lanka. Watching live cricket on TV allowed the elite, the middle and lower social classes, including labourers, domestic servants, and the young and old, to form a composite, sitting together and sharing time.

The enjoyment of watching cricket, especially when the National team was winning, was a conduit by which people transcended social constraints and inequalities of their state. Some non-British whites of Dutch origin (Burghers) and the local non-whites (Sinhalese, Tamils, Malays, Colombo

Chetty, and so on) saw the sports arena, especially cricket, as a theatre to 'show their colours' to the rulers (Roberts 2008).

Despite the unifying nature of cricket, it was also a significant factor that caused deep divisions among some multi-ethnic actors, including cricket clubs and rival schools in Sri Lanka. As noted by Perera (2000), Roberts (2008), and Brookes (2022), the first cricket clubs formed in Colombo were defined by the Colombo 'elite' groups in Ceylon, in those days.

The affluent clubs were divided along ethnic lines for decades before they expanded. Examples are clubs, such as the Sinhalese Sports Club (SSC), Burgher Recreation Club (BRC) and the Tamil Union. Similar to what James (1963) described in the Caribbean, such clubs were initially exclusive to cricketers by birth: Sinhalese, Burghers or Tamils. Such exclusivities lasted for decades before they disappeared. Suvendrini Perera (2000) noted, 'Contrary to imperial mythologies, cricket in the colonies, as in the colonising country, has been a source not of unity and cohesion, but of division and antagonism' [17].

* * *

Growing up, I was schooled in two elite Buddhist schools (Sri Sumangala College, Panadura, and Ananda College, Colombo). Leaders of both schools played significant roles in the Buddhist revival on the island before and after independence. Nonetheless, both schools warmly created an atmosphere catering for their cricket-mad kids.

I wasn't the only one seduced by cricket, although I might have stood out. In the 1950s and '60s, cricket received very little support from the island's post-independent national government. Indeed, cricket in Ceylon developed mainly with funding from 'upper-class' enthusiasts, various associations and networks of the plantation sector, especially tea planters, and the dominant missionary schools.

My father also had 'anti-colonial' sentiments, common in post-independent Ceylon. Nearly everyone had had enough British and wanted what they left behind to change quickly. Interestingly, cricket wasn't one of those elements. The nationalist elements in Ceylon baulked at cricket, calling it a part of Britain's imperialistic expansion.

---

[17] Politics and cricket didn't mix well in Sri Lanka. The island is still deeply affected by political corruption since the terrorist war ended in May 2009. Suvendrini Perera's scholarly piece (2000) referred to the killing by the *Tamil Tigers* (LTTE) a certain Chellia Anandarajah, a Tamil national, who attempted to organize a cricket match between Jaffna schools and the Sri Lankan Army. In killing Anandarajah, the LTTE interpreted the slain man's attempts as politically motivated and not related to promoting cricket.

I doubt whether the rulers introduced cricket to their colonies as a part of an ideological extension to win favour with the locals. Instead, it was a pastime that sailors and other servants of the empire engaged in. Cricket was also a way to develop social networks in the colonies and spend a few happy hours away from work. However, the locals saw winning against the coloniser as more than a win –a form of resistance.

As a kid, I recall that some of the elite clubs and cricketers were derided by the nationalist elements on the island using the term 'Kalu-Suddhas' (Kalu refers to black, i.e. native Ceylonese; Suddha refers to the white, British rulers). The term 'Kalu-suddha' referred to the archetypal 'native Ceylonese' who supported the rulers and wanted to create a little bit of Britain on the island, a sentiment hated by the nationalists.

As youngsters, we mocked some other kids as 'Kalu-Suddhas' when they preferred to play rugby or tennis and spoke endlessly in not-so-perfect English. This was not the kids' fault but their upbringing in the elite Christian schools in and around Colombo and other major cities. Kids from wealthy families in our schools often prided themselves on displaying their possessions (such as shiny shoes, starched uniforms and bats and balls). Families from the middle and lower social classes usually could not provide comparable luxuries for their kids.

* * *

My interest in cricket was so great that even my father, by no means obsessed with cricket, usually started the day reading the *Ceylon Daily News* from sports news on the last page. Checking cricket scores was one of the first things to do in the morning. I often sneaked in to look at the back page and get the scores. I could hardly speak English at the tender age of 10 years. But that did not entirely deter me.

One of the most dramatic transformations the politicians in the newly independent island made was to change the language instructions in schools from English to Sinhala and Tamil, the two dominant native languages. Around 1956, this change got entrenched with legislation, alienating the non-Sinhala-speaking people (Tamils, Muslims and Burghers) on the island. Hundreds of Burghers, including some famous cricketers from Ceylon, left the island and consequently migrated to Australia, the UK, Canada and other countries.

This change also meant that learning to speak and read in English in schools needed some dedicated effort for most kids of my generation. Many schools at that time were poorly equipped to teach English. That also didn't matter much to me as I learned English quickly by reading about cricket in newspapers and magazines like *Sport & Pastime*, *Wisden*, and *The Cricketer*. Learning to speak and write in English also developed concurrently with my passion for cricket.

In the 1950s and '60s, newspapers were the primary means of knowing what was happening around the globe in all aspects. Like my grandfather, avid readers read the daily paper for 2-3 hours. For a cricket freak like me, they were of great value. But at home, I had to be patient and get my hands on the paper after my grandfather finished reading in the mornings [18]. Apart from sports, a bit of music on the radio and movies, there were not too many other distractions in the 1960s for a kid growing up in Ceylon.

Roberts (2008) said that fluency in English gave the middle class more 'cultural capital'. In schools, kids who played rugby were more fluent in English, although it was full of slang. Rugby dominated sports in some Christian schools. But, in most of the island's schools, cricket was much more available for kids from all backgrounds.

Many who came up through the school system and clubs in recent decades and then went on to represent the island's cricket teams could hardly speak English. Also, the same race, caste and class clashes that James (1963) referred to were evident in Ceylon before and after independence, as traced by Nicholas Brookes' book (2020) on Sri Lanka's cricket history – *An Island's Eleven*.

* * *

When I studied in the U.K. from 1980-83, my colleagues realised that a cricket-mad scholar had arrived from Sri Lanka. They respected me for my cricket knowledge. Cricket allowed me to converse with people wherever I went – all kinds of University staff, from the cleaners, drivers, tea ladies, and technicians to the professors. It was great fun to talk about the cricket personalities – a conversation maker in every sense. Speaking cricket, I made friends with the locals much more quickly than other scholars from the sub-continent.

There are great cricket writers and commentators that I read, listen to and admire. Many, but not all, are cricketers themselves or are professional journalists. It would be folly to compare myself with them because I've not even been a serious amateur cricketer. I am just an armchair cricket fan. Still, my training in science allows me to be a bit more than a superficial analyst and critic.

---

18 Harte and Whimpress (2008: 369) explained that in the 1930s Newspapers offered page upon page of cricket and 'it was a poor newspaper that did not employ at least three former Test players as correspondents'.

I delve deeper into how cricket has changed, how it is played today, cricketers as people, and cricket's social evolution. Learning from history, as a cricket connoisseur, I also have strong opinions on how the game should be played. In this technological era, among the lay cricket fans, only a handful critically analyze and write about the game. Fast-moving lifestyles are, perhaps, the reason for that.

In the past, giants in Test cricket, like Jack Fingleton, Bill O'Reilly and Keith Miller from Australia, and E. W. (Jim) Swanton and John Arlott from England, criticised what they saw wrong in cricket in their respective countries or overseas. Nowadays, columnists criticising officials must be careful because they might lose their commissions.

Harsh criticisms don't go down well in Australia. As a result, the journalists who write critical accounts are often accused of being anti-Australian by their detractors. In recent times, Ian Chappell and the late Peter Roebuck have been rare exceptions because they critically analyzed the attitudes of cricketers and trends in cricket and didn't shy away from calling it for what it is. They also paid a price for reporting without fear or favour. Alan McGilvray was also highly critical of some Australian teams for being disrespectful towards opponents.

* * *

John Arlott, the English journalist, was the 'perfect voice' with his thoughtful delivery, long pauses and vivid descriptions of what was happening in the middle and surroundings. Arlott's rasping voice was distinct (the Hampshire burr). He often criticised the snobbish English upper class, including the elitist MCC, the owner of Lord's and the guardian of the Laws of the game in those days. A champion of the working class in Britain, Arlott wanted the MCC to be a more inclusive club. He was a former policeman who taught himself journalism.

Although appearing dogmatic on many issues, his delightful articles are full of sarcasm and wit. A recent critical analysis by Stephen Fay and David Kynaston (2020) of the impact of Arlott and Swanton, two of the greatest cricket writers, confirmed my recollections. Arlott and Swanton didn't like each other. They often battled for the soul of English cricket during the significant social changes in the 1960s, '70s and '80s. They were both excellent journalists, and their writings painted colourful images of the Tests they reported on in my mind.

Wallowing in cricket's rich history opens one's mind to the game's finer points, rumblings, and politics. Without such knowledge to draw from, there will be no future to build on and develop cricket. One way to understand parochialism entrenched in cricket and its role in shaping a society's culture is to probe deeply into the history of cricket.

Thankfully, my extensive collection of books and magazines allowed me this privilege. The writings of Cardus, James, Arlott, Swanton, Fingleton, O'Reilly, McGilvray, Bailey, Blofeld, Ian Chappell, Cozier and Roebuck gave me this knowledge. These gentlemen are endearing in my cricket-mad heart because they wrote so passionately. They poured their own true spirit of the game into my soul.

Arlott said Sir Neville was cricket's own 'Shakespeare': 'Before him, cricket was reported. With him, it was the first time appreciated, felt and imaginatively described' (Agnew 2013: 434). Cardus showed how to put cricket observations to paper with opinions backed by analyses mixed with metaphors and poetry. In so doing, he personalised the game for his readers. Cardus encouraged all cricket writers to expose their hearts and souls. He once wrote: 'We remember not the scores and the results, after years; it is the men who remain in our minds, in our imagination...The scoreboard is an ass'!

Describing early 20th Century batting heroes, such as W.G., Jack Hobbs, Frank Woolley and Pelham Warner, Cardus said that such men were 'Artists' who 'performed on the canvas called cricket'. In Days In The Sun (1924) and Good Days (1934), two of his early books (Cardus 1949a;b), he explained why Cricket is more than a game! Invoking cricket's unquestionable 'Englishness', Cardus wrote:

If everything else in this nation of ours were lost but cricket, it would be possible to reconstruct [from it] all the eternal Englishness which has gone to the establishment of the Constitution and the laws.

In nearly 150 years of cricket reporting (Moult 1935), no one can match Cardus for marrying poetry and the power of prose to paint a picture as an Artist would. Clearly, other prolific writers learned from Cardus how to report on matches invoking the atmosphere and not just dull scoreboard. In a tribute, *Wisden* (1965b) recorded:

It may be true that cricket was always an art, but no one until Neville Cardus presented it as an art with all an artist's perception. Because of him, thousands of people enjoy watching the game more than they would have done if he had not lived and written.

Many hundreds of cricket books have been written by past players.

Some are autobiographies written with the help of journalists. Such books provide details about what went on in the players' minds and the team as they engaged in Test battles. Until the floodgates opened about 20 years ago, I read many biographies and didn't miss much.

Some recent books are not helpful for the discerning reader. The narrators twist their stories to even glorify their dubious behaviours. That's the flip side of slick marketing of players. Narratives based on poorly conducted interviews, pouring out one's own, usually skewed opinions, are bad for a cricket book. A good cricket book must link the player to history, contemporaries, opponents, countries, playing conditions, crowds and the environment, all of which are relevant.

Cardus was a master of this craft; he actually invented it. Many of his articles describe the conditions surrounding a match and even how players and journalists travel to a game. Before he dealt with the scorecard, it was important for Cardus to illuminate to his readers the background and the atmosphere in which a match was played. Arlott followed this style of writing. They wrote without fear or favour because they believed they were duty-bound, as journalists, to speak out on behalf of cricket lovers about the good, bad and ugly in cricket.

* * *

For the sharp reader, the poorly written biographies are of little value. When the perspectives are presented from a narrow frame of mind, one cannot always believe what's written. A few books I've read insult the great traditions of cricket writing. Nowadays, many ghostwriters benefit from luring a player for a few interviews and creating a shallow narrative. One of the latest silly trends is to pen biographies even when a player is still in the middle part of a career.

Decades of soaking in cricket meant I became adept at instantly picking up errors made by commentators and mistakes in cricket photos printed in books. The errors made by the so-called 'experts' on TV and radio are laughable and unacceptable to connoisseurs like me.

I can't help but laugh at mistakes that have crept into books and magazines, photos printed the wrong way, cricketers misnamed in the captions. Alas, commercial pressures in the modern era have resulted in even editorial scrutiny dipping below the required standards.

I can easily pick those errors because of the thousands of hours spent looking at cricket photographs. The access to film footage has also dramatically sharpened my ability to recognize cricketers even as they move around in the field or in still pictures.

CHAPTER 5

An Uncontrollable Passion

My uncontrollable passion for cricket began in 1963-64. I was under 10 years of age. On our super-fantastic Grundig Radio (thanks to the brilliance of German technology!), I recall receiving short-wave broadcasts from England, beamed across the continents to be received in Ceylon. These were then relayed by Radio Ceylon. It was called Colombo Radio in those days, and it was initiated in 1923 as an experiment by engineers in the pre-independent Ceylon's Telegraph Department. The first radio equipment included a transmitter salvaged from a captured German submarine. Importantly, Colombo Radio was initiated three years after the BBC was established in London.

Of Batting and Batsmanship

Three concepts are relevant to my perspectives in re-telling this Doug Walters story. They are batting, batsmanship and genius. All were introduced to cricket by Neville Cardus in his early books. The ideas were expanded later by James (1963). Cardus and James were the most transformative cricket writers the world was privileged to experience.

The difference between batting and batsmanship, Cardus said, was that one is utility, meaning essential and useful, and the other is an Art. He admitted that most cricket fans would shift uncomfortably in their seats if someone said cricket is an Art. Those who saw 'cricket as an 'art form' were the educated 'highbrows', whom Sir Neville contrasted with 'lowbrows', the working class in industrial Britain [19].

Batting is the basis of run-scoring; without it, there would be no game of cricket. Batting is based on good hand-eye coordination, good footwork

---

19 In Sri Lanka, the words to differentiate the two groups were *'Kultur'* ('cultured') versus *'Haramani*s' or shortened as *'Hara'* referring to peasants from a village. Haramanis is a common name of a male farmer or a peasant in rural areas. It is also a common name of domestic servant.

What divided the *Haras* from *Kultas* was knowledge of English, western clothes and manners. The English language, used by *Kultas* was referred to as *Kaduwa*, which means *Sword* in Sinhalese. The weaponized term *Kaduwa* acts as a strong deterrent as a weapon of war, keeping people apart, or *cuts down those that aspire above their current status.*

to go forward or backward and often a straight bat rather than a cross bat. But Cardus said that 'real batters know that all but a few of the noble cricket strokes can be made with a straight bat. No one can cut, hook or pull without a cross bat'. Good batting also requires patience to build an inning. Batting could be just the ferocious attack on a bowler, as displayed by Gilbert Jessop, Learie Constantine, Garry Sobers, Clive Lloyd and Viv Richards, or defensive play, as by those who valued their wickets (accumulators).

The accumulators from Doug's playing era would be Bob Simpson, Bill Lawry, Geoff Boycott, John Edrich, Sunil Gavaskar, Zaheer Abbas and Glenn Turner. They were 'Impersonal compilers of runs' (Cardus 1935: 42-43). These 'star' players piled up runs and 'got the job done' for their teams. Undoubtedly, the 'utilitarian batters' gave pleasure when they made big scores and won accolades when their teams won.

Their deeds often saved the countries from defeat. But, in drawing a contrast between batting and batsmanship, Cardus (1935: 41) said, 'One could be excused for sometimes being bored with them'.

* * *

'Batsmanship' is a much loftier concept that alludes to the mastery of a craft. Both Cardus and James argue that cricket is an art similar to a masterpiece created by a great artist. It includes deft footwork and many other beautiful things at the crease. In displaying batsmanship, the great batter expresses genius at work. He leaves an unforgettable image in the minds of those who saw it.

Most Test batters fall between utilitarians and artists. The crowds who flock to see the artistry of specific individuals would attest to this 'phenomenon'. In expressing his 'genius', the scoreboard is irrelevant to the artist. Batsmanship, therefore, is batting plus the intense expression of creative genius at the crease.

Expanding the concept, James described the 'regal presence' of his heroes at the crease. He invoked Grace, Trumper, Bradman, Headley, Constantine, Walcott, Weeks and Worrell as great batting artists. James also said that the Miller and Lindwall bowling partnership and Hutton and Compton batting together were pure artistry (Cardus 1963: 279).

Limiting to only Doug's playing era batters, Sobers, Graeme Pollock, Clive Lloyd, Viswanath, Majid Khan, the Chappell brothers, Barry Richards and Viv Richards all had this 'magnificent presence' at the crease. As champions, they frequently went up from a normal batting mode into a 'savage' mode and murdered the bowling.

* * *

The artistry, power and energy such batters put into batting made them unique. In Cardus's reckoning (1935: 43-44), Bradman was the epitome; Trumper and Jessop were not far behind, 'best of the best power-hitters the game has ever seen'. You instantly knew something would happen when they were at the crease and dared not stop listening or watching! They often broke the bowlers' hearts.

Mortals, they may be, but their immortal displays of batting mastery were not something in the abstract; it was real; the strokes were true; the batters were a 'visible manifestation' of a man's capability and an 'expression of his soul' 'Footwork and faith in oneself! Get to the ball, and then deal with it according to one's instincts' (Cardus, 1935: 45).

As a cricket fan, I thank Sir Neville for differentiating between batsmanship and everyday utilitarian batting. It gives me a handy framework to analyse my idol, Doug Walters, who was an artist for an extended period in Australian cricket. As I explore in the book, elegant stroke play was a hallmark of his batsmanship as he notched up a Test century in a session three times in his career. Doug's muscular forearms and wrists, combined with deft footwork, gave him an uncanny ability for timing and placement of the ball where he wanted.

Cardus eloquently described the artistry in the batting of Victor Trumper, considered nonpareil among batters of the era, who tragically died in 1915 at the age of 37 years. Similar descriptions of Jack Hobbs, Don Bradman, George Headley, Learie Constantine, Everton Weeks, Clyde Walcott, Frank Worrell, Denis Compton, Garry Sobers and the like are plentiful in the literature, written by those who saw them in action. Not many batters, over 150 years of modern cricket, can be placed in the above unique category of artists at the crease.

Cricket is 'More than a Game' - Cardus again!

Sir Neville explained that while batting was transformed into batsmanship, the delight given by the great cricketers was so infectious that cricket became more than a game. It became an essential summer pageant. It allowed Englishmen to 'See the game but also live it' with various forms of cultural expression, including art, paintings and poetry. He wrote that 'playing cricket was an active tool to build "character" in human endeavours, especially in youngsters'.

Defining a genius in cricket, Cardus (1949b: 30) invoked the performances of several players, including Grace, Ranjitsinhji, Headley and Constantine. Below are some excerpts from Cardus (1949b):

Genius is "originality"... In Cricket, the main is a genius who does a thing superbly, masterfully, and entirely in a way that is his own. His play must make us cry out, "Nobody else could do it!" We must feel and know that without it [genius], the game would be short of some quality or power necessary to fulfil all its delightful parts and possibilities.

Cricket is more than a simple game and certainly not an abstraction. This is because it involves two teams of 11 players each, using bats, wickets and a ball for the implements. The Test cricket we love as a people the wide world over is the sum total of ALL the personal skills and character which have been put to it by great men who have played it and who, by giving to the technique and form some turn or push of their own...and have kept development alive and in touch with the people, decade after decade.

Grace demonstrated the art of placing the ball and how to play forward and back in one comprehensive system of footwork. Ranjitsinjhi demonstrated the leg glance and expressed the genius of his race. In other human endeavours, we identify a genius as someone with remarkable creative and intellectual power to produce something original and immortal. The often-cited scientific geniuses include Da Vinci, Galileo, Isaac Newton, Albert Einstein and Stephen Hawkins. Genius also applied to Beethoven, Bach, and Mozart in music.

Doug Walters is also a cricketing genius who came very close to the above definition. There were loads of days when Doug brought crowds to their feet with his brilliant batting. In my research, I couldn't discuss Doug's batting style separated from the man himself. He was a quintessential Australian lad from the bush, endowed with the mastery of batsmanship. While demonstrating this trait, he didn't forget to enjoy and make others enjoy the game.

The Lure of Cricket - A Madness

Bob Simpson's Australians made a 'whistle-stop' tour to Ceylon in 1964, which intensely aroused my interest in cricket. The team had sailed on a ship – the Orcades – on 9 April 1964. It was the last touring team to use a ship to travel. They were on their way to England for the 1964 Ashes. The team played a single match in Ceylon on 15th April. They then flew from Bombay on the 17th of April and arrived in London on the 19th of April. Jet air travel only began after 1964.

I recall the match they played at the P. Saravanamuttu Stadium, which we called The Oval. Several well-known Ceylonese cricketers (Buddy Reid, Mano Ponniah, Norton Frederick and Darrell Lieversz) made their international debuts that day. Conroy Ievers (C. I.) Gunasekera captained the local side. The Ceylon team had several well-established and famous cricketers (Neil Chanmugam, Abu Fuard, Anuruddha Polonnowita, Herbert Fernando and Lasantha Rodrigo).

Batting first, the Australians scored 249, with runs from Cowper (65), O'Neill (49) and Burge (32). Ceylon responded with 3-103 in 101 minutes when rain halted play. Coming in at 3-35, young Michael Tissera belted 12 fours and was 51* in just 34 minutes. Tissera showed exceptional batting skills against the attack, comprised of Graham Corling, Neil Hawke, Johnny Martin, Tom Vievers and Simpson.

The visitors paid a high tribute to how the locals played their cricket. It was the last time C.I., a national hero in post-independent Ceylon, captained the country. The mantle of captaincy passed on to the young star, Tissera, by August 1964. Michael first represented Ceylon in 1959 and had already impressed several touring teams with his brilliant batting. He was a crucial figure in the island's cricket journey and was captain for over a decade until the mid-1970s.

* * *

Following the Australians in the 1964 summer, one of my earliest memories is listening to Simpson making his monumental 311, batting for over two days, at Old Trafford in the fourth Test (23-28 July 1964). Lawry made 106 in an opening stand of 201 with Simpson. I thought Simpson was finally bowled by Barry Knight, a medium-pacer, but my memory was wrong. Simpson was actually caught behind by Jim Parks off Knight. Despite being incorrect in my 60-year-old memory, I correctly remembered Ken Barrington making 256 and Ted Dexter's imperious 174 in England's first-inning reply.

Many commentators described the fourth Test as a turgid disgrace for its slow batting. Australians batted first and made 8-656 in 255 overs. England batted even slower, replying with 611 from 293 overs, which left only two overs for Australia's second inning. Simpson's 311 was his first Test hundred at the 52nd attempt. It was the longest wait for an Australian batter to score a century.

As an avid young fan, it didn't occur to me that slow scoring of around 200-250 runs in a day of Test cricket kept crowds away. I thought this was the norm. However, Australians were criticised by the English press for batting too long in the fourth Test. Having won the third Test at Headingley by seven wickets, Australia was 1-0 up when they went into the Old Trafford Test. This explains why Simpson batted England out of the game to keep his team's lead.

I do not recall more about this early event except where the Grundig radio was placed at home and where I sat alone, listening to the monumental knocks from Simpson, Barrington and Dexter. As kids, when we played competitive backyard cricket in those days, we mimicked our favourite batters, and Bob Simpson was mine.

Australia won the rubber 1-nil in 1964 by winning at Headingley, Leeds (7-9 July 1964), thus retaining The Ashes. With four other Tests drawn, this single win was due mainly to Simpson. He had imbued his men with a fine team spirit after Australia's cricket had been weakened by the exits of Benaud, Davidson, Harvey and Ken Mackay. In England, Simpson lost the toss four times to Dexter but won it when it mattered most, in the vital Old Trafford Test, in which he batted England out of any chance of winning the match.

* * *

In those days, the Grundig radio did much work for our families. It was technology at its best in the 1950s and 60s. We were thrilled when we saw its bowels through the back panel, which was occasionally removed for fresh batteries to be put in. We learnt that the receiver was 'wireless' because no wires linked it to the transmitting station. It was called 'radio' because it received signals from the transmission in some electromagnetic waveform.

With an excellent bandwidth, the Grundig received medium wave and short wave signals. Sometimes, these signals were weak, had high background noises and frequently faded. But I didn't mind their inconsistency. I thoroughly enjoyed the BBC Test Match Special broadcasts, beamed from the UK and ABC broadcasts from Australia, which the radio easily picked up.

Back then, the ethos of both these prestigious institutions was to beam news across the continents using these radio waves. It was undoubtedly a relic of the war years when radio communication was critical. As the war ended and the world settled into a calmer and rebuilding period, the radio authorities saw continuing the broadcasts as an essential responsibility for the world.

The cricket-loving public and those like me benefited greatly as Test cricket commentaries were beamed across continents. Much to our dismay, by the 1990s, these broadcasts were abandoned as economic rationalism and market forces began to rule how organizations were run. Sadly, public interest in sports then became unimportant.

Sambandan (2006) reported that broadcasts from Radio Ceylon were crucially important in the Asian region in the 1930s and '40s. Ceylon's broadcasts, including English music, were extremely popular in pre-independent India. Verified by many sources, Radio Ceylon programmes were much more diverse than what Indians could listen to via Air India Radio, which mainly had localized content in different languages, such as Hindi, Tamil or Malayalam.

* * *

After Bob Simpson's marathon triple hundred, the following day, I read a report with a photo of him with that beaming smile in the Ceylon Daily News. I liked the audacity and determination of his batting. A few years later, I found it hard to believe that the triple century at Old Trafford, Manchester, was Simpson's first Test century. However, he had been opening for Australia for a few years before becoming captain in January 1964.

Once hooked in, I followed Simpson's career closely, through his premature retirement in 1969 and subsequent return to lead Australia in 1979 after the Kerry Packer's World Series Cricket (WSC) debacle during 1977-79. I also followed Simpson's tenure as Australia's coach through the 1980s, during which he brought a confident, hard-nosed attitude to physical fitness, fielding, planning, dressing room and on-field player behaviour and overall team management.

Reg Edwards (1977b), writing his series of articles on Masters of Cricket, said cricket fans were pleased when Simpson returned to Test cricket and helped Australia rebuild the team with younger players. Someone with experience was needed. At the end of the Ashes tour in 1977, the core of the senior players, including Greg Chappell and other established players like Dennis Lillee, Rod Marsh and Doug, had been banned from Test cricket after they signed up with Packer's WSC.

At 41, Simpson was still playing grade cricket in NSW for the Western Suburbs in Sydney when he was persuaded to return to Test cricket in 1977 by the Australian Cricket Board (ACB). With Jeff Thomson as his deputy, Simpson led an Australian side with young players against Bishen Bedi's Indians in the summer of 1977-78.

The series was marred by the Indians criticising the Australian umpires. There was also some dislike between the two teams. Indians were at full strength and believed they could beat the weakened Australians, and they nearly did. But the Australians won by a close margin of 3-2, mainly because of Simpson. Although he started shakily, the old stager showed that experience counted as he scored 539 runs at 53.9. In scoring 176 in the second Test in Perth, Simpson became the oldest Australian player to hit a century at home.

* * *

However, Simpson wasn't 'everyone's cup of tea', as Vivian Richards, the great West Indian, stated. Richards called Simpson 'A moaner, a bad loser and a very sour sort of guy' for whom he had 'no respect'. Simpson was the Australian coach in the acrimonious tour of 1990-91 to the Caribbean when Allan Border-led Aussies clashed with Richards-led Windies. Hostility between the two teams, verbal abuses and disputed umpiring decisions marred the series. The Australian tour to the Caribbean in 1990-91 was the worst in cricketing relationships between the two nations (Hutchinson and Ross 1997: 559).

Simpson played it tough and wasn't apologetic for his actions. In general, even within Australia, Simpson hasn't been a popular figure in cricket circles, despite fans admiring him for his gritty batting and slip-catching. When Australian cricket fell into a post-WSC hole in the mid-1980s, Simpson came back as coach (from 1986 to 1996) to assist, firstly, Allan Border and then Mark Taylor, to restore the country's cricket reputation once more to number one (Perry 2000: 242).

Simpson's disciplined planning laid the foundation for much of Australia's success in cricket over the next two decades, even after he finished as a coach. It is not that previous captains didn't do any strategizing before a tour or Test series. However, Simpson took planning to another level. His considerable influence on Australian cricket, including fitness and fielding, came during his second stint as Australia's captain in 1979, before his coaching tenure in the mid-80s. Simpson brought fitness as the core foundation of rebuilding Australia's cricket. It is a legacy credited to him that endures to date and is appreciated by all countries in the global cricket circuit.

As revealed by Doug, Ian Chappell's daring leadership and influence on the team were also critically important factors in Australia's resurgence and becoming the most dominant force in world cricket in the 1970s. Ian, too, isn't very popular among many Australian cricket fans because of his forthright and no-nonsense attitude to everything, including cricket. Ian pulls no punches when he says something, much like his grandfather, Victor Richardson, who also captained Australia.

* * *

The next best recollection of those distant and impressionable days was listening to a Test match in India in 1964. As a kid, I was seated on my father's lap; I believe it was a Saturday afternoon (10 October 1964). Tom Vievers, the muscular leg-spinning all-rounder from Queensland, and Barry Jarman, the burly South Australian wicket-keeper, were batting for Australia. Both made half-centuries, saving Australia from humiliation in the second Test.

Bapu Nadkarni's left-arm orthodox slow stuff on spin-friendly wickets troubled the Aussies in India. I remember asking my father about what was happening as the crowd's excitement and cheering could be heard, drowning the commentary occasionally. He couldn't answer. Later on, it became clear that father had only a passing interest in all of this. He knew not much about spin-bowling and uncovered pitches in those days. Still, at that crucial moment, etched in memory, he explained that the Australians were trying to save a match in India.

Nadkarni was already famous for bowling 131 balls (nearly 22 six-ball overs) in a row without a run being scored off him in a match against England in Madras in 1963-64. In this world record of tight bowling, on 12 January 1964, Ken Barrington and Brian Bolus 'stonewalled' as the crowds 'went to sleep' (Sengupta 2016).

A set of old *Sport & Pastime* gave me a thorough insight into how Simpson's Australians fared in 1964. I recall keenly reading the magazines that I still have. The photographs are still sharp and vivid.

The India-Pakistan legs of the tour came at the back of the Ashes battles in England, only after a short rest for the touring Australians on their way home. Only Test matches were played in the sub-continent, crammed into October 1964 (*Wisden* 1965a). In the three Tests played in India, each side won a game while the third was drawn. The game was drawn in the only Test match played in Pakistan.

* * *

In the first Test at the M. A. Chidambaram Stadium in Madras (2-7 October 1964), Australia won by 139 runs with two hours to spare. They paid the penalty of taking liberties with the accurate slow left-armer, Nadkarni (5/31 in 18 overs), when they won the toss and were dismissed for 211. Lawry (62), Simpson (30) and O'Neill (40) didn't go on with their good starts, and the last six wickets fell for 50. India also recovered after being 5-76 through a partnership between the captain, Nawab of Pataudi (128) and Chandu Borde (49), who added 142 for the sixth wicket. Pataudi's was a splendid century, while McKenzie claimed 6/58 in a tireless bowling effort. The Indian total was 276.

Australia cleared the arrears of 65 during an opening stand of 91 between Simpson (77) and Lawry (41). Burge (60) and Veivers (74) also batted well. Nadkarni bowled 54.4 overs, taking another haul of 6 wickets for 91 runs to finish with a bag of 11 for 122 in the match. Set to get 333 to win, despite defiant knocks from Hanumant Singh (94) and Vijay Manjrekar (40), India never looked like winning as the rest of the batting faltered. They were bowled out for 193. McKenzie took 4/33 for a ten-wicket match haul. Wally Grout, the great Australian wicket-keeper, got hit on the chin and was replaced by Barry Jarman for the following two Tests (*Wisden* 1965a).

* * *

Checking my recollection about the broadcasts received in Ceylon via All India Radio, I found that the second Test was played at the Brabourne Stadium in Bombay from 10-15 October 1964. Australia batted first and declared at 9-320.

O'Neill was suffering from a stomach virus and was hospitalized. So, Australia was one key batter short. Peter Burge made 80, but the Australians struggled at one stage at 5-146. Tom Vievers (67) and Barry Jarman (78) then put on 153 for the sixth wicket, rescuing the team from the tight spot. The fastish leg-spinner, Bhagwat Chandrasekhar (4/50), was the main wrecker. Nadkarni (2/65) troubled the Aussies again, but Vievers had hit him for three sixers, which I didn't recall.

The second innings saw Australia struggle again to reach 9-274. Bill Lawry (68), Brian Booth (64) and Bob Cowper (81) resisted stoutly on the turning wicket. Both Vievers and Jarman, who batted so well in the first innings, were dismissed by Chandrasekhar (4/73) for naught each.

Nadkarni spun his way to four more wickets for 33. India, then, scored the required runs (8-256) to win the match by two wickets and square the series. Dilip Sardesai (56), Pataudi (53), Manjrekar (39) and Borde (30*) ensured that they reached the target with half an hour to spare before a cheering crowd of 42,000. Vievers bowled 91 overs in oppressive heat and doubtful umpiring, bagging 4/150. Commentators said that the result might have been different if O'Neill had been able to bat (Hutchinson and Ross 1997: 356).

* * *

The third Test at Eden Gardens in Calcutta (17-22 October 1964) was ruined by rain, which washed off play on the last two days, leaving the series drawn at 1:1. The first innings of each side saw both teams troubled by spin. When Australia was put into bat, Simpson and Lawry opened with 97. Still, the rest of the batting collapsed, and the innings ended with a score of 174, the last nine wickets falling for only 77 runs.

This time, the Afghan-born Salim Durani, the left-arm orthodox spinner, troubled the Aussies, taking 6/73. Durani, a tall, charismatic athlete, was an all-rounder with a reputation for aggressive batting and bowling, which had a lot of variations.

Dilip Sardesai (42) and M. L. Jaisimha (57), whose large-sized colour pictures still adorn my scrapbooks, began well for India. Still, the off-spin of Vievers (3/81 in 52 overs) and Simpson's leg-spin (4/45 in 28 overs) caused a collapse. Chandu Borde, then, came to the rescue with a determined innings of 68* as India scored 235.

Australia batted a second time, 61 runs behind, but was again indebted to Simpson and Lawry, who opened with 115. With Australia at 1-143 at the end of the third day's play, rain ruined the match.

* * *

The three Test matches were marred by seriously inconsistent Indian umpiring and under-prepared, spinning wickets. The Australians protested strongly, to no avail. Simpson's *Captain's Story* (1966) and Lawry's *Run Digger* (1966) give absorbing insights into the competitive nature of this series. It was a pivotal series in my life. I got well and truly hooked on cricket after listening to the broadcasts from India.

While the hosts weren't affected, the heat in India and sickness, mainly due to food and drinks, affected many Australian players. Reports indicated that getting good food and clean water was a problem, and almost the entire team had stomach trouble at one time or another. It took India another three decades to resolve issues related to providing high-class hotels for visiting teams.

Lawry supported Simpson well, and their first-wicket partnerships in India of 66, 91, 35, 59, 97 and 115 enhanced their reputation as a top-class opening pair for Australia. However, neither made a century in the Tests. The only centurion in the series was the Nawab of Pataudi, with his gritty 128 in the first Test, which India lost.

The series showed how difficult batting was on uncovered and grassless pitches in those days. Run-scoring was often painfully slow. Pataudi (270 runs at 67.5), Simpson (292 at 49) and Lawry (284 at 57) were the leading batters of the series. Listening to the matches, I recall thinking that Test cricket, as slow as this, was the norm. As it turned out, the next few decades showed how wrong I was!

The bowling efforts of Graham McKenzie (13 wickets at 16) and Tom Vievers (11 wickets at 24) contrasted with Nadkarni's miserly figures of 17 wickets at 13.7 runs. Chandrasekhar, a legendary Indian spinner, did a lot of bowling in the two Tests he played for a series tally of nine wickets at 15.5.

* * *

Bob Simpson's account (1966) shows that, following his batting form in England, he enjoyed a successful time and showed no sign of staleness, which affected some of his other players. When the team moved from India to Pakistan, after just a few days of rest, the Australians played a single Test match at the National Stadium in Karachi (24-29 October 1964).

Simpson surpassed himself in this drawn Test, making 153 and 115, while the rest of Australia's batting failed. I recall the match well. In the Test, the Pakistan opener, Khalid 'Billy' Ibadulla, who played for Warwickshire, made a brilliant 166. Ibadulla had an opening stand of 249 runs with another debutant, a 20-year-old wicket-keeper, Abdul Kadir, who made 95. This stand remained the first-wicket Test record for Pakistan for decades.

If anything, the huge Pakistan opening stand showed the lack of penetration in the Australian attack. However, McKenzie bowled his heart out, taking 6/69 in 30 overs. Pakistan was dismissed for their highest Test score at that time of 414. McKenzie took two more wickets in the second innings for a match bag of 8/131. Several Australian bowlers, including Neil Hawke, were jaded by this time at the end of a long tour (Hutchinson and Ross 1997: 358).

The Australian reply (352) was built on Bob Simpson's second Test century (153). Australia conceded a lead of 62 runs. In the second innings, Pakistan declared at 8-279 with Javed Burki (62), Hanif Mohammad (40), Majid Khan (35) and Asif Iqbal (36) anchoring the innings, but it was a slow crawl. That left Australia with 342 to win in four and a half hours, which was never on. Bob Simpson used the time to notch up another century (115), the first Australian to do so in Pakistan and the fourth Australian to achieve the feat in Test cricket up to that time.

The Test match in late October 1964 also saw Pakistan play six debutants under Hanif Mohammad. Two of them, Majid Khan, who was not yet 18, and Asif Iqbal, about 21, became globally-admired cricketing legends. Majid and Asif, incredibly gifted batting all-rounders and handsome athletes, opened the bowling for Pakistan with their medium pacers. Both played most of their cricket in England.

Majid, a Cambridge Blue, played for Glamorgan, and Asif played for Kent for decades, building hugely successful careers. These two handsome young cricketers became my heroes after this Test. Majid and Asif became household names within a few years due to their daring batting and exploits.

I enjoyed how they transformed Pakistan into a strong Test-playing nation within a few short years.

* * *

In the same year, 1964, the Sri Lankan cricket team, led by Michael Tissera, defeated what was virtually a Pakistan Test side in a low-scoring match at The Oval (later, P. Saravanamuttu Stadium, in Borella) in Colombo. I later checked the dates, 28-30 August.

I recall listening to this victory with the whole family seated around the dinner table where we placed the Grundig. Sri Lanka was emerging into competitive cricket in the early 1960s. Surprisingly, cricket received little funding and support from the government in those days (which I was unaware of). The game developed mainly due to funding and support from cricket enthusiasts and institutions like missionary schools and planters' associations (Roberts 2008; Brookes 2022).

Before Sri Lanka achieved Test status in 1981 and played their first Test in 1982, the All Ceylon side played unofficial Tests in the 1960s. These were four-day affairs that were recognised as first-class matches. India and Pakistan were the only countries that invited Ceylon for these matches, supporting the island's campaign for Test status.

I remember well how we huddled around the radio and listened with great interest to some of the matches broadcast by Radio Ceylon. If we didn't get the broadcasts, we would eagerly listen to the radio for evening news at 6 pm (Sinhala News) or 7 pm (English News) to get updates on scores. Newspapers were vitally important when Test matches were played in the sub-continent. We read every word of a match report and dreamed about how our heroes performed.

Following the cricketing successes of the National team was a part of growing up on the island. Our cricketing heroes made us proud, enthralled and wedded to cricket. In the 1960s, Sri Lanka had not yet become a Test-playing country, nor had we beaten India in an 'unofficial' Test. However, in January 1965, well before the Test status, an All Ceylon team beat India, led by Nawab of Pataudi, in Ahmedabad in a one-off unofficial Test (a four-day game).

The Indian team included several batting and bowling stars, such as Dilip Sardesai, Farokh Engineer, Hanumant Singh, Abbas Ali Baig and Srinivas Venkataraghavan (Tiruchelvam 2013). Michael Tissera, the young captain of Ceylon's team, instantly became a great hero for us. He also won the respect of all Indian cricket fans and cricketers.

Many articles in the *Sport & Pastime* magazine showed that the Indians highly appreciated the charm, courage and spirit of the island's cricketers. The emerging stars also proved that cricket in Ceylon was of a very high standard and stable across the different ethnic groups, who were well-represented in the national team. India and Pakistan were confident that by the end of the 1960s, Ceylon should have Test status.

Cricket development in Ceylon paralleled how West Indies cricket developed in the Caribbean, particularly in the decades between the two World Wars (the 1920s to 1950s). The brutal suppression of the native populations by the British rulers defined the trajectory of cricket's evolution in the colonised countries, which includes India and Pakistan (both East and West Pakistan). It was East Pakistan, which became Bangladesh after 1971.

Those countries' geography and cultural histories also played a part in cricket's development. Not all sub-continental natives were easy to subjugate. The British encountered severe defiance pockets in both India and Ceylon. Cricket's rich history proves that the dislike for the British often translated into beating the rulers at their own game whenever the opportunity arose. By all accounts, cricket was a sport that allowed the natives, mixed in ethnicities, to excel.

* * *

In those days, I didn't know much about how cricket was organized across the Test-playing countries. But I quickly learned that cricket was controlled by the Imperial Cricket Conference (ICC), with Australia, England and South Africa as its founding members (Williamson 2005a). It was founded at Lord's on 15 June 1909.

In the beginning, only Commonwealth countries could join. India, New Zealand and the West Indies joined in 1926, and Pakistan joined in 1953 after the partitioning of India. In 1961, South Africa resigned from the ICC after leaving the Commonwealth. Still, it played Test cricket until their international exile in 1970 (ICC 2023).

Despite years of demonstrable talent and effort, Sri Lanka didn't get full membership in the ICC until 1981, which was a great shame. Zimbabwe became a full member in 1992 and Bangladesh in 2000. South Africa was re-admitted to full membership in 1991. In 1965, the Conference was renamed the International Cricket Conference.

The acronym ICC was retained. New rules permitted the election of countries outside the Commonwealth for the first time. The first Associate Members (Fiji and the USA), who had diluted voting rights, were admitted. However, foundation members retained a veto over all resolutions and were deeply resented by all other countries.

As the power (and money) of Asian countries started to dictate, England and Australia's dominant influence on the international game waned rapidly, and the organization began to change. The Conference was renamed in 1989 without changing initials (Williamson 2003a).

The 'new' International Cricket Council was formed, bringing together many member countries. In 1993, the new ICC gained its own secretariat and a Chief Executive. However, its headquarters remained at Lord's. The category of Foundation Member was abolished, and the West Indian – Clyde Walcott- became Chairman. He was also the first non-British (non-white) chairman of the ICC.

In 1997, the ICC became an incorporated body with an executive board and a President instead of a Chairman. The ICC remained at Lord's for over a decade, with a commercial base in Monaco. However, in 2005, it moved to Dubai, mainly for tax advantages.

Twelve countries qualified to play official Test matches are now full members of the ICC. They are Afghanistan, Australia, Bangladesh, England & Wales, India, Ireland, New Zealand, Pakistan, South Africa, Sri Lanka, West Indies and Zimbabwe. Additionally, the ICC has more than 100 Associate Member nations. These don't play Test cricket but are from geographical areas where cricket is firmly established, organized, and played following the Laws of Cricket (ICC 2024).

* * *

My next crucial memory was the short trip that Mike Smith's England Team of 1965 made to Colombo en route to Australia for the 1965-66 Ashes contest. It was the first time in history that an English team had travelled by air instead of sea. When Ted Dexter wasn't available for the tour for business reasons, the team was led by the bespectacled 32-year-old Michael John Knight ('MJK') Smith, a be-spectacled former English Rugby International from Warwickshire.

With a schoolteacher appearance, Smith had a calm attitude, somewhat like a diplomat. He was highly respected by fellow cricketers as an astute skipper and a gentle soul with a flair for making speeches.

Smith's team, comprised of some revered names in cricket circles and some newcomers, was on the way to Australia for the 1965 Ashes battles and stopped in Ceylon for a few games. Introducing each English player, the Ceylon Daily News carried large-sized portrait pictures of the English team, one picture each day, with their brief biopics. These portraits instantly became my prized possessions, and I still have two sets of these newspaper cuttings, which have faded with time. I can still reel off the names of the team etched into my memory: Mike Smith, Colin Cowdrey, Ken Barrington, David Allen, Bob Barber, Geoffrey Boycott, John Edrich, Eric Russell, David Brown, Ivor Jeffrey Jones, David Larter, John Murray, Ken Higgs, Jim Parks, Fred Titmus, Peter Parfitt and Barry Knight.

I also remember, to this date, the counties those players represented and other tiny details about them because I was so fascinated. In later years, I keenly followed the careers of many of them, whom I liked, particularly Boycott, Edrich, Cowdrey and Barrington.

However, I was too young to recall how the Englishmen fared in Ceylon. They didn't do too well on this 'whistlestop' tour. Playing just two one-day games, the MCC team was dubbed the 'Marylebone Cricket Clowns' by an unkind local press (Clarke 1966).

As chronicled by Tuberville (2021), commenting on the tour, Jim Parks, England's wicket-keeper, said: 'The stopover in Ceylon produced some forgettable cricket – two drawn one-day matches. It was monsoon weather'. The second match was rained off after MCC was bowled out for 127. Reminiscing about the game, Parks said: 'We played in Wellington boots – it was just a bit of fun. Then, after Singapore, we landed in Perth on October 21'.

Most importantly, I collected all the pictures from the Daily News and other local newspapers. Sixty years later, I still have the pictures, now jaded with time, stuck onto a Cricket Pictures book. This was really the beginning of becoming a cricket fanatic. I recall looking at these portraits daily for weeks and studying every detail about the cricketers.

Around 10 years of age, I needed my father's help to make cricket scrapbooks using brown paper. The papers, folded into two, were sewn by a large needle with twine. Later, I made books by myself. As my father had taught me, I used to dissolve 'gum Arabic' crystals in an old ink-pot and use the gum to stick the cuttings on my scrapbooks. Occasionally, I would spill gum over the pictures and destroy some. Over time, I've lost some old scrapbooks and cuttings, but I still have several books from the mid-1960s. Time has dulled their gloss, but the scrapbooks remain a testament to my boyhood obsession.

I also recall a date, 8 March 1965, which I had written with the unsteady hand of a child on the front page of one scrapbook. Even in those days, I was interested in committing to memory-specific details of Test matches and remembering the actors and the associated histories and chronologies of those clashes. Thus, was born a cricket freak!

* * *

After the early memories of 1963-65, my attention fully turned to the England vs. Australia 1965 Ashes series, played during the Australian summer of 1965-66. I recall great moments of anticipation.

I have also read the stories of Ashes battles hundreds of times in subsequent years. Test cricket between Australia and England has been played since 1877, when the first Test was played in Melbourne from 15-19 March, which Australia won by 45 runs. England then won the second Test in Melbourne (31 March-4 April 1877) by four wickets. In those days, the general consensus was that 'Cricket has no higher calling than a Test match between England and Australia'.

Test matches between England and Australia are played for the Ashes urn, a much-sought-after trophy to win because of the historical rivalry between the two countries. The 'Ashes' came about after Australia defeated England in 1882 at the Oval (28-29 August 1882) in an only Test match by just seven runs in a low-scoring game.

The Australian fast bowler Fred 'Demon' Spofforth, a much-unheralded cricketer, was the leading architect of Australia's win by a slender margin with his match bag of 14 wickets for 92 runs in the two innings. Australia scored only 63 and 122, while England's replies were 101 and 77, respectively, in their first and second innings.

Historical accounts (Smith 1996: 16-17; Frith 1997: 20; Harte and Whimpress 2008: 125) show that Spofforth was indeed 'The Demon Who created the Ashes'. People all over England lamented the decline of English cricket. Nevertheless, 'British humour' also surfaced after the defeat, which prompted a young English journalist, Reginald Shirley Brooks, of the Sporting Times in London, to print a mock obituary of English cricket. It read as follows:

"IN AFFECTIONATE REMEMBRANCE OF ENGLISH CRICKET,
WHICH DIED AT THE OVAL ON 29th August 1882
Deeply lamented by a large circle of
Sorrowing Friends and Acquaintances. R.I.P.
N.B. – The body will be cremated, and the Ashes taken to Australia".

Australians kept the little joke alive. During the 1882-83 tour, a group of Melbourne women presented a tiny terracotta urn to the English Captain Ivo Bligh, which allegedly contained the ashes of some cricket items. It is also possible that it was a perfume bottle containing the ashes of a burned cricket bail (Willis 1982; Frith 1997: 23).

The story is that on Christmas Eve 1882, the urn was presented by Lady Janet Clarke to Ivo Bligh, admired as an 'all-conquering English Captain', as a jest. This was after a friendly match between Bligh's team against staff and guests on Sir William Clarke's rural estate outside Melbourne. One of the ladies involved was the governess of the Clarke residence, Florence Morphy, who later married Ivo Bligh.

A website – The Ashes Bail – has now been created, dedicated to keeping the mystique of the Ashes love story alive for posterity (2019). The reports show that Sir William Clarke, President of the Melbourne Cricket Club, sponsored the English team's tour to Australia in 1882-83.

Sir William and Lady Janet were generous hosts to the tourists. Ivo Bligh, in particular, became a regular house guest at their 'Rupertswood' Mansion during the 1882-83 tour. The urn was presented again at Easter in 1883 after England won the series (Pollard 1992: 77-80; Frith 1997: 23). After Ivo Bligh died in 1927, Florence presented the urn to the MCC, the owner of Lord's Grounds in London, because they were the 'guardians' of the game's Laws (Willis 1982).

The original small Ashes' urn resided in the Long Room at Lord's before it was moved to the Lord's Museum in 1953. In 1998, the MCC assigned a look-alike trophy that was played for in the Ashes series between Australia and England. The trophy, a larger replica of the original urn, is not used as the official trophy. Instead, replicas are given to the winning side at the end of each series.

The original urn, a delicate object, remains at the Museum, displayed alongside a scorecard from the 1882 match that started it all. The young sports writer – Reginald Brooks' cheeky obituary, 'making fun of the English cricket team's defeat', is still remembered more than 140 years later because the 'Ashes' are still being symbolically regained and lost, series after series.

* * *

In 1962-63, England made another bid for the Ashes, which they had lost in 1958-59. The ensuing years hadn't been kind to them. In 1961, Richie Benaud's Team fought hard against Peter May's England and retained the Ashes. Ted Dexter's touring side, dubbed 'a team of gentlemen', played some attacking cricket but drew the 1962-63 series in Australia, 1:1 against Benaud's side.

Benaud said (ABC 1976: 85-91; ABC 2006): 'It was almost one of the greatest series of cricket between the two nations, except for the fifth and final Test'. It was the beginning of a new era for England with 'Lord Ted' Dexter adopting an attacking style of cricket.

Benaud responded cautiously, which he later stated was something he didn't enjoy. In the fifth Test (15-20 February 1963), the Sydney crowd of about 54,000, the highest on record for 34 years, abused the Australians for the boring cricket played. The series then was locked at 1-1, and the match billed as the big Test turned out to be the big flop.

Richie Benaud regretted failing to take up Dexter's challenge with a sporting declaration. Dexter looked for a win on the last day and asked Australia to make 241 runs in 240 minutes. Australia did not take up the challenge and drew the match, scoring 4-152. The series was also severely criticised by the public in Australia as dull and drab.

Benaud wrote about how miserable cricket was, especially in the drawn final Test (ABC 1976: 86). It prompted cricket authorities to call for brighter cricket all around. This series established the Simpson-Lawry opening partnership, which served Australia well for many years.

The final match in late February 1963 ended the illustrious careers of Neil Harvey and Alan Davidson, two of Australia's greatest cricketers (ABC, 1976: 96; Davidson 1963; ABC, 2006). My collection still has a Ceylon Daily News article from 1963, in which the caption says: 'Harvey Hits Out' with a classic picture of a Neil Harvey on-drive.

* * *

Bill Lawry's reputation as a brick wall also became established when Australia played for a draw in the final Test. An Australian newspaper in Sydney (21 February 1963) described that Lawry was 'barely alive' at the crease. People were 'dying in their seats' in excruciating pain, watching him take 36 minutes to move from 40 to 41 runs. The papers wrote, 'Not even a bomb would have blown Bill Lawry off the wicket yesterday' (Hutchinson and Ross 1997: 345).

Writing his own account, in Run Digger, Lawry, a plumber by trade, described his stubborn batting, explaining the opener's handicap when facing the new ball. Lawry asserted that a good opener must curb stroke play. He said that dashing batters coming in later benefit from a solid opening stand that lays the foundation for risky strokeplay. An opener, he said, has a job; sometimes, it can be a hard grind.

In the 1950s and '60s, coaches taught young cricketers never to show they had been hurt hit by a ball, even if a hand was too numb to hold a bat. It was a time without helmets, armguards, thigh pads, painkillers, or the magic spray to numb painful welts (Perry 2000: 252). Like John Wayne and James Bond, Lawry and others were supposed to be macho heroes. As a kid, I also learned that it was a male sin to show pain and, heaven forbid, to cry. If you did, you'd be branded a wimp. We didn't show that we were hurt if we were hit by a ball.

* * *

Concerned about the public losing interest in dull and drab cricket, in May 1963, Bradman, as the Chairman of the Australian Board of Control for International Cricket (later, the Australian Cricket Board), urged all State cricket authorities to bring about changes to play 'brighter cricket' for the benefit of the game.

The 1962-63 summer also saw cricket's hallowed grounds invaded by advertising billboards for the first time. 'Moving with the times', the ABC negotiated sponsorship deals with Shell Petroleum and the British Tobacco Company 'obtaining a slice of the corporate pounds and pence' for sports (Hutchinson and Ross 1997: 345). Where the money came from didn't matter, as cricket needed help with marketing.

Bob Simpson became Australia's next captain during the summer of 1963-64 when Benaud retired during the South African tour of Australia. Simpson's touring side to England in 1964 was dubbed the second worst after the 1912 team. It included 10 players with no previous experience playing Test cricket in England.

Simpson, O'Neill, Lawry, Booth and Burge provided a 'core' of good senior batters. Redpath and Cowper were the main emerging batters. The team had four promising fast bowlers, Graham McKenzie, Alan Connolly, Neil Hawke and Graham Corling, plus Tom Vievers as the spinner. But they outplayed England under Ted Dexter and won 1-nil, retaining the Ashes. Still, the series saw four drawn games and defensive cricket from both sides (ABC 1976: 93-100).

In those days, cricket was an amateur sport; the cricketers played by invitation only; they were not paid professionals. Cricket continued for decades without fully understanding how vital spectators were to keep the game alive. The policy of playing results-oriented cricket evolved only in the mid-to-late 1960s. Australia was at the forefront of this change, making the games more exciting and drawing spectators.

The limited-overs cricket (One-Day Internationals, ODIs) had already been played in England in the 1960s. U.K.'s Gillette Cup 'knockout' competition was the first played since 1963. In the early days, spectator numbers were low because the games were played mid-week in the early days. Nevertheless, the format was described as the 'financial saviour' of the game as it took hold (Selvey 2013).

'This Is Radio Australia'

As an ardent fan, I quickly learned how to tune in to the ball-by-ball commentaries on Radio Australia, relayed by Radio Ceylon in those days.

Thousands of fans in Ceylon tuned in to the broadcasts each day when a Test match was on. The lure of cricket was a bit crazy. Walking along the streets in my hometown, Panadura, one could hear the radios tuned to cricket, with noises fading intermittently. The ABC's introduction went something along the following lines:

> *This is Radio Australia, transmitting the overseas service of the ABC, bringing you ball-by-ball descriptions of the first day's play in the First Test Match, Australia versus England, being played at the Gabba, in Brisbane. Now, over to our commentator at the 'Gabba, Alan McGilvray.*

Shortwave radio was a powerful transmission mode over long distances in those days. That signal was the only way cricket could be heard in Ceylon, 7000 kilometres from Australia. As a child, I didn't know that the shortwaves were bouncing off the turbulent and ionized gases of the 'ionosphere', hundreds of kilometres above the earth. The loud crackling noises and a signal that mysteriously disappeared and reappeared a few seconds later did not matter.

As recently as 25 years ago, shortwave radio has been a significant source of international news in Australia, Europe, and North America via the BBC World Service, Voice of America, and Radio France Internationale. The BBC estimated the global shortwave listenership at that time to be more than 120 million weekly.

I was so keen to listen that I learned quickly to fine-tune the Grundig to pick up this capricious signal. I perfected this tuning as an art form! The shortwave broadcast from Australia came with the crackling sounds of 'swooooosh....sweeeeesh...' that still rang in my ears. However, the re-lay by Radio Ceylon in the 1960s cleverly improved our listening pleasure. Those were good days in Sri Lanka, a troubled country now.

Back when there was no Internet and no satellite TV or live streaming. Shortwave radio broadcasts were where many news-hungry people went first. In the 1950s and 60s, everyone had a radio, and radio listening was a universal occupation. From the 1930s decade before World War II, families clustered around an ornate family radio, a defining 20th-century image familiar to people. As an adult, I later realised the significance of this early-morning dose of cricket.

The cricket-mad natives of Ceylon didn't mind the English channel blaring off cricket at 5:30 a.m. as the country woke up to the daily grinds of a day. Cricket broadcasts were even at the expense of other news, turbulent post-independence politics or news of the unchanging weather of the island. My mother and grandfather had hardly any interest in cricket. But they didn't mind me switching the radio to cricket early in the morning when a Test match in Australia was on.

My father was happy to occasionally inquire, and I kept him informed about the progress of a game before he went to work and after he returned. I suppose my parents didn't mind, so long as this cricket madness didn't interfere with my education.

My English improved by leaps and bounds due to the long hours of listening to cricket and reading copious amounts of cricket material. I used to walk around the house, giving commentaries and imitating McGilvray, Arlott, or Brian Johnson. Those were fun days as I became obsessed with history, dates and chronologies of events due to cricket.

Alan McGilvray - A Golden Voice

Despite the steady, pulsing crackling sound of the shortwaves emanating from Australia and received in Ceylon, I loved to hear the golden voice of Alan McGilvray. 'Mac', as he was fondly called by everyone, covered all the Test matches Australia played between 1938 and 1985, notching up a tally of 185 matches. He was the pre-eminent voice of Australian cricket for nearly 50 years.

Alan's authoritative voice forever rings in my ears. The class and quality of his persona, projected through the broadcasts, impacted my young mind. The game will never be the same without Mac at the microphone. Like Cardus's influence on cricket writing, McGilvray's broadcasting influence was incredibly significant.

Alan McGilvray had already mastered the techniques of cricket broadcasting and was the leading commentator in Australia. With his distinct Australian accent, he put a great deal of emphasis on giving facts and figures, defusing the dry objectivity of stating the scoresheet.

The sophisticated and polished delivery projected his own anxieties and those of the players doing battle. The job of a radio commentator is to transport the listener to the playing field and paint a picture through words of the playing field, the weather, the crowd and, above all, the action. Both McGilvray and Arlott were masters of this Art. Their descriptions not only transported the listener to where the action was but also allowed fans like me to live it.

* * *

Before radio, cricket enthusiasts had to rely on newspaper reports for scorecards of the day's game. However, Alan's book (1985: 58-59) described that there was no such thing as ball-by-ball coverage in those pre-war years. Still, the broadcasters' descriptions of the games were 're-created' based on information received from overseas.

He described in his book that ABC Radio developed an ingenious system called synthetic cricket, first used in 1934. The commentators, seated in the ABC studios on Market Street, Sydney, synthetically recreated the game as it was played in England, with the details of a match sent via telex from the ground to the studio.

The system had been initially experimented with in 1934. It began to be fully used in 1938 by commentators, including Alan and Vic Richardson (O'Connell 2018). A radio operator decoded the signal and passed the information by phone via a second operator within 45 seconds to the commentary team sitting in another office.

One minute later, the commentators would broadcast the descriptions, complete with the sound of a pencil striking the desk and sound effects of a crowd. Such synthetic descriptions were extremely popular among listeners in those days and kept Test cricket alive [20].

* * *

Alan was a peerless broadcaster and a great personality indeed. He captained NSW several times in 1934-37 when the regular captains weren't available and played with or against cricketing greats like Don Bradman, Alan Kippax, Monty Noble, Sid Barnes and Bill Woodfull. While thousands of people admired Alan for his eye-witness tour accounts, he was often criticised back in Australia by his detractors for being too critical of Australian players for their behaviour.

One example when Alan contradicted everyone else was his defence of Charlie Griffith, called a 'chucker' by Simpson's Australians during the acrimonious 1964-65 series in the Caribbean. Alan defended Griffith's action as within the rules and pointed out that no umpire had called Griffith for throwing (McGilvray 1985: 147-149).

Keith Miller defended Alan's viewpoint in his newspaper column in Australia. He wrote that Griffith's action was 'as pure as the driven snow' (Lawry 1966: 81). When Miller spoke, thousands of people listened.

---

20 The ABC's 50th Anniversary Celebration – *The ABC Photo Album, from 1932 to 1982 (compiled by Jack* Bennett et al. 1982) carries accounts of the role cricket broadcasts played in the development of radio in Australia. The book has historical photos of how the synthetic cricket broadcasts were carried out (p. 21) and also highlights McGilvray as the premier cricket broadcaster of the era.

The stand that the two great friends – McGilvray and Miller – took annoyed many in Australia, including some at the Australian Broadcasting Commission (ABC) and the chief selector, Bradman. The throwing allegation against Griffith was first made in an Australian newspaper (*Sydney Sun*) and in the Jamaican paper – *Gleaner* – by Benaud during the match in March 1965. The article caused a huge uproar in the Caribbean, as the West Indies cricket administrators and the Jamaican press took it badly (Hutchinson and Ross 1997: 360).

Even to his end, Benaud believed that 'Big' Charlie threw, at least, his faster deliveries. Even in the History of Australian Cricket interviews, depicted in four CDs (ABC 2006), Benaud calls Griffith a 'chucker'. However, this view is strongly refuted by Wes Hall in the same History. Watching the footage, I am not sure whether Griffith chucked. But I believe Griffith was as fast, if not quicker, than even Hall, and he intimidate batters. Hall clarified that it was different to his style.

In Bill Lawry's book Run-Digger (1966: 77-89), Chapter 11 is titled 'A Man Called Charlie'. In it, Lawry said Griffith generated extra pace with his bumpers and yorkers. The Australians feared getting injured. Griffith also bowled at the batters' bodies. He hit Brain Booth, Norm O'Neill and Grahame Thomas in the first Test (Sabina Park, Kingston, Jamaica, 3-8 March 1965).

Lawry recalled that everyone who got hit needed medical treatment. This led to the batters taking reckless risks against the other bowlers as they looked for runs. However, he stopped short of calling Griffith a 'chucker and a cheat', as O'Neill did in a newspaper article. I recall that not everyone agreed Griffith chucked. Some journalists reported that it was only occasionally, the much faster delivery, that Griffith 'threw'.

* * *

On 10th December 1965, the time would have been 5:30 am in Ceylon, a humid morning on the island, but a hot, dry summer day in Brisbane. It was school holiday time in Ceylon in December, and I was at home, awaiting the beginning of the Ashes series. I was keenly following the reports of the English team after they flew out of Ceylon.

This was the first time an English team had flown by air to Australia with a brief stop-over in Colombo. Flying to Australia considerably shortened the time available for acclimatization to the hot conditions the team encountered, having left the cold autumn conditions in the UK. It is thought that the lack of time for acclimatization might have affected their performances. As the

1965-66 Ashes series battles were about to begin, I may not have even slept well the previous night.

A man called Doug Walters was about to enter my young life. Was it Alan McGilvray commentating on that day – 10th December 1965? I guess it was most likely him. Of course, hundreds of times in later years, this most distinguished 'voice' of Australian Cricket was a feature in my life. His golden voice still reverberates in my mind. I learned cricket by listening to McGilvray's voice! Doug confirmed that it was the same for him as well. So, for both of us, here is a shared experience. Doug and I watched cricket on the radio, and McGilvray was a crucial part of it.

As far back as 1965, McGilvray made an indelible mark on me and influenced my young and developing mind. Alan was often like a preacher, espousing the virtues of decency, integrity, honour and respect for opponents, regardless of colour and creed. Amazingly, his advice on moral behaviour came through the radio!

It wasn't a surprise when Doug confirmed how prominent Alan McGilvray was in his life, too, as a great NSW cricketer, gentleman, and personal friend. Alan advocated strongly for impartiality and 'fair play' without resorting to ugly tactics in cricket. I recall no irrelevant chatter when Alan was commentating.

McGilvray was a master of his trade and knew almost instinctively how much cricket broadcasts mattered to his listeners. His great skill was to describe cricket in a manner that would make fanatics like me enjoy the game's beauty as a contest unfolded on the playing field.

Throughout the 1970s, I was confused when I heard Alan criticising the overly hostile attitude of Australian teams and how some players behaved. Alan also lamented the atrocious crowd behaviour at cricket, baying for opponents' blood. He objected to poorly managed tours, inadequately prepared pitches, the selectors and even the press and other broadcasters (his own kind) who didn't care much about the decline in the way the game was played. He wanted more people to object if they felt that the standards were declining but had support only from O'Reilly, Fingleton and Miller.

* * *

Alan McGilvray was critical of Australian selection debacles, poor captaincy and the fact that umpires were not stricter about bad on-field player behaviour. His critiques did not go down well in his own country. Many of his detractors at home had their knives out for him. However, his opinions were valued by those who had played with or against him and his employer, the ABC. Most Australian teams in the 1960s, '70s, and '80s had a high opinion of McGilvray's reporting and broadcasting. While he understood the need to make the sport a commercially viable enterprise for the sake of cricket, its fans and the players, Alan disapproved the over-commercialization of the game and was critical of officials who were 'only interested in filling their coffers'.

Later, my confusion was clarified when I read Alan's books (McGilvray 1985; 1987), which provide many examples of the highs and lows of Australian cricket. The two books are sad accounts of what went wrong in Australian cricket in the 1970s and '80s, as commercialization took precedence over genuine regard for the game.

Nonetheless, McGilvray provided some delightful insights into Australia's most outstanding cricketers and how the game evolved. Having played at the highest level as NSW State captain, Alan didn't mind changes so long as they were positive for the game. McGilvray got into trouble in Australia by disputing that Griffith 'chucked' and for describing the 'unfriendly atmosphere, which always appeared when Australia played against other teams'.

The late 1960s and early '70s were also an era in which anti-British sentiments were strong in Australia. 'Ten-Pound Poms' had been streaming into Australia. Not taking kindly to new arrivals, Australian fans, most of whom preferred to wear thongs and singlets to watch cricket in the warm summer conditions, took great pleasure in mocking the stuffy propriety of the British, who tended to wear slacks and business shirts. Poms were ridiculed whenever possible at sports venues.

The Australian crowds became famous for anti-authoritarian behaviour at cricket matches. Hurling insults at opponents is now accepted as part of playing in front of large Australian crowds. Before some controls were initiated (such as low-alcohol beer), booze flowed at the cricket grounds. Most ugly incidents at cricket venues are caused by intoxicated spectators disregarding rules and regulations.

It was evident to me that there was not much love lost between the Australians and the West Indies, mainly due to the heat generated by the afore-mentioned Griffith's 'chucking' controversy in March 1965, when Simpson's team was in the Caribbean. News about the acrimony in the series was blazed across the newspapers worldwide.

A couple of years later, in the 1968-69 series in Australia, I listened to vivid descriptions of Australians' robust argument with the Windies, where Griffith was again in the spotlight. This time, it was for allegedly impeding

Ian Redpath, which resulted in a runout in the fourth Test in Adelaide (24-29 January 1969). Listening to these unfortunate incidents in Ceylon, I was greatly bothered because I was fond of both teams.

* * *

For many decades, my cricket-mad life had a meaning as I listened to the broadcasts from ABC and BBC overseas. Every word appeared to have the power to incite melodrama in my mind. Alan McGilvray and Lindsay Hassett formed an awesome pair for the ABC. The BBC commentaries, led by John Arlott, Brian Johnson and Henry Blofeld, with expert comments from Fred Trueman, Trevor Bailey, Jim Laker and Tom Graveney, brightened my life. Using overseas broadcasters, such as Tony Cozier from the Caribbean and McGilvray from Australia, added spice to the BBC's Test Match Special broadcasts.

Fay and Kynaston (2018: 115) noted that Arlott and McGilvray didn't like each other. Arlott's style of commentary met with Alan's disapproval. 'Mac' insisted that 'Arlott should give the scores at least three times during an eight-ball over'. In contrast, Arlott was more concerned about describing the 'mood and colour', as Cardus did. Nevertheless, both authoritatively 'talked cricket', keeping up a flow of intelligent remarks even when not much was happening in a match.

They had the gravitas to attract admiring listeners, including me. With their historical knowledge and analytical minds, both McGilvray and Arlott could get inside a batter's, bowler's or captain's mind and decisively describe the state of play. Their sophisticated voices and economic speaking styles were therapeutic for me.

Those were also the days when columns written by great cricketers sold newspapers. They praised a worthy performer or a team when they deserved it but were scathing in their criticisms when warranted. Cricket writers wrote relatively unbiased accounts from an observer's vantage point in those days. In the pre-Internet era, their columns had to reach a global audience via news agencies such as Reuters. Until the ugly tendency of using 'ghost writers' came about in the 1990s, most former greats, like Bradman, Fingleton, O'Reilly, Miller, Hassett, Harvey, May, Dexter and Bailey, penned their own columns.

* * *

McGilvray (1985: 162) said that Doug 'didn't do everything by the book' as he had often shown with his daring strokeplay. Like McGilvray, Doug was an old-school traditionalist. Doug's 'attitude to cricket was not entirely orthodox, but it was effective most of the time and pretty exciting all the time'. Alan also said that 'Doug gave "colour and character" that were simply irreplaceable' to Australia's cricket and that his success came from his 'laid-back attitude', as much as anything else. McGilvray (1987: 61) also praised Doug for being such an ally for his captain, Ian Chappell, with whom he developed a close bond.

> *Doug understood the fine points of the game more than most people were prepared to accept – his outwardly casual nature was a little misleading, for he was often a source of valued counsel to his skipper.*

Alan's view of Ian was that he was made in the same mould as his fiercely combative grandfather- Victor Richardson, whom Alan admired. Like Vic, Alan observed that Ian wasn't a sentimentalist; he was often hot-headed and quarrelsome but also quite generous.

Although Doug was never rude to his opponents, he was good at beating England at their own game. Unlike the two pacemen – Lillee and Thomson – who terrorized England in the 1974 Ashes, Doug wasn't a violent executioner. Instead, Doug was a classy cricketer who delivered at crucial times, mostly in batting and bowling.

In influencing my developing outlook on life, both Alan McGilvray and Doug Walters were more than just cricketers for me. I never got a chance to chat with Mr. McGilvray. It would have been one of my life's highest points if I had met Alan. However, conversations with Doug about 'Mac' filled this void to some extent.

* * *

Listening to cricket broadcasts is a joy for thousands of cricket fans worldwide. I, too, vent my dissatisfaction with the poor quality of radio and TV cricket broadcasts in the last decade or so everywhere. Many people say that the commentaries are not worth listening to anymore because they are full of inane stuff, bad jokes, constant giggles and ego-driven drivel of individuals. Even the so-called 'experts' all too often make listeners cringe with topics unrelated to cricket.

Commentators have lost touch with what they are supposed to do. Even in the recent Australian summer Tests, there was much pointless chatter among the commentators. In one instance, I timed that no scores were given for more than 8-10 minutes while the match was on. The public has little say in this, and most choose not to listen.

I look back, nostalgic, to those days when the civilized voices of the great commentators brightened my days. Their descriptions, occasional wit and cakes brought cricket alive! Sadly, the world hasn't found substitutes for

Arlott, McGilvray, Brian Johnson, Henry Blofeld, Chris Martin-Jenkins or Tony Cozier, to name just a few.

The quality of ABC Radio broadcasts has declined markedly from the past because of the useless prattle the broadcasters engage in. BBC still fares better than ABC because the commentators are still old-school traditionalists who give the score every two minutes. The BBC teams also include real Test 'stars'.

Using former Test stars as reporters by TV networks, rather than actual 'experts' who can analyze a game, gives the viewers a distorted picture of the events. Working in the media is not for everyone. A world-class athlete, even one who has dominated a sport, isn't always good at media work. So, to use a former player's 'star power' to lure TV audiences doesn't always work.

Most of the time, people must endure the ego-driven babble of some former Test players covering cricket in Australia, both on the radio and TV. The decline in the quality of broadcasts can be attributed to the commercial nature of the proceedings, partisanship and a blatant tendency to excessively glorify the home team's performances.

The decline in the quality of the opponents Australians have faced in the last decade also contributes to a degree of contempt, which comes through in the broadcasts. Some may argue that the prejudice is unintentional and is a small matter, but for freaks like me, it DOES matter!

I must also add that most radio and TV commentators everywhere make the same mistake of displaying too much allegiance to their own countries. In the past, the Indian commentators, with their emotive descriptions, were accused of a bias towards their own team. However, since the 1990s, the trend has become widespread, even in ABC and BBC broadcasts. In the past, we wouldn't dare switch off the radio when a Test match was on for fear of missing something exciting.

Nowadays, it is blissful not to listen to banal ramblings often, and I am not the only one incensed by this. Endless advertising breaks have to take most of the blame. Still, individual commentators cannot be absolved of the poor quality of cricket broadcasts. They would have realised their follies if they had listened to their performances behind the microphones and asked around for feedback from listeners.

CHAPTER 6

Comeback

'K. D. Walters, the Australian all-rounder, returned from compulsory military service to play in the Third and Fourth cricket t Tests against India, and his scores of 93, 62 not out, 94 not out and 5 speak in no small measure of his consistency with the bat. Besides, he is a more than useful medium-fast bowler and a fielder in the best Australian traditions' Sport & Pastime, Vol. XXII (8) (24 February 1968, India).

Resuming Cricket against Visiting Indians (1967-68)

The visiting Indians played some bold cricket in the 1967-68 summer under Mansur Ali Khan – the Nawab of Pataudi. However, they lost 4-Nil in the series. Bob Simpson retired as Australia's captain after the first two Tests, in Adelaide (23-28 December 1967) and at the MCG (30 December 1968-3 January 1969). Cricket wasn't stopped in that era for Christmas or New Year because of the profits that could be made by attracting bigger crowds on such holidays.

I was laid low with Mumps, the viral disease that affects the salivary and parotid glands. With a swollen face and fever, I was isolated in a bedroom. Even with the discomfort of fever and swelling, I was happy to miss school for a while. Still, I delighted in the opportunity to follow the broadcasts of each match, ball-by-ball, while I lay in bed. The household had a small transistor radio that belonged to an aunt by this time, in addition to the Grundig. I believe I was glued to it.

I enjoyed listening to Simpson making his centuries in the first and second Tests (103 and 109, respectively). On both occasions, he was bowled by the left-armer Rusi Surti. In Doug's absence in the first two Tests, resolute batting by Lawry, Sheahan, Cowper and Ian Chappell ensured that Australians won those Tests handsomely. The Indian captain, The Nawab, had been injured (hamstring) and didn't play in the first Test, which weakened the team.

Returning to the side after Simpson's retirement, Doug scored heavily in the third Test, in Brisbane (19-24 January 1968) and the fourth Test in Sydney (26-31 January 1968). His scores were 93 and 62* and 94* and 5, respectively. Doug's batting was praised by the leading Indian magazine – *Sport & Pastime*, a copy of which I still have. But, listening to the broadcasts at home, I was disappointed when Doug couldn't get to the two centuries he deserved.

I enjoyed some fightback, particularly from Ajit Wadekar, a left-hander who would become the next Indian captain and the all-rounder Rusi Surti. Other notable performers were the Indian captain, the One-eyed Prince and M. L. Jaisimha, the lone centurion of the series. I recall that Jaisimha was flown in to replace the injured Chandu Borde and scored 74 and 101 in the third Test. But Jaisimha failed to make an impact on the fourth and final tests.

The decline of Borde, a mainstay in the Indian batting line-up for several years, was a crucial factor in India's series defeat. I also recall another favourite, the Mysore Captain – Venkataraman Subramanya – who batted valiantly in the first Test in Adelaide, making a well-struck 75 even though India lost the match.

Part of India's royalty, the 26-year-old 'Tiger' Pataudi was a tall, handsome, graceful figure on a cricket field and India's youngest Test captain [21]. As Pataudi didn't play in the first Test, Borde captained the team and scored his only fifty in the series. Pataudi was not fully fit, but he returned to lead the side in the second Test, saying that with the injury, he 'couldn't play forward, but he could play back'; that he certainly did! His valiant efforts (75 and 85 in the second Test, 74 and 48 in the third, 51 and 4 in the fourth) and cheerful leadership won the hearts and minds of the Australian public (Raghavan 2022).

The Press praised Pataudi's batting at the MCG second Test 'not just with one eye but on one good leg, in dim light and on a green-tinged first-day pitch'. In Pataudi's obituary, David Frith (2011) noted that this performance made former Australian captain Lindsay Hassett compare The Nawab with the peerless Bradman. High praise indeed!

Doug didn't play in that game in Melbourne but remembers Pataudi's gutsy batting in later matches. Doug said the graceful Prince was a delight to watch. However, he was often subdued because he had to bat to rescue his team from precarious positions (Walters 1971: 33).

At just 32, Simpson's retirement mid-way through the series surprised

---

21   *The Nawab of Pataudi* played most of his cricket without the sight in his right eye, which he lost in a car accident in England in 1961. He captained India 40 times in 46 Tests between 1962 and 1975, scoring 2793 runs and six centuries. In 1962, when he became captain, he was only 21 years and 77 days old, a record as the youngest Test captain in the world. Pataudi remained a much revered and popular figure in Indian cricket until he passed away in 2011.

Australia as he was the country's best batter then. Concerned about the meagre income from cricket, Simpson had signalled to the selectors that he wasn't available for the forthcoming tour to England and for Australia to find its next captain. Simpson followed Benaud's example of indicating early retirement while continuing to play and making the transition to a new captain easier.

Despite Simpson making himself available, he was overlooked for the third Test, which allowed Doug to be slotted in. However, the selectors (Don Bradman, Jack Ryder and Neil Harvey, 1967-70) allowed Simpson a farewell final at his home ground, the SCG, in the fourth Test by dropping Ian Redpath. Doug was retained in the team as an all-rounder and first-change medium-pacer.

* * *

Bill Lawry captained Australia for the first time in the third Test. He was immediately labelled an uncompromising character. Lawry was well experienced, having captained Victoria for six years before becoming Australia's captain. He was also renowned for not conceding an inch to the opposition.

The selectors made the unusual decision to leave out not just Simpson but also McKenzie from the third and fourth Tests. The move was to audition a 'new boy', the South Australian fast bowler and Australian Rules footballer Eric Freeman, as an opening bowler for the upcoming England Tour (Hutchinson and Ross 1997).

The non-selection insulted the lion-hearted McKenzie, who was only 26 years old. Since Alan Davidson's retirement, he had tirelessly carried the country's bowling workload. In the second Test at the MCG, McKenzie's 10-wicket haul floored the Indians. His figures were 7/66 in the first inning, and at one stage, he had the tourists at 5-26.

I recall how hard India fought back, with Wadekar's 99, The Nawab's 85, while McKenzie took another 3/85 in the second inning. With 174 wickets, McKenzie was catching up with Benaud's Test record of 248 wickets. Players were also concerned that it was unfair for a full-time professional like McKenzie to lose match payments.

The Australian selectors often deviated from the policy of picking the best available players and threw up surprises. They discarded Dave Renneberg quickly after the first three Tests against India. They were looking for a fourth paceman to support McKenzie, Hawke and Connolly for the 1968 England tour. Doug bowled as the first change in two Tests and supported the faster men well. Doug bowled 24 overs but took only two wickets in the third and fourth Tests for 86 runs. Both Freeman and Renneberg made the tour to England in 1968.

Struggles in England (1968)

A glut of premature retirements of Australian stars since 1965-66 took its toll in the 1968 Ashes series in England. Only three players – Lawry, Jarman and McKenzie had prior Test experience in England. Apart from the promise of John Gleeson, Doug, Paul Sheahan and Ian Chappell, the Australian party for the 1968 tour 'looked decidedly moderate' (Haigh 2006). It was the youngest average age of any touring team, tagged 'the weakest' of all time to leave the Australian shores.

Ten of the 17-man squad had never toured England before and were unfamiliar with the conditions. Much was, however, expected of the young guns. The *Wisden* Editor (Preston 1969) said that 'despite being called a 'weak' team, they succeeded in their main objective of retaining the Ashes with a 1-1 drawn series, thus extending their hold of the urn to ten years. The series result was mostly an outcome of Lawry winning the toss more than anything else'.

After M. J. K. Smith's tenure, Cowdrey became England's captain. Lawry's relatively inexperienced team faced a surplus of more established English players, including Barrington, Edrich, Boycott, Graveney, Brown, Snow and Knott. England was also riding high after outstanding performances in the Caribbean, overcoming tough conditions and recording a series victory (1-nil) over Sobers' West Indies in the five Tests series in early 1968.

* * *

I listened to all the Ashes Tests in the 1968 English summer via the BBC broadcasts relayed directly to Sri Lanka. At home, I was glued to the Grundig radio and would listen deep into the night. Rain played a significant part in the drawn series. Ian Chappell's emergence, Doug's batting and those of another favourite, Paul Sheahan, thrilled me.

While Doug and Paul arrived in England with excellent reputations, Ian Chappell excelled on the tour (Haigh 2006: 286). After Lawry promoted him to bat at No. 3, Ian prospered as a batter and ended the tour as the highest run-getter in first-class matches (1,261 runs at 49). Ian also emerged as a potential future Australian captain.

Surprisingly, against the odds, Australia won the first Test of 1968 at Old Trafford, in Manchester, by 159 runs. Rain hampered the rest of the series, with three consecutive draws. In England, pitches were not fully covered then, and wetness affected those Tests. But England won the final Test by 226 runs with 'Deadly' Derek, almost unplayable (7/50) on a rain-affected wicket. Australia crumbled in the second inning for 125 runs. D'Oliveira's brilliant 158, combined with Edrich's 164 in the second inning, enabled England to save the series 1-All.

Doug experienced the gloomy English weather and unpredictable pitches for the first time on the tour. He also struggled with the moving ball and the accuracy of Underwood, Illingworth, Snow and Brown. However, while Doug didn't make a century, he did well in the Tests (343 runs at 38) with a highest score of 86 in the first Test plus two other half-centuries (81 in the first and 56 in the fourth Test). His series tally was only a few runs short of Chappell's (348 at 43.5).

The tour brought forward Ian Chappell's credentials as the next likely Australian captain. The story goes that on one occasion, in a bar in Kent, while the players were fooling around, drinking and telling yarns, the Team Manager and ACB Chairman Bob Parish had told Ian to curb his swearing if he ever wanted to captain Australia.

In Chappelli (1992: 80), Ian said he hadn't given any thought to captaining Australia. He said this to Parish in no uncertain terms. His words were: 'Well, Bob, I've been swearing since I was nine, and I don't see any point in stopping now because I don't expect to be captaining Australia'.

* * *

Few believed Australia would win the first Test at Old Trafford (6-11 June 1968). Still, in the event, Lawry's men rose to the occasion, whereas England failed. England surprised everyone by leaving out Underwood, Cartwright and Brown and played only three front-line bowlers (Snow, Higgs and Pocock). Australia chose a much more attacking line-up, with Hawke, McKenzie, Gleeson, and Connolly.

Lawry won the crucial toss and elected to bat. Australia's healthy 357 was built on two large stands: Lawry and Doug (third wicket, 144) and Sheahan and Chappell (sixth wicket, 157). At No. 4, Doug made a classy 81 in his first Test inning in England with 13 fours before Barber trapped him LBW. At No. 5, Paul Sheahan was impressive with an elegant 88. Ian Chappel made 73 at No. 6 before he ran himself out.

The second and third days were rain-affected, and England struggled to only 165 in the first inning. Cowper (4/48) and McKenzie (3/33) were the main wicket-takers. Lawry didn't enforce the follow-on, and Australia batted a second time, posting 220. Doug made another half-century, this time, 86, with five fours and a six. Barry Jarman smacked five fours and a six in rattling up 41, which helped Australia to a healthy lead of 413. With his off-breaks, Pat Pocock took 6 for 79 in 33 overs. England had a day and a half to get the runs, but the lead was formidable, and the crumbling wicket did not help.

England lost wickets regularly in the second inning. On the last day, the task looked beyond them; they were 5-105 at one stage. Barber (46), batting at No. 6, then had an 80-run partnership with D'Oliveira (87* with 13 fours and one six), but their stand was insufficient. England could only manage a total of 253 and was beaten. McKenzie and Connolly took two wickets each. Cowper bowled 39 overs of off-spin, capturing 2/82, and John Gleeson bamboozled England with his leg-breaks and googlies and took 3/44 in 30 overs.

The young Australians had beaten the highly-rated England by 159 runs to lead the series 1-0. By winning the first Test, Australia was already practically assured of retaining the Ashes, for never had England won the rubber in the past 70 years after being beaten in the first match in England. Listening to the BBC, I was thrilled with Australia's win, especially Doug's form.

In *The Cricketer*, John Woodcock (1968a) praised Doug, 'only 22 years of age', for his maturity and classy batting, particularly when the ball was turning in the second innings. He also reported that Australia performed beyond expectations because 'Walters, Sheahan and Chappell all produced their best form when it was most needed'.

The mid-1960s saw cricket boards looking for sponsors to support cricket and incentivise players to play more entertaining cricket. 'Like showmen, cricket must give the public what it wants' was the argument. Peter Moss (1968) reported that the value of cash awards went up to £38,000 in 1968 in an attempt to play 'brighter' cricket in England. After the Test, Doug, Cowper, D'Oliveira and Pocock picked up £100 each for their performances and 'impact'. These were the first cash awards ever given by a sponsor and were by Horlicks. Lawry picked up £1000 for his team's win given by an insurance company.

* * *

The second Test (20-25 June 1968) was the 200th between the two countries and was fittingly played at Lord's. However, instead of a celebration, it became a nightmare for Australia due to poor batting on a damp pitch. Woodcock (1968b) described the 200th Test as a 'cruel frustration' for the spectators. There were full-capacity crowds at Lord's on some days, who were bitterly disappointed because of rain interruptions, which allowed only 15 hours of play over the five days.

Following the first Test defeat, England needed a victory and was stopped from winning only by the weather. England dropped Higgs, Amiss, and Barber. They added the hard-hitting Colin Milburn, from Northamptonshire, to support the batting line-up, which also had Barrington, who was fit again. The English selectors again surprised everyone when they left out its most successful batter and bowler from Old Trafford, namely D'Oliveira and Pocock. The Australians were unchanged from their winning line-up. Cowdrey won the toss and decided to bat, which looked like the wrong call as the pitch was lively.

After several rain delays, things improved for England as Milburn muscled his way to a thrilling 83 in two and a half hours (two sixes and twelve fours), which entertained the spectators. Barrington scored his 2,000th run in Ashes contests while making 75. Cowdrey declared with England on 7-351. Australia, then, collapsed to only 78 all out in 33.4 overs. England's bowlers exploited the overcast conditions, with Brown (5/42) and Knight (3/16) being the main destroyers. Doug was the highest scorer with 26, made over an hour. Only Doug and Gleeson managed to achieve double figures.

Cowdrey enforced the follow-on. Australia needed 273 to avert an innings defeat. However, the pitch was not as lively as in the first few days, as England fancied their chances of levelling the series. To their frustration, the final day was also affected by rain. Resolute batting by Lawry (28), Redpath (53) and Cowper (32) saved Australia. Doug faced only 12 balls and was bowled by Underwood for a duck. Sheahan defied for 52 minutes without scoring. However, reports said the Australians were lucky to escape defeat. The Australian score was 4/127 when time ran out to end the rain-affected match in a draw.

* * *

By the time of the third Test at Edgbaston, in Birmingham (11-16 July 1968), Milburn was injured. The uncapped Keith Fletcher, a prolific scorer from Essex, took his place in the squad but didn't play. Illingworth, the Yorkshire all-rounder, played after his 69* and eight wickets for Yorkshire against the tourists. This was another Test left undecided due to the weather.

There was no cricket on the first day and only 90 minutes of play on the last day, when, as in the previous game, England did its utmost to force a victory. This was also the 100th Test of the gentleman of English cricket – Colin Cowdrey, described by the Times as 'too nice a chap to be a dominating cricketer' (Hutchinson and Ross 1997). Cowdrey, the first in history to play 100 Tests, celebrated it with a century.

Once more, heavy rain dampened Australia's efforts. No play was possible on the first day. Cowdrey once again won the toss, and in between rain delays, England scored 409. The score was built around Cowdrey's first century in Ashes contests in England (104) in his 100th Test, made in four hours (15 fours) before Eric Freeman bowled him.

Edrich scored a slow 88, taking five hours. *Wisden* (Preston 1969) recorded that Cowdrey played beautifully. But, the agile Australians, notably Redpath, Sheahan and Walters, saved many runs. With Graveney (96), Cowdrey added 96 but tore a thigh muscle and used a runner for the last part of his innings. He didn't play in the second inning, and Graveney deputised as captain. Australia enjoyed a fine debut from Eric Freeman (4/78). Alan Connolly also took 3 for 84.

Australia was soon in trouble when Lawry broke his finger and retired. He was hit by a rising snorter from Snow. A century partnership between Chappell (71), fast becoming the success of the touring side, and Cowper (57) steadied Australia's ship. In making 46 in two hours, Doug also batted responsibly, hitting five fours. But Australia collapsed to be 222 all out. The wily Underwood (3/48), changing his pace, took the vital wickets of Doug and Sheahan, exposing Australia's frail batting. Illingworth also claimed 3/37.

In the second innings, England batted brightly, and Edrich scored another fifty. Cowdrey declared on 3-142, leaving Australia to chase 329 in a little over a day's play. Unfortunately, when Australia was at 1-68, the rains came again and washed out England's hopes of squaring the series. Sharing the Grundig with the family, who were keen on listening to other early-evening radio programmes, I was frustrated by the rain interruptions, which ruined my listening pleasure.

* * *

Due to injuries, Lawry and Cowdrey didn't play in the fourth Test at Headingley (25-30 July 1968). So, Tom Graveney led England, while Barry Jarman captained Australia. Incredibly, the two deputies had also been doubtful starters. Jarman was recovering from a broken finger, and Graveney from a hand injury.

Boycott, Milburn and Cowdrey were also unavailable due to injuries. England recalled Ted Dexter, the former England captain who had played little first-class cricket in the previous three years. However, he had returned to form with a double-century for Sussex against Kent, silencing his critics and earning a recall. England also called up Roger Prideaux and Keith Fletcher, who made their debuts.

Determined to retain the Ashes, the tourists concentrated solely on avoiding defeat and succeeded in their objective. Of all the five Tests played, this match suffered the least from the weather, with only one hour lost on the fourth day. Jarman was ultra-defensive in his tactics in the absence of Lawry. The West Australian, John Inverarity, debuted and opened with Cowper. Cowper batted stoutly, scoring just 15 runs at lunch when the total was 1-75.

Australia's first innings total (315) was dominated by Redpath's sparkling 92, made in three hours (14 fours). Chappell (65), Doug (42) and Sheahan (38) also batted carefully, while Underwood (4/41) and Snow (3/98) captured the wickets. As in the previous Test, the scoring rate was painfully slow (2.3 runs per over).

When England batted, they were even slower, scoring only two runs per over, much to the discontent of a crowd of 25,000 people. In his first Test, Prideaux (64) shared an opening stand of 123 with Edrich (62) before England collapsed from 3-209 to 302. Barrington (48) and Graveney (37) batted stubbornly, but Connolly took 5/72 in 39 overs.

Ian Chappell batted particularly well for his 81 in the second inning. Doug made a cautious 56, taking over three hours. But Redpath (48) again batted well, and Sheahan, making 31, took Australia to 312 and a lead of 325. The scoring rate was again slow, just around two runs an over, as Australia saw the opportunity to play for a draw and thus retain the Ashes. Illingworth bowled 51 overs, taking 6/87, and Underwood bowled 45 overs for his miserly figures of 2/52.

An England win became unlikely as the final day progressed. Still, they required 137 by tea in the final session. Surprisingly, resuming after tea, Barrington (46*) and Fletcher (23*) played for a draw rather than attempting to win, and the game ended with England reaching only 4/230 in 84 overs. This meant that Australia was guaranteed to retain the Ashes as England could now do no better than draw the series in the final Test. I was puzzled as to why England wasn't interested in winning on that final afternoon.

Strangely, Jarman didn't ask Doug to bowl in that session, as Barrington and Fletcher blocked everything. In fact, Doug didn't bowl in the match at all. Jarman relied primarily on McKenzie and Connolly, whom he over-bowled (25 and 31 overs, respectively). At the same time, Jarman under-bowled his spinners. Collectively, Gleeson, Cowper, and Chappell bowled only 21 overs. It was a bad call because the English spinners, Illingworth and Underwood, had already done so much bowling and taken eight wickets in Australia's second inning.

The team knew that Lawry was pulling the strings, watching from the balcony, and Jarman became very defensive (Mallett 2008: 90). It was a match that they should have pushed harder to win. At an after-match press conference, Lawry said: 'We came here to hold the Ashes, and we've succeeded'. Lawry typified how Test cricket was played when 'safety came first' instead of winning.

* * *

England came into the final and fifth Test at The Oval, in Surrey (22-27 August 1968) 1-nil down, needing a win to square the series and regain some dignity. The press severely criticised the team for their performance in the fourth Test, as they gave up on the chances of ending another series without winning the Ashes. England won by 226 runs with six minutes to spare, and they squared the rubber 1:1, with three matches drawn, but The Ashes stayed with Australia.

Cowper was injured, but Lawry was fit again. Ashley Mallett, the offspinner, debuted. England brought in D'Oliveira to replace Prideaux, who was sick. Milburn was fit again and returned to the side. Cowdrey was also back as captain. Brilliant centuries by Edrich (164 with 20 fours) and D'Oliveira (158 with 21 fours) and a crisp half-century by Graveney (63) allowed England to reach 494. They were helped by sunshine, quite a few dropped catches and some indifferent Australian bowling. Mallett, in his debut, took 3/87 in 36 overs.

Australia knew they needed to bat well to minimise England's chances of winning. Lawry did his best to achieve that by taking almost six hours to reach a century. Snow and Brown bowled at top speed and had Australia reeling at one stage at 6-1. Between a rest day, Lawry batted on for seven and a half hours to score 135. Early on day four, when given out caught behind off an inside edge, Lawry left no one in doubt that he disagreed with umpire Authur Fagg's decision. He stopped to speak to the umpire on his way back to the pavilion.

An unkind English writer described Lawry as a corpse with pads on. However, John Woodcock of the Times appreciated Lawry's powers of concentration: 'Lawry is a great battler and a wonderfully sound judge of length. All too often, he has been the rock on which England have floundered' (Hutchinson and Ross 1997: 377).

Doug failed on this occasion, caught behind by Alan Knott off Brown for only five. However, the Australian tail wagged on day four with a rousing rear-guard action led by the debutant Mallett (43*). This allowed Australia to avoid the follow-on and reach 324. England led by 170. Some of the best cricket came when England sought to score quickly in their second inning.

England mustered 181 in only three hours, looking for quick runs while they looked for an unbeatable lead. Connolly (4/65) and Mallett (2/75) contained them.

England's lead of 351 meant that Australia could win on the final day if they scored at a rate of 54 an hour, which was a difficult task. But survival quickly became their concern as they lost Lawry and Redpath before the end of day four. When play resumed on the final day, Australia lost Chappell, Doug and Sheahan before lunch on the final day to be 5-65 and in real trouble. A nailbiter was on the cards as John Inverarity, the opener, dug in. With great apprehension, I recall hurrying home to catch the final few hours of play that evening.

The English weather had been a curse for Australia throughout the 1968 summer. But rain became Australia's saviour as the heavens opened up just before lunch, and torrential rain flooded the ground. However, miraculously, the ground staff at the Oval, assisted by more than 1000 volunteer 'groundsmen' from the crowd, managed to get rid of the water after the fierce storm, and the sun came out to help.

Mallett (2008: 91) recalled that the ground authority offered people seven shillings and sixpence for their mopping efforts. Film footage shows the England captain, Cowdrey, helped inspire the effort by parading about the ground under a large umbrella. As far as I can recall, it was a scene not witnessed again in a Test match.

Play resumed by late afternoon, at 4:45 pm, which was well past 9 pm in Colombo, as I listened. In the dramatic 75 minutes of remaining play, *Deadly Derek* (7/50) bowled England to an impressive 226-run win. Australia crumbled for 125 just six minutes before stumps. This was Underwood's best bowling figures in Test cricket; he headed the bowling averages for the series with 20 wickets at 15 runs apiece.

Wisden (Preston, 1969) said, 'No praise could be too high for the way he seized his opportunity on this unforgettable day'. Inverarity was the last man out after his gritty defiance over four hours, making 56.

The *Wisden* Editor, Norman Preston (1969), gave Australia credit for their sportsmanship. They averaged twenty overs an hour when England was pressing for runs. Their batters quickly emerged from the dressing room as wickets fell and passed each other on the way to the wicket, even in that hectic final period.

Facing defeat, the Australians didn't waste time by gardening or other delaying tactics – almost hard to believe, based on what we see on TV these days. After listening to the nerve-wracking final hour, I didn't sleep well that night. But the 'the most gripping finish since the war' as the win was described, even on a rain-affected pitch, restored some pride for England (Rippon 1982).

* * *

The English press was highly critical of the England team, who were often on top for much of the rain-affected 1968 series but barely saved the series 1-all. While the Australian batting was patchy, their youth and athleticism gave them the edge in a critically important area – fielding. In summing up the series, Jack Fingleton wrote: 'The English are slow and unsure. The flannels of the two teams tell the story. The English leave the field spotless at the knees, whereas the Australians have green stains because they fling themselves at the ball'.

In the 1968 Ashes, they had firmly set a fielding benchmark that the rest of the cricket-playing countries had to catch up to. One of my favourite cricketers, Paul Sheahan, won £100 as the best fielder for his athletic and brilliant fielding throughout the series. For a few years, Sheahan excelled in the field and, by many accounts, was even better in the covers and mid-off region than the very agile Clive Lloyd.

The series wasn't satisfactory for several players, including Doug. Only Bill Lawry made a century on the fifth Test that Australia lost. Lawry later pointed out that the English summer in 1968 was so damp and miserable that his team could bat long enough to score only about 7000 runs in the tour. This sharply contrasted with the previous 1964 team under Simpson, which made 14,000 runs on the tour.

Preston (1969) wrote that 'the best was not seen of Walters and Sheahan. Both had moments of sheer brilliance, but they never came to fruition'. In such a wet summer, they didn't do themselves justice. Each played his highest Test innings in the first match at Old Trafford, but batting on suspect surfaces, neither did well in English conditions.

In summing up the 1968 series in which many of Australia's good players under-performed, Neville Cardus (1968b) wrote: '

> Nature and the genius of cricket lavish gifts in equal and generous quantity in all periods and all seasons. It is the way they are used that counts. We may be sure that, after some lean years recently, the Australians of 1968 will not allow inborn potentialities to run to waste for want of their ancient will to win.

* * *

Doug did most of his best work in the Tests, and his supporters had hoped that this experience would help him regain his pre-Army form. His form against Sobers' West Indies, in the following summer at home, showed that Doug was back to his old ways of plundering runs (Edwards 1977a). Analysing Doug's performances, Mallett (2008: 92-94) gave one explanation for Doug's relatively low scores in the Ashes series, which is an anomaly. He suggested that Doug's hand-eye coordination was so good that on the slower, seaming English wickets, he caught up with the ball with his reflexes a fraction too early.

Mallett said that Doug saw the seam movement early off the hand of a fast bowler and knew how to play it well. However, when the ball was right on the stumps, Doug's reaction was too quick and 'good enough' to get a nick to a ball if it moved away much after pitching. 'Less-gifted, mere mortals', Mallett said, would have played and missed.

Having watched a few of Doug's dismissals and seeing how the English play on their seaming wickets, Doug might have benefitted if he learned to leave the ball more like Geoff Boycott. Boycott trusts his judgement when dealing with the off-cutters, seaming away, leaving many deliveries. Mallett recalled (2008: 94-95) that Boycott just played straight, 'down the line' and didn't care how many balls he missed.

If the ball moved, he missed it, sometimes by a considerable margin, but the bottom line was that even though he played and missed, he survived to bat on. The experience of watching how Boycott plays got Doug thinking long and hard about his batting technique in England.

With his tendency to not be bogged down, Doug wasn't inclined to let too many balls go. He took risks with the moving ball that caused several of his dismissals. Doug also never had the patience of Sunil Gavaskar, the Indian great, who was a successful batter in England.

Gavaskar had the Boycott-like patience to wait for the loose ball and let many deliveries on the stumps go to the keeper. It sounds simple but hard to implement. Doug recalled that he, too, learned by watching how Boycott bats in England. Given the pronounced swing in often overcast conditions, it becomes clear that batters in England must master the technique of not going hard at every ball.

* * *

One of the most critical events in cricket history came after the result of that thrilling final Test match at the Oval. Basil D'Oliveira's swashbuckling 158 helped England win, saving the series. However, on the same night (27 August 1968), when the English selectors picked the team for the forthcoming South African tour, D'Oliveira's name was missing. Critics raged that the selectors had yielded to South Africa's demand that as a 'coloured' player, D'Oliveira would not be welcome in the tour party.

In the parliament, South African Prime Minister John Vorster said that his country will not receive a team forced upon her by people with specific political aims. The non-selection of a 'non-white' player ignited the debate of racism in sports. More importantly, it brought South Africa's distasteful apartheid policy of racial segregation to the world's attention.

In September 1968, the 'D'Oliveira affair' simmered like an angry volcano for weeks. Newspapers in Ceylon also carried various articles, which I read with great interest. Doug Insole, the chairman of selectors, took the unprecedented step of having a press conference (uncommon in those days) to explain to the public that he and the other selectors regarded D'Oliveira 'as a batter rather than an all-rounder. We put him beside our seven batters, along with Colin Milburn, whom we also had to leave out with regret' (Melford 1969).

However, when Tom Cartwright, primarily a bowler, pulled out of the tour due to injury, and the final team was announced on 16 September, the selectors included D'Oliveira. Insole explained that D'Oliveira had previously been considered only a batter (and omitted).

Still, his inclusion in the team was now as a bowler or bowling all-rounder. The South Africans thought this was the final proof of political motivations driving team selections. After much debate, the tour was cancelled on 24 September by the M.C.C. Committee (Melford 1969).

Some writers pointed out that 'if Jarman hadn't dropped D'Oliveira when he was 31, no one would have considered the latter's omission from the touring squad 'unjustified'. Then, the tour of South Africa would have gone ahead. Cricket lovers everywhere might have enjoyed years of watching South African greats play Test cricket against the world's best. The cricket world might have been written differently if this extraordinary galaxy of superstars had played more Test cricket.

I can't help thinking this was a perfect example of The Butterfly Effect in cricket, whereby small events and incidents can have surprisingly large and sometimes entirely unexpected outcomes [22].

---

22   The *Butterfly Effect* (a term coined by Edward Lorenz, a meteorologist) explains how small events can have dramatic effects. For example, it explains how a small decision and action (such as people reducing waste, recycling materials or reducing fossil fuel usage by cycling or walking) can have positive, ripple effects on climate change, habitats and populations of varied species.

CHAPTER 7

Looking for Runs and Enjoying It

In Doug's 1971 book 'Looking For Runs', he clarified how he always looked for runs and enjoyed them. Doug's best advice to any aspiring youngster wanting to play serious cricket was to play attackingly and enjoy the game to the utmost. After all, he said, 'If you are not going to enjoy, there is no real point in taking part' – a philosophy Doug had tried to follow back in 1954 at that 'little place called Telligra'.

Plundering Garry Sobers' West Indies (1968-69)

I was glued to the radio as I listened to the Australians handing out a battering to the Garfield Sobers-led West Indies in the home series in 1968-69. The two sides were playing for the Frank Worrell Trophy, which had been established after the 1960-61 series in which a Test match ended for the first time in a tie.

The Worrell-led West Indians played some unforgettable cricket in Australia. The Australian public loved the Caribbean cricketers' cavalier style and appreciated Worrell's leadership on the tour. Fittingly, the trophy was named in Worrell's name as an honour and has been contested between the two countries.

It was a series where Doug's batting prowess was richly displayed while the mighty West Indies were on the wane. Throughout the series, they played poorly, as the team depended too much on their captain, Garry Sobers. Sobers, often dubbed the King of Cricket at the peak of his career, was the greatest all-round cricketer the world has seen.

A tally of 8,032 runs from 160 innings (93 Tests) at 57.8 with 26 centuries placed him among the all-time great batters. Bowling 3500 overs, Sobers also took 235 wickets at 34 and 109 catches (Wooldridge 2019). Arlott (1975) argued that 'no other cricketer in modern cricket has delivered so much entertainment for cricket lovers as Sobers did'.

Sobers played for Barbados for 21 seasons, in English professional league cricket for five (Radcliffe in the Central Lancashire League, 1958-62), for South Australia in the Sheffield Shield for three (1961-62), and

Nottinghamshire for seven (1968-74). In addition, he turned out regularly for the Cavaliers on Sundays for several years before the Sunday League in England.

Sobers made nine tours for West Indies, consecutively playing 89 of his 93 Tests, averaging more than four yearly Tests for 20 years. In between Tests, he led the Rest of the World XI twice (1968-69; 1971-72). Arlott (1975) was spot on when he said, 'The wonder was not that the spark grew dim but that it endured so bright for so long'.

Arlott (1979) also observed that by 1974, on his farewell circuit in England, Sobers was weary:

Anyone who ever matches Garfield Sobers's performances will have to be an extremely strong man – and he, too, will be weary'. 'Because he could do so much, he was asked by various people to do it too frequently; Sobers was a victim of his own talents.

As a kid, I could not quite fathom why the Windies would fail so badly when they were led by Sobers. Since 1965, I had read many articles and reports on how well Sobers had been batting and bowling and how his team had easily beaten other Test teams.

Clive Lloyd (1980: 47) explained that many West Indian players were on the wrong side of 30 and knew this tour down under would be their last. Lloyd lamented: 'They were also not as fit as they used to be, not as keen, not as dedicated, and, in many cases, not as good' and 'it was a formula for disaster' and also pointed out that Sobers had never been a disciplinarian; it was not in his nature.

Sobers expected all his big men to impose self-discipline as players representing their country. Sobers failed to realise that not everyone has the genius he possessed. As it was, old age had finally caught up with the speed merchants – Hall and Griffith. Brilliant batters – Kanhai, Nurse and Butcher – didn't score runs with their old consistency. The younger batters, Clive Lloyd, Steven Camacho, Roy Fredericks and Charlie Davis, didn't quite meet expectations. With the sharp edge of pace absent from the pace attack, Lance Gibbs often came on only when the Australian batters were well on top (Blofeld 1970).

* * *

Garry Sobers (2002: 174) admitted that 'all the cricket was beginning to take its toll'. After his Test debut at 17, in 1954, he played continuously for 14 years and had been captain since 1965. I recall well how brilliantly Sobers batted throughout the series. He made centuries in the fourth and fifth Tests, and his series tally was 497 runs at 49.

Sobers's wicket was the most vital one for the Australians. Despite niggling knee trouble and pain in the left shoulder, he also opened the bowling in several Tests, making up for the leading fast-bowler, Wes Hall's absence in three out of five Tests. Sobers bowled 206 overs with his medium-pacers, taking 18 wickets, but at 40.7. His effort was second only in the bowling effort to the off-spinner Gibbs (292 overs for 24 wickets at 38). Sobers also fielded brilliantly, taking 12 catches.

Despite the presence of Sobers, the Windies suffered greatly from the ageing team and declining fast-bowling stocks. Hall played in only two Tests (8 wickets at 40) and Griffith in only three (8 wickets at 54). The third fast bowler in the squad, a Barbadian – Richard Edwards, played only in two Tests and took only three wickets at 91. I recall that Joey Carew, primarily a batter, did a lot of bowling in each Test match along with Sobers's cousin – the off-spinner David Holford.

The hopeless fielding of the ageing West Indies also let them down in the series. Lloyd (1980: 48) said, 'We dropped so many catches that you needed a calculator to total them up'. They missed at least 35 chances in the five Tests. Sobers also recalled (2002: 177) how different the series would have been if his team had held those catches.

Lloyd said that the team management did not consider organizing training or net sessions or catching practice sessions for the team. Team meetings were a shambles without discussions on how to bowl to Lawry, Chappell and Doug, making piles of runs. Lloyd felt that Sobers was a bit distracted. Perhaps the West Indian tour manager should have better managed the players and activities, such as organizing net practices during a few days of Sobers's absence for family reasons in the middle of a tour.

Although the West Indies opened the tour with a convincing win in the first Test by 125 runs, Australia won the series, crushing the visitors 3-1. The end of the period of West Indies' dominance saw a significant shift in the balance of power in world cricket. Blofeld (1970) reported that the famous Windies side of the previous decade disintegrated against the younger and physically fitter Australians. The Australian team itself was nearing greatness by the end of the series. The West Indies also learned a bitter lesson – that success in cricket comes not from individual brilliance but from a team effort.

* * *

Doug suffered from a hamstring injury and didn't play in Brisbane in the first Test (6-11 December 1968). His replacement was John Inverarity, who was later dropped. The West Indies started the tour well with a convincing win by 125 runs. In the first inning, they began with 296, with Kanhai (94) and Joey Carew (83) scoring the most.

Australia started well with a 217 partnership for the second wicket between Lawry (105) and Ian Chappell (117). But they collapsed to be all out for 284. Sobers desperately called upon Lloyd, a part-timer, to try and break the Lawry-Chappell stand as he suffered from shoulder discomfort. 'With a blink of an eye', Lloyd's slow, medium pacers dismissed both centurions caught by Sobers. Australia ended up with a 12-run deficit, as Gibbs took 5/88 (Sobers 2002: 175).

In the second inning, for the Windies, Lloyd produced a power-packed century (129) in three and a half hours, hitting eighteen fours and a six. Carew (71*), Sobers (36) and Camacho (40) helped the tourists pile up 353. The wicket was taking spin at this stage, and Johnny Gleeson ended with 5/122 off 33 overs.

The Australians were set to make 366 to win but could not counter Sobers's mighty effort (6/73 in 33 eight-ball overs) and that of Gibbs (3/82 in 30 overs) on a spinning wicket. Despite the resistance from Chappell (50), Stackpole (32), Sheahan (34) and McKenzie (38*), the home team was bowled out for 240 and lost by 125 runs.

* * *

Australia bounced back in the second Test, played at the MCG in Melbourne (26-30 December 1968), to win by innings within four days. The Windies made three changes, bringing in three debutants – Richard Edwards, a fast bowler for Griffith; Roy Fredericks replaced the injured Lloyd; and Charlie Davis, an all-rounder, for David Holford. Doug returned to the team for Australia, replacing Inverarity, and Eric Freeman replaced Ashley Mallett.

McKenzie bowled brilliantly, taking 8/71 in 28 overs, and the Windies managed only 200. Sobers was bowled by McKenzie for 19, the bowler's 200th Test wicket, a highly-prized scalp. Roy Fredericks, on debut, made 76 in almost five hours, and Basil Butcher (42) showed some pluck, but the rest of the batting collapsed.

In the reply, Lawry made a double-century (205 with one six and 12 fours), and Ian Chappell scored 165 (16 fours). They put on 298 for the second wicket in even time. Just turned 23 years old, Doug batted at No. 4 and plundered 76. Doug's 76 was a grand inning and the start of a fantastic summer harvest of runs for him. Although his timing was not quite right, Doug helped Lawry to add 123 for the third wicket as Australia amassed 510 runs. The tourists' bowling stocks were depleted without Hall and Griffith. Sobers bowled 33 overs, taking 4/97, while Gibbs bowled a marathon 43 overs, taking 4/139.

In the second inning, West Indies collapsed again, mainly to Gleeson's spin (5/61) and were bowled out for 280 runs. Nurse (74), Sobers (67) and Fredericks (47) batted well but couldn't stop Australia from winning. Nurse and Sobers put on 134 for the fourth wicket until a freakish catch ended Nurse's innings. Nurse pulled a Gleeson long hop, which cannoned off the short-leg fielder Freeman's head into Stackpole's hands at square leg. Australia won the match by an inning and 30 runs in the last over of the fourth day.

* * *

Sobers (2002: 175) described the defeat in the second Test as a severe setback to the team's low morale due to the injuries that Hall and Griffith were carrying. It showed in the third Test at the SCG in Sydney (3-8 January 1969), which Australia again won comfortably. The West Indies brought in Lloyd and Hall for Camacho and Davis.

In the first inning, they were bowled out for 264, with McKenzie (4/85) and Freeman (3/57) doing the damage. Sobers was bowled by Freeman for 49, which he made in 90 minutes, while Lloyd, returning to the side after injury, made a rapid 50, striking nine fours.

When Australia replied, Doug was at his best, scoring 118 in just three and a half hours, hitting twelve fours. Mallett (2008: 99) said:

> *Here was Walters at his finest: he cut and pulled the fast bowlers, making the shots look ridiculously easy because of his swift footwork. And he used his feet to skip down the wicket to get to the pitch of the spin of Gibbs, a number of times thumping the off-spinner wide of mid-on with power-packed on-drives.*
>
> *The crowd rose as one on Sydney Hill when he played Gibbs with his famous 'come to attention' shot, sending the ball careering to the fence in front of the M.A. Noble Stand.*

While Redpath (80), Stackpole (58), Freeman (76), and Sheahan (47) made the other bulk of the runs, the last-wicket pair of Gleeson (42*) and Connolly (37) added 73. With 541 runs on the board, Australia were ahead by 277. The Windies batted better and scored 324 in the second inning. Basil Butcher scored a fluent 101 in just four hours, while Kanhai

(69) and Fredericks (43) made runs. Sobers fell for 36 after looking well set, caught by Ian Chappell in the slips off Gleeson.

In the *Wisden* report, Henry Blofeld (1970) argued that Sobers erred by persisting to bat at No. 6 when a player of his ability should have gone in earlier to set the example and to remove some of the pressure. Gleeson's finger spin, delivered with the right-hand middle finger tucked under the palm, bamboozled the West Indians again.

Gleeson bowled 26 overs, taking 4/91, while Freeman showed his all-round worth, capturing 3/69. Stackpole and Sheahan quickly knocked off the required 42 runs, and Australia won by 10 wickets.

* * *

Inconsistencies of the West Indies showed again in the fourth Test in Adelaide (24-29 January 1969). For this match, they brought back Griffith and Holford for Edwards and Hall, while Australia kept its winning side. After winning the toss on an easy-paced pitch, the West Indies threw their wickets away with careless strokes.

Despite a run-a-minute century from Sobers (110), the tourists mustered only 276 in the first inning. Sobers' innings included two sixes and 15 fours. At times, he hammered the bowlers with disdain. Butcher (52) and Carew (36) batted well while others faltered. This time, Freeman (4/52) and Gleeson (3/91) were the wreckers.

Another Doug Walters century (110), batting at No. 5 in just over three hours, with 13 fours, led the Australian reply of 533. Lawry (62), Stackpole (62), Chappell (76), Sheahan (51) and McKenzie (59) all made half-centuries. Sobers opened the bowling again and toiled 28 overs for his 1/106, while Gibbs took 4/145 off 43 overs.

The Australians had a 257-run lead, and it looked like the Windies faced another humiliating defeat. Sobers (2002: 176) recalled that the team had been stung by the criticism in the press. So they hit back with determination, scoring 616 in the second inning. Everyone got runs, led by another Basil Butcher century (118 with 18 fours). Carew (80), Kanhai (80), Holford (80), Sobers (52), Lloyd (42), and Hendricks (37*). Gleeson belted out of the attack and ended with 1/176 in 35 overs. Still, Connolly took 5/122 and McKenzie, 3/90.

Chasing 360, Australians were cruising to another victory at 3-298 with the top-order batting firing. Ian Chappell (96), Lawry (89), Stackpole (50) and Doug (50) made it look easy until a spate of runouts stalled their progress. Redpath, Doug, Freeman and Jarman were all runouts. Redpath was controversially run out for a duck by Griffith, who did a 'Mankad' without prior warning [23].

Charlie Griffith's running out of Redpath in 1969 was the second 'Mankading' instance in Test cricket. For decades, 'Mankading' was considered 'not within the spirit of the game'. However, it is now accepted as a legitimate run-out within the ICC rules. Nevertheless, most umpires prefer a prior warning to a batter persistently backing up too far before the bowler attempts a 'Mankad'.

Sobers said he was disgusted with Griffith for not warning the batter before the dismissal. Still, as Redpath left the field run out for nine, Sobers didn't recall him (2002: 176-177). Perhaps he should have. The mistake can only be explained by the possibility that the noisy heckling by the crowd distracted Sobers. Sobers later apologized to Lawry for Griffith's action (Hutchinson and Ross 1997: 380).

I recall the incident well as I listened to the proceedings attentively at home. Having read accounts of the incident in various articles, I think Griffith, a quietly spoken and dignified human being, was hard done by what happened. He was doing his best for his team under the existing rules and regulations; nothing more, nothing less.

Australians were at this stage teetering on the brink of defeat at 9-333 but were saved by the last pair, Sheahan, 11* and Connolly, 6*, who batted out the last 26 balls. The match ended in a thrilling draw with Australia at 9-339; they were 21 runs short of victory. Sobers said 'it was indeed the most exciting Test match he had played since the famous tied Test in the 1960-61 series' [24].

---

23   Doing a *'Mankad'* is the name given to a method of dismissal whereby, instead of delivering the ball, a bowler runs out a batter at the non-striker's end when the non-striker is out of their crease, backing up too far. This form of dismissal was first used by the Indian all-rounder Vinoo Mankad in the 1947-48 series between Australia and India, in the Sydney Test. Manka ran out Bill Brown, the non-striker, who was out of his crease as the bowler ran in.

24   Jack Fingleton (*'The Greatest Test of All'*, 1961) wrote that in one of the most electrifying finishes on record, Australia and the West Indies created history when they tied in the first Test match at the Gabba in Brisbane (9-14 December 1960). It was the first time in 83 years, and after almost 500 matches of Test cricket that a match tied.

Sobers was a key member of Frank Worrell's 1960-61 team that featured in the 'Tied' Test and made a fabulous 132 in the Windies first innings, which the Australian paceman, Alan Davidson, described 'as the greatest inning he had seen in Australia'. The Windies scored 453 in the first innings. A majestic 181 by O'Neill anchored the Australian reply of 505.

In the second inning, the Windies scored 284 and Australia was chasing 233 for a

* * *

As the series had not been decided, the final Test at the SCG in Sydney) was played over six days (14-20 February 1969). Sydney had received a lot of rain before the match, and the curator of the SCG had not been able to mow the grass or use the rollers to produce the wicket he wanted (Piesse 2013a). As it turned out, Australia again outclassed the tourists, who revealed their familiar failings. Griffith replaced Holford and partnered with Hall for the last time in a Test match.

Sobers won the toss and sent Australia in, and at one stage, Australia was 3-51. Doug, batting at No. 5, then joined Lawry. But the West Indies lost the opportunity to press home the early advantage when Lawry, who was 44 then, drove at Sobers and was dropped by Nurse at second slip. Lawry went on to make 151. In eight hours, Doug scored a monumental first double-century (242 with 24 fours).

His inning was full of uninhibited and daring strokeplay. More than 25,000 fans went into raptures as Doug played his way into record books, and he received the most stirring ovation given to a batter since Bradman. When he reached 200, hundreds of children ran onto the ground to congratulate Doug, holding up play. With Australia at 5-453 and his score at 242, Doug tried to cut Gibbs off his stumps; he missed and was bowled. Freeman (56), Taber (48) and Gleeson (45) took Australia to a massive score of 619. It was the fourth Test in a row that Australia posted a 500-plus total.

The wicket-keeper, Jackie Hendricks, dropped Doug off Hall when he was 75, and the tourists paid a heavy price for this. The Lawry-Walters stand of 336 was the second-highest for Australia against the Windies for any wicket. It also became the fourth-highest stand in Test cricket up to that time. The partnership ensured that Australia won back the Frank Worrell Trophy.

Hall (3/157 in 36 overs), Griffith (3/157 in 37 overs), Sobers (2/94 in 28 overs), and Gibbs (2/133 in 40 overs) toiled as the Australians batted for over two days. Sobers used Carew's part-time leg-spin and Lloyd's gentle medium-pacers on the first day to dislodge Lawry and Doug. Still, they only bowled 12 overs between them.

---

win. Ten minutes before stumps, they needed only seven runs to win when Wes Hall began the last over. In the last over, the last man for Australia, Lindsay Kline, came to the wicket after Wally Grout had been run out on the sixth ball. The scores were tied at this stage.

Kline deflected the seventh ball to square-leg. Ian Meckiff raced down the pitch but was out of his ground when a return from Joe Solomon shattered the stumps and the end came with each tide scoring 737 runs. A total of 3,142 balls had been bowled and 1,474 runs scored over five days, yet these two fine teams could not be separated.

Keith Miller severely criticised this move by Sobers: 'What were Joey Carew and Clive Lloyd doing bowling in a Test match on the first day with Australia's score still under 200? Neither would get a bowl in a second-grade Saturday afternoon match' (Piesse 2013a).

With their chance of victory gone, the West Indies once again carelessly threw away their wickets. However, they were given a fine start by Carew (64) and Fredericks (39), who put on 100 in under two hours. Then, only Lloyd (53) and Kanhai (44) showed any fight, and they were all-out for 279, finishing 340 runs behind. Sobers promoted himself to No. 4 but only made 13. Connolly (4/61), McKenzie (3/90) and Gleeson (2/53) shared the wickets.

With the series already won and mindful of the Windies' recovery at Adelaide, Lawry didn't enforce the follow-on, and Australia batted again. Redpath batted down the order and made his maiden Test hundred (132). Doug benefitted from Lawry not enforcing the follow-on and plundered a second century (103) off the tiring bowlers. He had a 210-run partnership with Redpath for the fourth wicket. Doug later said: 'Not a bad match that one for me!' (Piesse 2013a).

The uncompromising Lawry had no pity for the suffering the tourists and declared his second inning at 8-394, setting up a small matter of 735 to win. Lloyd (1980: 51) wrote that it was 'just about the last straw' for the West Indies. However, instead of wilting under Australia's glut of runs, Sobers (2002: 177) recalled that they refused to roll over. Despite the impossible target, batting at No. 7, Nurse scored 137, a powerful inning with 18 fours and a six.

Sobers batted at No. 5 and smashed 20 boundaries in his 113 in 140 minutes of a dazzling display. When he was out, the score was 6-220, and he had scored more than half of the team's runs. The West Indies scored at a phenomenal rate of 5.5 runs per over but were bowled out for 353 in just 64 overs to lose the match by 382.

It was mayhem for a while, as I recall. I even remember where I was standing in my hometown with a transistor radio held to my ears. Australia won quickly on the sixth morning. Batting to save the match was out of the question for the Windies. The persistent Gleeson took 3/84 in 15.2 overs, and McKenzie claimed 3/93 in 16 overs.

* * *

Doug was at his best in this home series, and his four centuries in three of the four Test matches he played made him a superstar. An injury kept him out of the first Test. Doug was only 23 when he became the first batter to achieve the unique feat in Test cricket, a double-hundred and a second-century in the same Test. Not even The Don achieved this feat. In the four Tests and six innings, Doug's series aggregate was 699 at a phenomenal average of 116.5. This placed him among the most incredible post-war Australian batters.

In a newspaper article, Frank Tyson described Doug as 'the supreme example of an eye player in superlative form' (Hutchinson and Ross 1997: 380). Describing Doug's 242 in Masterly Batting, Piesse (2013a) noted that coming into the 'stellar' Test of his career, Doug fell down a flight of concrete steps at his apartment in Parramatta. He had several days of physiotherapy before he was declared fit to play [25].

After the inning, Bradman wrote a personal letter to Doug in which he extended hearty congratulations for this monumental inning. The great man was not known for giving praise easily. But Bradman acknowledged Doug's record-breaking knock, which surpassed his highest score against the West Indies, a double-century (223) he made in Brisbane in January 1931.

Bradman was delighted that Doug broke his record because of how Doug goes about the business of scoring runs. He had been watching Doug closely since 1965-66. A brief excerpt from Bradman's letter printed in full by Mallett (2008: 106) reads as follows:

It is essential in the interests of cricket that batters are alive to the necessity to play shots and be aggressive. This does not imply any lack of soundness, but in the end, with discretion, the stroke-maker will get more runs…Keep it up!"

* * *

Ian Chappell, vice-captain, made hundreds in the first and second Tests and reached a series aggregate of 548 at 68.5. Lawry plundered three centuries (105, 205 and 151 in the first, second and fifth Tests) for a series aggregate of 667 at 83. Lawry's batting was unglamorous but as compelling as ever. With such a good side under him, Lawry became a more flexible tactician (Blofeld 1970).

The series win by a margin of 3-1 meant that Australia wrested back Test supremacy from the beleaguered West Indies, who had been the most

---

25 *Masterly Batting*, by Patrick Ferriday and Dave Wilson (2013) was an analytical exercise to rank the significance of 100 of Test centuries. A panel marked each of the candidate centuries in 10 categories, including the impact on the match and the series, quality and condition of the pitch and bowling attack, weight and speed of scoring, chances given and runs scored as a percentage of the total. The panel was asked to give each category a weighting in terms of how they deemed the relative importance of the inning to create an overall score.

dominant force up to that time. No team in the modern era has had such an impact as the West Indians since 1960-61.

Why the Windies suddenly fell from the stellar heights of the past wasn't clear to me until I read the autobiographies of Lloyd (1980) and Sobers (2002) about how the series went. The gallant efforts of the captain were not enough to beat the Australians playing at home, as the West Indies suffered from atrocious fielding lapses, inconsistent batting and bowling, which lacked penetration.

I still have vivid memories of the series. The Windies' defeat disappointed me because I greatly liked the 'lion-hearted' Sobers and the Caribbean team. Sobers was criticised for not being a good leader on the tour, being distracted by golf, flying off to Melbourne and leaving his team in Brisbane without much to do.

By this time, the 33-year-old Sobers had married an Australian lady, Prudence Kirby. Their marriage occurred two months before the Australian tour, on 12 September 1969 at Nottingham. Sobers had met Prudence 18 months prior when she was promoting an Australian fruit in England while he was playing for Nottinghamshire.

In *The Cricketer*, Bryan 'Bomber' Wells (1969: 25) decried the attacks on Sober as 'manifestations of the ugly side of human nature'. Angered by the criticism, Wells wrote, 'Those "experts" who criticise Sobers do not even qualify to tie his shoelaces'.

In the same vein, lamenting the mounting pressure in the West Indies for Sobers to be replaced as captain, C. L. R. James (1970: 11) reminded the cricketing world that 'Sobers represents the summation of the game – and what a man can do for it'.

Garry Sobers is in trouble. That means all of us are in trouble, particularly people interested in the future of cricket as a public spectacle…Sobers is the living embodiment of what cricket used to be, what it can be, what it has to be – if it is once more to hold its place in the civilization of the [British] people.

In the article, James re-invoked what he had written earlier in *Beyond A Boundary*: 'A great batter is a special organism; it must be so for they are very rare, as rare as great violinists'. He cautioned the West Indian authorities if Sobers is not handled carefully, 'it could result in the deterioration of a rare organism'!

However, Australia's ascendency, especially Doug's batting, greatly pleased me. Jarman was replaced as wicket-keeper by an agile Brian Taber in the fifth test. McKenzie remained the 'beating heart' of the Australian attack with 30 wickets at 25. Gleeson, Connolly and Freeman (26, 20 and 13 wickets, respectively) contributed to Australia winning the Test series.

Writing in *Wisden*, Blofeld (1970) predicted that beating this Australian side would take a lot over the next six years. 'Blowers' felt that the team was strengthened by Taber as wicket-keeper and predicted that Mallett would soon become a regular team member.

Visiting Ceylon and Troubles in India (1969-70)

By 1968-69, politics had a say in cricket as the 'D'Oliveira Affair' unfolded (Haigh 2006: 296). The apartheid policy in South Africa affected all cricket-playing countries. Australians undertook the 1969-70 tour of India, Sri Lanka and South Africa under its shade. It really was a turbulent time. The cancellation of rugby and cricket tours and the boycotting of South Africa dominated the news.

The pressure was high on the South African government to get rid of its distasteful segregation policy. The stubborn refusal by South Africa to not accept a 'coloured' person in a touring team was the real issue. The South African cricket authorities and the government decried that selecting D'Oliveira as a late substitute for the injured Tom Cartwright was the 'Anti-Apartheid' Movement at work and not a decision based on the merits of the player involved. The ACB was, however, quite happy to accept South Africa's invitation for a full tour.

* * *

Initially, Bill Lawry's men were to have completed the brief tour to Ceylon and India before a Test series in Pakistan. However, the itinerary changed as the tour couldn't work financially because of the Pakistani government's strict exchange controls. On 27 October 1968, the Pakistan Cricket Board rescinded its invitation for the Australians to tour there. The South African Cricket Association (SACA) offered to fill the void (Mallett 2008: 142-143).

The ACB accepted the invitation as a substitute for the Pakistan leg. During General Ayub Khan's dictatorship, Pakistan was politically quite unstable in those days. On the other hand, Ceylon was a peaceful haven in 1969, and all journalists who accompanied tours were unstinting in their praise for the island's hospitality. The players had no hesitation in accepting the offer to spend some time in Ceylon before embarking on the Indian leg of the tour. It wasn't a 'whistlestop' tour but an official Australian team's first extended tour to the island.

I recall that only a few players came through well in the three-day match played in Colombo, and there were three one-day internationals; two played in Colombo and one in Kandy. The Australians looked like they were not keenly contesting the battles like the English visitors a few years earlier. On the other hand, the highly motivated island's cricketers showed the Australians what they could do. The home team had a point to prove; they loved what they did and always played attractive cricket with passion and dedication.

The three-day match was played at The Oval in Colombo from 24-26 October 1969. It was a full-strength team from the visitors as they wanted match practice as much as possible. One of the umpires was Fitzroy De Mel, whom I mentioned earlier (p. 48).

'Mighty Australians Humbled', said Ceylon The Daily News headline as the visitors could only manage 197. Doug scored 49, while McKenzie swung the bat for 52, saving face for the visitors. With off-spin, Neil Chanmugam took 5/47 and held a brilliant catch in the covers to end Doug's inning.

Tight bowling from the Australians and poor batting restricted the island's reply to 148. The home side struggled for nearly six hours, facing 90 overs. The opener, C. Balakrishnan, a Tamil, scored 55, while David Heyn, a Burgher, made 26. The locals surprisingly couldn't get on top of the Australian bowling. The two Australian spinners did the bulk of the bowling. Ashley Mallett (3/35 in 18 overs), John Gleeson (2/63 in 35 overs) and McKenzie (2/8 in 13 overs).

In the second inning, Australia rattled up 6-158 and declared. Lawry hit 70, Ian Chappell 29, but Doug scored only 11. Chanmugam took 3/43, including Doug's wicket. In the time remaining, the locals made 5-132, with the skipper Michael Tissera stroking an impressive 53*. Gleeson took 3/32 in his 15 overs.

Doug recalled that it was quite a pleasant experience on the island, and the team was treated as royalty. They stayed in Colombo at the famous Galle Face Hotel, which was grand in those days. Despite the heat and humidity, Doug said that the island's cricket officials, players, support staff, media, broadcasters and spectators bent backwards to make the tour unforgettable.

* * *

The Australians also lauded the locals for their keenness. Bill Lawry and the manager – Fred Bennett, picked Chanmugam as a world-class bowler and praised Anura Tennekoon for his batting technique, David Heyn for his fielding and Michael Tissera for batting and leadership.

The recognition by the Australians was an essential step in the island's journey towards Test status. Both England and Australia, with veto powers, stood against Sri Lanka's bid for Test status for more than two decades. It took another 12 years, after the visit by Lawry's team, for the island to become a full ICC member in 1981. There were no Australian visits in the intervening decade until Kim Hughes's team visited Sri Lanka in 1981, on the cusp of that elevation.

I recall that even after a tremendous show of talent and capability to perform under duress at the 1975 World Cup, Sri Lanka's application for Test status was denied by England and Australia in 1979 using veto powers. They required 'further evidence of the standard of cricket on the island'! Many commentators clearly rated the Sri Lankan team as one of the top four teams in the 1975 tournament.

The West Indies, New Zealand, India and Pakistan favoured the elevation of Sri Lanka by 1979. However, before that, Sri Lanka's journey towards Test status was hampered every time the application came up for discussion at the ICC meetings. One absurd reason, given repeatedly, was that 'it was already difficult to schedule tours even among the present "Big Six" Test countries'.

Another reason for delaying the upgrading was the concern expressed by the West Indies in 1977 that individual islands like Jamaica, Barbados, Trinidad, and even Guyana, on the mainland of South America, would also seek separate Test status. They argued that such a move would break up the West Indies cricket establishment.

I remember that Sri Lankan cricket fans found it hard to put up with dithering by the ICC during this period. The likely reason for the continual rejection of Test status for Sri Lanka, even in 1979, was the doubt about finances. Despite the new 1977 Sri Lankan government issuing an assurance about finances, England and Australia doubted whether their touring teams could be guaranteed the income they sought on an extended tour.

The Windies, Kiwis, India and Pakistan, supporting Sri Lanka's case, objected, pointing out that 'the scrutiny was not tight when they were admitted'. The much-awaited Test status for Sri Lanka came in May 1981. But it was too late for many of the island's brilliant cricketers. World-class players, including Michael Tissera, Anura Tennekoon and Sunil Wettimuny, missed out on playing Test cricket. It was entirely a case of neglect by the international body.

* * *

The Australian visitors were keenly awaited by the Indians. The unique attraction was the fact that the team had up-coming batting stars, like Ian Chappell, Doug Walters, Paul Sheahan, Keith Stackpole and Ian Redpath, who had given a hammering to the West Indies a season earlier in the home series. They were also keen to see the 'mystery spinner' Johnny Gleeson. Sundaresan (1971), reporting for *Wisden*, said that the daily attendance for the four Tests in India ranged from 35,000 to 50,000 people. Only the limitations of space at the venues kept out many more thousands.

Doug's accounts in *Looking for Runs* (1971: 28-45) show that the Indian tour didn't go well for the Australians under Lawry. The Aussies came under pressure as troubles with rioting crowds erupted many times and were not limited to the Test matches. In addition to rioting and incidents of stone-throwing at the players during matches, there were also death threats to the team and clashes with the Indian press.

The Indian media also pounced on Lawry for every transgression. Benaud was most annoyed in Australia and questioned the veracity of reports from India. Apparently, no English or Australian reporters were covering the tour, and every incident report by an Indian reporter blamed the Australians for everything. Doug said (Mallett 2008: 142), 'Missing in India was the presence of Australian journalists. No one turned up, not even the ABC's Alan McGilvray. We had no independent witnesses to the dreadful conditions we had to endure'.

* * *

The Nawab of Pataudi captained India in the series. Bill Lawry's poor public relations skills came to the fore in the first Test. In the first Test at the Brabourne Stadium in Bombay (4-9 November 1969),

Batting first, India scored 271. Pataudi's 95 anchored the inning. Uncharacteristically, he battled doggedly for over six hours but hit 14 fours (Walters 1971: 34). Ashok Mankad ground out 74. McKenzie impressed with 5/69, and Gleeson's finger spinners troubled the Indians as he took 3/52 in 35 overs.

In replying with 345, the Australians came across three of India's world-famous spinners – the left-arm spinner, Bishan Singh Bedi and the two right-arm off-spinners, Erapalli Prasanna and Srinivas Venkataraghavan. A well-compiled Stackpole century (103) anchored the visitor's inning. Redpath (77) and Doug (48) put on 118 runs for the fourth wicket. Like the Indians, Australians also batted slowly, averaging only two runs per over. Prasanna took 5/121 in 49 overs; Bedi wheeled away 62 overs, more than half of them maidens, and 3/74, while Venkat bowled 35 overs, taking 2/67.

Indians, batting second, quickly got into a mess due to some fine bowling by Connolly (3/20) and Gleeson (4/56). When the score was 7/89,

Venkataraghavan ('Venkat'), who later became a much-respected Test umpire, joined Ajit Wadekar, defending stoutly at the crease.

The pair added 25 runs, and the score was 7/114 when Venkat 'played forward to a leg-cutter and missed it by a long way' but was given out by umpire Shambhu Pan on an appeal for caught behind off Connolly. It was evident to all players on the field that the umpire had made a mistake, as Taber, the keeper, had not even appealed.

Stackpole, at second slip, appealed, saying that he had heard a noise. Both Taber and Venkat couldn't believe their eyes when, after a long pause, the umpire raised his finger. A 'true gentleman, Venkat left the crease without showing dissent. Devraj Puri, the commentator for All India Radio, made the startling announcement that the umpire made an error and Lawry should be a sportsman and recall the batter.

This angered the Mumbai crowd, who heard it over the thousands of transistor radios they held to their ears. It was a scene not too dissimilar to what I've experienced. The crowd got angry within a few minutes and demanded that Lawry withdraw the appeal and call Venkat back immediately. While most Australian players felt Venkat was 'done by an error', Lawry didn't accept the request.

He insisted on continuing with the game even as a riot broke out. Responding to the turmoil, a 50-man-strong gang of riot squad police asked for play to be stopped for some time to bring the situation under control. Film footage shows that the play was stopped for a while.

Taber said that Venkat missed the ball by at least a foot. Mallett (2008: 117) said the ground, teeming with thousands of people with their ears pressed to their transistors, heard the radio commentator say: 'Venkat was not out. Lawry is a cheat. The Australians cheated'.

Bonfires were lit, with deck chairs stacked high. Stones, chairs, fruit and other missiles were pelted on the ground. Behind the stands, cars and tyres were also set on fire, as thick smoke enveloped the ground. Mallett (2008: 109) recalled:

> *As smoke surrounded the ground and visibility became so poor, a little man in a grey suit, carrying a leather briefcase, raced onto the field, complaining to Lawry that he was the scorer. He could not see what was happening and that he was actually going home!*

The scorer earned a sharp rebuke from Lawry: 'Piss off, pal. We're trying to play a Test match here'. That was typical uncompromising and insensitive

Lawry at his worst! Apparently, the radio announcers took over the official scoring. Doug recalls that the last hour of play was sheer hell as a couple of Australian players were hit by flying missiles. Fortunately, none of them suffered injuries.

Mallett (2008: 118) recalled that when he was bowling, he realised that Doug, Sheahan and others were facing the crowd, keeping a close eye on the bottles being hurled at them. At the height of the riots, a vast mob, an estimated 15,000, began to push the high cyclone fence, which separated the playing area from the spectators.

Ian Chappell suggested to Lawry that leaving the field might be a good idea. But the captain refused, saying he wanted a wicket and insisted on continuing the game amidst thick smoke and rioting crowds. When the next batter – Prasanna, walked in after play was stopped for 10-15 minutes, he was accompanied by the Chief of Police!

The turbulent day ended with India reeling at 9/125 (Hutchinson and Ross 1997: 384). I recall listening to the broadcasters, particularly Pearson Surita, who was in anguish as he described the rioting, which continued for a long time [26].

The next day, Australia won the match by eight wickets by bowling out India for 137. Indian officials had to restrict the number of spectators allowed into the ground on the last day to control riots. In eerie silence, Australia scored the 87 runs required for the loss of Lawry and Stackpole. Ian Chappell and Doug, unbeaten on 31 and 22, respectively, knocked off the runs required.

However, the Australian victory provoked another bout of throwing missiles and chairs by the crowd. The Indian press took the position that while the volatility of Indian crowds was well-known, Lawry could have helped defuse the crisis rather than add fire to it. Lawry was also condemned for prejudice and for constantly looking out for umpiring mistakes. The press claimed this was probably due to Lawry's bad previous experiences in India on the acrimonious tour in 1964.

* * *

The second test passed without crowd trouble, and India managed a draw

---

26 I loved listening to Pearson Surita, the respected Indian commentator. He was an American by birth and an executive from India's tea industry. Surita's commentaries were pure joy because of his polished English accent, melodic voice and choice of words and phrases. I also recall the highly accented and emotive commentaries of other Indian broadcasters, particularly Balu Alaganan, Anant Setalvad and V. M. Chakrapani. Their descriptions of the Test matches in India were so emotionally charged, yet delightful, that they nurtured my inquisitive cricketing mind.

at Kanpur (15-20 November 1969). The Indian selectors dropped Chandu Borde, Dilip Sardesai, Rusi Surti and Abid Ali. They brought Eknath Solkar, Subrata Guha, Ashok Gandotra and a fresh-faced youngster – Gundappa Viswanath ('Vishy').

I remember the Test well as I listened to the emergence of the 20-year-old Viswanath, who became the next Indian batting star. He was out for a first-innings duck, caught by Redpath off Connolly, but made a brilliant debut hundred in the second. Cricketing 'experts' in India and overseas who know Viswanath well call him the embodiment of a 'gentleman' in cricket, in exalted company with Colin Cowdrey.

India won the toss and batted first. They scored slowly but totalled 320, with Engineer (77), Mankad (64), Solkar (44), and Pataudi (38) scoring the bulk of the runs. Connolly took 4/91, and Mallett, bowling 51.5 overs, claimed 3/58. The Australians replied with 348. Anchoring the middle, Paul Sheahan made his debut century (114). He hit 20 fours, batting for just over four hours. Batting at No. 4, Doug hit eighth fours in his 53 before he was deceived and bowled by Bedi. Redpath, at No. 5, also made an impressive 70. Venkat took 3/76.

Vishwanath flayed the Australian attack when India batted a second time, hitting 25 fours in his inning of 137 before Mallett bowled him. Viswanath was the sixth Indian batter to score a debut Test century [27] McKenzie took 3/63 in 34 overs. India declared at 7/312 on the final day, and Australia played out the time left (0-95) with Lawry (56*) and Stackpole (37*), and the match fizzled out to a draw.

* * *

Spinners ruled supreme in the third Test at the Feroze Shah Kotla Grounds in New Delhi (28 November-2 December 1969). This saw India fight back to win the Test by seven wickets with a day to spare. After their improved performance in the second Test at Kanpur, the victory brightened the image of Indian cricket, which was at a low ebb before the series. The architects of the win were their 'Spin Kings' – Bedi and Prasanna – who took match bags of nine wickets each. The match was a fascinating duel between bat and ball.

Batting first, Australia scored 296. Ian Chappell (138, with 21 fours) hit his second century against India, the first being in Melbourne in 1967-68. Stackpole (61) and Taber (46) also scored well. Doug fell cheaply, caught at

---

27 Five other Indian batters made debut Test centuries before Vishwanath: Lala Amaranath (1933), Dheepak Shodan (1952), A.G. Kripal Singh (1954), Abbas Ali Baig (1955) and Hanumant Singh (1964).

short-leg by Solkar off Prasanna for just four runs. Bedi (4/71 in 42 overs) and Prasanna (4/111 in 38.4 overs) tormented Australia, as Doug recalled.

An impressive 97 by Ashok Mankad and his bright opening stand of 85 with Farokh Engineer (38) gave India hope of a good reply. This wasn't to be, as the rest of the batting collapsed to Mallett's off-spin (6/64 in 32 overs). India's total of 223 ended well short of the Australian total. But the Australians collapsed in a heap in the second inning on day three to be all out for a paltry 107 in 58 overs. Only the obdurate Lawry fought the spinners off (49*), carrying his bat. Doug failed again, this time bowled by Bedi for a duck. Bedi took 5/37 in 23 overs, and Prasanna 5/42 in 24.2 overs.

Led by a fluent Ajit Wadekar knock (91*) and another dashing inning from Vishwanath (44*), India scored 3-181, registering a solid win by seven wickets on the fourth day. Listening to the match, ball-by-ball, I recall the tension as India moved towards their victory. This courageous knock cemented Wadekar as the next Indian captain. I also remember that the Indian spinners were backed up by some splendid close-in catching by Wadekar, Solkar and Venkat.

* * *

Thus, the series was interestingly poised, with one match each, when the two sides met at Calcutta. In those days, it was a city with a dominant population that supported the Communist Party of India, which sided with the North Vietnamese (Viet Cong) in the Vietnam War. As a result, a large crowd protested against Doug Walters, the 'Vietnam Soldier' who had 'killed women and children in the Vietnam War'. Without anyone in the Indian media clarifying the matter, the crowd believed that Doug had gone to fight in the Vietnam War.

Posters saying 'Doug Walters – Go Home' had been plastered all over the city, alleging that he had taken part in killing women and children in Vietnam. The truth that Doug had never been on duty in Vietnam didn't matter to the protestors. Doug never passed North Queensland in his army stint (Walters 1971: 40).

Doors and windows of the Great Eastern Hotel, where the Australians stayed, were smashed by the protestors in the skirmishes with the police. However, Doug said he didn't get too flustered by what was happening around him. He kept his regular drinking routine at the hotel bar and watched from inside. These tensions off the field added to Lawry's already heightened worries.

When the match was in progress, crowd disturbances began mainly aimed at the organizers, as black marketing of tickets was rampant. Many people had been duped into buying fake tickets. The Indian administrators had issued only 8,000 tickets for spectators in an attempt to control the crowds. But Mallett (2008: 133-134) and Doug recalled that possibly 20,000 tried to get in. The ire of spectators peaked when the Indian batting collapsed in the second inning, and the angry spectators invaded the playing area.

Australia won the toss and sent India in. Lawry was happy as McKenzie bowled impressively (6/67 in 33 overs) in overcast conditions, breaking through at crucial times. India crumbled to be all out for 212. Mallett took 3/55. The young Viswanath sparkled again (54), mastering McKenzie's swing and pace in the heavy, misty air. Solkar stubbornly resisted, making 42.

The Australians replied with 335, with Ian Chappell missing out on a hundred (99). He batted for over five hours and hit 16 fours, 'combining defence with judicious aggression in an innings full of character' (Sundaresan 1971). Lawry grafted for runs (41) with Stackpole (35), while Doug made 56 in two hours before he was stumped by Engineer off Bedi. Doug still remembers how Bedi's command of line and length mixed with his cunning flight. It was the fourth time Bedi had taken Doug's wicket in the series.

Sheahan made 32, while Connolly, the last man, used the long handle, striking three sixes off Prasanna and one six off Bedi in his knock of 31. Bedi was most impressive, taking 7/98 in 50 overs with 19 maidens, while Prasanna went wicketless (0/115) in 49 overs.

India was 123 runs behind and had to bat well to save the match. But much to the crowd's dismay, on day four, they crashed on the fourth day to be all out for 161. Eric Freeman (4/51) and Alan Connolly (4/ 31) were the main wicket-takers. For India, Wadekar alone batted well, making 62. Australia had just 39 to get and was on the way to scoring these runs when the crowd invasion stopped play.

During the ensuing melee, Lawry pushed a photographer to the ground with his bat, resulting in him becoming the centre of the wrath of spectators and the press. An unrepentant Lawry justified his position by saying he only tried to prevent the photographer from entering the playing area. Australia eventually scored the required runs and won the Test by ten wickets. It was also a Test marred by crowd disturbances and unruly behaviour, mainly aimed at the visitors.

* * *

Before the fifth Test, there were calls in Australia for the tour to be called off due to the alarming newspaper reports about the risks of the physical danger posed to the players. However, the position of the Australian Board of Control was that it hadn't received any such request from Fred Bennett, the team manager. So, the tour continued.

India's defeat in the fifth Test, played at the Madras Cricket Club Grounds in Madras (24-28 December 1969), frustrated the home crowd as the Indians had opportunities at various stages to wrest a win. Mallett spun Australia to win by 77 runs one hour after lunch on the fourth day. The Test was scheduled for six days, according to the playing conditions, as at the end of the third Test, the series was level at 1-all. The victory gave the visitors a 3-1 margin in the series.

Australia won the toss but scored only 258. A century by Doug held the innings together on the first day, but he should have been out at four. Engineer missed a stumping chance off Bedi. Doug took advantage of the opportunity and scored 102, his only century on the tour. It was a power-laden display on a spinner's wicket (two sixes and fourteen fours). Bedi then claimed Doug's wicket for the fifth time in the series with a flighted delivery, which took the edge and was brilliantly caught by a diving Vankat, the lone slip. Prasanna bowled 40 overs for his 4/100, Venkat 34 overs, taking 4/71. Apart from Doug, all the other Australians struggled against the spinners. [28]

The Indian batters failed again. Scoring only 163, India conceded a lead of 95. Mallett's off-spin (5/91) caused the collapse. India struggled at one stage at 5-96 before Engineer (32), batting down in the order at No. 5, and Pataudi (59) attacked the bowling. But, when restraint was required, the Indian batters failed. They thought an attack was the way to go about it. It didn't work on the day.

In the second inning, Australians were soon in trouble. Prasanna's had the visitors reeling at six for 24, but as in the first inning, fielding lapses cost India dearly. Redpath was missed twice but batted with grit, saving his team with his 63. Doug was caught by the 'ever-so-sharp' Solkar, diving at short-leg off Prasanna for only one.

The Australian reply of 153 was made in 80 overs at a crawling run rate, which showed the spinners' stranglehold. Prasanna finished with 6/74 and a match tally of ten wickets for 174. Set to make 249 to win, the Indian batters failed, apart from a good stand of 102 for the third wicket between Ajit Wadekar (55) and Gundappa Viswanath (59). While they were on together, India hoped for a win, but the inning collapsed once this stand was broken.

---

28 In my interviews, Doug always said that Bedi was a better bowler and harder to attack than Prassana, although Ian Chappell rated the two bowlers the other way around.

Again, the collapse was caused for the second time in the match by Mallett (5/53 in 29 overs), who matched the Indian spinners. Mallett's match figures were ten for 144 as India lost by 77 runs. In the *Wisden* report, Sundaresan (1971) noted that Farokh Engineer's poor wicket-keeping in the Test was vital in India's defeat. He missed easy chances to stump Doug in the first inning and Redpath in the second.

* * *

Doug scored 286 runs in the five Tests at 41 and was third in Test averages to Stackpole (368 runs) and Chappell (324, averaging 46). The Australians batted better than the Indians, using footwork more effectively in the spin-dominated series.

There were four Australian centurions (Stackpole, Chappell, Doug and Sheahan) but only one century from an Indian (Vishwanath). Perhaps the absence of the more experienced batters, like Sardesai, Borde and Surti, may have been a factor in the later Tests. All three were dropped after only the first Test as the Indians were looking ahead to re-build the Test squad under Pataudi.

The tour is remembered mainly for unruly crowd-rioting, burning chairs and smoke and other disturbances rather than the 3-1 win for the visitors. Doug recalled that the frailty of batting on both sides made the series much closer than the results.

India fought hard in the home territory's 'heat and dust', and their 'Spin Kings' revealed themselves to the world in almost every match. Often, the trio of Bedi (21), Prasanna (26), and Venkataraghavan (12) penetrated Australia's batting, claiming 59 of the 70 wickets (94%) that fell to bowlers. They also bowled 73% of the total overs in the Tests. Their domination of the Tests and Mallett's 28 wickets (at 19) for Australia made the series a contest of the spinners.

Although Australia won the India series, Doug said it would be 'flirting with the truth' to say that India was an enjoyable experience. The five rancorous Tests and other disasters on tour involving the press, photographers and rioting spectators proved how wrong the chief Australian selector, Don Bradman, was. His lofty expectation – that 'cricket is unrivalled in its ability to 'harmonise' the people in the two countries on a common level' – was completely dashed.

While travelling, the Australian bus was also pelted with stones at various times, forcing the players to hit the floor. Instead of being a superior form of diplomacy, cricket became a 'crucible of strife' on tour. This prompted Lawry to recommend to the ACB that there should be no further double-tours and that future visits to the sub-continent should only take place with guarantees about the standards of hotel accommodation, travel and security (Haigh 2006: 315).

Ian Chappell's account, given in an interview with Simon Lister (Chappell 2009), provides an insight into what he thought about the ACB at the time. Without blaming anyone in particular, Chappell said:

There's no doubt that the bulk of us were pretty pissed off. The Board refused to put us in good hotels to save money. We didn't blame the Indians but the ACB. We knew there were much better hotels because we bloody drank in them. Then we heard what Bradman, a selector, if not the chairman of selectors, had said about my brother, Greg.

He was asked why Greg wasn't on tour and replied: "He's better off making runs in Australia, not getting ill in India".

Then we found out that if we died on tour, our families would be offered something like 400 dollars. There were a whole bunch of other things, too. We were sold up the river, and the board didn't give a damn.

Certainly, the seeds of disenchantment were sown there...but the history of Australian cricket is littered with blues between players and administrators.

Ian's criticism sounds very much like the columns I had previously read from Fingleton, Miller and O'Reilly, who often criticised the selectors for bizarre decisions. Alan McGilvray's books also document that the selectors 'too often got it wrong'. Amazingly, at a subsequent annual Board meeting in September 1970, the tour manager Fred Bennett failed to support Lawry's views and report.

According to Bennett, the whole tour, including the unpleasant time in India and the disastrous South African leg, was 'neither too long, nor imposed undue strain', a view with which all players vehemently disagreed (Mallett 2008: 140).

Despite taking such an absurd position, Bennett continued to be a manager of Australian teams for many more years. He managed six Australian tours between 1969 and 1981, although most also ended in controversies (ESPN Cricinfo 1995). Bennett also became the ACB Chairman from 1983-87, a turbulent era when Kim Hughes resigned in tears as Australian captain and the rebel tours of South Africa surfaced.

In Mallett's book on Doug (2008), Chapter 6 gives a detailed account of the agonies of the Indian summer, including the unhygienic conditions in some hotels where the team stayed. Doug recalls that players were upset because they could have been given better food, hotels, transport and more time for relaxation. The team felt the players' welfare was not a priority for the ACB while they Board raked in substantial profits'tour profits.

In those days, a liquor permit was needed to buy alcohol, even from a hotel bar in India. Prohibitions existed in many states, and foreigners were the only ones allowed to buy a drink legally with a permit. Any visitor would be surprised by how much things have changed now.

Doug was critical of the ACB (Walters 1971: 44)., which made a great deal of money out of the tour. However, they paid little attention to what the team went through in India. Doug said that because of the Board's stupidity, the team experienced only the ugly side of 'grime, dust, poverty, bad hotels and food' in India, and it was such a pity.

Thankfully, in subsequent tours to India, the Australian teams have stayed in the best of India's hotels. Many are on record as having genuinely embraced the sub-continent's food, hospitality and rich culture. The situation is almost entirely the opposite now as so many Australians are now attracted to stay for several months in the sub-continent, playing in the lucrative Indian Premier League (IPL).

Thrashed by the Springboks (1970)

In *Looking for Runs*, Doug (Walters 1971: 46-71) gave an account of the thrashing Bill Lawry's team received in South Africa. Doug recalled that when the players flew out of India on New Year's Day in 1970, they were physically and mentally drained despite their good work in the bitterly contested series. Reading newspaper reports of the tour, as the Australian team moved from the Ceylon-India legs to South Africa, I was also aware that the team was tired. But, no one expected the debacle that unfolded for the Australians.

Doug recalled that moving to South Africa after India was a relief. The team had been unhappy with the food, drink and hygiene they encountered in the hotels and during travel. The team was also hounded in India wherever they went by the press and hordes of photographers, which made the players edgy.

All players on the team were underweight, sick, or both. McKenzie had shed a stone, and Connolly suffered from pneumonia. When Alan McGilvray met the Aussies at Johannesburg's Airport on 2 January 1970, he noted, 'They looked haggard; their eyes seemed to be standing out of their sockets, and some of them looked positively yellow'.

As soon as they flew into Nairobi, Kenya, before continuing to Johannesburg, at the hotel, Doug and most others let go of three months of careful eating in the Indian sub-continent and gorged on an enormous meal of 'Western' food, which had an adverse effect on their stomachs. Doug described it as 'one of the strangest days of his life'.

The team ordered enormous meals but couldn't get through even half of them because they lost their appetite as their stomachs had shrunk. It was an odd effect. Other touring teams to the sub-continent had suffered the same effects before (Walters 1971: 47-48).

It obviously took a while before the team could pick themselves up. Four days after the team arrived, McGilvray walked past the Australian enclosure at the multi-sport venue (Berea Park, Pretoria), where he found most of the team still asleep on benches half an hour after the start of play. In contrast to the Australians, South Africans, who had not played a Test for three years, were rearing to go.

Their thirst for success in sports made cricket an advertisement for national pride (Haigh 2006: 308). Moreover, South Africa also possessed some world-class players, such as Graeme and Peter Pollock, Barry Richards, Eddie Barlow, Lee Irvine, and Mike Procter. This was a tremendous all-round side with brilliant batters right down the list and bowlers who could do well on most pitches. Nevertheless, McGilvray noted that Australians were so weary that the contrast between the two teams could hardly have been more acute.

* * *

After arriving in South Africa, Lawry made a mistake when he said that the Australians were: 'A very good side and would fight hard'. He also claimed his vice-captain: 'Ian Chappell is equal to any batter in the world on all types of wickets'. This proved an embarrassing claim as Chappell scored only 92 runs at 11.5 in four Tests.

The South African press ruthlessly ridiculed Australia as the home team cracked open the tourists' batting line-up several times, and their batters hammered the visiting bowlers. Lawry admitted later that his team was 'simply not good enough' against the 'best team in the world'. Thrashed by a 4:0 margin, it was the worst Australian defeat in more than 90 years of Test cricket (Haigh 2006: 308).

Interest in South African cricket was very high during the 1960s. The effects of apartheid and racial segregation were headline news everywhere. In Ceylon, as a youngster, I read these stories without entirely understanding the issues of racism and riots that were burning the South African society.

I was well aware of their cricketing prowess, having read about the Pollock brothers, Mike Procter and Eddie Barlow, particularly in *The Cricketer* magazines. Doug said the South Africans gave Australia 'one of the most awful thrashings ever taken by an Australian cricket team either in Australia or overseas'.

Only three players – Redpath (283 runs at 47), Connolly (20 wickets at 26) and Gleeson (19 wickets at 39) acquitted themselves with some credit. In contrast, all others, including Doug, failed to deliver. Lawry could not win a single toss in the four Tests, which resulted in the side never being able to get off to a good start.

In just about every game, the Australian batting collapsed. None of the Australian pacemen got much out of any wicket. In contrast, the South Africans bowled well even on the pitches that offered little or no assistance to bowlers.

Doug recalled how brilliantly the South Africans fielded, backing up their bowlers. As the team took a hammering, Australia's once-famous fielding also deteriorated. They dropped at least twenty catches in the four Tests alone. Australians were clearly tired after a long tour, visiting three countries and having ups and downs on the way.

I remember reading that one of the saddest sights on the tour was the decline of the lion-hearted McKenzie, who had been Australia's premier paceman for many years. He played in only three Tests in South Africa and bowled 110 overs for a single wicket at 333!. McKenzie was never the same bowler again.

* * *

In the first Test, at Newlands, Cape Town (22-27 January 1970), South Africa won convincingly by 170 runs. Barry Richards made his debut. Batting first, South Africa scored 382, with Eddie Barlow striking his fourth century (127) against Australia in 11 Tests. Ali Bacher (57), Graeme Pollock (49), and Lee Irvine (42 on debut) boosted the score. Mallett took 5/126 in 55 overs.

Australia, then, collapsed to 6-92 against some fine bowling by Peter Pollock (4/20) and Mike Procter (2/30). This pattern persisted throughout the series when similar collapses occurred in at least one inning of each Test. Doug made 73 with four fours and a six, playing his best innings of the tour. He was the only batter to indicate his ability as the Australians were humbled and bowled out for 164.

Led by Alan Connolly (5/47) and Gleeson (4/70), the Australians restricted South Africa to 232 in the second inning. Graeme Pollock (50), Mike Procter (48) and Barry Richards (32) scored the most for the home team. In the second inning, Australia battled to stave off defeat. Lawry (83 in over three hours) and Redpath (47* in four hours) received little support from others, and Australia, all out for 280, fell short by 170 runs. Doug fell for only four runs. Procter (4/47), at the peak of his bowling prowess, broke through at crucial times.

* * *

A masterful knock by Graeme Pollock set the scene for Australia's defeat in the second Test at Kingsmead, Durban (5-9 February 1970). Pollock (274) hammered 43 fours in a seven-hour inning. Barry Richards, only in his second Test, joined him and blasted 140 in three hours with 20 fours and a six. Experts have described both innings as 'almost perfect batting displays'.

Pollock's 274 was the highest-ever by a South African in Test cricket, surpassing a 17-year-old record (Jackie McGlew's 255* against New Zealand in 1953). The total, 9-622, was the highest for South Africa in the 170 Tests they had played up to that time. For Australia, Gleeson bowled 51 overs, taking 3/160.

The demoralized Australians collapsed for 157. Doug made only four; Only Sheahan (62) batted with some resolve. Barlow took 3/24, initiating the collapse of the inning. When Australia followed, Doug fought hard and scored 74, hitting eight fours and a six. Stackpole (71) and Redpath (74*) resisted stoutly for over four hours. But their efforts were in vain as the South African bowlers repeatedly penetrated the batting. Barlow again staged a repeat performance (3/63).

The match ended with South Africa 2-nil up in the series with a full day to spare. Doug recalled that the margin of the defeat by innings and 129 runs in the second Test deflated the team. He was critical of the selectors not playing Mallett to partner Gleeson in this Test and opting for Freeman, an all-rounder who made no impact.

* * *

South Africa continued its winning streak in the third Test at the Wanderers Stadium in Johannesburg (19-24 February 1970). They won by a massive margin of 307 runs. The match was vital to Australia if the series was to be saved. Laurie Mayne replaced McKenzie, the man who had been the backbone of the Australian attack for many years.

Denis Lindsay regained his place as the South African wicket-keeper. I recalled how dominant Lindsay's batting was in the 1966-67 home series against Simpson's Australians, in which he scored 606 runs at an average of 86.6. His return strengthened the home side further.

Ali Bacher again won the toss, and the Springboks batted first. Barry Richards (65), Graeme Pollock (59), and Lee Irvine (72) were among the runs in the total of 279. Gleeson took 3/61, and Doug bowled five overs, taking 2/16 runs. Australia, then, struggled against Peter Pollock (5/39) and Procter (3/48) and were bowled out for 202. Doug was the highest scorer, grinding out 64 in nearly three hours. Sheahan (44) and Chappell (34) made runs, but all others failed.

In South Africa's second inning, Barlow scored his second century of the series (110), his sixth Test century. Pollock (87), Irvine (73) and Procter (36*) attacked the bowling as the home side made 408. Bacher left his opponents another formidable target- 486 to make in eight hours. Once again, Australia collapsed and was dismissed for 178.

Doug was bowled by Procter for only five. Redpath resisted batting for nearly four hours for his 66 with 11 fours. The last man, Alan Connolly, swung his bat to make 36. Procter's 3/24, Trevor Goddard's 3/ 27 and Barlow's 2/17 ensured a quick victory for the home team, which was 3-nil up at this stage, demoralising the visitors.

* * *

In his first series as captain, Ali Bacher was determined on a clean sweep for the first time in South Africa's history. On the other hand, Australia was looking for a win to salvage its damaged prestige. After a three-week lay-off, McKenzie replaced Freeman in the fourth Test (played at St. George's Park, Port Elizabeth, 5-10 March 1970). An opening stand of 157 by Barry Richards (81) and Barlow (73) set the pattern as South Africa scored 311 in the first dig.

For the Australians, Connolly took 6/47, his best in 28 Tests. In reply, Australia made a dismal 212, their highest first-inning total in the four Tests. Only Redpath (55) and Sheahan (67) played with any certainty. Lindsay stumped Doug off Pat Trimborn for just one. Peter Pollock (3/46) and Mike Procter (3/30) did most of the damage.

Barry Richards then played another quality inning (126 with three sixes and 16 fours). But he was dropped twice. Solid knocks from Lee Irvine (102), Ali Bacher (73) and Denis Lindsay (60) made the Australian bowlers toil. Irvine was dropped three times and Lindsay once before the latter plundered 35 runs off two overs from Gleeson, who lost control (1/142 in 30 overs). Laurie Mayne took 3/83. South Africans declared at 8/470 with a lead of 569. Procter, then, ripped through the Australian batting, taking 6/73 in 24 overs.

Bowled out for 246, Australia was defeated by a massive margin of 323 runs. Lawry (43), Sheahan (46), Doug (23) and Taber (30*) resisted. The differences between the two sides were starkly evident by the winning margins of 170 runs, innings and 129 runs, 307 runs and 323 runs in the four Tests, respectively.

* * *

Doug described how Eddie Barlow's all-around influence was significant in the series. Barlow was often the cause of the collapse of Australian batting when it seemed they had weathered early storms. Doug also thought that the absence of all-rounders of the calibre of Davidson or Benaud in the lower order was a deficiency in the Australian batting line-up, which folded quickly. It must be said that Doug, Stackpole, and Ian Chappell were more than capable bowlers and were genuine all-rounders when they broke into the national team.

Perhaps their bowling skills were underutilized by Lawry, who was often reported as aloof and isolated. The team underestimated the skills of the South Africans, who were so eager to show the world what they were capable of. The weariness of the long tour of nearly six months (October 1969 to late March 1970) affected the Australians. I recall reading the dismal news about the failures, day after day, as the series unfolded. In those days, the team on tour was not managed well, and the players were not paid well, which added to their frustrations.

* * *

Beaten by a 4-nil margin, the Australians moaned about this series loss for many years. The differences between the teams made an indelible blot on Australia's Test history. The Australian critics were scathing in condemning the team's lack of application. Far worse was how newspapers in England rubbed it in. *The Times* in London wrote:

> *If the Australians could catch a ship out of Port Elizabeth this evening, unseen and unsung, that is probably what they would like. In all their history, Australia has never received such a drubbing.*

The London Star's report (Mallett 2008, p. 163) included ridicule:

> *Out-thought, out-bowled and out-batted is the story of Australia's performance in this series. Seeing a talented bunch of cricketers reduced to such impotence was pathetic. But worst of all, seeing how easily they accepted it, was shattering.*

The emergence of Barry Richards, a 'handsome, blond athlete from the

Durban High School' (Haigh 2006: 310), as a batting star (508 at 72.5) was critical to South Africa's dominance.

Australians also couldn't match the consistency of Graeme Pollock (517 at 74) and the all-rounders – Eddie Barlow (360 at 51 and 11 wickets at 23) and Mike Procter (209 at 35 and 26 wickets at 13.5). Nor could any Australian bowler come near Peter Pollock's bowling (15 wickets at 17). Other South Africans, like Lee Irvine (302 at 50), also made crucial contributions to a team led well by Dr. Ali Bacher.

Apart from Redpath, only Doug and Sheahan had batting averages above 30. Lawry was well below his best, scoring only 193 at 24, while Stackpole failed, scoring only 187 at 23.

The persistent failure of the top batters was a reason for unsettling the lower order and the team's abysmal batting. Doug said the disaster would have been worse if not for Redpath's 283 at 47 and Sheahan's 247 at 31. Doug was the second-highest scorer in the Tests (258 at 32), putting into perspective how the South Africans flattened the Australians. The series defeat was one of the lowest points in Australia's proud Test history.

* * *

The friction between the Australian players and the ACB became visible from those days in 1969-70. Although unsupported by the team manager Fred Bennett, Lawry wrote a scathing critique of the ACB's handling of tour arrangements. McGilvray, who covered the South African part of the tour, attested to the weariness of the players and pressed the need to look after them a great deal more. His accounts reinforced Lawry's arguments, but the selectors were unimpressed.

There was also a messy fallout at the end of the gruelling tour. The South African Cricket Association proposed an additional fifth Test by scrapping two first-class matches and extending the tour.

Under Bennett's insistence, Lawry put the proposal to the players in February 1970, after the first Test match had been lost. Doug said that most players didn't want a quarrel with the Board. But Ian Chappell led an internal revolt, demanding at least $500 when the ACB offer was only $200. This caused a rift within the team, but the refusal to accede to the ACB's demand received strong support from Keith Miller:

The Australians lost the first Test but won their greatest victory in years. They thumbed their noses at the Australian Board of Control by deciding against playing a fifth Test...The days of playing for the honour and glory of your country have long passed. (Haigh 2006: 310).

Mallett (2008: 161) said Lawry was a man of high principle. He decided to write to the Cricket Board outlining the players' concerns, criticising the itinerary and the lack of care for the players' welfare. Chappell and Redpath pleaded with Lawry to have everyone in the tour party sign the protest letter. However, Lawry stubbornly insisted it was his responsibility as the captain and no one else's. The actions probably placed Lawry on the Board's little black book.

In an article titled 'When They Were Kings', Hartman (2005) said it was the very best Test team South Africa ever fielded. As it turned out, it was also the last Test team the country fielded for 21 years. All these great players, at their peak, left Test cricket for good. The 'golden age' of South African cricket abruptly ended with this series because of the apartheid policies of its government.

South Africa had been without Test cricket for three years since their 3-1 triumph over the Australians in 1966-67. So, the matches were played to capacity crowds, segregated by race. The 'blacks' turned out in large numbers, and many supported the Australians, while the 'whites' relished the home team's dominance.

The frenzy of interest around the series was so great that newspapers worldwide reserved front-page slots for the cricket daily. In my teens, I keenly read these reports, relayed worldwide by Reuters, struggling to understand all the political ramifications. The political noose tightening around South Africa's neck motivated its cricketers. The Springboks were united in their desire to win for the sake of their country. The cricketers were incensed at being victims of apartheid. Crushing the opponents was their way of demonstrating that, despite apartheid, the world could not turn its back on them, as they were capable of the highest quality cricket (Hartman 2005).

In the wake of the bloodbath in South Africa, a new batch of hopefuls broke into the Australian Test team. Before the 1969-70 summer ended, on tour to New Zealand in an Australian 'B' team, a young West Australian quick, D. K. Lillee, and a South Australian with a copybook style of batting, G. S. Chappell, emerged as potentials.

Greg Chappell had already made a name for himself in Somerset, making tons of runs during the 1968-69 seasons. The history of cricket knows how vital these two superstars were in the next decade for Australian cricket. For better or worse, their performances changed how cricket was played in Australia and also around the globe.

CHAPTER 8

Plundering Runs

Doug made plenty of runs in the 1970s but also had ups and downs. On his day, he would take any attack apart and do so without an attitude; that is why he is so liked by opponents. In his own words, he wasn't too interested in traditions but firmly believed in entertaining the spectators.

Doug also enjoyed the excitement and pressure of a closely contested game. He played the way he did because of his belief that people who pay their money at the turnstiles should be the most important in the sport; if people were not entertained, the very lifeblood of cricket would drain away. 'Without the support of people, cricket as a sport would be killed off'.

England Tour Down Under (1970-71) - Bouncers and Beer Cans

Australia held the Ashes for six straight years after the 1-1 drawn series of 1965-66 and 1968. Then came Ray Illingworth's 'die-hards' who played exceptionally well in Australia during the summer of 1970-71. Although Australians were combative, they were soundly beaten by a superior team. England won back the Ashes with a series win by 2-1. This win down under was only the third time in 50 years after 12 long sterile years for England. The series was decided in the seventh Test in Sydney after the third Test in Melbourne was washed out.

I was now in the upper school, and through a small transistor radio, I listened to all the Test matches, even during school hours. The broadcasts began at 6:30 am, as we travelled to school on our bus. With friends listening to the broadcasts, our endless chatter was full of 'armchair' opinions of players that we 'liked' or 'disliked'. Most of us cheered for the Australians as England wasn't our favourite team. Even as kids, we didn't forget that the English were once our rulers.

* * *

After some fine performances in the county circles, Ray Illingworth, a born fighter from Yorkshire, ascended the throne left vacant by M. J. K. Smith, Colin Cowdrey and Brian Close. Illingworth had bravely led England to a 2-0 victory against Garry Sobers's West Indies in 1969 (Mason 2021). He also kept the job the following summer (1970) when South Africa's abandoned tour was replaced by a series against a Garry Sobers-led Rest of the World XI team packed with great players.

England lost 4-1 to the World team. Still, Illingworth again led the team brilliantly, infusing a dynamism that had long been absent in the England team. He also had a superb series with the bat; only Sobers bettered his aggregate of 476. Illingworth was an astute cricketer whom John Woodcock described: 'A shop steward rather than a cavalier, a sergeant-major, not a brigadier: the personification in fact of the modern game'. Arlott (1979: 118-122) also had high praise:

No one else – certainly not in such a short period – achieved as much as a Test and a county captain as he did...Illingworth was always a utilitarian player who filled in where needed. So he took a hundred wickets in each of ten seasons, scored a thousand runs in eight, and performed the double in six.

Cowdrey was offered the vice-captaincy but asked for time to think it over. Realising Cowdrey's concerns, Illingworth encouraged: 'Colin is one of the best batters in the world and the best in England'. Cowdrey eventually said yes. England's selectors had overlooked Brian Close when they gave Illingworth the job.

Both were in the same mould as Douglas Jardine and Len Hutton, strong-willed leaders who had previously won the Ashes in Australia. The decision to make Illingworth the captain wasn't popular. Most people knew that Illy had an anti-establishment streak, was already 37 years old and had only played 30 Tests spasmodically.

After reading so much about Close (Yorkshire and Somerset) and Illingworth (Yorkshire and Leicestershire) in *The Cricketer* magazines, I liked these two gallant cricketers. They didn't like each other, but their 'never-say-die' attitude enriched English cricket, which wasn't healthy in the 1950s. However, both got into trouble with cricket officials for speaking their minds. On the other hand, Cowdrey was always an amiable figure who was well-liked by everyone [29].

---

29 Brian Close captained England (1966-67) in seven Tests, one against Sobers' West Indies and six against India and Pakistan, winning six of them and one draw. In a

Colin Cowdrey wasn't seen as a dynamic leader and had to endure an injury in 1969. He was deeply disappointed to be overlooked a second time for the job as captain of the England team on an Ashes tour. In 1965, Cowdrey was the deputy to Mike Smith's touring squad when Doug entered Test cricket and was England's captain in the summer of 1968 against Bill Lawry's side.

The backgrounds of Illingworth and Cowdrey couldn't be any more different. The university-bred Cowdrey had a principled approach to the game's ethics. He baulked at confrontations and held the view that hostility in cricket should have its limits. Contrastingly, Illy was 'the epitome of a Yorkshire fighter' (McGilvray1985: 108) who 'welded into his team an obsessive lust for conquest and victory'.

A hard-nosed professional, Illingworth exploited the weaknesses in Australian batting with his own bowling. He also managed to coax the best out of the mercurial John Snow. As events turned out, the English selectors were fully vindicated in their belief that Illingworth would carry the fight to the Australians rather than Cowdrey.

* * *

After the debacles in South Africa, the Australian selectors made some drastic changes. Lawry was one target as he had challenged the Board. Mallett (2008: 169-171) wrote that a player who stood up to the Board was akin to 'Oliver Twist asking for more porridge' in those days. However, Lawry kept his place, as did most of the batters. Two fast bowlers on tour, Freeman (11 Tests) and Mayne (six Tests) and two others, Jock Irvine, from Western Australia and Ray Jordan, from Victoria, were all totally discarded from Test cricket.

Australia introduced Alan 'Froggy' Thomson, a right-arm, fast bowler from Victoria, to share the new ball with McKenzie. This 'Thomson', who delivered the ball off the wrong foot, was heralded as the great white hope when picked to play in the 1970-71 summer. He had taken 100 Sheffield Shield wickets in 16 matches before he was called up. But 'Froggy' Thomson failed badly, playing in four Tests only in the series, taking 12 wickets at 54. He also never played Test cricket again.

Mallett (2008: 170) said that even his spot was in danger despite the 28 wickets (at 19) he took in four Tests in India. But in South Africa, Mallett

---

match against Warwickshire he got into trouble for delaying tactics as he forced a draw by slowing down the over rate. It led to his dismissal as England's captain. Close played in 22 Tests. After leaving Yorkshire, Close joined Somerset, where he made a lasting impression on cricketing greats, none more so than the young Vivian Richards and Ian Botham (Marks 2015).

played only a single Test and took only six wickets at 34. Two leg-spinners also claimed their baggy-green caps in the 1970-71 summer – Terry Jenner from South Australia and Kerry O'Keeffe from NSW. Greg Chappell from South Australia came in as an all-rounder. A West Australian, Rod Marsh, replaced Taber as the wicket-keeper. The series also introduced another West Australian, Dennis Keith Lillee, to Test cricket in the sixth Test [30].

* * *

It was the batting of Geoff Boycott (657 at 94), John Edrich (648 at 72), Brian Luckhurst (455 at 57), and John Snow's bowling (31 wickets at 23) that gave England superiority over Australia. Stevenson (1978: 1-3) noted that Snow was the critical difference between the two sides. No Australian bowler could match Snow's control and hostility.

He often bowled short at the batter's throat and was frequently warned by the umpires. However, McGilvray (1985: 108) said he didn't overdo it but had an uncanny ability to make the ball lift sharply from a good length and 'intimidate batters without being intimidatory'.

The tour's success would have been risked if Illingworth hadn't handled Snow's mercurial persona well. He backed Snow throughout the series when the bowler was warned for too many bouncers. Bailey (1973) said that Illingworth didn't back down and constantly argued with the Australian umpires about the definition of a bouncer.

The captain insisted that Snow, with his height and muscular forearms, lifted the ball sharply up to chest high from just short of good length where the wicket had some bounce. 'It wasn't quite a "bouncer" that would normally bump over the batter's head'.

In my interviews, Doug agreed that Snow's bowling was the crucial factor that decided the Ashes. McGilvray (1985: 108-109) also noted that Ian and his brother, Greg, smartly revised their approach to batting and developed defences against the delivery at the throat due to Snow's aggressive bowling. They learned how to quickly evade!

As recorded by Smith (1996), Doug had observed that Snow was:

> *The first of the modern-day bowlers who intimidated batters. He was so accurate that he didn't waste a delivery. Snow never bowled a bouncer a yard over your head. It was always at your head and came off a fair length, too.*

* * *

---

30 Dennis Lillee, a controversial figure, went on to become one of the greatest fast bowlers the world had ever seen. He played 70 Tests from then on for Australia and took 355 Test wickets at 23.9.

In the first Test at the Gabba (27 November-2 December 1970), Stackpole made a brilliant 207 (25 fours and a six). His score, along with Doug's 112 (nine fours) and Ian Chappell's 59, lifted Australia to a sizeable 433. However, after being 2-372, Australia collapsed to a raging Snow (6/116) and the spin of Underwood (3/101).

England's determined batting became a hallmark of the contests. Solid knocks by Brian Luckhurst (74), Alan Knott (73), John Edrich (79), Basil D'Oliveira (57), Geoff Boycott (37), Keith Fletcher (34) and John Snow (34) saw England get ahead, to reach 464. But they batted slower than the Australians, so Australia held out to a draw. Doug added to his runs by taking three wickets for 12 runs.

A dogged second inning by Lawry (84) held the side together as Australia were bowled out for 214. Ken Shuttleworth took 5/47. Doug made only seven, but Redpath batted more than two hours for 28, as the last five wickets fell for just 21 runs. England had only an hour left on the final day to score 172, and the match was drawn.

Stackpole was 'lucky' as TV replays (which were unavailable to the umpire in those days) and photographs showed that he was clearly run out when he was only 18. The English press castigated Lou Rowan, the Australian umpire who said, 'Not out'. Marsh didn't do too well for Australia, making his debut as the wicket-keeper, letting many byes go and dropping some catches. It earned him the nickname iron gloves.

* * *

The 22-year-old Greg Chappell's debut hundred (108) was the highlight of the drawn second Test (11-16 December 1970) in Perth. It was Perth's first men's Test match, played on the grounds of the Western Australian Cricket Association (WACA). Nearly 85,000 people attended. The spectator number was nearly twice that at Brisbane, and gate receipts in the region of £50,000 were almost three times as large.

Graham McKenzie, the Western Australian paceman, was playing in his first Test match at his home ground. Ten years had passed since his Test debut in 1961. He bowled the historic first ball at the WACA from the Farley Stand End to Boycott. A century by Luckhurst (131 with 13 fours), supported by Boycott (70), Edrich (47), Cowdrey (40) and Illingworth (34), saw England score 397 in the first inning. McKenzie took 4-66, but Australia dropped five catches in the inning.

Snow (4/143) broke through early in Australia's inning, causing a collapse despite a 50 from Ian Chappell. Redpath became the saviour, hitting 171 (over eight hours, with 14 fours). His 219-run stand with Greg Chappell (108 with

10 fours) allowed Australia to reach 440. Greg's runs came in about half the time Redpath took. Marsh made 44. Snow bowled tirelessly, taking 4/143 in 33.5 overs.

England declared its second inning at 6-287. It was built on a match-saving century by Edrich (115*) and a half-century by Boycott (50). Gleeson (3/68) troubled the English batters on the WACA wicket, which began to crumble on day four. Illingworth declared, challenging Australia to make 245 in 145 minutes. But Australia made no effort and was 3-100 at the end, in the drawn match. Lawry (38*), as obdurate as ever, saw out the 32 overs, scored his 2000th Test runs against England and 5000th Test runs (Frith 1997). Doug failed with the bat twice but took a wicket each (1/35 and 1/28), bowling 18 overs in the match. The Perth Test also saw several confrontations between Illingworth and umpire Rowan as they could not agree on the definition of a bouncer.

* * *

The New Year's Test (third Test), scheduled for 31 December 1970 to 4 January 1971 at the MCG in Melbourne, was entirely washed out. It was later announced that a 40-over match would be played on the last day of the Test and that an additional Test would be inserted into the programme in place of the four-day return match against Victoria.

* * *

England won the fourth Test in Sydney (9-14 January 1971) with quality batting and Snow's fiery bowling. Bob Willis, flown in to replace the injured fast bowler Alan Ward, made his Test debut. The consistency of England's top order was again on display in the first inning with runs from Boycott (77), Luckhurst (38) and Edrich (55). Late-order rallies by Snow (37) and Peter Lever (36) got England up to 332, while Mallett took 4/40 and Gleeson 4/83.

When Australia batted, Underwood's spin (4/66) caused a collapse. Making only 236, Australia conceded a 96-run lead. Only Redpath (64) and Doug (55) withstood the England attack. Both escaped chances dropped in the slips off Lever. Boycott (142*) played a crucial inning when the tourists batted a second time. While he anchored the inning, quick runs came in his stands with D'Oliveira (56) and Illingworth (53). Illingworth declared England's inning at 5-319, with a lead of 415, leaving a day and a half to dismiss Australia a second time.

Facing a fiery spell by Snow 7/40 in 17.5 overs, Australia fell over for just 116 to lose by 299 runs. The stubborn Lawry carried his bat (60*). McKenzie had his nose smashed by a lifting ball. Doug was out for only three. Stackpole resisted, making 30, at No. 6. Snow's figures were his finest in Tests. The pitch was without pace, but Snow still made the ball kick viciously from a good length. David Frith (1997) reported that: 'the Australians seemed not to know which way to turn against such hostility from Snow' as England went 1-0 up in the series.

* * *

The fifth Test at the MCG in Melbourne (21-26 January 1971) was drawn. Australia dropped McKenzie and Connolly and played another right-arm seamer, Ross Duncan, from Queensland, to open the bowling with Alan Thomson. The match was marred by unpleasant Australian crowd behaviour. The NSW leg-spinner Kerry O'Keeffe debuted as Mallett was made the 12th man.

Australia won the toss and batted. Lawry (56) was hit on the hand by a lifting ball, retired with a damaged finger, but later returned to bat. Eight dropped eight catches, four by Cowdrey at slip, allowed Australia to declare at 9/493 on day two. Cowdrey dropped Ian Chappell off Snow when he hadn't scored and again off D'Oliveira on 14.

Capitalizing on the chances, Ian Chappell made his first Test hundred (111 with 12 fours) against the old enemy. When he reached his hundred, a stampede occurred. About 2000 spectators, mostly children and many beer-drinking adults, ran onto the pitch. They stole Chappell's cap, Cowdrey's hat, and a stump in the scuffles. Wellings (1972) reported that the crowd behaviour 'tarnished' the match.

After settling down, Ian Chappell partnered with Redpath (72) in a stand of 180. Later, Doug made 55, also benefitting from a dropped catch. Doug was nowhere near his best and scored most of his runs off the bat's edge, as he did again in the second innings. The new wicket-keeper, Marsh, thumped the ball hard for over three hours, hitting 12 fours in his 92*. Marsh also gave two chances in the sixties.

On the verge of Marsh's debut century, late on day two, Lawry declared the inning, to the batter's dismay. Even the commentators were surprised, as I recall. Lawry's defence was that he put the team's interest ahead of an individual's. With the declaration, at 8-493, Lawry deprived Marsh of the chance of becoming the first Australian wicket-keeper to score a Test century in an Ashes series. Marsh later said that he never forgave Lawry for this decision. The declaration was typical of the way Lawry played his cricket.

Lawry's unimaginative captaincy gave his side little chance of squaring the series. England stumbled at 3-88, but Luckhurst steadied the inning (109, over five hours), batting with a broken little finger. A forceful D'Oliveira century (117 with 11 fours) and Illingworth's gritty 41 allowed England to reach 392, as Gleeson took 3/60. Alan Thomson took 3/110, bowling 34 overs. Doug bowled five overs and clean-bowled Luckhurst. Ross Duncan bowled 14 overs for 30 runs and went wicketless. He never played Test cricket again.

Australia, then, failed to capitalize on their first-inning performance. They scored way too slowly to force a result. Stackpole batted for 90 minutes to make 18; Lawry took 180 minutes to score 42; Ian Chappell took two hours to make 30. Doug made 39* in an hour and a half, as Lawry declared the second inning at 4-169 on the final day.

Declining the invite to make 271 to win in four hours, Boycott and Edrich batted out the time (0-161) to draw the match. Snow was warned several times in Australia's second inning for over-using the bouncer by umpire Max O'Connell. The bowler and captain stubbornly argued with the umpire. In the *Wisden* report, Wellings (1972) said that Alan Thomson bowled more bouncers than Snow despite receiving no warning.

* * *

Dennis Lillee, the young firebrand who became one of the greatest fast bowlers in cricket, debuted in the sixth Test at the Adelaide Oval (29 January-3 February 1971). Australia needed to push hard to win to square the series, but England defended their series lead stoutly. As the battle intensified, listening in Ceylon, I didn't miss much.

England won the toss and batted well on the first day. Cowdrey was replaced by John Hampshire. Luckhurst was injured, which allowed Boycott (58) and Edrich (130 with 14 fours) to resume their opening partnership. They did so well, putting on 107. Fletcher (80), Hampshire (55), D'Oliveira (47) and Snow (38) then helped England reach 470.

On his debut, Lillee bowled quicker and better than anyone else, taking 5/84 off 28 overs. Mallett (2008: 183) recalled that Lillee was 'A sight to behold as he stormed in from his long run-up, impressing all and sundry'. With Lillee's appearance on the scene, the 'changing of the guard' for the Australian attack was underway.

Although Stackpole played a stroke-filled inning (87 with 11 fours), Australia's batting was spineless around him, and wickets fell steadily to the English pace attack. Ian Chappell, Marsh, and Mallett got good starts (scoring 28 each). Still, the three English pacemen – Peter Lever (4/49), Snow (2/73) and Willis (2/49) restricted Australia to 235.

Illingworth didn't enforce the follow-on as he knew his pace bowlers were tiring, and he had to think about the final seventh Test starting in a week. The added Test meant that the same bowlers would likely quickly tackle an unprecedented string of Test matches. However, this decision let Australia off the hook.

England scored 3-233 in the second inning in four hours before Illingworth declared. Boycott scored another century (119* with 12 fours). He also put on another century stand (103) with Edrich (40). Illingworth promoted himself, swung the bat, hit eight fours and made 48*, showing his leadership. Australia had eight hours to make 469 but never made the effort. They batted cautiously to avoid defeat.

Stackpole made 136 in seven hours; Ian Chappell batted for over five hours for his 104. They ensured Australia didn't lose the match by staying together for more than five hours while adding 202. Redpath then brought the game to a dreary end by plodding two hours for 21*. Doug, too, was cautious (36*) at the end, batting for 100 minutes.

Australia ended with 3-328. Lawry, facing the formidable opponent, 'blinked' first. The English bowlers were weary towards the end of the match; they had been playing continuous cricket on tour for over three months. Yet, Lawry lacked the courage to trust his batters and order them to go for a win, which his team needed. Sadly, the Test was Lawry's swan song, as he was sacked at the end of the drawn Test.

* * *

The seventh Test in Sydney (12-17 February 1971) saw Ian Chappell lead Australia for the first time. But the big news was the bombshell dropped by the selectors in sacking Lawry as captain. It was an abrupt end to the career of a cricketer who was a truly great servant of Australian cricket for a decade or so, sometimes under the most trying conditions. But the public knew that he had run his last race.

This was the last Test XI that Bradman presided over as the selection panel chairman. He had been a selector since he first captained the team in 1936-37 (Mallett 2008: 183). The selectors made four changes, dropping Lawry, Alan Thomson, Gleeson and Mallett. They introduced Ken Eastwood, a left-handed opener from Victoria. Eastwood failed and never played Test cricket again. Tony Dell, a left-arm fast bowler from Queensland, also debuted. Dell bowled with pace in the Test but played only one more Test in his short career.

England, without the injured Boycott, was bowled out for 184, spun out on the spin-friendly SCG by the two spinners, O'Keeffe (3/48) and Jenner (3/42). Australia replied with 264, anchored by Redpath (59), Greg Chappell (65), Doug (42) and Jenner (30).

Crowd trouble began when Jenner ducked into a rising delivery from Snow, who was then warned by Lou Rowan for bowling too many bumpers at tail-enders. Jenner retired to the pavilion, blood oozing from the cut on his head. Hooting and abusive threats rang out from the notorious Hill at the SCG. Lillee was on strike when Snow received the first warning from Rowan, to which his loud response was: 'That's the first bouncer I've bowled this over – your blokes have been bowling seven for an over'!

Incensed by the warning, both Snow and Illingworth rounded on Rowan. An ugly argument ensued, with the English captain wagging his finger at the umpire, watched in horror by countless TV viewers. Illingworth disputed Rowan's claim that Snow had no right to bowl a bouncer to a tail-ender. However, Jenner was a capable bat with a century under his belt in a Shield match and was the fourth-highest scorer in the Australian inning (Stevenson 1978: 2-3). Illingworth argued with Rowan whether 'one bouncer per over' was fair for the English when the Australians had bowled so many per over and escaped warnings. Two repeat warnings would have cost the captain his most precious weapon, and Australia might have even squared the series. The captain had a reason to be angry. He was also upset about the non-ending hoots from the crowd.

After the angry exchanges with the umpire, Snow retired to deep long leg. This resulted in a volley of bottles and beer cans thrown at Snow and onto the ground. A foul-mouthed and drunk spectator also grabbed Snow at the picket line and wouldn't let go until others hauled him back, aided by a shove from Snow.

Tirades of abuses were hurled at Snow, along with waves of beer cans. The sorry sequence of events, the manhandling of Snow and player safety caused Illingworth to lead his team off the field for 15 minutes. When play resumed, the Australian inning ended with a lead of 80 runs (Stevenson 1978: 5).

Opinion was deeply divided on whether Illingworth was right in his decision to go off the field in protest. Having witnessed the turbulent day and the event, Doug agreed that Illingworth was quite right to do so. Norman Preston (1972), the Editor of *Wisden*, was prompted to write about the erosion of the 'spirit of cricket' due to the incident. Although he disapproved of Illingworth wagging his finger at the umpire and for not fore-warning the umpires of his intentions to lead the team off the field, Preston said that the captain did the right thing.

England batted resolutely in the second innings, led by Edrich (57), Luckhurst (59) and D'Oliveira (47) to reach 302. Australia needed 233 to level the series but collapsed again and was bowled out for 160.

Illingworth, incensed by what happened in the field during the match, 'schemed out' Doug by getting him caught at third man by D'Oliveira for a single off Willis. Illingworth knew Doug wouldn't resist an uppercut to a rising, short ball and placed his fielder there. When the Australians were five wickets down for 96, Stackpole (67) and Greg Chappell (30) were the only two between England and the Ashes. Leading from the front, Illingworth (3/39) bowled 20 eight-ball overs straight and dismissed both.

* * *

As England regained the Ashes, the seventh Test was a great contest. However, it was marred by the arguments and atrocious crowd behaviour. The match had been arranged behind the backs of Illingworth and the players by the tour manager – David Clark, and 'Gubby' Allen, the MCC treasurer. It was supposedly 'to give Australia an extra chance of retaining the Ashes' (Stevenson 1978: 6).

Having been on an extended tour of several months, McGilvray (1985: 109) noted a great deal of disquiet about extending the tour in the England dressing room. However, it may have galvanized the team to win. It also took some time for the players to obtain an agreement from MCC for an extra match fee.

Booing by the crowds whenever Illingworth came out to bat or bowl was a sad experience to listen to. The English press castigated the Australian umpires for not calming the noisy crowds.

Doug didn't contribute much to the series except for some valuable runs. His series aggregate (373 at 37.3) included one century (112) in the first Test and two half-centuries (55 each in the fourth and fifth Tests). Doug also took seven wickets in the six Tests at 26. Illingworth became the first English skipper to win back the Ashes in Australia since Jardine did in 1932-33 in the ill-famed 'bodyline' series.

* * *

Douglas Jardine, a hard-nosed English captain, devised an attacking form of cricket called bodyline bowling to thwart the Australians from making huge scores. Those who experienced it agreed that it was a tactic to stop the phenomenal run-scoring of Bradman and others who batted around him. James (1963: 188) noted, 'Jardine seemed to be at war not with the Australian XI but all of Australia'.

Even the governments were involved in the furore as Australians protested against the English paceman, Harold Larwood, who was ordered by Jardine to bowl at the body with several fielders placed on the leg side for catches. The assault peaked during the third Test at the Adelaide Oval (16 January 1933). The ploy worked in England's favour as several Australians, including the captain William Woodfull, were hit on the body and were caught on the leg-trap while defending.

Bradman described the game as a 'regrettable affair' (Smith 1996: 43). England won the match by 338 runs. Bradman scored eight and 66 in the game, and his average in the series was a low 56. He later said: 'The man never lived who could consistently and successfully combat the 1932-33 bodyline attack as employed by England that summer' [31].

Bodyline bowling, defined as 'persistent and systematic bowling of fast, short-pitched balls at the batter standing clear of his wicket', was banned by the MCC as 'not in the interest of the game'. After the series, Jardine never captained England again. Larwood, the leading English fast bowler involved, also never played Test cricket again.

* * *

The 1970-71 series was a watershed for Australian cricket. By the second Test, Greg Chappell, with so much elegance, had won a permanent place in the team. His masterful batting ensured he joined his famous grandfather (Victor Richardson) and elder brother Ian, who claimed an indelible place in the country's cricket history.

The first Test saw the new wicket-keeper, Rod Marsh, behind the stumps. I recall the catches that went begging and wondering who this guy was. Marsh, from Perth, then took the initiative to adjust his techniques and become Australia's No. 1 keeper for the next decade.

The sixth Test saw Dennis Lillee, a tearaway fast bowler from Perth, earn his spurs. In his debut, Lillee bowled tirelessly, taking 5/84 in England's first innings, showing his potential for spearheading an Australian attack one day. Marsh and Lillee were destined to play a huge part in Australia's success over the next 13 summers. They were crucial members of the resurgent and dominant Australian team of the early-to-mid-1970s under the new captain, Ian Chappell.

Lawry's batting form was not very high in the series (324 runs at 40 with a highest score of 84), but he was still a man whose wicket was valued most by England's bowlers. The sacking of Bill Lawry as Australia's captain was inevitable. Lawry was a dour campaigner and never a popular leader. His

---

[31] Fingleton's book *Cricket Crisis* (1947) is one of the finest ever written on a series. '*It Isn't Cricket, Sir!*' – the title of Chapter One, starts off the account. The *Bodyline Series* is recorded in cricket annals as a 'war' between the two nations, unleashed by cricket passions. The phrase: *This Isn't Cricket* is very much a part of cricket's lexicon nowadays, under the 'Spirit of Cricket' discourses. Jack Pollard's *History of Australian Cricket* (1992: 273-290) gives a comprehensive account of the Bodyline Series and its aftermath.

approach was known to be partisan and often favoured Victorians over anyone else.

Doug confirmed that Lawry's behaviour sometimes annoyed others in the team as he usually preferred his own company and sat aloof and alone. Doug told me that even when having a drink or at dinner, after a day's play, Lawry used to call over his Victorian colleagues (Redpath, Stackpole, Connolly and Sheahan) and sat with them.

The others, from other States, including Doug, Ian Chappell and Brain Taber, had to find their own way and sit separately. Critics also said Lawry was not a born leader. He could not simply motivate others. Stories about his gloomy demeanour had been around for a long time. Still, I respected him for his commitment to his team and doughtiness.

Doug said he was upset by the way Lawry was sacked. The selectors were unkind to a man who provided yeoman service to Australia for over a decade. Shamefully, the national team's skipper had to hear the news of his removal on the radio while the Test series was still on.

The first time Lawry heard about his sacking was when he got off a plane to be besieged by reporters. However, as a man known for some unpopular decisions, it was typical of Lawry to say: 'The selectors' decision was on par with their policies towards tough decisions'.

Alan McGilvray's book *The Game Goes On* (1987) dedicated a chapter entitled *'The Selectors At Fault'* to show how insensitive and uncommunicative they were. He said it was a 'closed shop' concerning team selections. Alan pointed out many mistakes the selectors had made over decades of his broadcasting career. One of the top four outrageous selection mistakes Alan highlighted was the sacking of Lawry and not selecting him for the next Ashes tour to England.

Lawry could hardly be blamed for the Ashes defeat to a better side, which 'hummed like a well-oiled machine' around the talents of batters Boycott, Edrich and D'Oliveira, and bowlers of the calibre of Snow and Underwood, to say nothing of the aggressive and astute captaincy of Illingworth' (McGilvray 1987: 174-75).

Ian Chappell, who inherited the captaincy, took a dim view of Lawry's off-hand treatment. Lawry played first-class cricket for one more season before hanging his boots permanently. Cricket fans know that selectors worldwide make huge errors all the time. Sometimes, these mistakes are illogical and mind-boggling.

When England won by 299 runs in the fourth Test, Lawry carried his bat through the second Australian inning to remain 60*. He also had other scores of 84, 56 and 42 to his credit and a series aggregate of 324 at 40. Broadly, it was wrong for selectors to blame Lawry for the team's batting failures against some determined bowling by Snow and others. McGilvray (1987) noted that Lawry fell afoul of the selectors mainly because of his attitude. He became too conservative in outlook, bogged down in batting, and appeared unwilling to play strokes.

Soon after, Lawry entered the broadcasting world, first with the local channels, before moving to Kerry Packer's Channel Nine TV network in 1977. He soon became a famous commentator, developing an entertaining commentary style.

Lawry was famous for colourful and idiosyncratic utterances, 'GONE!' and 'GOT 'IM', expressed in a distinctive, high-pitched screaming voice when someone got out. Lawry was a constant fixture in the commentary box of Channel Nine for 41 years before he retired. He was honoured by being inducted into Australia's Cricket Hall of Fame in 2010 (ESPN Cricinfo 2010).

* * *

The 'new' Australian selection committee – Neil Harvey, Sam Loxton and Phil Ridings – decided to give youth a chance and picked Ian Chappell for the captain's job for building a new era. Chappell had already made a name for himself as a combatant in all departments.

The selectors thought appointing Chappell as captain would be their best chance of winning the Ashes back. While that was a fair decision, McGilvray said they should have asked whether Lawry would play under Ian. Alan speculated that Chappell would have been glad to have Bill along as the two got along very well (McGilvray 1987: 176).

In my interview, Ian Chappell praised Lawry as an astute captain who always allowed others to prove themselves. A classic case was Lawry surprising everyone by asking Stackpole to open the inning. Stackpole became a highly successful player after he became Australia's regular opener for several years.

Lawry's yardstick to measure others was his resolve, which no one ever questioned. Everyone knew that he was a hard taskmaster. His problem was his defensive batting style. It always made him think of safety first and a win as the second option. One cannot blame Lawry too much; it was how Test cricket was played in those days.

The 1970-71 Ashes series ended the Test careers of Graham McKenzie and Alan Connolly, two long-serving, fast-bowling greats of Australia. By the time his Test career ended, McKenzie was two short of the record then held by Benaud. He took 246 wickets at 29 in 60 Tests between 1961 and 1971. The tall Victorian Connolly took 102 wickets at 29 in 29 Tests between 1963 and 1971. Trying to earn a living in a semi-amateur cricket economy, these two lion-hearted bowlers had bowled themselves into the ground (Haigh 2006: 294).

McGilvray (1987: 174) said 'experience was such an irreplaceable commodity'. He said not taking McKenzie on the 1972 Ashes tour to England was a huge selection blunder. The selectors were wrong to try too many 'new things' under a 'new captain'. They 'short-changed' Chappell by not sending McKenzie on tour [32]. Alan argued that Lillee, who later became a force, had only two Tests in 1971 to his credit, while the other pacemen in the touring team (Bob Massie, David Colley and Jeff Hammond) had none.

Against Garry Sobers's Rest Of The World XI, 1971-72

The World XI team captained by Sobers toured Australia in the 1971–72 season. The hurriedly organized series replaced the proposed Test tour by South Africa, which the ACB cancelled in 1971. Despite the global anger over apartheid, the tour of Australia by South Africa in 1971-72 was still officially on, as late as September 1971.

However, during South Africa's rugby tour in June, massive political unrest and disturbances in Australia came to a head. They led to a state of emergency being declared in Queensland. With planned direct action announced by various protest groups, authorities knew a Test series with South Africa in the summer was impossible.

Faced with an inevitable non-violent-direct-action to disrupt matches, flashing mirrors to distract batters, and blockading the team into its hotel, the ACB withdrew the offer to South Africa seven weeks before the scheduled start. Reactions to apartheid brought politics well and truly into the sports arena (Williamson 2005b).

The ACB heard the concerns of politicians, police, religious leaders, and trade union officials, all of whom suggested that anti-apartheid demonstrations were planning massive interruptions if the South African tour went ahead. It was indeed an awful time for world cricket. A month earlier, England had also cancelled a tour of India and Pakistan because of security concerns. Back in Sri Lanka also, the newspapers screamed about anti-apartheid protests by people.

Faced with financial losses and needing strong opponents to prepare

---

32   McKenzie's yeoman services to cricket were honoured later as he was inducted into Australia's Cricket *Hall of Fame* in 2010 (ESPN Cricinfo 2010).

the Australian team for the 1972 Ashes tour, the ACB had to find someone to replace South Africa. After weeks of negotiations, the Board assembled a Rest of the World XI to undertake a tour in October. The team included some of the world's best cricketers at that time (i.e. Garry Sobers, Rohan Kanhai, Graeme and Peter Pollock, Clive Lloyd, Bishan Bedi, Intikhab Alam and Farokh Engineer).

It also included stars, like Sunil Gavaskar, Zaheer Abbas and Tony Greig. Sobers (2002: 174) recalled that Bradman had invited him to captain the World XI. Assembled at short notice, the 17-member squad was 'not in any way the best of the Rest of the World' (McGilvray 1985: 144). Due to other commitments, players like Snow, Knott, Boycott, Procter and Barry Richards were unavailable. The wicket-keeper was England's Bob Taylor. The depleted bowling side had Richard Hutton from England, Bob Cunis from New Zealand, and Asif Masood from Pakistan.

It was clear that the bowling depended on the all-around talents of Sobers and Greig and the spin of Bedi and Intikhab. All of them played in all five matches. The South African paceman Peter Pollock played in only two games and got poor returns for his efforts.

However, the matches were financial successes. Records indicate that attendance increased as the series progressed from 14,800 people in the first unofficial 'Test' match to 23,000 in the second. Each game had a profit of about $19,000. About 133,600 spectators attended the third match in Melbourne, paying more than $103,000. Attendance in the fourth and fifth matches was also high (91,000 and 61,000, respectively, for incomes exceeding $100,000. The series was an exceptional financial success for the ACB (ESPN Cricinfo 2009).

In his foreword to Ian's book *The Cutting Edge*, Sobers wrote that the series was one of the most enjoyable he had ever played in, mainly because the two captains had similar approaches to the game. Both were willing to take chances to achieve a win. 'It was an example the players followed, making for wonderful cricket' (Chappell 1992).

Unfortunately, the World XI matches were not granted Test status. They were called 'unofficial Tests' and only counted as first-class matches. The reason was that 'A "Test" match had to be played between two nations'. The World XI won the series 2-1. Ian Chappell captained his side with aggression, hit four centuries and made a glut of runs (634 at 79). His brother Greg played only in three matches but topped the averages (425 at 106) with two centuries.

Stackpole and Doug also made two centuries each. Doug played only in the first four matches, making 355 runs at 71. Dennis Lillee, the West Australian, emerged as a fearsome fast bowler and a tireless workhorse for Australia in this series. Lillee took 24 wickets at 20 with two five-wicket hauls and one 12-wicket haul in the second match at his home turf at the WACA, in Perth (10-14 December 1971).

After becoming captain a few months earlier, Ian Chappell had already embarked on getting the Australian team out of a slump and moulding a competitive outfit. Dennis Lillee and the West Australian wicket-keeper Rodney Marsh also emerged in this re-building effort.

Both Marsh and Lillee developed quickly as Chappell's closest allies. They helped the captain form a highly competitive Australian outfit that went on to great success. Both players became pre-eminent forces but controversial figures in Australian cricket over the next decade.

Aggression and combativeness characterized the team under Ian. I recall that much of the hostility was directed at the Old Enemy, England. However, there is no question that Chappell's charges were determined to play cricket in a combative but fair manner, following the way great Australian teams had played in the past. Much of the time, they respected the opponents engaged in battles with them.

* * *

The first 'unofficial Test' was at the Gabba in Brisbane (26 November-1 December 1971). It was a rain-affected draw with no play on day two. Australia's first innings (4-389) was built on centuries by Stackpole (132) and Chappell (145) and Doug's unbeaten 75. The World XI replied with 4-285, including centuries by the South African Hylton Ackerman (112) and the West Indian Rohan Kanhai (101).

Aided by a second Ian Chappell century (106), Australia declared the second inning at 3-220. The tourists then played out the time, making 4-108. Sobers (2002: 187) said he noticed how Dennis Lillee bowled with fire in the first match. In the first inning, he was surprised as Lillee took a bowling run-up of more than 20 yards and was *quicker than expected*, even on a slow Brisbane pitch.

* * *

The second match, at the WACA in Perth (10-12 December 1971), was over in three days and embarrassed the World XI. Australia batted first and made 349 in only 73 overs as Doug bashed his way to a century (125). The World XI bowlers were put to the test by both Stackpole (55) and Ian Chappell (56), who also batted aggressively.

When the tourists batted, they were bowled out for 59 in just 90 minutes and in only 14.1 overs. Lillee, bowling fast on his home ground, was the wrecker. Helped by some drift and the pitch, he ruined the visitors' batting lineup, taking 8/29 in just 7.1 overs. The press denounced the visitors for taking matters too casually.

Sobers (2002: 188) said that up to this point, his only concern was that the teams' bowling stocks were depleted, which meant that he had a lot of bowling to do. The bouncy Perth wicket had been covered overnight by a tarp, plastic and canvas. Aided by high temperature and sea breeze from the south-west (called the *Freemantle Doctor*), the Perth track had changed overnight. Sobers (2002: 189) wrote that he had never seen anything like that: 'The wicket was quick and bouncy, and it looked like the ball taking off after it had pitched'.

When Sobers came into bat with a score of 5-46, Lillee let fly a series of short-pitched deliveries. Sobers gloved the third delivery to the keeper Marsh and was out for a duck. Chappell enforced the follow-on. Kanhai (118), Zaheer (51), Lloyd (32) and Sobers (33) prevented a second collapse, but the visitors were bowled out for 279. Lillee (4/63) and McKenzie (4/66) were the main wicket-takers as Australia won by an innings and 11 runs to lead the series 1-0.

Sobers said that Lillee's bowling in that series was the fastest he had ever seen. He reckoned that Frank Tyson, the English paceman of the '50s, was 'Consistently faster, but on the Perth wicket, Lillee bowled faster than anyone else he had played against in his life'.

* * *

The third match, which started on New Year's Day in 1972, was played at the MCG in Melbourne (1-6 January 1972). The game has a special place in cricket history because of Garry Sobers' innings, hailed by Sir Don Bradman as 'the greatest-ever innings played on Australian soil'. Sobers won the toss and batted, but the World XI batters again failed and were all out for 184. While Lillee again took 5/48, only Tony Greig (66), Sunil Gavaskar and Intikhab Alam (38 each) resisted.

Lillee again bowled a barrage of bumpers at Sobers in the first inning, and Sobers edged the third ball, which was caught by Stackpole in the gully for a second duck in the series. A well-known story is that in the evening, after the day's play was over, Sobers went into the Australian dressing room and let his opposite number know that he was taking the short-pitched stuff seriously (Sobers 2002: 190):

That evening, I went to the dressing room where Ian was sitting, and

> Dennis Lillee stood nearby. I said to Ian, 'You've got a fellow by the name of Lillee. Every time I come in, he bowls me bouncers. I want you to tell him that I can bowl quick, too. Tell him I can also bat a bit better than he can and to look out for me when he comes into bat.

The Australian reply was 285 with a classic Greg Chappell century (115*). Greig bowled aggressively, and in picking up 4/41, he bowled Doug for 16. When Lillee came into bat, goaded by Greig, Sobers bounced him but kept the ball outside the off stump. Lillee, apparently, turned pink as the first ball he faced flew past his nose; Lillee holed out for a duck in the next ball (Sobers 2002: 190).

Trailing by 101 in the second inning, the World XI had to bat well to save the match. They were 3-146 when Sobers entered the arena and took control of the game. The tourists were 7-344 when day three ended with Sobers 139*. Lillee bowled like an 'enraged bull, looking for blood' but got flayed by Sobers. Batting was made to look easy that afternoon as Sobers struck 21 fours. After a rest day, on day four, he resumed his masterclass, hammering two sixers and 35 fours in making 254, one of the epic batting displays in cricket history.

McGilvray (1985, p. 144) noted that Lillee and Massie bowled like lions. But the harder they tried, they got slaughtered. Sobers's 186-run stand with Peter Pollock (54) for the eighth wicket put the match beyond Australia. Finally, a miscued pull caught by Doug at mid-on, off Greg Chappell, ended Sobers' knock.

Wooldridge (2019) described the inning as 'an unforgettable display, combining such elegance of strokeplay, power and aggression that the crowds were ecstatic. It was a throwback to the dominance of Sobers in other years'. According to McGilvray (1985: 144), Bradman, 'who is not often given to handing out praise', called the innings 'probably the best ever seen on Australian soil'. Bradman went on to say:

> The people who saw Sobers enjoyed one of the historic events of cricket. They were privileged to have such an experience...With his long grip of the bat, high backlift, and free swing, Sobers hits the ball harder than anyone I can remember. This helps to make him such an exciting player to watch because the emphasis is on power and aggression rather than technique – the latter being the servant, not the master.

McGilvray (1985: 142-143) described Sir Garry as a 'ruthless carnivore who gobbled up bowlers'. He added that:

This knock was the best expression of unbridled talent I had ever seen. A supreme master of the batting art, Sobers had no inhibitions and played without thought of risk. Every shot was struck truly and gloriously...and it was an inning upon which it would simply be impossible to improve.

However, Alan also wrote that the Sobers' inning 'developed almost accidentally because it was a 'manufactured series' and he 'batted with freedom of approach like beach cricket at home'. Willimson's account (2006) noted what Tony Greig remembered and publicly stated:

Garry had problems on the home front. His wife and little boy, who lived in Melbourne, had left him. My lasting memory is when he walked off the ground, and his wife agreed to return and speak to him...People in the whole stadium were on their feet except one person. And that was his wife. Sobers went straight downstairs, and the two of them reconciled.

Sobers is admired worldwide by millions of cricket fans for how he played his cricket with unimpeachable sportsmanship. I've listened to many Test match broadcasts that described his singular impact. I doubt we will ever see such a great all-rounder again in cricket for the number of runs scored and wickets and catches taken.

Australians fought hard to save the match, trailing by 413. Doug's second consecutive century (127) led the effort with Ian Chappell (41) and John Benaud (42), but they failed to save the match. The spinners took hold on the final day, with Bedi (4/81) and Intikhab (3/83) bowling the visitors to victory by 96 runs, levelling the series 1-1.

ABC did not broadcast the matches across other countries then. So, all my knowledge comes from different sources, including a film called Salute to Sobers, a special tribute to Sobers's magnificent 254. Michael Manley (1988: 203) wrote that it was one of the most remarkable films ever made in sports. In the film, Bradman analyses every aspect of Sobers' batting, stating that 'he is describing a genius at work'.

The film used 'freeze-frame' technology to show Sobers' strokes at different points, beginning with the backlift, the stroke, the follow-through and the use of the wrists, aptly and analytically described by Sir Donald. The film of this remarkable innings was widely publicized in all other cricket-playing countries. It was shown in various towns in Sri Lanka free of charge. I recall going to a church hall (Methodist Church) in my hometown, Panadura, in mid-1972, sitting among hundreds of cheering admirers and watching the film in awe. Anyone who needs to see what batting genius is should watch this Sobers' inning.

In his autobiography, Sobers (2002: 193) lamented that the film was made into a commercial property without anyone telling him. While he did not receive any penny in royalties from the Don or the ACB, the film had been used for coaching. Sobers said he had to buy a copy from the MCC Bookstore in London!

* * *

In the fourth match (8-13 January 1972), the World XI was saved by rain, which washed out play on the final day. Ian Chappell won the toss for the third time, and Australia batted first to make 312. It included a Stackpole century (104) and half-centuries from Marsh (77) and John Benaud (54). Doug was dismissed cheaply for eight. Bedi (4/85) and Intikhab (3/75) did the damage. When the World XI batted, they could muster only 277, with Massie taking 7/76. Late-order resistance from Intikhab (73*) and Greig (70) saved the face of the visitors. Sobers only made 15 before he was caught by Marsh off Massie.

The Australian reply was a massive 546, with over 400 runs scored on day three. Stackpole started with a bang (95). Ian Chappell's aggressive 119 was followed by a blazing Greg Chappell knock of 197* as the Australians plundered the visitors' bowling. Doug missed out, bowled by Intikhab for four. All of the visiting bowlers were hammered. Only Intikhab returned respectable figures of 4/132. Set to make 582, the World XI limped to 5/173 by the end of day four with Gavaskar 68*. But the rain spoiled an almost certain Australian victory.

* * *

After several limited overs and State games, the final match for the World XI was played at the Adelaide Oval (28 January-1 February 1972). Despite making centuries in the second and third matches, Doug was made the 12th Man for the match. Lillee also didn't play, and the off-spinner Mallett replaced Jenner. Ian Chappell won the toss for the fourth time, and the Australians scored quickly to reach 311.

Quick scoring became a hallmark of Ian's approach to cricket. He reasoned that any team wanting to get into a winning position must score quickly and try to dominate the opponents' attack. Also, Ian insisted on scoring 300-330 in a day as a method to make Test cricket more appealing to spectators. Looking to score more than 300 runs per day is almost a standard in Test cricket these days.

A rapid 99 by John Benaud was bolstered by aggressive batting from Greg Chappell (85) and Rod Marsh (54). While the spinners took some hammer,

Tony Greig's effort (6/30 in 15 overs) contained the Australians. When the World XI batted, they were 3/74 at one stage. Then, Graeme Pollock, the South African batting star, unleashed his genius on the Australian attack in a typically blistering 136.

With Zaheer making 73, the visitors scored 367 and were ahead by 56 runs. Mallett, who played only in this match in the series, took 4/116 in 35 overs. Sobers was taken in the slips off Massie for only two runs. Batting a second time, the Australians inexplicably collapsed to the spin of Intikhab (4/78) and Bedi (3/54). As the innings folded for 201, Ian Chappell stood head and shoulders above, carrying his bat to be 111*. The match ended on day four, with the World XI quickly chasing down the required 146 runs. Ackerman was 76*, and Gavaskar made 50. Winning the game, the visitors led the series 2-1.

* * *

The hastily arranged series was a watershed in many ways, although the games were not afforded the 'Test' status. Apart from getting into the world's cricket annals because of Garry Sobers' brilliant 254, the series firmly established Ian's leadership as Australia's captain.

Not only did Ian make a glut of runs (634 at 79 with four centuries), but he also stood out as a captain whose approach was quite different to the two previous Australian captains, Bob Simpson and Bill Lawry. In sharp contrast to the Simpson-Lawry era, when 'scoring big and keeping the match 'safe' was the priority' (McGilvray 1985: 107).

Ian Chappell's approach to getting results was hinged on taking calculated risks, leading from the front, scoring quickly and aiming to win all the time. The batting of his brother Greg (425 at 106), Doug (355 at 59) and Stackpole (507 at 47) helped Ian's cause, each of them hitting two centuries each in the series.

In a tour match with South Australia at the Adelaide Oval (17-18 December 1971), Lloyd got seriously injured while diving for a catch at cover off a drive from Mallett. He landed on his shoulder and injured his spine. Some thought he would never play again. But physiotherapy helped Lloyd to recover fast, and he was back playing cricket within a few months. Manley (1988: 204) said, 'Luckily for cricket, Lloyd, a man of immense courage, fought to survive and did come back to play by 1973 and by 1975, he was captain of the team'.

CHAPTER 9

Making Runs - Ups and Downs

Failures in England Again, 1972

Towards the end of the 1960s decade, after the pounding dished out by the South Africans, for several years, Australian cricket in the international scene was at a very low level (Preston 1973a). Confidence in their cricketing abilities was lacking, and public interest was also low.

In the fiercely fought 1970-71 Ashes series in Australia, in which Doug played in all of the Tests, the Australians, led by the determined but unimaginative Bill Lawry, surrendered the Ashes to Ray Illingworth's much more professional and superior team. Ian Chappell took over as captain in the seventh Test in the 1970-71 series after Lawry was unceremoniously sacked. This was a time to re-assess the available talent and resources and rebuild the team.

Following the battles with the World XI in which the beaten Australians still glistened, Ian saw the potential of several players. He began to put together a 'new fighting force' of Australians for the 1972 tour to England. Chappell's ability to get the best out of his team was appreciated by all his other teammates (Sheahan 1979).

His opponents also shared the same view. In his autobiography, Lloyd (1980: 182) said that his team always knew they'd be in for a scrap when Chappell was in charge. Ian succeeded in getting his team to play entertaining cricket that would draw crowds.

Overall, the 1972 Ashes tour was somewhat of a failure for the Australians and a low point of Doug's Test career. Well into my teens, I listened to the BBC broadcasts late into the night, following Australia's fortunes closely. I also collected pictures of the trendily dressed Australians (Preston 1973a; *Wisden* 2020).

Ian Chappell's 'young' team was well-noticed in England for their stylish 1970s hairstyles, hair over the ears and thick and long sideburns. Several players also had drooping moustaches to go with the long hair.

The English press, in general, were unimpressed with the flashy outfits – flared trousers, pink-coloured shirts and trendy suits that the Australians wore. Nevertheless, Chappell insisted that his 'young guns' should dress up flashy and stylishly. He encouraged his charges to walk about and always speak, oozing confidence in their cricketing abilities.

Doug confirmed that Chappell never missed an opportunity to impress the on-lookers and photographers. The team strutted around, full of self-confidence, giving the impression that the team was ready for a battle and wouldn't be pushovers. The team also wore baggy green caps, which have since become an Australian icon.

As they went around various counties and venues on the 1972 tour, the English press noticed the young team's 'carry-ons, yelling, laughing, pranks, the beer and the cigarettes and cribbage games'. Grudgingly, they said that 'it wouldn't have happened in the good old days' (Hutchinson and Ross 1997: 399).

* * *

The English were dumbfounded when the chosen seventeen Australians excluded Lawry, Redpath and McKenzie, in particular. Only seven of the players who toured England in 1968 had been retained. They were Ian Chappell, Doug, Sheahan, Inverarity, Gleeson, Mallett and Taber. Many in Australia thought taking four fast bowlers (Dennis Lillee, Bob Massie, David Colley and Jeff Hammond), who had no previous experience in England, was a huge gamble. But it paid off as Lillee and Massie dominated the series (ABC 1976: 10).

The odds were 3-1 against Australia winning the series (Preston 1973a). However, Chappell's team did much better than everyone expected them to do. The tour successes were Lillee (31 wickets at 17), Massie (23 wickets at 18), Marsh (23 dismissals; 242 runs at 35, Ross Edwards (291 at 48), Greg Chappell (437 at 48) and Ian Chappell (334 at 33).

Dennis Lillee was the real find of the tour as he established a record for an Australian bowler in England. Lillee's haul of 31 wickets beat the 29 wickets each in a series, taken by Clarrie Grimmett in 1930 and Graham McKenzie in 1964.

Although nothing much went right for Doug in the Tests, he did pretty well in other tour matches., making three centuries – 109 against Derbyshire and 154 against Warwickshire, both before the first Test and 150 versus Kent, after the Tests were over. Doug's tour aggregate of 935 runs in first-class matches suggested that his decline on the big occasions might be only temporary (Preston 1973a).

He didn't get much chance to bat for long in the earlier matches on tour. However, approaching the first Test on 8 June, he was in form with the two centuries he made on 31 May and 3 June. However, the Test series was a low point in Doug's career, and he was dropped for the fifth Test match at The Oval.

The tour was a notable one for Western Australia. In their history, they had staged only one Test: when Illingworth's team played in Perth in 1970-71. Now, the Sheffield Shield champions for the third time, six team members (Lillee, Massie, Graeme Watson, Ross Edwards, Marsh and Inverarity) who played in the final Test were West Australians. With Doug dropped for the final Test, for the first time in Australia's cricket history, NSW State had no player in that match.

In *Wisden*, the Editor (Preston 1973a) wrote that the influence of Tony Lock, the English left-arm spinner who captained Western Australia for several seasons in the late 1960s, might have shifted Australia's cricketing power balance.

* * *

In the first Test at Old Trafford (8-13 June 1972), affected by rain, Australia was beaten by the competent home side led by Illingworth, who became 40 years old on the opening day.

England was bowled out for 249 and 234 in the first and second innings. Edrich made 49 in the first inning, and Boycott, 47 in the second inning. But Tony Greig, South African-born, six feet six inches in height, the tallest cricketer to play Test cricket at that time, impressed everyone. On his debut, the future England captain showed considerable skill and energy. Greig hit two half-centuries (57 and 62) and took two catches and five wickets in the match for 74 runs.

The 22-year-old Lillee announced to the world that he had 'arrived' by taking 6/66 in England's second inning. For his match bag 8/106, Lillee bowled 59 overs at a menacing pace, indicating to the Australian selectors that they had found the bowling spearhead for the future. However, England held the upper hand throughout the match, thanks to their more reliable batting and accurate seam bowling.

Australia batted dismally in the first inning to be put out for 142. Snow (4/41) and his new partner Geoff Arnold (4/62) exploited the seaming conditions well. Doug failed twice for low scores (17 and 20). Stackpole (53 and 67) batted resolutely twice for Australia, while Ian Chappell was dismissed cheaply twice as he hooked impulsively.

In a recent article, '*Captain Hook*' explained how the 'hooks' were vital to him and his batting style (Chappell 2015). Needing 341 to win, Australians stumbled to 8-147 when Marsh made a belligerent 91, striking nine fours and four sixes in just two hours. He nearly became England's first Australian keeper to make a Test century. The effort was only a late gesture of defiance as Snow (4/87) and Greig (4/53) kept their heads to bowl Australia out for 252.

England won comfortably by 89 runs on the last day, the first time in 42 years they had taken the first Ashes Test in a home series. With Lillee's impressive bowling, something notable in cricket emerged for Australia. The dismissals, known as 'Caught Marsh-Bowled Lillee', were also established in the match, as Marsh took four out of his six catches off Lillee's bowling. The Lillee-Marsh pairing was a crucial factor in Australia's ascendancy in the world of cricket in the 1970s.

* * *

It appeared as if Chappell's young Australians were in for a torrid time as the home team capitalized on early summer, dampness and overcast conditions. But then came the Lord's Test (22-26 June 1972), in which Australians avenged their defeat in the first Test. While Lillee wrecked the top order, it was the swing bowler – Bob Massie, a 25-year-old West Australian, on his Test debut, who put his name on the record books for perpetuity. Massie was unfit and did not play in the first Test, but what a debut it was in the second Test!

Incredibly, Massie lost all form and would play just five more Tests for his country, taking a career total of only 31 wickets at 21. Within 18 months of his Lord's debut, he was also dropped by his State. Glued to the radio, I listened in awe as Massie swept through England's batting with the staggering 16 wickets in the match for 137, setting up a world record by a bowler on debut, still unbroken. Massie took 8/84 in 32.5 overs in the two innings and 8/53 in 27.2 overs.

Glued to the radio, I recall that the heavy atmosphere was ideally suited for swing bowling. Massie maintained an excellent length and direction, but his late swing troubled the English batters. None of them could combat the late-curving ball, the only exceptions being Greig (54) and Alan Knott (43). England was bowled out for 272.

Australia began disastrously, losing both openers (Stackpole and Bruce Francis) with just seven runs on the board. But the Chappell brothers then steadied the inning. Ian made 56, with six fours and a six, hooking 'to do some damage' (Chappell, 2015). Greg stroked a fighting century (131 with 14 fours), showing complete command at the crease. This was an inning that Greg Chappell later described as his finest.

Doug failed again, making only one, while Marsh thrashed a half-century (50), again hitting out with six fours and two sixes. The total of

308 gave Australia a small but significant lead of 36. Snow (5/57 in 32 overs) commanded great respect from the Australians.

England then crumbled in the second inning, all out for 116, crashing under Massie's 'magic spell'. Edges of the bemused English batters, beaten by the curving swing, were caught in the slips or behind the stumps. Only M. J. K. Smith, recalled to the side at 39, made a fighting 30 batting for nearly three hours.

While Massie took 16 wickets for 137 in the Test, Lillee took a match bag of 4/140. Preston (1973a) noted how important Lillee was to Australia's victory. Lillee was fast, sending far fewer loose deliveries than in the first Test. Massie capitalized on Lillee's hostility. Australia quickly chased down the required 81 runs to win by eight wickets. The series was tied at 1:1 at this stage.

The Lord's Test saw the batting prowess of the younger Chappell. But the Test match would forever be remembered as *'Massie's Test'*. Never before had a bowler taken 16 wickets in a Test debut. No Australian had ever taken so many wickets in a Test. At the same time, Lillee was on the way to a series tally of 31 wickets, thus launching a colossal career (McGilvray, 1985: 110).

Over 100,000 people attended the match over five days. The gate receipts £82,914 were a world record for a Test match then (Preston 1973a). When Massie touched great heights at Lord's, he came close to Jim Laker's remarkable achievements against Australia at Old Trafford in 1956. The English off-spinner claimed 19 wickets for 90 runs in the fourth Test (26-31 July 1956).

Laker's figures were 9/37 and 10/53 in the two innings. Reminiscing about Laker's outstanding performance, in *The Golden Age of Cricket*, Neville Cardus (1968) wrote:

> *In July 1956, at Old Trafford, the most wonderful of all happenings took place, the most wonderful in all the recorded annals of cricket. Laker's 19 wickets in one and the same Test match, v. Australia, with Tony Lock bowling nearly 70 overs at the other end; here was a performance staggering credulity.*
>
> *The analysis of Laker's ten wickets in Australia's second innings strains belief to this day: 51 overs, 2 balls, 23 maidens, 53 runs, 10 wickets. Here, for certain, is a record that will remain unbeaten.*

* * *

The third Test at Trent Bridge, in Nottingham (13-18 July 1972), was a disappointing draw for the Australians. Winning the toss, Illingworth sent

Australia in, but a Keith Stackpole hundred (114) steadied Australia, helped by some dropped catches. In the late order, Marsh (41) and David Colley (54) hit out as the tail wagged, and Australia reached a respectable 315. Snow was again imperious, taking 5/92, but suffered from fielding lapses. Doug also failed in this Test, scoring only two and seven in the two innings.

England then struggled for over a day, making 189, with Edrich (37) being the highest scorer. The English were under constant pressure from Lillee (4/35) and Massie (4/43). This has been described as batting at its 'most abject'. The openers scored only 40 runs in one session. I remember well how painfully slow it was. Luckhurst (23 in two hours), a capable opener, was so clueless about how to score that he reached double figures only after two hours. In the subdued England inning, Marsh held five catches behind the stumps.

Australia's second inning increased the pressure on England. Ross Edwards, opening in place of the injured Bruce Francis, scored a brilliant 170* with 13 fours and a five. Edwards had two crucial stands – 124 with Ian Chappell (50) and 146 with Greg Chappell (72). The Australians declared at 4-324. It set England up to survive nine and a half hours or win by making 451.

With some rain around, the chase was never on. England batted out the time on a pitch that offered no assistance to the Australian bowlers to draw the match reaching 4-290. The escape was mainly due to Luckhurst, who made 96 in five and a half hours and middle-order resistance by Peter Parfitt (46), D'Oliveira (50*) and Greig (36*). England's escape meant the series was still locked at 1-1.

* * *

The fourth Test at Headingley, Leeds (27-29 July 1972), dubbed the *'Fusarium Test'*, was over in only three days of play, as the Australians were twice routed by England's spinners. With the win, England went up 2:1, thus retaining the Ashes. The Test produced a huge debate, in which England was accused of 'pitch-doctoring' (Williamson, 2015b). McGilvray (1985: 111) revealed that when he and the Australian team examined the pitch, they were stunned by its condition.

The pitch was devoid of grass. The ground staff claimed that the rain had affected the pitch a few days earlier, which had ignited a Fusarium fungal infection, killing off the grass. The *London Times* described the pitch as 'bare as a baby's bottom' (Hutchinson and Ross 1997: 399). A drenching before the Test began also prevented the heavy roller from being used.

Mark Nicholas recently mused (2023), quoting Greg Chappell: 'It was uncanny that it (the fungus) affected only a strip 22 yards by eight feet and was a 'whitish' pitch with dead grass, while the rest of the ground remained lush green and perfectly healthy'. The ball hardly bounced on the pitch, and the conditions were better exploited by England, who won by nine wickets. England dropped Norman Gifford after the first three Tests and selected Derek Underwood to play. When the team was announced, the selection prompted McGilvray to report that he had 'smelled a rat'. Underwood's ten-wicket haul (4/37 and 6/45 in the two innings) ensured that England won easily.

Batting first, Australia made a gritty start with a Stackpole half-century (52) and then slumped to be all out for 146. The wicket began to take spin on day one, and both English spinners bowled before lunch on day one as Illingworth read the signs correctly. Underwood (4/37 in 16 overs) and Illingworth (2/32 in 21 overs) exploited the conditions well. Doug was bowled by Illingworth for just four runs.

England, too, struggled to be 6-112 by lunch on day two but recovered due to resolute batting, firstly by Edrich (45) and then by Illingworth (57) and Snow (48). The pitch slowed by the hour and did not help Lillee and Massie. But Mallett gave a good account of himself, bowling 52 overs and taking 5/114. England batted the whole day on day two for safety, scoring only 209 runs.

England's reply of 263 gave them a handy 117-run lead, and it became clear that Australia would struggle again on the pitch, on which the ball was turning sharply. Not surprisingly, trapped on a spinner's wicket, Australia collapsed in their second dig to be all out for 136.

Underwood (6/45) and Illingworth (2/32) wrecked the batting. At one stage, in a deadly dozen overs, Underwood took 5 for 18, tearing the heart out of the batting line-up. Only Sheahan resisted firmly (41*). Doug's miserable run continued. He made only three in the second inning before edging Underwood to be caught at slip by Parfitt.

The angry Australians accused the groundsmen of 'pitch doctoring' to make it a rank turner, to subdue the pace and swing of Lillee and Massie. The fact remained that the English spinners, the combination of 'Deadly' Derek and Illingworth, did better on the turning pitch than the Australian spinners.

In the inquiry, the Pitches Committee of the Test & County Cricket Board (TCCB) cleared the groundsman of any blame for the condition of the pitch. The committee concluded that *Fusarium oxysporum*, a well-known fungal disease of plants, spread when the covers were on during the deluge, killing much of the grass before the ground staff had an opportunity to treat it (Preston 1973b).

* * *

Australia's defeat in the fourth Test meant that England had retained the Ashes, but this did not spoil the attraction of the final Test, which was contested over six days (The Oval, 10-16 August 1972). It was also the first Test match televised live in Australia through satellite communications. On three days, the gates were closed, and the crowds enjoyed an epic battle in which Australia prevailed. England's luck ran out as Illingworth, Snow and D'Oliveira – couldn't bowl and were out of action due to freakish injuries.

Doug was left out because of his poor form. The performances in the four Tests were indeed the lowest point in his career. In seven innings, Doug had managed only 54 runs at 7.7, with the highest score of 20. Ian also under-bowled him as Doug rolled his arm over only for five overs without taking a wicket. Doug said dropping him for the fifth Test was the right decision ((Mallett 2008: 197).

England's first innings of 284 owed little to the specialist batters and much to Alan Knott's fighting 92, made in just over two hours of attacking batting. Knott smacked 17 fours, and his inning saved England. The innings fell away after several good starts by the top-order batters – Peter Parfitt (51) and John Hampshire (42). Lillee was fiery, taking (5/58), and Mallett took 3/80.

The solid Australian reply of 399 was built on the centuries of the Chappel brothers – Ian (118 with 20 fours) and Greg (113 with 17 fours), combining in a partnership of 201. Ian batted for five and a half hours, and Greg batted for only four. They became the first brothers to score a century each in Test cricket. Ross Edwards also contributed 79. Underwood wheeled away, taking 4/90, and Geoff Arnold (3/87) bowled 36 overs tirelessly, preventing a more significant deficit. Snow bowled 35 overs but was unlucky, taking only one wicket for 111.

A fighting 90 by the debutant opener, Barry Wood, a second half-century by Knott (63), and Basil D'Oliveira's solid 43 helped England reach 356. Lillee was again the pick of the bowlers, taking 5/123, which gave him match figures of 10/181. As Australia sought a win, Illingworth bowled only six overs before he sprained an ankle on a foothold and was carried off the field; Snow could bowl only six overs because of a damaged shoulder (he was hit by a Lillee bouncer), and D'Oliveira did not bowl due to a strained back.

This left Underwood to do the bulk of the bowling, supported by Arnold and Greig. Without Illingworth, Edrich led England. Stackpole (79) and Ian Chappell (37) then put on 116 for the second wicket, making the target of 241 look easy.

As the match headed towards an end, I was on a bus heading home. But I got off the bus about 10 km from my hometown. Filled with tension, I hastily went to a friend's home to listen to the last hour as Sheahan (44*) and Marsh (43*) joined in a 71-run stand. They took Australia to victory (5-242) by five wickets, levelling the series 2-2.

In the two innings, Rod Marsh added four catches to take his series dismissals tally to 23, setting up a new series record. Altogether, Marsh had 10 catches in the five Tests off Lillee. The dismissals labelled 'Caught Marsh-bowled Lillee' were recorded 95 times in Tests over the next decade, giving rise to one of Australia's great cricketing legends.

* * *

Stackpole, the vice-captain, served his side well with consistently effective batting in the Tests. He struck 114 at Trent Bridge and passed fifty on five occasions, averaging 54 for the series. Greg Chappell came close behind Stackpole in the Tests, scoring 437 runs at 49. Having spent two seasons with Somerset, Greg was well-versed in English conditions. His centuries in the two Tests Australia won, and other fine knocks, left no doubt that in him, Australia possessed a high-quality batter who would stand them in good stead for a long time.

On many occasions, Ian Chappell led from the front, scoring 334 runs at 33. *Wisden* reported (Preston 1973a) that Ian was happiest with the bat when the situation permitted freedom of strokeplay. Although he fell to the first ball he faced in the first Test to a fine catch in the deep, when hooking a bouncer, he used the hook frequently in the series as a profitable stroke (Chappell 2015). He got his head down to serious business in the final Test when the brotherhood produced the match-winning double-century stand.

Ross Edwards was often the sheet anchor in the middle order. But his most crucial inning of 170* came as the make-shift opener in the Trent Bridge Test. A series aggregate of 291 runs at 48 in four Tests showed his value. Edwards's performances were crucial for Australia, as Doug didn't deliver much in the middle. Sheahan, third in the tour averages (41), played only in the last two Tests and did well in both. He fought doggedly on the difficult Headingley pitch. He batted at the death of the final Test when his 44* won the match for Australia.

* * *

The 2:2 drawn series was an enthralling one, as I remember well. It enabled

England to retain the Ashes, which Illingworth's team had won in 1970-71. But batsmanhip in England was in severe decline at this stage, which is a reason for Illingworth's cautious approach.

No English batter averaged more than Tony Greig's 36 in the series, and he scored only 288 runs. Lillee and Massie proved the old adage: 'Bowlers win matches'. Preston (1973b) explained that England's poor batting displays were due to their inability to cope with Lillee's sheer speed and bounce and Massie's skilful control of length and swing.

While a few slip catches went amiss, the 'young' Australians lived up to the high reputation of their predecessors in the field. As Doug was in the deep, Ross Edwards and Sheahan were outstanding fielders in the covers. With Rod Marsh establishing a new record with 23 dismissals (21 caught and two stumpings), overall, the Australian slip-catching, throwing and ground fielding was far superior to England's.

After all their fine batting in Australia 18 months earlier, Boycott (72 at 18), Edrich (218 at 22) and Luckhurst (168 at 24) failed with the bat. Their meagre contributions meant none of the wins came easy for Illingworth. An injury kept Boycott out of the last three Tests. Still, even in the first two, he wasn't happy facing Lillee's fast and furious short-pitched deliveries.

The all-rounders, Greig (288 at 36), D'Oliveira (233 at 29) and Knott (229 at 29), were the only batters who held the side together, along with the gritty Illingworth (194 at 32). While stressing England's dismal batting, the *Wisden* Editor (Preston 1973b) wrote:

> *The Australians possessed one priceless virtue. They were a young set, and they improved all the time, whereas England relied on the old brigade-- dubbed Dad's Army in some quarters. For the first time in the history of five-day Tests against Australia, England had no century to their credit.*

However, with four of the five Tests ending in a result, each country winning twice, spectator interest was high. Both captains received praise for some of the most exciting Ashes cricket in history. Both showed their first aim was to win, but when the odds were against them, they goaded their teams to fight for a draw (Preston 1973b). Ian Chappell's young Australian team won accolades for entertaining the public with competitive and results-oriented cricket. They had played their cricket with a fierce determination that had been rarely seen previously in Australian teams.

Pakistan Tour Down Under (1972-73)

Pakistan's Team, under the leg-spinner Intikhab Alam, visited Sri Lanka in November 1972 before travelling to Australia. The Sri Lankan team, under Michael Tissera, managed to scrape a draw in the three-day match at The Oval in Colombo.

I listened to the broadcasts on the radio but didn't get to see the match. Pakistanis were careful not to lose the game to the 'underdogs' but played some enterprising cricket. They scored 8-262 in the first inning, helped by Majid Khan (69), Zaheer Abbas (63), Mushtaq Mohammad (35) and Asif Iqbal (39).

The Sri Lankans replied with 133, spun out by Intikhab (5/34 in 9.2 overs). Only David Heyn (49) and the wicket-keeper Russel Harmer (35) batted well for the home side. Pakistan showed great respect for Sri Lanka, which had already built enduring diplomatic and political relationships with the country over a few decades. Pakistan had been helping Sri Lanka in many ways, including supporting the claim of Test status. So, much camaraderie between the teams and players was visible on the cricket field and in how the tours were conducted. As a kid, watching these friendly interactions, I naively believed that cricket would continue to be played like a gentleman's game!

* * *

Upon arrival in Australia, the tour didn't go well for the Pakistanis in the Australian summer of 1972-73. These matches were also broadcast to the sub-continent by ABC, and I managed to listen to the commentaries via shortwave transmissions. Boasting acclaimed batting stars like Zaheer, Majid, Asif and the Mohammad brothers – Sadiq and Mushtaq, the Pakistani team was considered the 'best team' ever to set foot in Australia (Hutchinson and Ross 1997: 404). However, they were soundly beaten 3-0 by a much stronger Australian team.

The youthful Australian team had just returned from England and was well-settled under Ian Chappell's leadership. Having played well in the Ashes battles, they were rearing to go in front of home crowds in their first summer back with the newly found confidence and competence. At this time, the public's interest in cricket was also high.

In the 1972 summer, Australia unleashed Jeff Thomson ('Thommo'), a paceman from NSW, who was soon destined to become Lillee's partner. The 'Lillee-Thomson' pair became an Australian legend as they terrorized their opponents for several years.

The series, however, was marred by tight scheduling, which meant three Tests were played in three weeks. Both sides complained about the punishing schedule caused by the Australians needing time to accommodate the upcoming Caribbean tour in February 1973.

* * *

Mallett (2008: 204-205) explained that back in Australia after his horrors in England, Doug did as he always did, regardless of his form; he looked forward to the new summer, although the season didn't start well for him. As the season 1972-73 unfolded, Doug made a duck against Queensland in Brisbane, six and 106 against Western Australia in Perth, 14 and 0 against South Australia in Adelaide and a duck and 10 against South Australia in the return match in Sydney.

Far too soon, the critics called for his head after those early-season failures. Then came the NSW second innings against Western Australia at the SCG. Doug hit a brilliant 159, belting Lillee and Massie into submission to hand NSW a victory over the Sheffield Shield holders.

Phil Wilkins (1972), reporting in the *Sydney Morning Herald* on 6th December, wrote, 'Once a champion, always a champion'. He emphasized that Doug Walters 'has answered his critics and a host of disbelievers' with his 159 as NSW beat the Sheffield Shield holders by four wickets at the SCG. The inning silenced his critics and put him back in the frame to be recalled to the Australian team.

While not playing in the first two Tests, Doug scored 133 versus Victoria in Melbourne, followed by 43 and 176 for NSW in a return game with Victoria at the SCG. The selectors recalled Doug for the third Test, but he scored only 25 runs in the match (Mallett 2008: 205).

* * *

Lillee (4/49) and Massie (4/70) tore through the Pakistan batting line-up in the first Test at the Adelaide Oval (22-27 December 1972). Massie swung the ball well, while Lillee was extremely hostile. Talat Ali, the debutant opener, had his thumb broken by a Lillee delivery. But resolute late-order batting by the skipper Intikhab (64) and Wasim Bari, the wicket-keeper (72), saw them recover to a final total of 9-257.

Australia then scored a huge first-inning score of 585. Ian Chappell scored a brilliant century (196), hammering 21 fours and four sixes. In under three hours, Rod Marsh hit his first Test century (118). Ross Edwards (89) and Kerry O'Keeffe (40) also added to the score, made at a fast rate of 5.8 per over. The Pakistani bowlers toiled on a wicket their pacemen (Asif Masood and Salim Altaf) couldn't exploit. While the captain Intikhab's leg-spinners did not have much impact (0/115 in 18 overs), wickets, Mushtaq's leg-spin brought him 3/67 in 11 overs.

Pakistan resisted again with gutsy batting but couldn't prevent an Australian win and was bowled out for 214. Sadiq, the left-handed opener, resisted (81), aided by his brother Mushtaq (32), Saeed Ahmad (39) and Intikhab (30). Mallett was at his best on the bouncy and spinning Adelaide wicket, his adopted home turf. He took a career-best 8/59 in 26 overs, bowling Australia to a win by innings and 114 runs.

The Pakistanis were pretty unhappy with some umpiring decisions by Norman Townsend, including a catch at the wicket by Ian Chappell when the batter was only five. In the second inning, the umpire erred in giving Saeed Ahmed out lbw to Mallett at 39, and Majid, claimed caught by Chappell off Mallett for 11. The Pakistan team manager was forced to complain about the team's dissatisfaction in his official report to the Australian Cricket authorities. This was the only Test that Townsend, a Navy veteran, ever umpired.

* * *

In the second Test at the MCG (29 December-3 January 1973), two Australian bowlers who became legendary cricketers – Max Walker and Jeff Thomson – made their Test debuts. Massie was omitted, despite his four wickets on the first test, as the selectors (Phil Ridings, Sam Loxton, and Neil Harvey) wanted to find a long-term partner for Lillee. From Sydney, Jeff Thomson, a fast bowler with a slinging action, was introduced only after playing just five first-class matches.

Both sides scored a glut of runs, but the home side won the contest by 92 runs. At the same time, Pakistan, from a position of considerable strength, somehow managed to waste the chance to win. Batting first, Australia scored rapidly at 5.2 runs per over, ending day one at 4-349. The leading scorers were Redpath (135), Greg Chappell (116*), Ian Chappell (66) and Marsh (74) before the declaration at 5-441.

The Pakistani reply was strong (8-574 declared), a position from which it was hard to imagine how they could lose, which they did. The total was built on brilliant centuries from Sadiq (137 with 15 fours) and Majid (158 with 18 fours). Saeed Ahmad (50), Zaheer (51), Mushtaq (60) and Intikhab (68) contributed to the total. Jeff Thomson was ineffective in his debut Test (0/100 in 17 overs). In comparison, Max Walker (2/112) and Mallett (3/124) were the picks of the bowlers. Lillee struggled, bowling only 16.5 overs, taking 1/90.

Trailing by 133 in the first innings, the home team batted again strongly as the Pakistani bowlers failed to capitalize on the first-inning lead. Sheahan (127 striking 12 fours) and John Benaud (142, including 18 fours and two sixes) made rapid centuries. Benaud was playing in only his second Test match. Reports showed that John Benaud (Richie's younger brother) was furious when he played this inning after hearing that he had been dropped for the third Test in Sydney. However, he did make the tour to the Caribbean a month later.

Greg Chappell also hit a half-century (62) as Australia made 425. This left Pakistan to score 292 to win, and given their first-inning batting, it appeared as if they would achieve the target. However, an erratic batting display resulted on the final day. Only Majid (47), Intikhab (48) and Asif Iqbal (37) showed application. Walker took 3/39 as Pakistan were bowled out for 200, handing over an improbable victory to the Australians by 92 runs.

* * *

In the third Test, played at the SCG in Sydney (6-11 January 1973), Pakistan again got into a winning position but still lost the match. The Australians made five changes to the side that played in Melbourne, trying out players who might make the team for the Caribbean tour. They dropped Thomson after just the single Test to bring Massie back. Stackpole returned as the opener to partner Redpath. Ross Edwards and Doug were back in the team, replacing Sheahan and John Benaud.

By this time, Sheahan and Mallett had indicated their unavailability for the tour for personal reasons. They knew that there was no money in cricket. Sheahan was a school teacher and focused on building his teaching career. Mallett took up a job as a journalist in a newspaper, which he preferred over selling advertisements (Mallett 2008: 206).

Ian Chappell insisted that Doug be recalled in preparation for the West Indies tour. Dropping O'Keeffe, the selectors chose John Watkins, the NSW leg-spinner, as the side's only spinner. This was the only Test Watkins ever played. However, a few months later, he went to the Caribbean with two other leg-spinners, O'Keeffe and Jenner.

Batting first, Australia scored 334 in the first dig, with Redpath (79), Ross Edwards (69) and Ian Chappell (43) scoring the bulk of runs. Batting at No. 6, behind Edwards, was not Doug's usual position. He was subdued, batting for an hour before being bowled by Asif for only 19. The two Pakistani pacemen, Sarfraz Nawaz (4/54) and Salim Altaf (3/71) bowled better and thrived under Australian conditions.

The Pakistanis replied with 360, led by Mushtaq's brilliant 121 and an enterprising knock from Asif (65). Massie took 3/123 on what turned out to be his final test. Lillee delivered only 10 overs before leaving with his back problem. Greg Chappell took most of the wickets with his medium-pacers on the greenish wicket (5/61).

In Australia's second inning, Salim (4/60) and Sarfraz (4/56) swung the ball on a helpful SCG wicket, bowling the hosts out in just 53 overs for 184. Doug was lbw to Salim for six. Australia was 8-101 at one stage, and if not for the brave rear-guard by No. 11, Massie (42), and the all-rounder, No. 9, Watkins (36), they would have been humiliated.

Pakistanis only needed 159 to win. But they somehow got into a 'tangle' with Max Walker, who produced an exceptional spell. After Lillee and Massie broke open the innings, Walker took over. In his last 30 balls, Walker's mesmerising spell gave him five wickets, ending with 6/15 in 16 overs. Only Zaheer (47) batted with determination in this strange innings, as Pakistan collapsed for 106 in just 46 overs.

Lillee returned to aid his team and bowled non-stop for 23 overs at a reduced pace, taking 3/68. The Australians, who faced defeat, were ecstatic. Most commentators said such a star-studded team's collapse could only be explained by disunity in the dressing room.

* * *

The series showed that Pakistanis were beaten by the better-acclimated home team. They were not helped by poor fielding, erratic bowling and disunity within the team. The batting was sometimes brilliant but inconsistent. The team was dubbed unkindly as *'Panikistan'* by the Melbourne Age (Hutchinson and Ross 1997: 404).

Intikhab, as captain, tried hard to maintain cohesion in the dressing room as the team struggled with the busy schedule. He performed creditably, scoring 237 at 38, but had poor returns for his bowling (four wickets at 77). Intikhab was replaced by Majid as captain after the tour ended. The unfair sacking of Intikhab displeased me immensely.

Pakistan made Australia fight to such an extent that they appeared probable winners of the last two Tests until the end of each game in the 1972-73 series. In the end, Australia won the series, taking all three Tests. Inadequate preparation time and playing three Tests in successive weeks in separate States were found to be too demanding for both teams. Both captains complained about the arduous itinerary.

Imran Khan (1988: 130) was heavily critical of the Pakistan team's performances in Australia on that tour. He said that the team wilted under pressure quickly, even from winning positions, because of a 'negative attitude'. They were not used to winning. Imran also stated that most Pakistani players were self-centred, worried too much about personal failures (Zaheer was the example he showed) and always put their own performances ahead of the team's interest.

The expectations of a large, cricket-mad population at home affected Pakistani cricketers. The insecurity of erratic selections may have been a factor. The captains were also too defensive for fear of losing. Nonetheless, for Pakistan, the defeat in Australia was painful.

Although several players excelled, the tour was marred by dissent within the team. This was mainly caused by the interference of the Pakistan Board of Control President – Abdul Hafeez Kardar (Oborne 2014: 236-238). The way Saeed Ahmed, a veteran of 40-odd Tests, was sent home for claiming that he was not fit enough to play in the third Test destabilized the team and affected its morale greatly.

Peter Oborne documented in *The Wounded Tiger* (2014: 236-238) how Kardar interfered with the team with dictatorial decisions conveyed via telegrams from Pakistan. The messages confused the team and undermined its cohesion. Kardar was Pakistan's first Test captain in 1952. He drew power from his friendship with Zulfikar Ali Bhutto, Pakistan's President (1971-73) and then Prime Minister (1973-77).

The mercurial Kardar terminated Intikhab's reign as captain by telegram and appointed the up-coming star – Majid Khan, a Cambridge Blue. Majid was taken completely by surprise when he heard the news. Majid lasted only one home season and was again replaced by Intikhab for the next season before Mushtaq became Pakistan's captain in 1975. They were undoubtedly tumultuous times in Pakistan cricket.

However, Wilkins (1974) noted that the Australian leg of the tour provided the Pakistanis with the experience of being well-armed on the second leg of their tour to New Zealand. Battling the Kiwis, Pakistanis drew the three Tests 1-1. The tour also proved that Pakistan would soon beat Australia, in Australia. They achieved that in their next tour in 1976-77 under Mushtaq's aggressive and astute captaincy.

Mallett (2008: 206) said that Doug was back on the big stage, although he didn't do much in the third Test. Ian Chappell wanted him for the Caribbean Tour because he knew Doug's genius on slow, turning pitches. Ian also knew that Doug was due to get some Test runs sooner than later and was a great 'team player' to have on tour.

Battling the West Indies in the Caribbean (1973)

Ian Chappell's charges to the West Indies in 1973 were unproven. The team appeared strong in the pace department. Max Walker and Jeff Hammond backed up the Lillee-Massie combination, which had triumphed over England the previous summer.

But the events turned out differently. Massie didn't play a single Test, ending his career with only the six Tests he had played before the tour. Lillee was a shadow of the fast bowler who had taken 31 wickets in the 1972 Ashes only six months before and played only in the first Test. The stress fractures in his put him out of business (Blofeld 1974).

Garry Sobers, 36 years of age, was recovering from a knee injury, pain in one shoulder due to a floating bone and an eye infection. As he refused to undergo a fitness test, the selectors omitted him, declaring that Sobers hadn't proven his fitness and a new captain had to be found. So it was the Guyanese-born, Rohan Kanhai. Where Sobers had a laissez-faire attitude to captaincy, Kanhai was a disciplinarian. He was also determined to build a competitive team (Manley 1988: 204).

The absence of Sobers took the edge off the series (McGilvray 1985: 163). Sobers refused a fitness test and argued with the West Indies Board of Control for Cricket, stirring a hornet's nest in the Caribbean. The Prime Minister of Trinidad and various others tried to persuade the great man to comply with the Board's request.

Sobers defended his position, saying that his record was such that 'if he said he was fit, that should be good enough'. By this time, Sobers had an incredible unbroken run of 85 consecutive Test appearances for the Windies. He had also been the captain in the last 39 of those.

Lloyd (1983: 61-62) wrote that he was almost left out of the 1973 series against Australia for not playing in the Shell Shield back at home. At the time, Lloyd was playing for South Melbourne in Australia, and a few months earlier, he had been in England playing for Lancashire.

In that account, Lloyd recalled how the Guyanese Prime Minister, Forbes Burnham, took an unusual step by writing to the Australian Prime Minister, Gough Whitlam, to use influence and have South Melbourne release him. This was successful, and Lloyd returned in time to play a few Shell Shield games and be eligible for selection. By this time, the West Indies Chairman of selectors, Jeffrey Stollmeyer, had written to Lloyd to be on 'stand-by' in case Sobers didn't make it.

* * *

In the first Test at Sabina Park, Kingston, Jamaica (16-21 February 1973), Australia declared 7-428. Stackpole (44), Redpath (46), Greg Chappell (42), Edwards (63), Doug (72) and Marsh (97) did the scoring. On day one, Gibbs throttled them; they scored only 4-190. But on day two, Doug and Marsh cut loose. Doug hit 13 fours in his inning, and Marsh slammed 17 fours. Gibbs bowled 41 overs for 4/81.

The Windies replied with exactly the same score of 428, with the Jamaican Maurice Foster making 125 and joining a select band of debut centurions. Kanhai (84), Lawrence Rowe (76) and Kallicharran (50) also batted well for the home side. Max Walker (6/114) and Jeff Hammond (4/79) shared the wickets. Despite suffering back strain, Lillee bowled 26 overs for 112 but went wicketless.

Batting a second time, Australia was not in danger of defeat as the Windies pacemen (Vanburn Holder, Uton Dowe and Maurice Foster) were simply non-threatening. Stackpole belted a century (142 in four hours, with 22 fours and two sixes), and Chappell made a token declaration at 2-260. The West Indies batted out the time (3-67), and the match was drawn with honours going even to both sides.

Uton Dowe, the Jamaican fast bowler, was prone to being wildly erratic. Stackpole mauled him in both innings to such an extent that the crowd erected banners proclaiming an 11th Commandment: *'Dowe shalt not bowl'*, a joking insult, well-reported in the news worldwide.

* * *

The second Test, played at the Kensington Oval, Bridgetown, Barbados (9-14 February 1973), was also drawn. Australia batted first, making 324. Greg Chappell (106), Ian Chappell (72) and Marsh (78) steadied the inning. Gibbs dismissed Doug for just a single. A 19-year-old left-arm spinner, Elquemedo Willet, debuted for the Windies. He was the first cricketer from the Leeward Islands (Nevis) to play Test cricket. But Willet had meagre returns of 2/124 in the two innings.

The West Indies replied with 391, which included a subdued Rohan Kanhai century (105). He batted down the order at No. 5 and ensured safety for the West Indies; Kanhai struck 11 fours and a six. This was after a belligerent knock by the opener Roy Fredericks (98 with 12 fours and a six). Derryk Murray, the wicket-keeper, made 90 and had a 165-run stand with Kanhai for the seventh wicket. Without Lillee, Max Walker led the attack for Australia, and his 5-wicket haul for 57 and Terry Jenner's 3/65 contained the West Indies.

In the second innings, Australia batted yet again with fortitude. Stackpole made a solid half-century (53), but Redpath was painfully slow in making 20 over three hours. Coming together at 2-108, Ian Chappell (106*) and Doug (102*) had a huge unbroken stand of 192 in even time. Each struck 15 fours and a six. This allowed Chappell to declare at 2-300. Having watched Doug's batting from the other end in the second inning, here is what Ian Chappell said to me:

Doug Walters is the best player of spin bowling I've ever seen. If you look at his record. In his first two test centuries, they had Allan and Titmus on the side, you know? Good, good off-spin bowlers. I saw him get 100 in a session in Trinidad against Lance Gibbs. Fine off-spinner...

And he got a century on a minefield in Madras. Then, that was against Prasanna. So yeah, on his day. He didn't just survive against good off-spinners. He belted him...He didn't just come down the wicket. He wasn't a three-paces-down-the-wicket player.

Yeah, but he was very quick on his feet. If he came out, he came out quickly. If he went back, he went back quickly and didn't just go straight back. Sometimes, he would go back a little bit towards the legside and make room.

I hear commentators say you don't cut off spin against the spin. It's the greatest sort of bollocks I've ever heard. Because Doug could cut off spinners... you see, that's the art of footwork. Footwork gets you into a position where you hit the ball, where you want to hit it, not where the bowler wants you to hit it...The bowler will place a field. So that you're hitting the ball to his field. But the idea of batting is to get into a position where you can hit the ball into the gaps, and that's what Doug was very good at.

There was one sequence that sums Doug up. Lance Gibbs was bowling to him in Trinidad when he got 100 in the session. There was a big hole right where an offspinner likes to bowl, and the ball might do anything out. Often, it might jump, turn might go along the ground, anything might happen...

Gibbs was very good at bowling accurately, and he had a 6-3 field, three on the off and six on the on-side, but he had no mid-wicket. Gibbsy pitched roughly where the hole was. Doug got quickly onto the back foot, and he hit him for four through midwicket. Gibbsy moved his field. He took point and put him over at midwicket on the fence. So he's now got 7-2.

The next ball landed in virtually the same place, and Doug went back to the left side and cut it straight where the guy had come from at point, and it went for four. And Gibbs, he got the ***s and brought the guy back and put him at point, and Doug hit the next ball, virtually pitched again in a similar place to midwicket for four.

Gibbsy just threw his hands in the air and said, "How do you bowl to this guy?" But that was Doug. If he was playing really well, he could manipulate the field.

Although Ian praised Doug's batting in Australia's second inning, McGilvray (1985: 162) acclaimed Ian Chappell's daring batting against Gibbs, in particular, in which he danced down the wicket frequently to attack. The batting of both Ian and Doug must have frustrated the vastly experienced Gibbs because of how they placed their shots. As Ian said, Doug pierced the field easily and frequently by using his feet and hitting the off-spinner to various places left vacant by a fielder who had just been moved. The Windies had only 19 overs to bat and replied with 0-36 in the drawn match.

* * *

Australia went one up in the third Test at the Queen's Park Oval in Port of Spain, Trinidad (23-28 March 1973). On the spin-friendly wicket, three West Indian spinners operated: the wrist-spinner Inshan Ali, Lance Gibbs, the off-spinner and Elquemedo Willet, a left-arm orthodox spinner. Keith Boyce was the only fast-medium bowler in the home team's attack, backed up by Clive Lloyd and Maurice Foster.

Batting first, Australia lost Stackpole for a duck, but Redpath (66) and Greg Chappell (56) took the score to 2-108 when Greg fell just before lunch, caught off Gibbs. It was three minutes to lunch when Doug walked in at No. 4. He went on to make another remarkable century (112), getting Australia to a score of 332. Doug was imperious, hitting 16 fours and a six in an inning that lasted only two hours and 28 minutes. Ian Chappell recalled how Doug belted the first ball he faced from Gibbs to the boundary:

> *I'd sprained my ankle, so I batted at six. Greg batted at three. Doug batted at four...Greg got out in the last over before lunch to Lance Gibbs off the second ball. So that meant there were four balls to start, you know, straight after lunch, and Doug came in, and as I said, there was this spot on the pitch, and Gibbsy used to just run up and come at it.*
>
> *Doug cover drove his first ball for four, which is the hardest shot on a turning track...the right-hander cover driving an offspinner...He was 102 at tea, so he got 100 in the. Session.*

The uneven and spin-friendly wicket was challenging to play strokes on with close-in fielders ready to catch. Yet, in the two hours between lunch and tea, Doug scored precisely 100, using his feet to attack the spinners. In the *Wisden* report, Blofeld (1974) said, 'It was a magnificent inning and the best of the series' in which Doug's 'driving was glorious, and he cut and pulled with power and certainty'. Gibbs (3/79) and Inshan Ali (3/89) were the main wicket takers.

The West Indies replied cautiously. Kanhai (56) and Kallicharran (53) made half-centuries. Murray (40) batted responsibly again as the Windies replied with 280, reducing the deficit to only 52. Jenner took 4/98 in 38 overs. The Australians also batted carefully in the second inning, scoring 281 on the wearing pitch. Ian moved back to his No. 3 spot and made 97; Redpath (44) and Doug (32) batted well when it seemed like the Windies spinners would win them the match. Gibbs took 5/102 in 48 overs.

Chasing 333 to win, the Windies were in a strong position at 3-219. Fredericks (76) and Kallicharran (91) batted well at the top. However, the rest failed to apply themselves as they collapsed to 289. O'Keeffe's spin (4/57) and Walker's tireless bowling (3/43) ensured the Australian victory by 44 runs. The West Indies were not helped by an injury to Lawrence Rowe, who didn't bat in either inning.

* * *

The fourth Test was played at the Bourda grounds in Georgetown, Guyana (6-11 April 1973). After winning the toss for the first time, the Windies scored 366. Batting at home, Clive Lloyd made 178 with 24 fours and a six, 'an absolutely commanding inning' (Manley 1988: 205). Blofeld (1974) said Lloyd's inning was of immense value, but 'it didn't contain the power or the variety of stroke common to his batting...he was never wholly at ease, and yet he stuck to his task'.

The fourth Test was also a significant match in Doug's career as he took his only five-wicket haul in Test cricket (5/66 in 18.2 overs). Doug's ability as a partnership-breaker was well-proven in the match as he helped restrain the Windies to 366. Australia replied with 341, with Ian Chappell (109) and Greg (51) at the top of the order.

Then, Doug made 81 and got close to what might have been a record-breaking three centuries in a row. Sadly, this was not to be. Blofeld (1974) reported another 'superb innings by Walters, whose footwork against the spinners was a joy to watch'. The tireless efforts of Gibbs (3/67 in 35 overs.) and Boyce (3/69) restricted the visitors.

The Windies were ahead in the first innings by 25 runs. But they collapsed for 109 runs in the second inning, playing recklessly. The collapse was caused by Walker taking 4/45 in 23.3 overs, while Hammond took 4/38. Used as a partnership-breaker, Doug chipped in with 2/23 runs, bowling 13 overs. Doug jokingly complained later to Ian that 'it is bloody time that you realised that I am a match-winner'.

Stackpole and Redpath knocked off the runs easily (0-135), and Australia won by 10 wickets. The Windies were humiliated. Every prime minister of the islands saw the collapse. Michael Manley (1988: 206), the Jamaican Prime Minister, said that the Guyanese Prime Minister, Forbes Burnham, even adjourned the Heads-of-Government meeting so that the leaders could see their team bat. Lloyd (1983: 64) said, 'The defeat threw West Indies cricket into melancholy'. The stands were empty when the team returned to Trinidad for the final Test. The ever-faithful public deserted their squad. Australians were 2-nil up at this stage.

* * *

The fifth Test was played at the same venue as the third Test (Queen's Park Oval) in Port of Spain, Trinidad (21-26 April 1973). Winning the toss for the fourth time in the series, Australia batted. With the series already won, the Australians accumulated runs slowly and reached 8-419. No one scored a century.

But Doug made a solid 70 (with eighth fours), while Ross Edwards (74), Ian Chappell and Marsh (56 each) and Greg Chappell (41) contributed strongly. The wickets were shared by the home team's spinners: Gibbs bowled 52 overs, taking 3/114; Inshan Ali (44 overs for 3/124) and Raphick Jumadeen, another slow, left-arm spinner from Trinidad (40 overs, taking 2/89) also did a lot of bowling.

The Windies reply (319) was anchored by Fredericks (73) and Lloyd (59). Walker (5/75) and Jenner (5/90) shared the wickets. Australian declared the second inning at 7-218, with Ian (37), John Benaud (36) and Doug (27) holding the innings together. Gibbs again did the bulk of the bowling (4/85), taking 26 in the series and 238 in all Tests.

Asked to make 313 in four and a half hours, the Windies played it safe (5-135) to draw the game. Ensuring his team didn't lose, Kanhai blocked for 100 minutes and, in the end, was 16*.

* * *

For the West Indies, there was no actual pace attack. Keith Boyce, the Barbadian all-rounder who bowled fast-medium, headed the attack in the last four Tests. He took nine wickets at 37. Gibbs claimed a series tally of 26 wickets at 26. Kanhai (358 runs at 51), Fredericks (381 runs at 42), Lloyd (287 runs at 59), Kallicharran (294 runs at 37), and Foster (262 runs at 43) batted responsibly but were not outstanding.

By the time the Australian tour was over, the Windies had gone for 20 Tests without a victory. They appeared to lack confidence in their ability to succeed in front of their crowds. In every match they played, the Windies had their moments but took the route of safety.

Issues destabilising the team included disagreements about Sobers's non-inclusion and Lloyd's delayed entry to the team. Reports said that the Windies feared losing a match because of the possibility of crowd rioting, as seen before. Beating the Windies by a margin of 2-0 showed that Chappell's men played with more resolve than the home side.

Ian (542 runs at 77) and Doug (497 runs at 71) topped the averages. Redpath, Stackpole, Greg Chappell and Marsh all averaged above 40. Walker was the most outstanding bowler with 26 wickets at 20. Jeff Hammond also bowled well, claiming 15 wickets at 32.

It was clear that the West Indies were in a rebuilding stage. Manley (1988: 206) said that Kanhai's disciplined approach showed positive signs that the team was on the right track, especially with the promise of the Guyanese left-handers – Fredericks and Kallicharran. However, the series revealed that Kanhai's captaincy was often too defensive.

On several occasions, when things began to go wrong, his instinct was to fall back on defence rather than look for ways to dismiss the opponents. In contrast to Kanhai's approach, Ian Chappell always tried to dismiss his opponents somehow (Blofeld 1974).

* * *

Ian Chappell said that Doug's century in a session at Port-of-Spain in the third Test of the 1972–73 series was the best Test century he had seen against a turning ball on a treacherous wicket (Mallett 2008: 2). 'Doug was the best player of off-spin bowling I have ever seen' was Ian's opening remark when I interviewed him.

Ian highlighted the Port-of-Spain inning and other times when Doug showed his exceptional skill, especially against the West Indian spinners on spin-friendly wickets. Doug also bowled well on the Test, taking seven wickets in the series at 14. After the failures in England, returning to form on an overseas tour was crucial for Doug.

McGilvray (1985: 161) paid tribute to Max Walker in his book, *The Game is Not the Same*, in a chapter titled '*The Achievers*'. Alan said Walker's 'awkward action unwinds like a windmill at the end', which earned him the nickname 'Tangles'. Alan said that people like Walker rise above the rest because they are 'real achievers and ultimate competitors on whom great teams are built'.

McGilvray (1985: 161) described that before the fourth Test in which Walker bowled Australia to victory, he saw that Max's feet were raw and bloody and advised him not to play. But Max responded, saying, 'Somebody has to do it, mate'. With his bleeding feet packed in foam rubber, Walker bowled 38 overs in the first inning and 24 in the second. The performance typified the outlook of the side. Walker's effort was 'true grit'. Regarding Ian's leadership, McGilvray said:

> Chappell was at his absolute best in the series, moulding a relatively unlikely bunch into a winning outfit. It was a tour in which skilful improvisation won the day. Ian managed to drag the best out of everybody.

It hardly seemed possible for Australia to win a series in the West Indies without Lillee and Massie, who were such a formidable pair in England just a few months earlier. Despite this, Ian's side was impressive in defeating the Windies in the third and fourth Tests.

Chappell's charges won because, collectively and individually, the players refused to accept defeat until it became a fact. On the other hand, the temperamental flaws of the home team caused more to their defeat than any technical shortfalls. Blofeld (1974) noted that in the West Indies, interterritorial rivalries often work to defeat the objective of producing the best available West Indies side.

The series represented the end of an era for the West Indies in that Sobers, who had been their captain since Worrell, didn't play. The Australians were handicapped by Lillee's injured back. Lillee had come to the West Indies as the world's fastest bowler. Lillee found no pace on the Caribbean pitches. He played in the first Test at Sabina Park, didn't take a wicket, but gave away a hundred runs. Blofeld (1974) wrote that Lillee was 'A pale imitation of the tearaway fast bowler he had been in England'.

The series established Lloyd as the most likely candidate to captain the West Indies after Kanhai. Lloyd sometimes sparkled with the bat, including the brilliant 178 in his home ground in Guyana, but struggled at other times, especially against the spinners. By his own account, Lloyd didn't like how he had to struggle to get back into the team.

But, taking over as captain, Lloyd led his team to a phase of unmatched world dominance. During his captaincy, the Windies won the ODI Cricket World Cup twice (1975 and 1979) and narrowly lost it to India in 1983. Lloyd played 110 Test matches between 1966 and 1985, scoring 7,515 runs with 19 centuries.

He also played 87 ODIs, making 1,977 runs with a best score of 102 in the 1975 World Cup final against Australia at Lord's. Nicknamed 'Supercat' because of his fielding prowess, Clive Hubert Lloyd, a dashing and dynamic batter and a brilliant fielder, is among the most respected cricketers in the West Indies and globally.

CHAPTER 10

Runs Win Matches

In his foreword to Mallett's book on Doug, Ian Chappell called Doug a 'great' player. He qualified the statement by describing that Doug belted a Test century in a session three times and repeated the feat even against a Rest of the World Xi team. 'Other than Bradman, no one else has surpassed these amazing feats. As the captain of a player with such extraordinary match-winning qualities, one tends to appreciate his contribution'.

'Doug was very good in the middle-order, often coming in at No. 5 or 6 and occasionally, at No. 4. He did his job well; if things were going well, he carried on the good work; in times of adversity, he helped his side out of trouble, carrying considerable responsibility. But he was his own man. He did it in his own way, as he had the skill, technique and confidence in his ability, which are great assets of a genuine batting all-rounder'.

Typically, like Bradman, Trumper or Sobers, Doug did not 'just' make a Test century in a session. He contrived extra drama on the field. That last ball six – Doug casually hooking a Bob Willis bouncer out of the ground in the Perth Test 1974 – was one example of this incredible talent. 'Timing is everything', so they say in every aspect of cricket. Timing was a critical element in Doug's batting and bowling.

His peers recognized that Doug wasn't interested in hanging around and plodding. He was the antithesis to accumulators like Boycott, Barrington, and Gavaskar, to name a few of the best players in the modern game regarding both total runs scored and their impact on protecting their team's position.

Doug's attacking style of cricket was also different from that of his teammates – Lawry and Simpson- and was closer to the attacking instincts of Ian and Greg Chappell. They often dictated to the bowlers instead of being dictated to. They all had the temperament and patience to read the match situation and adjust their strokeplay.

There was never a dull moment when Doug was batting. He always wanted to move things along and preferred to 'score or get out'. In that sense,

Doug had a more carefree attitude than the two Chappells with whom he played a great deal of cricket. Perhaps it was a weakness in Doug that great bowlers like Underwood exploited. They knew Doug would take risks even with the moving ball. Many of Walters' innings brought admiring crowds to their feet even as he walked to the crease.

It would be an error to think that runs did not matter to Doug; they did. But how the runs were made, and the team's position was far more important to him. Commentators often call Doug a Match-Winner. Any analysis of Doug's batting record would show that by consistently scoring quickly and methodically, Doug frequently got the team into a winning position within a short period, an hour or so of batting, a point that has been repeatedly attested to by Ian Chappell.

* * *

In the summer of 1973-74, Bradman instigated a change in the name of the governing body of cricket in Australia. The Australian Board of Control for International Cricket became The Australian Cricket Board. The word control wasn't acceptable by then (Mallett, 2008: 216). Since the Board's formation in 1905, its 'control' over the players sometimes reached absurd levels, such as the players' wives having to travel and live separately on overseas tours.

Bradman sensed a player revolution in the air, mainly after the tour to India in 1969-70. The players also refused to play a fifth Test match in South Africa at the end of that gruelling six-month tour. Also, Ian Chappell, who didn't always see eye-to-eye with Bradman, was now the undisputed captain of Australia.

Battles across the Tasman - New Zealand 1973-74

New Zealand's first major tour of Australia on a Test campaign in 1973-74 was a belated recognition of the Kiwis by the Australians (*Wisden* 1975a). Kiwis have never forgiven Australia for this slight.

The first-ever Test Australia played in New Zealand was in March 1946, when the visitors won by innings and 103 runs, bowling out the home side for 42 and 54 in reply to their score of 8-199. The match was over in two days. Since then, Australia deemed that the cricket in New Zealand wasn't up to the standard in other Test-playing countries.

New Zealand also toured Australia in 1967 and played matches with various states and an Australian XI. Still, it wasn't allowed a Test match. Although Kiwis had gained Test status in 1930, the Australians believed they were 'not good enough' to play Tests against Australia. Since then, the Kiwis bore a grudge against the 'older sibling' for not taking them too seriously in cricket and everything else. The two countries shared Britain as a common parent.

* * *

Australia played three Tests with the visiting Kiwis in the summer of 1973-74, followed by a visit to New Zealand for three more 'return' Tests in March 1974 (*Wisden* 1975 a, b). The Kiwis were known as the 'gentlemen' of cricket. Despite having some outstanding cricketers, they also never showed too much confidence in their abilities since the days of John Reid, the former captain (from 1955-65) and Bert Sutcliffe, the prolific left-hander who played from 1947 to 1965.

I didn't catch any Test broadcasts in New Zealand as they were not relayed to Asia. However, I followed the series via the daily newspaper reports. Bevan Congdon, one of New Zealand's finest all-rounders, captained the side in the twin series. Congdon was a reserved and thoughtful man. His personality completely contrasted with the rugged, vocal, aggressive Australian captain, Ian Chappell.

In the Australian leg of the series, the home team won by 2-0. In the return leg, the Kiwis won the second Test in New Zealand, beating Australia for the first time in their history, tying the series 1-all. The twin series saw ups and downs for both sides.

After their recent successes, Ian's side established a pattern of competitiveness, which the Kiwis matched with spirited displays. The battles across the Tasman Sea are fought with such intensity that they always spark great interest. The intense rivalry between the two Nations continues, not just in cricket but also in sports like rugby.

* * *

Australia won the first Test played at the MCG (29 December 1973 to 2 January 1974) easily by an inning and 25 runs. Gary Gilmour, a left-arm swing bowler from NSW, debuted for Australia. In a tour game, New Zealand's prolific run-getter, Glenn Turner, broke a finger. But Turner played in the Test, opening the inning only to be hit again on the hand by the Australian paceman, Tony Dell. Turner couldn't bat in the second inning and was forced to miss the second Test.

A Keith Stackpole century (122 with 13 fours) led the score as Australia rattled up 8-482 and declared. Doug made 79 in two hours, with nine fours. Half-centuries came from Ian Chappell (54), Greg Chappell (60) and Gilmour (52). The Kiwis dropped several catches, including dropping

Stackpole four times before he reached 50. Dayle Hadlee bowled well to take 4/102.

The Kiwi reply was 237. Ken Wadsworth, the wicket-keeper, made a resolute 80, and John Morrison made 44, but Gilmour (4/75) broke through at crucial times. Chappell enforced the follow-on, and batting poorly, the Kiwis were all out for just 200 runs.

Doug bowled well in the second innings, taking the first three wickets to fall, ending up with 3/26 in 13 overs. Mallett and O'Keeffe took match bags of 6/109 and 4/91, respectively. Gilmour announced that he could become a valuable all-rounder for Australia with his score of 52 and his first-inning wickets. Glenn Turner's experience was sorely missed by the Kiwis, and they requested backup. Jeremy Coney, a tall, right-handed batting all-rounder and a future New Zealand captain, arrived in time for the second Test.

* * *

In the second Test in Sydney (SCG, 5-10 January 1974), rain robbed New Zealand of a certain win. Sent into bat on a wet day, the opener, John Parker, made a century (108), steadying the Kiwi inning. Fighting knocks in the middle order came from Ken Wadsworth (54) and 21-year-old debutant Jeremy Coney (45), which helped New Zealand reach 312. As Gilmour and Walker struggled, Doug bowled 11 over as the second change. He took 4/39, picking up the first three wickets to fall consecutively for the second time in his career.

On the rain-affected second day, the Kiwi seamers bowled out Australia for a low 162. Only Ian Chappell (45) and Doug (41) batted well in the overcast conditions. Richard Hadlee took 4/33, while his brother, Dayle, captured 3/52. Rain washed out the third day's play.

The Kiwis batted with resolve in the second inning, enjoying a lead of 150 runs. Resolute batting by John Morrison (117) in only his second Test and Brian Hastings (83) allowed New Zealand to rattle up 9/305 and declare, making a bid to win the match. Walker didn't bowl in the second inning (groin injury), and Greg Chappell took the new ball with Gilmour. Each took three wickets.

Australia was 2-30 and on the ropes by the end of day four, with Richard Hadlee threatening to break through. However, the weather gods intervened and washed out the final day. The match confounded the critics as the Kiwis showed their mettle in matching the stronger Australian side, playing at home (*Wisden* 1975a).

* * *

Rain washed out one full day (day four) in the third Test (Adelaide Oval, 26-31

January 1974). But Australia won easily with an innings and 57 runs. Injuries to Walker and Gilmour allowed Geoff Dymock, from Queensland, and Alan Hurst, from Victoria, to lead the Australian attack. Having recovered from the hand injury, Glenn Turner returned to open for New Zealand.

Winning the toss, Australia scored 477. Doug was imperious, smashing 94 in just over two hours, hitting eight fours and two sixes (I bet he was looking for another century in one session). Marsh made his second Test century (132 with nine fours). He was helped by four dropped catches. O'Keeffe scored his highest Test score (85), and Greg Chappell scored 42, while poor fielding did not help the Kiwis.

The Kiwis replied with 218 in the first inning, with only Wadsworth (48) and Morrison (40) resisting. O'Keeffe took 3/55. Following on, 259 behind, Dymock's left-arm swing (5/58) destroyed the Kiwis, and they were bowled out for 202. Only the captain, Congdon, defied the bowlers, carrying his bat to 71*. Ultimately, it was a tense victory in the final hour on a rain-disrupted final day. O'Keeffe picked up another 3/51, proving his worth as an all-rounder.

The tour successes were most notably Ken Wadsworth, with both batting and wicket-keeping and the newcomer, Jeremy Coney, especially in slip-fielding. Dropped slip catches let the Kiwis down many times at crucial times. Centuries from Parker and Morrison also proved that the Kiwis had the talent to be a competitive Test side.

The Hadlee brothers carried the weight of New Zealand's bowling attack. Richard, the quicker, and Dayle, the more subtle, were quite formidable in the Sydney Test and used the conditions far more cleverly than the Australians. The players were also good ambassadors who helped reset the relations between the two countries. The Australians appreciated Congdon as a forward-looking leader.

* * *

A few weeks later, the Australians toured New Zealand for the return series of three Tests. The island's cricketers have always been quiet achievers. The zenith of their efforts came on 13 March 1974, when they beat Australia for the first time at their sixth attempt.

New Zealand had twice come very close to victory against England in 1973. At Sydney, only a few weeks earlier, they had been robbed by the rain of an almost certain win. So, the victory in Christchurch was the fruit of a long endeavour to sharpen their cricket (*Wisden* 1975b). It was a panacea for New Zealand and its cricket fans, who had been starved of success in the Test arena.

The highlights of the first Test at Basin Reserve in Wellington (1-5 March 1974) were an imperious Greg Chappell double century (247*) in under six hours, with 30 fours and a six) and a colossal stand the Chappell brothers put together (264 for the third wicket). Ian made 145 in just four hours off 207 balls, including 17 fours and a six. Greg took much less time, belting his first century in two and a half hours off 160 balls. *Wisden* (1975b) reported that nothing in the series compared to the mastery of strokes played by Greg on that day. Doug made 32 as Australia declared with a formidable total of 6-511, scoring at a rate of 4.8 runs per over. None of the Kiwi bowlers bowled well.

New Zealand also took advantage of a placid pitch when they replied with 484. For his sixth Test century, Congdon batted for seven hours (132 with 14 fours). Hastings also hit a century (101), while Turner (79) and John Morrison (66) made half-centuries. The Congdon-Hastings stand (229) was the third-highest in Tests for any wicket by Kiwis (*Wisden* 1975b). Walker took 3/107 and Dymock 3/77 as the Australian bowlers also toiled.

The Chappell brothers were again in spectacular form in the second innings, thumping centuries. This time, Ian struck 121 (13 fours and a six), while Greg made 133 in three hours, striking 18 fours. Redpath missed out on a hundred (93). Doug was dismissed cheaply for eight.

Without seeking a win, Australia batted out the time to reach 8-460, ending the match with a draw. The match total of 1,455 runs was a record for a Test match in New Zealand. The Chappell brothers scored 646 in the game for three dismissals, setting up a new record. With their twin centuries, the brothers also joined a select band of Australians who scored centuries in both innings of a single Test [33].

* * *

New Zealand recorded its first historic win against Australia in the second Test at Lancaster Park, in Christchurch (8-13 March 1974) in a low-scoring match. Although the game was mired in controversy, it was a fascinating contest until the last hour.

It was reported that no New Zealander had ever taken part in a more thrilling Test (*Wisden* 1975b). The win for the Kiwis was set up by a century in each inning by Glenn Turner, who had been playing for Worcestershire since 1964. He scored 101 and 110* in the match and became the first Kiwi to score twin centuries in a Test.

The Test also belonged to the Hadlee brothers, Dayle and Richard, the

---

33 The others, up to that time, were Warren Bardsley (1949), Arthus Morris (1946-47), Don Bradman (1947-48), Jack Moroney (1949-50), Bob Simpson (1964-65) and Doug himself, in 1969 against the West Indies.

two right-arm, fast-medium seamers. They combined to take 12 wickets between them in the match. In Australia's second inning, Richard took 4/71, while Dayle took 4/75, breaking through at crucial times. The two seamers bowled confidently on a home strip in helpful conditions, which yielded movement and a brisk but even bounce.

The match was affected by rain. After winning the toss, Congdon sent Australia into bat. The tourists scored only 223, with Redpath grinding out 71 and Marsh (38) being the leading scorers. Doug was dismissed for just six runs, bowled by Richard Hadlee (3/59). Richard Collinge, the tall left-armer, took 3/79, and Congdon, with his gentle medium pacers, chipped in with 3/11.

The Kiwi reply hinged on Turner's 101 made in nearly five hours. Others lingered around him long enough for the Kiwis to reach 255, a valuable lead of 32. Walker (4/60) and Dymock (3/59) bowled well on a pitch, which assisted seam bowling.

Australia had to bat well in the second inning. While Stackpole's dip in form continued, Redpath stepped up again with 58 batting for three hours. The Chappells failed this time; Ian fell for one and Greg for six. Australia was 3-33 at this stage. Ian Davis (50) steadied the inning with a 106-run stand with Redpath. Doug attacked (65 with 10 fours) to take Australia to 6-211 at the end of day three. However, after the rest day, they folded up for 259 due to Dayle Hadlee's inspired spell (4/75).

The Kiwis needed 228 for victory. They were soon subdued by Walker breaking through and were 3-62. Then came Turner's 115-run stand with Brian Hastings (46). Turner's second century (110*) took five and a half hours. Still, his landmark inning guided New Zealand to reach the target and register a five-wicket victory.

The Christchurch Test became a part of cricket history because of the historic New Zealand win and an unsavoury incident. Late on day four, Hastings hit a four, which was signalled as a six by umpire Bob Monteith. The non-striker, Turner, told the umpire that the ball had cleared the line, but the ball had actually bounced inside the ropes.

Before Monteith made a correction, Ian Chappell ran up to the umpire and protested vigorously. Doug recalled that Chappelli was a bit angry and told Turner where to get off in no uncertain manner.

In an article titled *'Beating the Big Brother'*, Turner claimed that he began to assure Ian Chappell that the error would be corrected. Monteith reversed his call to signal a four (ESPN Cricinfo 2011). But Turner alleged that Chappell abused him with some choice language and a one-digit gesture. Along with Turner, several other Kiwi players complained bitterly about the excessive sledging and abuse they received when batting, which 'exceeded the lines of decency'.

Congdon demanded an apology from the Australian camp for using abusive language. Ian refused. The Australian administrators also did not intervene. Chappell said, 'he wouldn't apologise because what happened on the field of play ended there' (Hutchinson and Ross 1997: 411). Doug disagreed with Chappell over this incident and felt he should have apologised to the Kiwis for some choice words used in the heat of the moment Mallett (2008: 220).

Neither team wanted to be seen as weak. By this time, the series had generated considerable public interest in both countries. The fierce rivalry continued as both teams carried their grudges into the next Test, which Australia had to win to square the series. This incident led the Kiwi press to tag the Australian squad as *'Ugly Australians'*. It is a derogatory reference that pops up every now and then in criticism of the hard-nosed way Australian teams play their cricket.

* * *

The third Test was played at Eden Park, Auckland (22-24 March 1974). Ian Chappell and his team were pumped up after the tensions between the two sides in the second Test. The game ended in three days on a poorly prepared pitch. Australia won by 297 runs. Eighteen wickets fell on the first day. The *Wisden* (1975b) report said Australia was saved only by an outstanding Doug Walters century.

Congdon won the toss and sent Australia to bat, expecting the pitch to bounce unevenly. The pitch was 'soft and damp' when the Test began due to some over-watering 'by mistake' by the curator and early morning dew. Although batting wasn't too difficult, the tall, left-arm seamer, Richard Collinge (5/82 in 18 overs), broke through Australia's top order as the ball often leapt from just short of good length. In the first hour, Australia was 4-37 when Doug, at No. 6, entered the arena.

The score became 5-64 before lunch. Batting assuredly, Doug made a century (104* with 15 fours) in the next two and a half hours. He was magnificent and hammered the Kiwi bowlers who didn't maintain length and direction. Mallett (2008: 221) wrote, 'This was vintage Walters and of all the players I've seen on the Test stage perhaps only he could have played that well on such a wicket'.

With Marsh (45), Doug added 86 for the sixth wicket to rescue Australia. With typical Australian spirit, Walker and Mallett lingered long enough for the last two wickets to realise 59 and for Doug to get to his century. With the pitch inflating the value of the runs, the total of 221 turned out to be a match-winning effort (*Wisden* 1975b). Congdon again bowled well and took 4/46 in ten overs.

From a position of strength, the Kiwis failed to capitalize as Richard and Dayle Hadlee bowled badly. When they pitched short, Doug square cut or pulled with fierce intent in a dazzling display. He drove effortlessly when the medium pacers pitched up (Piesse 2013b). An eyewitness, Don Neeley, a later New Zealand selector, lamented that:

> *The game was won and lost in those 75 minutes of batting mayhem from Walters and Marsh. The runs came at a giddy rate. If courage is defined as the ability to press on regardless of doubt and fear, then Walters and Marsh displayed it for all to see and admire...he [Walters] alone scored what Australia as a team should have been dismissed for.*

Doug's 104 came in 167 minutes as he pulled Australia back into the game, although they were bowled out within two sessions. Ian described it as 'an incredible piece of batting, especially on a wicket, which bounced and popped so much' (Piesse 2013b).

The batters' difficulties were highlighted when the Kiwis collapsed in the final session to 8-85. Eighteen wickets fell on the opening day. Against the pumped-up Aussie attack, Turner took the strike at the wetter end of the pitch, grinding out 41, as the Kiwis were bowled out for 112. Gilmour (5/64) and Mallett (4/22) were the leading wreckers.

When Australia batted a second time, an attacking Redpath century (159* with 20 fours) led the way to a score of 346 and a lead of 455. Batting around him, the Australians scored quickly. Ian (35), Greg (38), Marsh (47) and O'Keeffe (32) made runs. Doug was out for only five in the second inning. *Wisden* (1975b) described Redpath's inning as comparable in quality to Doug's.

Redpath became the seventh Australian batter to bat through an inning in a Test (ESPN Cricinfo 2024b). Leading by 456 runs, the Australians were unstoppable as the Kiwis were bowled out before the end of the third day for just 158. Walker reaped the rewards in the second innings for a tireless effort, taking 4/35. Australia won by a large margin of 297 runs, thus squaring the series 1-all.

* * *

With the Auckland win, in the six-Tests of the 1973-74 summer, Australia won three and lost the Christchurch encounter. *Wisden* (1975b) described that on several occasions during the tour, the batting of the Chappell brothers, Doug and Redpath, was 'masterful'. Redpath was the most reliable run-getter; Ian faded in the second half of the tour; Greg scored 380 of his 592 runs in one match.

Doug's returns were satisfying (220 runs at 44), including the classic 104* in the third Test. While the Australian batting was sometimes vulnerable, Kiwi batters fared worse after the first Test. The exception was Turner, who scored 403 runs in five innings at 101. One major disappointment of the tour for the Aussies was Stackpole, who had a miserable tour in New Zealand, scoring only 50 runs in six Test innings. He announced his retirement after returning to Australia.

Another highlight of the tour was Doug's remarkable inning in a match against Northern Districts in Hamilton towards the end. Doug made a century in the day's final session without hitting a single boundary but with great running between the wickets. Ian Chappell told me that in the inning, Doug 'hit the ball at just the right speed to pick up twos, whereas a ball hit harder would only get one run'. Doug ran the fielders ragged on that day. The unmown grass on the outfield meant that the ball didn't quite reach the boundary ropes.

Reflecting on the summer and the tour, Mallett (2008: 223) said how tough it was for an Australian cricketer in those days to hold down a job or get a company to agree to give time off without pay and then be 'paid the pittance of a rank amateur and be expected to perform like an elite professional'. Doug was luckier than others as he worked for Rothmans, who gave him leave to play cricket.

Pommie Bashing Down Under, 1974-75

By the time the 1974-75 Ashes clash began, I was studying at the University. Studies were never a distraction, as I followed cricket from early morning until the day's play ended. I used to run to the Boys' Common Room between lectures to catch the ABC broadcasts.

Often, I was the only one listening to the cricket on the radio in the Common Room. Away from home, I carried a small transistor radio as I travelled, listening to the broadcasts whenever possible. I had to hear through the speaker as there were no earphones then.

I was very much aware that the Aussies, under Ian Chappell, were now becoming a force in cricket and determined to win the crown back after drawing the previous 1972 Ashes series 2-2. By this time, Stackpole's retirement left a vacancy at the opening spot, and Massie had faded away. But Lillee was back on the side after recovering from a back injury after two years of being out of cricket.

After 36 Tests as England's captain, labelled by Bailey (1973) as the 'Keeper of Ashes', at 41, the gallant fighter – Ray Illingworth's reign ended in 1974. Looking around the counties for a captain, England gave the job to Kent's Mike Denness. Although he wasn't an automatic member of the England team, Denness had led Kent successfully and was also the vice-captain of the MCC team under Tony Lewis on the previous winter's tour to India and Pakistan in 1973. In the sub-continent, Denness acquitted himself well as a batter. He also served the team and Lewis well as the vice-captain (*Wisden* 2018).

England didn't have Geoff Boycott in the team because he had exiled himself from the tour. Boycott had indicated that he had lost his appetite for Test cricket, and the stress had become too much. Boycott's withdrawal has been attributed to him being less than impressed by being overlooked for the captaincy after Illingworth, as England selectors put their faith in Denness first and then Greig. During his self-imposed exile from international cricket, which lasted from 1974 to 1977, Boycott scored prolifically for Yorkshire.

England possessed a decent fast-bowling attack, comprised of Bob Willis, Mike Hendrick, Chris Old and Geoff Arnold, even though they omitted Snow, the hero of the previous tour. Even without Boycott, England had great hopes that the team, with prior experience in Australia, would safeguard the Ashes, which Illingworth's side had retained in the 1972 series. But it wasn't to be. Denness's touring team never had a chance, as Dennis Lillee unleashed a fearsome pace attack with his new comrade-in-arms, Jeffrey Robert Thomson.

* * *

England first saw Jeff Thomson, with his slinging action, in their tour match against Queensland but didn't think much of him. England didn't know that Thomson was under orders from Greg Chappell to rein himself in. Chappell had instructed the bowler: 'Don't show the English batters what you can do'.

Thomson admitted, 'I just toyed around and bowled within myself'. Even so, he let it rip in the second inning after Peter Lever and Bob Willis had peppered the Queensland tail with a barrage of short stuff. England was still surprised when Thomson was selected for the first Test (Williamson 2015).

He had previously played only one Test (the second Test) against Pakistan two seasons earlier and taken none for 112. So, the English appeared not worried about him when the series began. The English press also hadn't seen much of Thomson and they failed to warn the English team. As a result, they failed to warn the English team, which was getting ready for the impending clash. They thought all the talk of a fearfully fast bowler was good old Aussie propaganda. They were to get the shock of their lives!

Everyone's view of Thomson changed within a matter of hours once he started delivering his thunderbolts. With a slinging action, '*Thommo*' bowled much quicker than Lillee – as Doug described, he was very quick indeed – and on a pitch that offered some assistance, blindingly quick. Ian Chappell had told Mallett (2008: 228) that Thommo was the 'fastest bowler into the wind that he had ever seen'. It was no wonder Thomson's pace, bounce and aggression, combined with Lillee's relentless pace and accuracy, unsettled the English batters.

It was very much the *Lillee-Thomson Summer*, where the crowds bullied the English players. Often, the loud barracking from the raucous spectators called for blood to be spilt on the ground. In those days, without helmets and other protective gear, several English players feared being hit by the Lillee-Thomson barrage and getting injured. In the days before the Test, Thomson upped the hype in a TV interview when he said: 'I enjoy hitting a batter and hurting him more than getting him out. I like to see blood on the pitch' (Williamson 2015).

Film footage shows that some of the stuff was ugly and has been compared with the 'Bodyline' bowling in the 1932-33 Ashes in Australia. I was also amused when I heard the chorus of the partisan crowd giving loud support to the way Lillee and Thomson intimidated the opponents. The raucous spectators encouraged their aggression and hurricane speed, targeting the batter's bodies with barrages of well-directed bumpers. All in chorus, loudly the crowds chanted:

'*Ashes to Ashes – Dust to Dust…If Lillee don't get Ya – Thomson Must*'

Amol Rajan (2011) traced the Australian version, which he said was a bastardised version of the immortal lines the English crowds chanted in 1956 when Jim Laker spun England to the famous victory over Australia. In that series, the spin bowling pair from Surrey, Laker and Lock, often bowling in tandem, troubled the Australians greatly. The chanting, energized by the alliterative names, was:

'*Ashes to Ashes – Dust to Dust…If Laker don't get You – Lock Must.*'

Mallett (2008: 250) explained that it was the Australian cartoonist Paul Rigby who produced a wonderful image of a battered English lion in a coffin being swept through a field of beer cans, images of Lillee and Thomson bowling together in the shadow of the old SCG Members' Stand.

The cartoon carried the tagline: '*Ashes to Ashes, Dust to Dust – If Thomson Don't Get ya, Lillee Must*'.

Thomson was erratic at times but generated great speed with the unusual action. When he hit the right spots, most deliveries rose sharply from a short-of-length, making it difficult for batters. As he took 33 wickets in four and a half Tests, Thomson looked like he was on the way to breaking Arthur Mailey's longstanding record of 36 wickets in an Ashes series, which was in 1920-21. But Thomson hurt himself playing tennis on the rest day of the Adelaide Test and didn't bowl again in the Test or the remaining two Tests.

Reflecting on Ashes battles, Mark Nicholas (2023) recalled that Benaud had described Frank Tyson as the fastest bowler he had ever seen through the air. But Thomson was 'the fastest off the pitch'. Nicholas also said: 'The message of aggression and rebellion [of Lillee and Thomson] perfectly suited the age, in which popular culture and music had overtaken traditional boundaries and innate conservatism'.

I vividly recall that the world was unstable towards the end of the 1960s. Those years were dominated by the explosion of public protests against the Vietnam War, anti-communist rhetoric, the Cold War, the Civil Rights movement against slavery, rebellions and other forms of social unrest in many countries. Following these turbulent periods, the early 1970s was also a time of great social transformation. However, that decade was no less unstable.

* * *

Colin Cowdrey was flown over as a substitute batter only a few days before the second Test as several players were injured. Cowdrey, widely acknowledged as the epitome of a *cricketing gentleman*, was 42 years old. Having first toured Australia as a young man in Len Hutton's 1954 team, Cowdrey was making his sixth visit to Australia with an England touring side.

Amusingly, cricket writers noted that *Michael Colin Cowdrey* – with the initials MCC – suggested that his would be nothing but a cricketing life! Cowdrey played Test cricket for 20 years – from 1954 to 1974. At that stage, he was the first cricketer to do so. Since then, the feat has been achieved by 14 others, including Bob Simpson and Brian Close (ESPN Cricinfo 2024c) [34].

---

34 Lord Cowdrey (*Baron Cowdrey of Tonbridge*) is truly one of cricket's greatest players, not just for his elegant batting and slip fielding but also for maintaining the highest standards of cricket etiquette. He insisted on good behaviour from all his teammates and epitomized the same dignified conduct.

The MCC honoured Lord Cowdrey for his selfless service to both England and cricket, over a long period, by naming the annual lecture: *MCC Spirit of Cricket Cowdrey Lecture* – a highly anticipated event in the global cricket calendar.

Cowdrey was also the first to reach 100 catches, ending his career with 120 catches in 114 Tests. McGilvray (1985: 112) noted that Cowdrey lacked the killer instinct and was almost apologetic to the bowlers he punished. Sunil Gavaskar, the former Indian captain, delivering the third Spirit of Cricket Lecture (ESPN Cricinfo 2003) [35], paid tribute to Cowdrey, saying:

Colin showed that (cricket) could be played with great skill and grace in the toughest of conditions and against the hardest of opponents and still have a smile and appreciation for the opponent.

Six Tests were played in the 1974-75 series. The tourists were slaughtered in the first two Tests and lost the fourth and fifth Tests. England salvaged some pride by winning the sixth Test. However, Jeff Thomson, who had been terrorizing them, missed the Test with an injury on that occasion, and Lillee exited early. The series was remarkable as Australia 'brutally and unceremoniously wrenched' the Ashes urn out of England with a resounding 4-1 series win.

* * *

I distinctly recall the excitement as I waited for the series to begin. I was now in my second year at the University and quite relaxed about managing time between studies and following cricket; my wife would fondly recall that I was still quite madly in love with cricket!

The first Test was played at the Gabba in Brisbane (29 November-4 December 1974). When England batted, the Lillee-Thomson pair didn't take long to establish mastery over the batters. By this time, Lillee had recovered from the back injury that kept him out of part of the previous West Indies tour and made an effective comeback. The rain-affected pitch did not deter Thomson's pace, and he took nine wickets in the match, causing England to lose by 166 runs.

On a damp pitch, Ian Chappell courageously chose to bat first. He saw the openers – Ian Redpath and Wally Edwards fall quickly. At No. 3, Ian made a gritty 90, batting for nearly five hours on an uneven bounce pitch. His partnerships, 100 with brother Greg (58) and 97 with Ross Edwards (32), steadied the inning. With Walker hitting 41* in the end, Australia scrounged up to 309. Doug fell for three runs to Bob Willis (4/56), who led England's attack.

As the Australian tail wagged, Tony Greig, bowling briskly and generating

---

35 The *MCC Spirit of Cricket Cowdrey Lecture* is held at Lord's usually in July. The first lecture was given in 2001 by Benaud and the third, in 2003, by Sunil Gavaskar (https://en.wikipedia.org/wiki/Cowdrey_Lecture).

significant lift from his tall frame, bounced Lillee, who had hung around 40 minutes for 15 runs. The ball reared at his head, and Lillee could do no more than glove it to the wicket-keeper, Alan Knott.

An angry Lillee walked off and, returning to the dressing room, uttered the prophetic words: 'Just remember who started this...they did...but we'll bloody finish it'. Chappelli (1992: 20) said *he did finish it*!

Chappell (1992: 20) also described how erratic Thomson was, despite the pace, as opposed to Lillee's pace and accuracy. Most of Thomson's bouncers went harmlessly over the batter's head. However, some of Thomson's thunderbolts and dangerously intimidating bowling unsettled a few batters in the English camp (Williamson 2015).

The English Press made a grave mistake by thinking that Lillee had not fully recovered from his back injury in the Caribbean in 1973. Also, the press thought that what they had heard about the 'new' find – Jeff Thomson and his extreme pace- was just Australian propaganda. Both were serious errors, as the events proved.

Despite a gallant Tony Greig century (110, with 17 fours) and Edrich making 48 in over three hours, England was bowled out for 265, conceding a deficit of 44 runs. Walker (4/73), Thomson (3/59), and Lillee (2/73) shared the wickets. Greig's was an exceptional inning as he counter-attacked with some ferocity. Thomson broke Amiss's thumb in the first inning. With great speed, Thomson's deliveries exploded the ball chest-high at the batters from a full length, making the batters hurry. It also made them fearful of being hit. A rising ball from Lillee broke Edrich's hand just before he was out.

In the second inning, Australia declared at 5-288. Redpath scored 25 in two and a half hours, as they feared a collapse. Greg Chappell (71) and Ross Edwards (53) also batted for three hours each. Doug (62*) and Marsh (48*) hurried the score along in an unbroken stand of 98 before Chappell declared, inviting England to try and win with a target of 333 in a little over six hours.

However, England couldn't cope with Thomson's pace as he ploughed through the inning, taking 6/46 in 18 overs. England was bowled out for 166, and Australia won by 166 runs to lead the series 1-0. In the process, the Lillee-Thomson pair and Walker unsettled several English batters. The pattern of dominance of the Australian attack in this opening match was such that it hinted at the prospect of regaining the Ashes this time around.

England was affected by injuries, including Dennis Amiss's broken thumb and John Edrich's broken hand, both of which were hit by fast deliveries. The injuries to the top-order batters led England to send for Cowdrey as reinforcement, and the great man responded without hesitation. The way Lillee bowled in this first Test indicated that he had fully recovered and was bowling better and faster than before, which added to England's woes.

* * *

The second Test saw Aussies on a scoring spree and was a special match for Doug. It was played at Perth's fast and bouncy WACA grounds (13-17 December 1974). The match saw Australia's superiority in all facets of the game. The WACA pitch, with its reputation as the quickest in the world, was no comfort for the bruised England players. However, the Test is best remembered by history for a memorable inning by Doug – a hundred in a session, in which Doug displayed his idiosyncratic self and brilliant and skilful batting.

England made five changes to the side that lost in Brisbane. Old, Arnold and Titmus replaced Lever, Hendrick and Underwood. Australia dropped Jenner in favour of Mallett. A highlight of the match was Australia's fielding. The home team held 17 out of the 18 catches offered; Greg Chappell recorded seven catches, mostly at second slip. Australia won quite comfortably within four days by nine wickets.

Winning the toss again, Ian sent England into bat, and they collapsed under four hours for 208 after being 1-99 at one time before the fast bowlers began to break through. Thomson's fast deliveries hit both England's openers agonising blows. David Lloyd (49) was struck on the abdomen and groin so hard that his protective box turned inside out. 'You didn't feel fear', Lloyd later said, 'but you did feel hopeless at times, a feeling that you couldn't cope'. Luckhurst (27) was badly hurt, struck on the hand and had to bat lower down the order with a heavily swollen hand in the second inning (Williamson 2015).

The 41-year-old Cowdrey, flown in to replace the injured Amiss and Edrich, walked into an ovation from the large crowd at the WACA to play his 188th inning for England, the first after a lay-off of three and a half years. He then faced the fiery Thomson for the first time only four days after arrival and survived his first three balls.

While he showed courage under fire and his defensive technique against fast bowling, Cowdrey got hit on his chest and body several times but batted with courage for over two hours, making 22 before being bowled by Thomson. I recall listening to the enthralling battle, which was well described by the ABC commentators.

The conversation between Cowdrey and Thomson, as they met for the first time, is a legend in Ashes cricket. In a panel discussion with Mark Nicholas a few years ago, Thomson embarrassingly described how Cowdrey approached him and said: 'Mr. Thomson, I believe. My name is Colin

Cowdrey. Nice to meet you'. Thomson's angry and hostile reply was: 'That's not going to help you, fatso. Piss off!'

Mallett (2008: 230) said England was in dire straits at 6-132 when Titmus came out to bat. One ball from Thomson took off from just short of driving length, cleared Marsh's head and hit the bottom of the sightscreen at the Member's End on the full pitch. Such was the pace England faced at the WACA. As Thomson wreaked havoc (2/45), Knott fought bravely (51) and helped England limp up to 208. The wickets were shared between Lillee (2/48), Walker (2/49), and Doug, taking 2/13 in just two and a half overs, including Knott's wicket.

The Australians replied with 481. Greg Chappell batted brilliantly for 62. The score was 4-192 when Greg departed, falling to a lazy shot off Bob Willis, caught in the slips by Greig. It was only a few minutes before tea. Mallett (2008: 232) recalled that Doug entered the arena, walking out calmly, totally at one with the world. He joined Ross Edwards, again playing a typical sheet anchor role.

Doug recalls that as Greg passed him returning to the pavilion, he quipped: 'I've set it up for you to get a hundred in the last session'. It was a reference to what happened in the third Test at the Queen's Park Oval in Port of Spain, Trinidad (23-28 March 1973) when Greg fell to Gibbs just three minutes to lunch and in walked Doug, who made a spectacular hundred between lunch and tea on a turning wicket.

On this occasion, facing a few balls, Doug was three* at tea on the second day. Then, after tea, he went into another gear, plundering runs at will with spectacular pulls, cuts and drives. Doug's 50 came in just 48 minutes with seven fours. As recorded by Mallett (2008: 231), Doug's recollections of this 'almost perfect inning he ever played' were:

> *Right from the start, I middled the ball and felt in total control. I looked around the field and visualized the gaps. And I found myself placing the ball almost to perfection. Around the time I was in the 60s, I thought I had a realistic chance of scoring a hundred in a session. I was seeing the ball that well. I felt good, so confident that I believed I could make somewhere in the vicinity of 130 in the session.*

The century partnership with Edwards came in 85 minutes as Doug made a spectacular century – 100 exactly – between tea and the close of play. More than 23,000 people and Sir Don were on the ground watching the Walters' special unfold. I recall well where I was seated, listening with increasing excitement.

As Willis began the day's final over, Edwards took two off the first ball and three off the second. Doug, at 93, sensed that he could get a hundred in a session. The third ball was a bouncer, which Doug hooked. It flew over Knott's head to the boundary, taking him to 97. Doug couldn't score from the next few balls.

Ross Edwards tried to calm Doug, suggesting that Doug bat 'sensibly' in the final over and resume the innings the following day. That advice wasn't heeded! In the day's final ball, Willis again bowled a short one. Doug pounced on it and swatted it high over mid-wicket to achieve the remarkable goal of hitting a hundred in a session. This period in the final session was utter mayhem. Edwards later described the privilege he felt watching this display of raw batting skills from the other end and being part of it (Mallett 2008: 238).

Mallett's first-hand account said: 'There was something surreal about how he brought up the hundred in Perth. Few people there could believe the skill and the nerve required to execute such a shot at that stage of the match: it was to Doug very much a matter of a six or out'. Sometimes, it seems that bravado pays off!

It was something uniquely thrilling to listen to. I remember jumping up joyously as Doug hit that final ball for six. It was the third time Doug hit a century in a session. But was upset when Doug got out quickly on the following day. He edged Willis's second ball of the day to Fletcher at slip, thus ending this most remarkable inning.

Edwards, 79* overnight, scored the first Test hundred by a Western Australian at Perth, reaching 115. Doug's partnership with Edwards was 170. Old polished off the tail, and Australia's last six wickets fell for 129. The hundred re-invoked the 'Bradman tag' (Mallett 2008: 239). It also placed Doug on a special list of players who have hit centuries in a single session more than once in their careers [36].

Ian Chappell painted a picture of this outstanding performance:

We're back in the original order now. Greg's batting at four, and Doug's batting at six. Greg gets out with about five minutes to go before tea. As they crossed, Greg said to him, "I've given you a sight of it this time". That's all he said. So, Doug was three, not out at tea.

---

36 Ten players have achieved this feat up to 2023. Leading the list are Bradman (five times), followed by Trumper and Wally Hammond (three times each). Doug is among others who have achieved the feat twice. The List is Weeks, Brain Lara, Matthew Hayden, Adam Gilchrist, A. B. de Villiers and Ben Stokes.

He goes out after tea and belts them everywhere. At drinks, he was 60 or 70. So I told Terry Jenner, our 12th man, to check where the little bastard is and how he's going. So TJ takes the drinks out and gives Doug a drink, he said. "How are you going? And Doug said ....Ohh, it's a bit warm out here; and Terry said, "That's not what I'm talking about. Doug, how are you going?" And Doug said I've got a chance.

So it was never mentioned, 100 in the session, but he obviously knew what we were thinking. Anyhow, it comes down to the last over. He was 93*. Eight ball overs, Bob Willis to bowl. Everyone in that dressing room is saying, "He'll do it". So he had to get 10 in that over to get the 100 in the session. And we were all saying, "He'll find a way".

So, he hooks the first ball for four, and we all said, "Ahh, now he'll do it". He doesn't score off the next six. Still, I reckon everybody in that dressing room said, "He'll find a way", and as soon as he hit the last ball, we all said, "Jeez, the little bastard has done it" because you could see it flying in the air and it was heading over the ropes. So, as soon as he hit it, the kids ran onto the ground. But we pretty well knew it was a six from the time he hit it, and we all just said, "Shit, the little bastard's done it!

England was bowled on day four for 293. Opening the batting, Cowdrey (41) and David Lloyd (35), gave England a good start. Titmus, who returned to Test cricket after a lapse of five years, made 61. Greig (32) and Old (43) also showed courage as Thomson ripped the heart out of England's batting with 25 overs of sheer pace (5/93) to claim match figures of 7/138. Australia won by nine wickets on day four, scoring 1-23 and outclassed the tourists (Frith 1997: 294).

Chappell (1992: 21) recalled how umpire Tom Brooks told him that Luckhurst, batting at No. 7 in the second inning with a broken finger, would not receive bouncers. Although he disagreed, Chappell accepted the request. Luckhurst batted for over two hours for 23 before Mallett caught him in the gully off Lillee. Ian also recalled what happened after Doug made that hundred and returned to the dressing room:

So you can imagine. If you score 100 in Test cricket, people are standing and clapping...Here we are [in the dressing room]. Nobody is out at the front. Everybody is in the dressing room, so they can't see anyone clapping. And I just said to the guys, right, grab a beer. And let's go in the shower room. So there's no one here when Doug comes in; we've all gone somewhere out at the back.

Now we're all standing there, sipping on a beer for 10 minutes, and nothing happens. So, eventually, I told the guys that this is a waste of time. We better go back in. So we go into the dressing room, and there's Doug. He is just sitting. He is taking his hat off. The pads were probably off. And he is smoking a cigarette. TJ, the 12th Man, took the can of beer over to him and handed him the can of beer. Never forget Doug's words, he said: "Not before time, twelthy!

Anyhow, I went to Ross, who was batting with Doug, and asked, "What did he do when he came in and there was no one here?" Ross said he did what he always does. He said, "He just took his cap and gloves off. Put himself down. Lit up a cigarette. Then he took his pads off. Then Doug just sat there and smoked like he always does".

And I've always said that if you didn't see Doug bat, and you were in the dressing room and you just saw him come in the dressing room after an inning, you'd never know whether he made naught or 100 because he always did the same....he never threw the bat down, even if he got out for naught.

* * *

The third Test (The 'Boxing Day Test') at the MCG (Melbourne, 26-31 December 1974) was a cliffhanger of a game until Australia put up the shutters on a game they could have won. Not pursuing a victory kept the series alive. Ian knew everyone benefitted from the extra revenue as interest was already ignited. Australia was already 2-Nil up.

England was expected to play better on the sluggish MCG wicket. As Chappell put England into bat, they made 242 in the first inning. Batting cautiously, Cowdrey (35 in four hours), Edrich (49 in over two hours) and Knott (52) held the inning together, while Thomson took 4/72 and Lillee 2/70. Ian Chappell (1992: 22) recalled that the umpire Robin Bailhache asked him to stop Lillee from abusing Knott, who had made a complaint. It was, Ian said, thoughtful umpiring by Bailhache because years later, Knott had said he never complained!

In short, lively spells, Bob Willis then bowled fast, taking 5/61 and restricting Australia to 241. The Australians also found it hard going. Redpath (55) and Marsh (44) grafted for Australia, while Doug and Ian Chappell scored 36 each. It wasn't inspiring batting from either side on the first three days of the Test (Hutchinson and Ross 1997: 415).

On day four, in the second inning, England had their best opening stand of 115, with David Lloyd (44) and Dennis Amiss (90) weathering the attack. But the middle-order disintegrated as eight wickets fell for 67. Greig's 60 helped England reach 244. Thomson (4/71), Lillee (2/55) and Mallett (4/60) troubled England.

Australia needed 246 to win but didn't push for a win. After early trouble, Greg Chappell (61) steadied the innings. Redpath batted for four hours for his 39. When Doug got out for 32 after tea, Australia still needed 75 runs to win in 105 minutes, but Marsh (40) and Walker (23*) scored too slowly. Greig took four wickets for 56. Titmus bowled in pain after being hurt in the first inning, hit on the knee by Thomson. He still bowled 29 overs, taking 2/62. The match was a draw. Australia was eight runs short, and England was two wickets short of victory.

* * *

Australia won the fourth Test at the SCG in Sydney (4-9 January 1975) by 171 runs, recapturing the Ashes. The margin was 3-Nil already with two more Tests to play. Denness dropped himself because he was batting poorly and asked John Edrich to be captain.

Chappell won the toss, and Australia batted on a grassy Sydney pitch and reached 405. The debutant opener from NSW, Rick McCosker, made 80. Greg made a classy 84, and Ian made 53. Doug was out for just a single lbw to Arnold. The Australian tail wagged again (Marsh, 30; Walker, 30; Mallett, 31) as the score reached 405. Arnold carried the bowling honours (5/86), and Greig took 4/104.

England replied with some spirit, reaching 295. Edrich batted doggedly for four hours, making 50. Knott hit out spiritedly for his 82 (11 fours); Titmus (22) and Underwood (27) helped to reduce the deficit. The batting was wrecked by Thomson (4/74), Lillee (2/66) and Walker (2/72). Doug took 2/26 in seven overs.

In the second inning, Australia pushed for a win. Redpath (105) steered them into a commanding position. His partnership of 220 with Greg Chappell (144 with 16 fours) ensured a comfortable declaration at 4-289. Doug failed again; this time, Underwood bowled him for five. England had over four sessions to survive or score 400 to win.

Respite came in the form of a thunderstorm late on day four. Batting on the final day, England got up to 0-68 before a disastrous afternoon. After the openers departed, Edrich, at No. 4, had two ribs cracked by the first ball he faced from Lillee. He was helped off the field. Cowdrey was dismissed almost immediately for one. Fletcher only made 11 when he was hit on the head by Thomson, the ball flying to cover and was caught by Redpath. Greig (54) fought back bravely.

Edrich returned to bat with two cracked ribs and remained 33* as England was bowled out for 228. Lillee (2/65), Thomson (2/74), Walker (2/46) and Mallett (4/21) were relentless. It was a tight contest, with Australia winning by 171 runs in the tenth of the last 15 overs.

Going 3-Nil up in four Tests, the Australians won back the Ashes. The total attendance at the SCG was a record of 178,000. During the Test, 864,000 empty beer cans had to be cleared from the ground as the fans rejoiced (Frith 1997: 296). Mallett (2008: 250) recalled a group carrying a massive banner with the words *'The Doug Walters Stand'* during the Test. The sign was fixed at the Randwick end, and sometime later, Doug had a stand named after him at the SCG.

* * *

England was beaten for the fourth time in the fifth Test (Adelaide Oval, 26-30 January 1975). In England's second inning, Thomson didn't play. He sprained his right shoulder playing tennis on the rest day. Denness returned to lead his team again after showing some form, scoring 157* against Tasmania and 99 against NSW in tour matches.

After day one was washed out, Denness won the toss and sent Australia in on day two. Underwood then scythed through the batting (7/113), and Australia reeled at 5-84 at one stage. But Doug made 55 in 90 minutes, striking seven fours and a six. Australia reached 304 with the help of Jenner (74), Walker (41), Lillee (26) and Mallett (23*).

In reply, England folded up for a paltry 172. Only Denness (51), Fletcher (40), and Cowdrey (26) withstood the pressure. Lillee took 4/49; Thomson chipped in 3/58, and Mallett took 3/14 in only nine overs, wrecking England's hopes of getting a foothold in the match.

Australia declared its second inning at 5-272. The leading scorers were Doug (71*), Redpath (52), Ian Chappell (41) and Marsh (55). Underwood took another 4/102 for his match bag of 11/215. England was left to make 405. They could only manage 241, despite Knott's brave century (106*) and Fletcher's 63. Australia won by 163 runs. Lillee (4/69) and Walker (3/89) bowled Australia to victory and a 4-0 lead in the series. Knott's century was only the second hundred by an English wicket-keeper in 219 Ashes Tests. The first was also by a Kent player, Lesley Ames, in 1934 when he scored 120 at Lord's.

* * *

The sixth Test was played at the MCG in Melbourne (8-13 February 1975). Australia won the toss for the fifth time in the series and batted on a humid Melbourne morning but was routed for 152. Already 4-Nil up, Australia erred in batting first and was caught out on a wet pitch on one end caused by a groundsman's error when lifting the covers off before play. The left-arm swing bowler Peter Lever found the affected spot and rattled the Australians (Hutchinson and Ross 1997: 415).

Bowling with accuracy, Lever took 6/38 in just 11 overs. Australia stumbled to 4-23. Old also picked up 3/50. Only Ian Chappell's determined 65 spared Australia total shame (*Wisden* 1975b). Doug scored only 12 before he was caught by Edrich off Old. The innings were over in 36.7 overs, and it was a disastrous first day for Australia.

When England batted, they wobbled at 2-18. Lillee then hobbled off after six overs. Having already lost the Ashes by a wide margin, Denness (188), Fletcher (146), Greig (89), and Edrich (70) restored some pride in the final Test with some solid batting. Without the pacemen to worry about, England scored their highest score in the series, 529, a match-winning lead of 377. Walker took 8/143 in 42 overs, his best in Test cricket. Dymock bowled 38 overs (1/130), Mallett bowled 29 overs (0/96), and Doug 23 overs (0/83).

Trying to save the match, Greg Chappell (102), Redpath (83), McCosker (79) and Ian (50) batted cautiously. But the middle order collapsed on the final day, and Australia was bowled out for 373 to lose by an innings and four runs.. Doug was bowled by Arnold for three. Greig took 4/88. Arnold (3/83) and Lever (3/65) also contributed.

The Test showed how much of a psychological grip Lillee and Thomson had on the English. For the first time in the series, their absence gave England some freedom to bat freely. But England was a beaten team by this time. Rob Bagchi (2013), a sports editor for The Guardian, wrote that it was a case of 'mice playing when the cat is away'! The *Wisden* (1975b) called it a pyrrhic victory – A victory accompanied by such enormous losses that it may not be worth it.

* * *

The *Wisden* Editor (Preston 1975) noted the criticism from the press of the manner of Australian pace bowling in the series:

> *Never in the ninety-eight years of Test cricket have batters been so grievously bruised and battered by ferocious, hostile short-pitched balls as were those led conscientiously by Denness until, owing to his own lack of form with the bat, he handed over the captaincy to John Edrich in the fourth match at Sydney.*

In those days of no helmets and other protective gear, critics accused Ian of letting this happen. Chappell's defence (1992: 20-21) was that 'it was entirely a matter for the umpires', adding that a competent batter, with a bat in his hand, should be able to deal with short-pitched balls, even if they are aimed at the body. Chappell also said he never asked his bowlers to cause an injury to anyone's anatomy. Denness admitted that his team was 'shell-shocked' Williamson (2015):

As the plane left Australia for New Zealand, some of the lads said they were glad to get out alive, even if some didn't get out all in one piece. The team had spent three months fearing for their lives by being hit on the head!

Tyson (1975: 219) reported, I think with regret, what Thomson said: 'Truthfully, I enjoy hitting a batter more than getting him out. It doesn't worry me in the least to see the batter hurt, rolling around screaming and blood on the pitch'. Lillee had also said: 'he aimed to hit the batter somewhere between the stomach and the ribcage'.

* * *

The axe fell on Denness four months later in the English summer when the Australians returned to England. Cowdrey played his 114th and last Test at the MCG. His fans gave him a warm farewell in an impromptu gathering, hoisting a banner that read: *'M.C.G. Fans Thank Colin—Six Tours'*. I recall the lengthy cheering and this moment of gracious appreciation for a cricketer I admired greatly.

Ian Chappell raised the issue of too much cricket for the first time at the end of the gruelling 1974-75 season. He also went to bat for his players' remuneration, his bugbear for a long time. Chappell has been saying that paying the cricketers 'fish and chips money must stop while the board raked in huge profits'. Ian explained what he earned in 1974-75, only $4800 over six months of Shield cricket and six Tests.

Chappell was invited to attend an ACB meeting in Melbourne before the sixth Test. There, he argued for higher pay for his players, who 'were almost full professionals with the amount of cricket played'. He also wanted players to be given contracts to play for Australia. The Board granted some of Chappell's demands. The match fee went up to $557, comprising a $200 match fee, a $200 bonus, and a sponsor bonus of $157. This was a significant increase compared with the $180 per match the players received four years earlier.

However, the Board didn't agree to contracts for players at that time. Its position was that players are 'invited' to play for their country. Alan Barnes, the secretary of the Board at that time, made an absurd statement: 'If the players don't like it, there are 500,000 others who would love to take their place' (Mallett 2008: 318).

Twenty-two years later, in 1997, the Australian Cricket Association was formed, led by Tim May. They signed a Memorandum of Understanding (MOU) with the ACB. It led to players getting contracts for the first time (ACB 2000).

CHAPTER 11

Agonies and Ecstasies

Playing any sport at the elite level is all about striving to be the best. However, professional sport is unpredictable. So many critical moments are decided by sheer chance. As a result, every cricketer has his day and ups and downs. They are part of his or her everyday life.

Cozier (2015) reported what the great West Indian batter Everton Weekes once said: "Making runs is a habit...Why not enjoy it when you get into that habit, for there'll come a time, once you play long enough, that you'll lose that habit. I repeatedly told the young players I coached to learn to temper the ability to do well with the expectancy of failure as well".

Speaking with Doug, I don't doubt that he went through agonies and ecstasies. Even Bradman had some pretty bad days, as revealed in his autobiography 'Farewell To Cricket'. Cricket is similar to a life's journey in that sense. However, great players do not let the 'downs' affect their game too much. They know that the next 'up' is around the corner. The 'downs' build character, and the 'ups' feed the ego, which needs to be managed. Doug's persona allowed him to ride the challenges of both.

The Prudential World Cup, 1975

Cricket is a sport that promotes mateship across countries and cricketers and connection with the local communities. Cricket also provides the opportunity to promote social integration. The first-ever limited-overs World Cup was highly successful, proving such benefits abundantly. Doug played a crucial part in the first tournament, which Australia narrowly lost to the resurgent West Indies.

I listened to the BBC broadcasts of the first-ever, one-day World Cup Final between Australia and the Windies well into the night on 21st June 1975. The final was incredible: 'Clive Lloyd showed his class and took the game by the scruff of the neck' (Richards 1991). The enthralling match ended around 8 pm, London time. By the time the awards ceremony took place, it was around 3 am in Colombo. There was no sleep for me that night!

The 1975 Cricket World Cup (officially called the Prudential Cup) was the inaugural men's first major tournament in ODI cricket. It was played in England during 7-21 June 1975. Rob Steen (2014) explained that cricket was slow to initiate a global championship. Sports, such as soccer, ice hockey, table tennis and canoeing, got off the mark between 1949 and 1954. These were emulated by volleyball, motorcycling, water-skiing, badminton, basketball and rugby. By 1971, rowing, lawn bowling, and hockey also had international championships.

The first men's ODI tournament (1975) was a landmark event. However, the first women's ODI World Tournament preceded the men's event. It had already been held in the UK in July 1973. The success of the 1975 tournament guaranteed that ODIs would become a crucial part of international cricket. The concentrated action of the shortened game made it very popular worldwide in the ensuing years.

The tournament was sponsored with £100,000 by Prudential Assurance, an insurance company in the UK. It had eight participants: the six Test-playing teams (Australia, England, West Indies, India, Pakistan and New Zealand) and the two Associate ICC members, Sri Lanka and East Africa. The winners were to receive £4000, the runners-up £2000 and the losing two semi-finalists £1000 each.

Some matches in the tournament were played simultaneously using the six Test venues in England. There were altogether 19 matches condensed into two weekends. We received regular updates of all matches throughout the day on Radio Ceylon. As the Lankans were competing, the interest in the island was massive.

The eight teams were divided into two groups of four. Each team played each other in their group once; the top two from each group battled in the semi-finals, with the winners of the semis meeting in the final. They were 60 x 6-ball overs per side games, played in traditional white clothing and with red balls; all were played and ended in daylight.

England and New Zealand finished as the top two teams in Group A, while the West Indies finished at the top of Group B, ahead of Australia, as the four teams qualified for the semi-finals. Australia defeated England, and the West Indies beat New Zealand in the semis. In the finals, the West Indies met Australia at Lord's and won by 17 runs to become the first World Cup champions (Steen 2014).

* * *

More than 26,000 noisy spectators, paying £66,950 at the gates, saw the Windies beat Australia in that most thrilling final (Preston, 1976a). It was high drama and tragedy for the Australians. As I recall, the large crowd's cheering, singing and drum-beating drowned much of the commentaries. Clive Lloyd's 102, off 82 balls with two sixes and 12 fours, in the Windies' total of 291 has been hailed as 'one of the finest ever seen, not least because of the event itself but also because of the power and skill on display (Preston 1976a).

If Lloyd had fallen, it would have been impossible for them to post a competitive total. Australia's best fielder, Ross Edwards, crucially dropped Lloyd off a miscued pull short of his century. But it was Lloyd's day as he battered the Australian attack. Praising Lloyd's innings, Preston (1976a) wrote:

As soon as Lloyd came in, he showed himself to be a master of the situation. He hooked Lillee in majestic style, square for six, and then put Walker off the back foot past cover with disdainful ease.

I still remember Lloyd's decisive fourth-wicket partnership of 149 in 36 overs with the 40-year-old Rohan Kanhai, who made 55. A man greatly respected by all opponents, Kanhai was nearing the end of an illustrious career. Kanhai, therefore, had the extra motivation on that day to bat sensibly and help the Windies' cause.

When Lloyd got out, the score was 4-199, and Kanhai followed to make the score 5-205. Gilmour soon bowled Viv Richards for only five, and the Windies wobbled at 6-209. However, Boyce (34) and Julien (26*) lifted the score to a respectable 8-291. Lillee (1/55) and Thomson (2/44) were fast, but it was Gilmour (5/48) who troubled the Windies. Doug bowled five overs for 23 without any wickets.

The total didn't seem so big as the Australian batting line-up was in good nick in the tournament. They only needed to score a bit under five runs per over and were up against the pace of Roberts, Julien, Boyce and Holder and the gentle seamers of Lloyd. They knew that this Windies attack was nowhere near as fearsome as it later became.

Giving chase, the Australians started well, 1-80 off the first 20 overs, before trouble began as they tried to get sneaky runs. The brilliant West Indies fielders ran out five Australians. Viv Richards was a primary figure who caused the problem with deadly aim. Swooping on the ball like an eagle hunting prey, Richards threw down the stumps twice from a square leg position (*Wisden* 1976).

He got Turner (40) out first and then the crucial wicket of Greg Chappell (15). Australia were 3-115 at this stage, still with a chance of winning. Richards then enabled Lloyd to break the wicket at the bowler's end when Ian Chappell (62) set off for an impossible third run. Ian's mistake made Australia 5-162. These top-order mishaps and two more runouts at the end cost the Australians a match.

I recall how Doug made a valuable 35 before he was bowled by Lloyd with a gentle seamer. Australia faltered at this stage, at 5-170. Edwards (28) batted with his usual grit. Near the end, the last pair, Thomson (21) and Lillee (16*), added 41 in their attempt to win. Australia was 9-233 at one stage with seven more overs, but a final runout ended Thomson's innings. Australia fell short by 17 runs.

The *'Poor Man's Sobers'* Boyce took 4/50 (Manley 1988: 228) while Lloyd had the single wicket of Doug conceding 38. With five runouts, the other bowlers went wicketless. I admired the Windies' triumph and especially Viv Richards' fielding. The Australians made several fielding errors, contrasting with the Windies' brilliant fielding.

At the outset, the bookmakers made the West Indies firm favourites because of the teams' all-round strength and experience. Eleven players in their squad of 14 had been playing limited-overs games, especially in the Gillette Cup tournament in the county circuit. It came as no surprise that the Windies squad collectively held their nerve and pulled off the victory. But it still needed some super-human effort.

Lloyd and Richards outshone the others in this effort. Reflecting on the 'most significant and decisive acts of fielding' that turned a match, Haigh (2014) wrote: 'Richard's interventions did as much as Lloyd's to win the game and the inaugural World Cup title for his team'.

The World Cup victory in 1975 heralded a new era for the Caribbean. It restored respect for the overseas diaspora, especially in Britain. In the end, thousands of joyous West Indians transformed both The Oval and Lord's into Caribbean carnivals with their drums and whistles, bringing a particular type of excitement previously foreign to England. Achieving excellence with collective skills was critical for the West Indies to be globally recognized as a force in cricket.

The team's success represented the success of the people of the Caribbean islands in overcoming slavery and colonial rule, which had plagued them for several centuries. Cricket was critical for the islands to form a global identity. The profits from the tournament were distributed: 10% to the U.K. and seven and a half % to each of the seven other participants. The balance went to the inaugurators, the ICC, for distribution among the non-participating Associate Member countries, the International Coaching Fund and the reserve account for promoting the next International World Cup (*Wisden* 1976).

* * *

Doug did reasonably well in the World Cup tournament. His most decisive contribution came in the semi-final thriller against England at Headingley, Leeds, on 18 June 1975. The Headingley pitch was green and a seamer's delight. The atmosphere was heavy as Chappell sent England in. Gilmour was singularly the hero for Australia. With his left-arm swing, Gilmour took 6/14, bowling his 12 overs non-stop and combined with Walker (3/22) to rout England for 93 in only 36 overs.

At one stage, England was 8-52. Only captain Denness (27), Arnold (18*) and extras (14) reached double-figures. Australia was also in serious trouble at one stage, slumping to 6-39 when Old (3/29) and Snow (2/30) ripped into them. Doug (20*) and Gilmour (28*) batted resolutely and then had a 55-run unbroken partnership. Australians prevailed to reach the target of 94 and win by four wickets.

Doug received some good news from home before the World Cup Final. To his delight, he learned that he had been awarded an MBE for services to cricket. Doug said: 'It was a great surprise, totally out of the blue, because I thought that if ever I was going to get an award like that, it wouldn't come until after I retired' (Mallett 2008: 254).

* * *

I remember being glued to the BBC broadcasts relayed by Radio Ceylon, which had become the Sri Lanka Broadcasting Corporation (SLBC) by then. Doug did well in an earlier Group B match when Australia met Sri Lanka at the Oval (11 June 1975). It was the seventh match of the tournament. It will forever be remembered for gutsy Sri Lanka's cricketers who bravely faced the hostile Australian bowling. Australia won by 52 runs, but their victory didn't gain them any admirers, certainly not Sri Lankans, who were battered and bruised.

In the era when modern-day helmets or other protective gear were unheard of, the Lankans refused to be intimidated by the barrage of balls aimed at their bodies. In those days, even waist-high or face-high deliveries aimed at the batter's body were not no-balled by the umpires.

When the Sri Lankan captain Anura Tennekoon put the Australians into bat, he hoped his bowlers could exploit the conditions. This was not to be, as the Australian openers piled on 182 before the first breakthrough. Alan

Turner (101) and McCosker (73) combined in a 173 opening stand. Later, Greg Chappell (50) and Doug (59) put on 117 in 19 overs, flaying the Sri Lankan attack as the score mounted to 5-328 (a run rate of 5.5 per over.

The Sri Lankan bowling was mediocre. The two pacemen (Tony Opatha, 0/32 and Mevan Pieris, 2/68) were ineffective, as were the three spinners (Somachandra De Silva, 2/60; Lalith Kaluperuma, 0/50 and Anura Ranasinghe, 0/55).

Chasing 328, the Lankan batters, most of them short in stature, batted bravely against the hostile Australian attack. The openers, Sunil Wettimuny (53) and Ranjith Fernando (22), as well as the No. 3 Bandula Warnapura (31) and No. 4 Duleep Mendis (32), took on Lillee and Thomson at the early stages. They cut and hooked the short balls with skill and confidence. The crowds appreciated the brave show put up by the underdogs with loud cheering.

Around the halfway mark, at 32 overs, Sri Lankans were well on the way at 2-150, needing 179 off 168 deliveries. Frustrated by being unable to break the batters' resolve, Thomson unleashed a barrage of bouncers aimed at the batter's body. He caused two key batters, who were well set, to retire hurt. It was reminiscent of the way Thomson terrorized the hapless England tourists less than six months ago.

With the score at 2-150, the tiny Duleep Mendis was struck on the head when he ducked into a rising ball when he was 32 and had to be carried away by a teammate (Mevan Peiris) and the manager (Dennis Chanmugam) who rushed to the middle. There was no stretcher on the grounds. Mendis was in a bad way, eyes dazed and tears rolling down.

He admitted to being 'unconscious' while being carried away but recovered and resumed his innings after 10 minutes. Doug recalled: 'We gathered around the little bloke on the ground. He was lying on his back looking up at the heavens when Chappelli asked him if he was okay'. Tears rolling down his cheeks, he said, 'Please, Mr Thomson, I (am) going now'. The crowd booed Thomson for bullying the underdogs, but the bowler was unrepentant (Brookes 2022: 148).

At 2-164, Sunil Wettimuny, the opener, played a rising ball onto his body, which bruised his ribs; he needed a runner (Haigh 1997; Mallett 2008: 253). Wettimuny was hit by a toe-crusher on the right instep in the next ball. He was hurt badly. As he staggered in and out of his crease, Thomson threw down the wicket, appealing for a runout. It was disallowed. However, Thomson was left in the cold as his teammates, who initially coaxed him to throw down the stumps, kept their arms folded. Thomson fumed for a few minutes, cursing his teammates.

Sunil Wettimuny's brave inning ended in the next Thomson over as another toe-crusher hit his right leg. Sunil was carried off the field. The angry crowd continued booing Thomson. As the Lankan batters got hurt, it was high drama indeed.

In the mayhem, both Wettimuny and Mendis were rushed to a nearby hospital for treatment, but they soon recovered. Incredibly, Sri Lanka never gave up hope of winning, surprising the Australians. Like their predecessors, the captain, Anura Tennekoon (48), the former captain, Michael Tissera (52), got behind the ball's line and refused to be intimidated. They also fearlessly attacked whenever they could.

It is a great pity that there was no TV record of this remarkable effort by the Sri Lankans. Only the newspaper reports and first-hand accounts of several players illuminate what went on. With two of their best batters retired hurt, the Lankans nearly pulled off an improbable victory, scoring 4-275 in their 60 overs, falling short by 52 runs.

Wettimuny sustained a hairline fracture to one of his ribs, and his right foot was broken in the battering he received. He was also severely bruised on the thigh and hip. Both Mendis, who was hit on the head, and Wettimuny spent a night at the St. Thomas's Hospital in London.

Unbeknown to them, a policeman, who wasn't on duty at the game, had heard the tail-end of a radio report about two Sri Lankans being assaulted by an Australian cricketer at The Oval. Mendis later smilingly described how the policeman turned up at the bedside, holding his bobby's helmet under one arm, and quite seriously asked, '*Do you want to press charges against a Mr. Jeff Thomson?*' (Mallett 2005). It must have been hilarious, but Mendis's exact response is unknown.

* * *

Along with a million other Lankans who listened to the broadcast, I was upset with the loss. Still, I soon realised that this performance won the hearts and minds of thousands of cricket lovers worldwide. The team's bravery, fighting spirit and raw cricketing skills, on display at The Oval in 1975, played a part in the island's agonizing journey to become recognized by the ICC as a country worthy of playing Test cricket. There was recognition that the Sri Lankan team was the third-best performer in the tournament after the Windies and the Australians.

Six years later, on 21 July 1981, the island became the eighth Test-playing country. It was 30 years since the last newcomer was admitted to the Test ranks (Pakistan, in 1952). Despite consistently performing better against stronger opponents, England and Australia used veto powers for a long time to prevent Sri Lanka from gaining Test status. Support for the island came only from the Windies, Pakistan and India.

Seven months later, Sri Lanka played its first Test against the touring English team, led by Keith Fletcher, from 17-21 February 1982, at the P. Sara Stadium in Colombo. It was precisely 100 years after Ivo Bligh's team played cricket in Colombo on a short tour (Brookes 2022: 163).

Bandula Warnapura captained the home team on this historic first Test. It was a star-studded England team boasting Ian Botham, Bob Willis, Graham Gooch, David Gower, Derek Underwood, John Embury and Bob Taylor, all top-class Test and county professionals.

England won a tight contest by seven wickets. Sri Lanka, batting first, scored only 218, with Ranjan Madugalle (a current match referee) scoring a slow 65, batting for over four hours. The highlight of the inning was a bright debut half-century (54, including seven fours) by a schoolboy – Arjuna Ranatunga – future Sri Lankan captain. Underwood took 5/28 in 16 overs. But England also slumped to 223, with David Gower (89) and Keith Fletcher (48) being the leading scorers.

Only five runs behind, with three frontline spinners and the benefit of bowling last on a spin-friendly pitch, Sri Lanka was in the box seat. With some bright batting, the Sri Lankan top-order ran ragged English fielders under hot and oppressive conditions. Sri Lanka ended day three at 3-147. The No. 3 bat Roy Dias made 77, striking 11 fours.

However, on the fourth day, Embury stifled them, taking 6/33 in 25 overs, with Underwood adding another three wickets for 67 runs, bowling 37 overs. In 69 balls, the home team lost seven wickets for eight runs and was bowled out for 175. The greater experience of the English professional came through as the Test newcomers panicked.

Chris Tavare's patient 85 in just under four hours (with 12 fours), and David Gower (42) saw England home (3-171) late on day four. The Sri Lankans couldn't quite explain why they threw away what might have been a historic win (Brookes 2022: 170-171). However, David Frith, the *Wisden* Editor, watched the proceedings and was impressed with the hosts' performance.

On this birth of Test cricket in Sri Lanka, Frith wrote (1982: 26-29): '*The baby had been delivered without complications; heartbeat regular, breathing sound, if a little excited*' (Williamson 2012). Four years later, Sri Lanka recorded its first Test win. On 6 September 1985, they beat India in the second Test by 149 runs at The Oval in Colombo.

* * *

The first ODI World Cup event was monumental and highly successful as the first-ever ODI international tournament (Steen 2014). Sri Lanka's performances also kept thousands of us awake. However, we didn't receive the BBC broadcasts of every match the Lankans played. In Australia, the World Cup final was only the second big international match shown live on ABC TV, with millions watching. The high ratings made Australia's Channel Nine TV's Kerry Packer realise how cricket could be commodified and broadcast on his network to become a powerful profit-making tool.

'Ashes' Battles in England, 1975

Following the World Cup 1975, Ian Chappell's team remained in England to play a four-match Test series against England. This was only four months after Australia won the Ashes by crushing England down under. The *Wisden* Editor (Preston, 1976b) said the Australians 'rendered a great service to English cricket by staying in the country after the World Cup and playing four Test Matches'. The Ashes part of the tour was not in the original calendar.

The Australian team had McCosker, who quickly became the regular opener. The team had Alan Turner, a left-hander, as a new opening partner for McCosker. The backup bowlers for Lillee and Thomson were Max Walker and the left-armer, Gary Gilmour. Ashley Mallett was the only spinner in the team.

Even before the series began, Australia had an advantage over England, under Denness, due to the whipping his team endured a few months earlier. The Australians were also battle-ready despite the defeat at the World Cup Final. Denness had also been appointed as captain only for the first Test, which wasn't a vote of faith from the selectors. Denness later said he regretted accepting the captaincy under such conditions (*Wisden* 2018). Bagchi (2013) noted that the knives had been out for Denness before the summer. After the debacle in Australia, the press had been screaming, '*Denness Must Go*'.

The inquest into the disgrace in Australia led to three of the England selectors, under Alec Bedser, stepping down. The new panel of selectors comprised Bedser himself, continuing as chairman, Len Hutton, Ken Barrington and the former umpire Charlie Elliot. Only Bedser's casting vote led to Denness being appointed as the captain for the World Cup and the first Test. Tony Greig, the Sussex captain, who had been in impressive form, took over as the new England captain in the second Test and immediately had an impact.

* * *

In the first Test at Edgbaston (10-14 July 1975), England introduced Essex's prolific scorer Graham Gooch, a future England captain. At 21 years old, Gooch was the youngest to play for England after Cowdrey in 1954. I recall how Gooch began his career, bagging a 'pair' in his debut Test. The selectors also brought back John Snow, who was now 35. Snow had already taken 55 wickets against Australia in two series. Although he hadn't played Test cricket for two years, it was thought Snow could make a difference.

Australia won with a day and a half to spare, much to England's embarrassment, after Denness won the toss and sent them in to bat. Under overcast conditions, Denness had hoped that his seamers – Geoff Arnold, John Snow, Chris Old and Tony Greig – could exploit the conditions. It was a gamble that failed, and he 'signed his own death warrant', as Mallett recalled (2008: 254).

The English seamers found no response. Given that rain had been predicted for the next two days, Denness took the risk of his side being caught on a wet wicket, which was precisely what happened. There was also a harsh view from the press that the English batters were not too keen to face the fiery Lillee-Thomson pair and preferred to postpone the encounter. McCosker (59), the debutant Alan Turner (37), Ian Chappell (52), Ross Edwards (56), Marsh (61), and Thomson (49) made runs, enabling Australia to total 359.

England batted between more rain delays, but devastating spells from Lillee (5/15 in 15 overs) and Walker (5/48 in 18 overs) reduced them to 101. Only the veteran Edrich (34) resisted for three hours.

Ian Chappell enforced the follow-on. England was soon in trouble again as Thomson took 5/38 in 18 fiery overs. Lillee (2/45) and Walker (2/47) also chipped in. England could only scrape 173. Fletcher (51), Knott (38), and Snow (34) resisted to no avail. Australia won by an inning and 85 runs. This was England's first defeat at Edgbaston in an Ashes Test. Preston (1976b) wrote that 'the Australians took many remarkable catches true to their reputation for splendid fielding. It was a victory they so thoroughly deserved'.

Denness resigned as captain and was dumped for the rest of the series. *Wisden* (2018) remembered Denness as a conscientious and determined cricketer who won more Tests than he lost in the 19 he captained. But he was uneasy in the media limelight, which contrasted with the exuberant, South African-born Tony Grieg, who replaced him. The 29-year-old Greig, six foot six inches tall, had been scoring heavily in the county circuit. By this time, he had plenty of Test experience, with five Test centuries already in 39 matches.

* * *

The second Test was played at Lord's (31 July-5 August 1975). As captain,

Greig immediately affected England's selections. He asked the selectors who was 'the best batter of fast bowling' and 'the hardest to dismiss' in the county circuit. The answer was 'Geoff Boycott', who was unavailable because of his self-exile. When Greig persisted, 'Who is next?', the answer he got was Northamptonshire's David Steel.

The be-spectacled 33-year-old Steele then became Greig's first *Captain's Pick*. Mallett (2008: 259) recalled that the Australians derided Steele, calling him *Groucho Marks*, the American comedian with his famous glasses and bushy eyebrows. However, Steele stood up to the bullying by Thomson and Lillee and came out on top several times.

Barry Wood, a Yorkshireman playing for Lancashire, was recalled to open the inning, and Bob Woolmer, a cricket coach in Kent, made his debut at the age of 27 years. Clearly, England wanted to find new batters who might fare better against the Australian pace attack.

England won the toss and batted. But Lillee, bowling unchanged for 90 minutes, crashed through the top order. England was 4-49 when David Steele dug in for his half-century (50, with nine fours), anchoring a recovery. The erratic Thomson bowled 22 no-balls. Greig struck 15 fours in his 96, made in under three hours. Knott (69) also attacked the bowling, while Woolmer (33) batted patiently, helping England reach a score of 315. Lillee ended up with 4/84. Thomson (2/92), Walker (2/52), and Mallett (2/56) shared the other wickets.

When Australia batted, Snow, bowling at his inspired best (4/66), caused a collapse, reducing Australia to 7-81 before a recovery. Doug fell for only two. But Ross Edwards (99, with 15 fours) once again played a vital role in saving Australia but was unfortunate to miss a century, falling lbw to a yorker from Woolmer. Edwards added 66 runs for the ninth wicket with Lillee (73*). Lillee added another 69 for the last wicket, with Mallett (14) reducing the deficit to only 47. It was Lillee's highest Test score in a career of 70 Tests.

England batted with confidence in the second inning. Wood (52) and Steele (45) stayed with Edrich, who played a sheet anchor role. Edrich's seventh century against Australia (175, with 21 fours) took over nine hours. But it allowed England to build a sizeable lead.

Edrich's century was the second-highest at Lord's against Australia, surpassed only by Wally Hammond's 240 in 1938. The top-order (Greig 41, Gooch 31 and Woolmer (31) accumulated slowly (2.9 runs per over), allowing England to press for a win. When the score was 7-436, Greig declared, setting Australia a target of 484 in 500 minutes.

Bowling 147 overs, Australians toiled in the stifling heat in London.

Mallett took 3/127 in 37 overs. Doug bowled just two overs but had Steele caught and bowled for 45 when the score was 2-215. This was an instance of Ian under-bowling his potential match-winner. England had hoped for some rain intervention to help them push for a victory.

An hour was lost due to rain at the start of the final day. But the covered pitch behaved well enough when Australia batted. They didn't take up the challenge and were 3-329. Ian (86), McCosker (79), Greg (73*), and Edwards (52*) played for a draw. The drawn match left England needing to win both remaining Tests to regain the Ashes.

The match, played in stifling heat, attracted vast crowds to Lord's. The gates at Lord's were closed on the first three days, and 27,000 attended each day. The game was also remembered for cricket's first streaker, who ran into the ground wearing nothing but his shoes while England built its sizeable lead. With London's temperature hovering around 34oC, England was 6-399 with Knott and Woolmer at the crease when the streaker appeared and hurdled the stumps at each end while the bemused umpire Tom Spencer watched (Williamson 2013).

The streaker was a certain Michael Angelow, a cook in the Royal Navy. The time in the afternoon was 3:20 pm. Commentating for the BBC Test Match Special at the time, John Arlott got too excited and forgot the word 'Streaker'. He called the culprit a 'Freaker'! in one of cricket's most hilarious descriptions:

We've got a Freaker! We've got a Freaker! It's not very shapely, and it's masculine. The old ladies in the crowd are seeing what they haven't seen for years. He's masculine, well built, wearing plimsolls, and I'm sure if his mother is watching the television, she'll recognise him.

John Ashdown (2016) noted Doug's comments:

No one at Lords had seen a streaker before, but I'd seen quite a few back in Australia before that. They were really quite commonplace back home, but you certainly didn't expect that behaviour in England, certainly not in those days and at Lords of all places. It's probably fair to say that cricket in England was a bit formal. Times have changed since then, whether for the good or the worse.

Mallett (2008, p. 260) noted that Angelow was fined £25 the following day by the Magistrate in the St John's Wood Court. The streaker had bet his friends the same amount, £25, to streak at Lord's.

* * *

For the third Test (Headingley, 14-19 August 1975), Australia dropped Alan Turner, allowing the bowling all-rounder Gary Gilmour to debut following his outstanding performance at the same ground in the World Cup semi-final against England. Marsh was asked to open with McCosker. England dropped Amiss and the 'new hope' from Essex, Gooch, after the failures in the first and second Tests.

Yorkshire's John Hampshire was recalled after a long lapse, and Fletcher was also recalled. A newcomer, Phil Edmonds, an orthodox left-arm spinner, was to partner Underwood. Peter Lever was left out, and Chris Old was brought back. Woolmer was made the 12th man.

Batting first, England made 298 with gritty knocks from Edrich (62), Steele (73) and Greig (51). Gary Gilmour, the left-armer, made a conspicuous mark on his Test debut. He swung the ball late to take 6/85 in 31 overs, continuing his impressive form from the World Cup.

When Australia batted, Edmonds, on his Test debut, took 5/28 in 20 overs, taking all five wickets in the first 12 overs he bowled in Test cricket, sending the visitors packing for 135. Doug made only 19 before falling lbw to Edmonds. Doug prevented a hat-trick after the two previous Edmond's deliveries had dismissed Ian Chappell and Ross Edwards. England's lead was a sizeable 153 runs.

A single wicket to Underwood took him to 200 Test wickets, joining Alec Bedser, Fred Trueman and Brian Statham, England's past heroes who had previously achieved this record. John Snow continued his fine form, taking 3/22. Steele top-scored again with 92 when England batted a second time, showing his competence in only his second Test, top-scoring in both innings. Greig (49), Edrich (35) and Knott (31) helped England reach 291. Gilmour took another 3/72 (a bag of 9/157) and Mallett 3/50. This left Australia needing 445 to win.

Australia ended the fourth day sitting comfortably at 3-220. With McCosker settling down, Ian Chappell (62) hit a six and 11 fours and set the scene for a win. When the day ended, McCosker was close to his century (95*), and Doug was 25*. Australia still needed 225 runs to win with seven wickets in hand. Vandals then got in the act overnight, digging holes on the pitch and pouring oil, making it unplayable. It was the first high-profile pitch vandalism in cricket (Chappell 2016).

The vandals, from London's East End, were campaigning for the release of a jailed criminal. The incident angered all cricket fans, as the match and the series were well poised. There had been a night guard of a solitary policeman on duty at the ground. But he never saw the vandals. The game was abandoned without any play on the final day.

Following the outrage, officials decided that much greater vigilance would be needed to ensure that Test pitches receive better protection in the future. In any case, an Australian win was doubtful because of the rain at midday on that final day. Already 1-Nil up in the series, the draw meant that Chappell's men retained the Ashes (Preston 1976b).

* * *

On a placid pitch, in the fourth and final Test, at The Oval (28 August-3 September 1975), a brilliant Ian Chappell century (192) and McCosker's first Test century (127) set Australia up for a massive total of 9-532. The six-day Test was the longest match ever played in England. No one thought it would go the full distance.

The McCosker-Chappell stand was 282 runs as England's bowlers were ineffective. When the first day ended, Australia was 1-280. Doug scored his highest score of 65 for the series before Underwood bowled him. It was Underwood's single wicket (1/96), bowling 44 overs.

Thomson (4/50), Walker (4/63) and Lillee (2/44) then bowled England out for 191, a deficit of 341 runs. David Steel (39) withstood the pressure for a while. Ian Chappell enforced the follow-on, but Edrich (96), Steele (55), and Graham Roope (77) led a fightback before Woolmer took over with a patient century (149).

After his debut in the second Test, Woolmer had been dropped by the selectors but returned to the side for the fifth Test. His first Test hundred was the slowest for an Ashes century, but it ensured England's safety. All Australian bowlers toiled hard for little reward over nearly two days (Lillee 4/91 in 52 overs; Thomson 1/63 in 30 overs; Walker 0/91 in 45 overs; and Mallett 0/95 in 64 overs). When Doug was called upon to bowl, England was past 500. But Doug got Woolmer lbw for 149, Knott (64) caught behind, and two more wickets to finish with 4/34. With only 85 minutes left to make 198, Australians ended with 2-40 and drew the match.

* * *

Doug had an ordinary series, scoring only 125 at 31 in the four Tests. He was 25*. in the abandoned third Test. His highest score of 65 was made in the fourth Test. Ian Chappell (429 at 71), Rick McCosker (414 at 83) and Ross Edwards (253 at 51) were the main batters whose contributions ensured Australia's success in the series.

Australia's batting owed much to Ian Chappell and (*Wisden* 2020). In 11 matches and four Tests, each topped 1,000 runs on the tour. Most disappointing was Greg Chappell's lack of success in the Tests. In five games in 1972, he hit 437 at 49. In contrast, in the four Tests in 1975, he made only 106 at 21. Doug did himself no justice in the Tests despite heading the tour averages with 784 at 60.3 (Preston 1976b).

The 1-Nil result was explained by Australia being lucky to catch England on a rain-affected wicket in the first Test at Edgbaston, which they won, and their escape with the loss of the fifth day at Headingly, where England could have won if not for the vandalism.

Australia's brilliant fielding was a crucial factor in the success. An array of six in the slips and gully held hot catches. The close-in fielders were supported by Edwards 'swift as a hawk in the covers'. Far away behind the stumps, Marsh caught 14 while 'leaping hither and thither when the pacemen were wide off the mark' (Preston 1975b). The press dubbed Steele *'Stainless Steel'* for his batting in the series. Steele was named the BBC Sports Personality of the Year in 1975, the first cricketer to win the accolade since Laker in 1956. Nonetheless, England's batting was again unable to withstand the pace of Lillee (21 wickets at 22), Thomson (16 wickets at 28), and Walker (14 wickets at 34); the trio shared 51 wickets in the four Tests.

* * *

The new England captain, Greig, brought toughness that had been missing in previous teams under Cowdrey, Smith and Denness. However, Greig's captaincy tenure lasted only the next two years. At least for some time, his name became anathema in cricket because he became the leading recruiter for Kerry Packer's World Series Cricket. Later, as cricket recovered from the WSC debacle, Greig became a much-admired TV commentator.

During the Test, Ian Chappell surprised everyone by announcing that he would retire from the captaincy but not from cricket. Ian wasn't happy about the abrupt sacking of Bill Lawry, whom he regarded as a great servant of Australian cricket [37]. Ian commented, 'The bastards would never get him that way'(Chappell 2009). Interviewed by Simon Lister for Cricinfo in 2009, Ian explained:

> *Well, that's what I told my wife when I was given the job: "The bastards won't get me that way". So, I guess that indicated I would go early rather than too late. But actually, after The Oval Test here in '75, I was done. I knew I wasn't in the right frame of mind to lead the side against the West Indies so soon afterwards. I would have gone one more if I'd had six months off, but I was mentally done. I wasn't aggressive enough anymore. I didn't have it.*

---

37 When Lawry was sacked in 1971, the Panel of Selectors comprised Sir Don, Jack Ryder and Neil Harvey. After Bradman retired in 1972, Phil Ridings took over as Chairman. The other two in the panel were Sam Loxton and Harvey.

Doug at the age of 12 was known as a fast bowler

Doug photographed in 1965

The NSW Colts XI that played against a Queensland Colts XI. Doug (far left, front row, left) scored 140* at the SCG. Brian Taber is second from the right in the front row.

(Source: Doug Walters' Collection)

Doug with Don Bradman after the debut hundred [It was this photo that was published in 1965 in newspapers, which carried the caption 'Dairy Farmer's Son Goes the Milky Way'] (Source: Doug Walters' Collection)

Brian Booth (Australia's captain) and Doug Walters – 1965 after the debut century (Source: not known)

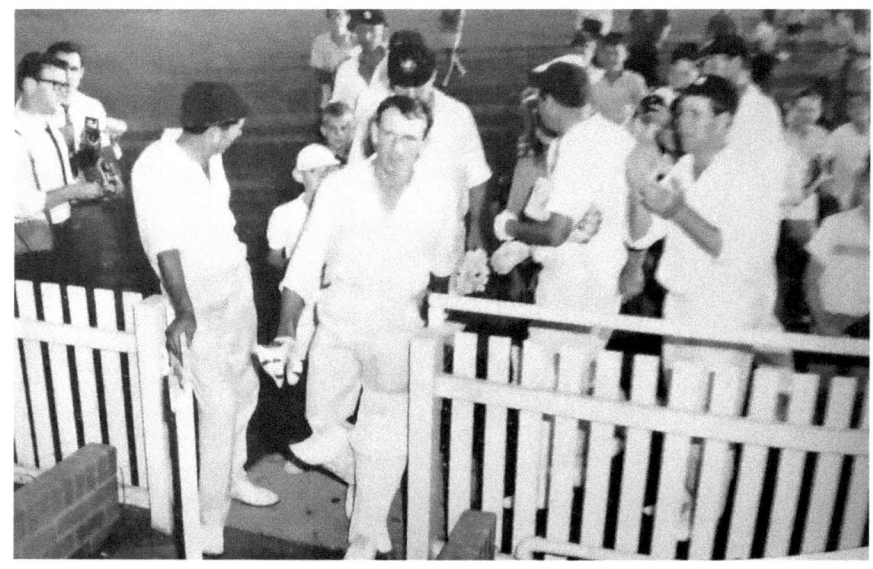

Doug returning to the pavilion after the debut century, to the applause of the English players. December 1965 (Source: Doug Walters' collection)

Doug playing cricket at home, around 1963 (Source: Doug Walters' Collection)

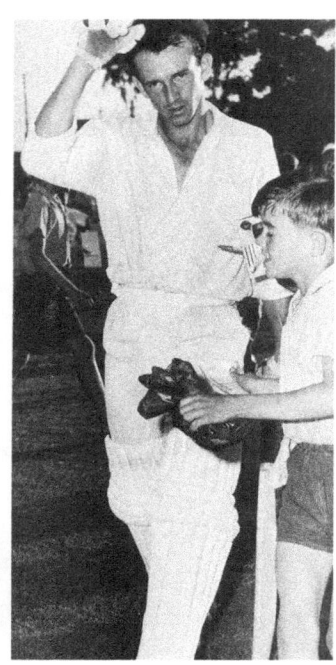

Doug mobbed by a young fan as he returned after the debut century (1965).

Doug with Caroline listening to a replay of commentaries of his debut century (Source: Doug Walters' collection)

Doug (1966) at Holsworthy training camp — after joining the Army. Doug played cricket whenever he could while in the Army (1966) (Source: Doug Walters' collection)

Doug padding up for a practice session (around 1963)
(Source: Doug Walters' collection)

Doug featured on the cover of The Cricketer (U.K.) January 1966 (Author's collection. With permission)

Pictures from Doug's debut century featured in The Cricketer (U.K.) January 1966 (Author's collection. With permission)

Doug featured on the cover of a Sport & Pastime Magazine, *India (24 Feb. 1968) (Author's collection. Photo source: not known)*

Doug in early 1965 (Source: Doug Walters' collection)

Image from Jack Pollard's 'Cricket The Australian Way' (1968).

Doug's stance (Left) with slightly bent front elbow and the toe of the bat behind the rear foot. Keith Miller (Middle) has the toe of the bat between his toes and because of his height,, the front elbow is not bent as much as Doug's. Both have hands together gripping the bat in the middle. Doug shows the forward defensive stroke (Right). Note the bat very close to the front toe, which points to where the ball will go.

Doug being introduced by Bill Lawry (covered) to Her Majesty The Queen in 1968. Next to Doug are Brian Taber, Paul Sheahan and Dave Renneberg (Source: Doug Walters' Collection)

Doug featured on the cover of The Cricketer *(U.K.) May 1968 (Author's collection. With permission)*

Cover photo from 'Looking For Runs' (1971) – Doug pulls, watched by Alan Knott. This image appeared in The Cricketer (U.K.) September, 1968 (Source: Author's collection. With permission)

Above - Doug bowling in a tour match in England (1968). Right — With Brian Taber on the Ashes tour (1968) (Source: Doug Walters' collection)

Doug in full flow in England, 1968. This picture first appeared on The Cricketer (U.K.) June 1972 cover. (Source: Doug Walters' Collection)

Doug (1968 in England)

Members of the Australian cricket Team take a tour of the sights of London (L to R) Ian Redpath, Graham McKenzie, Bob Cowper, Alan Connolly, Paul Sheahan, Neil Hawke, Ian Chappell, Eric Freeman, John Inverarity, Dave Renneberg, Ashley Mallett, Johnny Gleeson, Les Joslin, Doug Walters, Brian Taber and Bill Lawry (Source: Alamy Images)

Bob Massie returning to the dressing room after his phenomenal bowling spell, 1972. Others in the picture, from L-R, Rod Marsh (covered), Ross Edwards, David Colley, Doug Walters, Keith Stackpole, Dennis Lillee, Bruce Francis, Johhny Gleeson, Bob Massie and Greg Chappell (Source: from The Cricketer (U.K.) with permission)

The Australian team in England, 8th June 1972. L to R back - Graeme Watson, Ashley Malett, Bob Massie, Jeff Hammond, Rod Marsh. Centre row L to R - Physiotherapist D. McErlane, Bruce Francis, Greg Chappell, Ross Edwards, Fred Bennett (Assistant Manager), Paul Sheahan, David Colley, Dennis Lillee, D. Sherwood (Scorer). Front L to R - Brian Taber, Doug Walters, Ian Chappell (captain), Ray Steele (Manager), Keith Stackpole, John Inverarity, John Gleeson (Source: Alamy Images)

Doug's famous last ball hook off Bob Willis. 1974 at WACA, Perth (Source: Getty Images)

Ian Chappell (far right) with Rod Marsh, Doug Walters and Greg Chappell (R to L) outside the Kensington Hotel, London, Prudential World Cup, 29 May 1975 (Source: Alamy Images)

Doug bowling to Asif Iqbal. Prudential World Cup, Group B match (1975) (Source: Getty Images)

Prudential World Cup 1975 - Group B - Australia v Sri Lanka - The Oval. Doug Walters (Australia) sweeps Somachandra de Silva (Sri Lanka) to the boundary for four. Anura Tennekoon is at slip and Ranjith Fernando is the wicket-keeper (Source: Alamy Images)

Doug in the dressing room playing cribbage with Rick McCosker during the first Test match, Australia v. England at Edgbaston, 10th July 1975. Rod Marsh and Gary Gilmour are watching TV at the back (Source: Getty Images)

The Australian team for the Centenary Test (1977). Back row, from left: Ian Davies, Gary Gilmour, Rick McCosker, Gary Cosier, Kerry O'Keefe and David Hookes. Front row, from left: Max Walker, Rod Marsh, Greg Chappell, Doug Walters and Dennis Lillee (Source: Getty Images)

Doug Walters (Australia) batting, England vs Australia, 5th Test Match, The Oval, London, England 25-30th August 1977. Doug made only four before being bowled by Bob Willis (Source: Alamy Images

Doug (1977) – Front Cover Image from the 'World of Cricket' Monthly (Doug Walters' collection)

Doug in 1976-77 season. 'Found himself pressed into the NSW captaincy" (Reg Edwards, 1977). (Doug Walters' collection)

Doug driving Underwood in his inning of 88 in the second Test (Old Trafford, Manchester, 7 July 1977). Alan Knott is behind the stumps (Source: unknown)

A square cut from Doug – The Doug Walters statue to be erected at Dungog is based on this Photo. (Source: Doug Walters' collection)

Doug on the occasion of receiving the MBE (2011)
(Source: Unknown)

Doug in front of the 'Doug Walters Pavilion' at the Old Kings Oval in Parramatta, NSW after receiving the Member of the Order of Australia (AM) honours in 2022. The Doug Walters Pavilion is home to the Parramatta District Cricket Club.

(Source: Doug Walters' Collection)

Cover image of Ashley Mallet's book on Doug (2008)

Promotional material.
Source: Doug Walters' collection

Other 'Actors' prominent in the Book (Source: Public Domain images)

*Alan McGilvray –
The 'Voice of Australian Cricket'*

*John Arlott – BBC commentator,
a 'Golden Voice'*

*Sir Neville Cardus, among the greatest
of cricket writers (From*

*The Cricketer (U.K.), Author's
collection. With permission)*

*C. L. R. James, also among the greatest of
cricket writers (This 1974 picture is from the
120th Anniversary of his birth published by the
Duke University Press)*

Len Hutton and Don Bradman (1953)

Ray Lindwall, Sir Robert Menzies (Prime Minister), Lindsay Hassett and Frank Worrell

Keith Miller

Bob Simpson

Sir Garfield Sobers, the greatest all-rounder ever (Cover Picture from the Autobiography; Source: unknown. Author's collection.

CHAPTER 12

Triumph, Defeat, Mateship: All Part of the Game

As a cricket fan, I have been very much aware that the winning players feel proud if they can beat the Australians in their own backyard and be able to tell those tales to their grandchildren.

Peter Roebuck (2007) wrote: 'A tour to Australia counts amongst the most challenging experiences cricket offers. Teams visiting the antipodes and returning with the spoils of a series win feel rightly honoured by that experience....The reason is simple'.

'Among senior cricketing nations, Australia has the strongest sporting culture. Visiting teams know they are taking on a powerhouse. Australia may be beaten on its own patch from time to time. But only by a team capable of summoning and sustaining its mightiest effort. Australia's domination has been partly due to its single-mindedness and partly to the opponents' struggles. It is quite simply the game's ultimate testing ground. It tests the character of individual players and also the teams'.

Australians Humiliate Clive Lloyd's West Indies, 1975-76

When Australia's intended tour to South Africa was cancelled, the West Indies Board of Control agreed to send a side to Australia to play six Test matches two years before their next scheduled visit (*Wisden* 1977). With Jeff Thomson and Dennis Lillee on one side and Andy Roberts and several other fast bowlers on the other, it would obviously be a trial of strength between the best international sides of the time.

The series was highly anticipated because the West Indies beat Australia in the World Cup Final only a few months before. They had never won a series in Australia. It looked like this tour would give them that chance. With several high-quality players, at least on paper, the Windies looked like a formidable team.

As it happened, it was a monumental series that had a lasting impact on global cricket. But not in the way cricket fans expected. The humiliating defeat suffered by Lloyd's team changed cricket forever.

Lloyd's answer to the defeat was assembling a battery of fearsome West Indian fast bowlers far exceeding the menace of the Lillee-Thomson pair. The emergence of a quartet of legendary pacemen – Andy Roberts, Michael Holding, Colin Croft, Joel Garner, Malcolm Marshall and Patrick Patterson – directly resulted from the team's series defeat. Four fast bowlers, 'hunting in a pack', intimidated and mercilessly routed many opponents in the late 1970s (Becca 2010).

The fast bowling mantle was later expanded by Courtney Walsh, Curtley Ambrose and Ian Bishop, who led the Windies to an unparalleled domination of world cricket through the 1980s and 90s.

Lloyd's own assessment, based on the battering received from Lillee and Thomson, was that 'It was OK to face two pacemen who came at you hard; even three was just about manageable, but four – that made it nearly impossible to relax and take control of a match situation. Relentless pace throws your head into uncharted territory'.

* * *

However, the 1975-76 summer was disastrous for Doug as he got injured before the Test series began. Doug started the season wanting to make amends for yet another dismal Ashes series in England in 1975, despite some successes in the World Cup tournament. In the early season matches for NSW, Doug got 45 and 7 versus Queensland at the Gabba and 13 and 17 against Western Australia in Perth.

Then came the fateful Sheffield Shield match against South Australia in Adelaide. Doug got 56 in the NSW first innings. Set 266 runs to win, NSW would have cruised to victory had not fate taken a hand. The South Australian fast bowler Wayne Prior dropped one short when Doug was on five in the second inning. The ball came much slower off the pitch than Doug anticipated. As he went to hook the ball, his feet got caught in the cracks of the wicket. Doug's recollection (Mallett 2008: 267) was:

> While the foot stayed still, and my knee kept going. In trying to stop the shot, I lost balance and crashed heavily into the stumps. There was a loud cracking noise and excruciating pain. I thought a stump had broken off and had gone through my leg. The pain was so intense.
>
> Both ligaments had snapped, and my kneecap had fallen out of place and was around my shin bone. When the SA physiotherapist straightened my leg, he was able to manoeuvre the kneecap into place and strap it. Because both ligaments had snapped, there was nothing to hold the kneecap in place.

When Doug fell on his stumps, the opponents celebrated another NSW wicket, not knowing the extent of his injury. South Australia won the match by 21 runs. Reports said, 'The cost [of the injury] to the NSW captain and the Australian Test batter Doug Walters was far worse than a Sheffield Shield loss in the City of Churches'.

It took a full three months before Doug was fit enough to play. This meant he missed the entire six Test series against the West Indies. Doug was, therefore, fated to play just nine Tests against the West Indies, four in Australia and five in the Caribbean, scoring 1196 runs at 92, a remarkable record (Mallett 2008: 267).

According to Doug, while he didn't play in any Tests, he had another view of the game by doing TV commentary with ABC. He covered three Test matches. Doug also reported on the games for Sydney Radio Station 2UW. On one occasion, he said: 'It was much easier handling the West Indies fast bowlers from in front of a microphone rather than at the wicket!'.

* * *

This was a decisive series in world cricket as Lloyd's team lost to Greg Chappell's men by a substantial margin of 5-1. It resulted from a pace-battering handed out by Lillee and Thomson, under which the Windies buckled (ESPN Cricinfo 1977). I followed each match closely, listening to the well-received ABC broadcasts in Sri Lanka. The cricket was very competitive, and the series win was a kind of revenge for the World Cup loss Australia had suffered only a few months earlier.

Each side won one of the first two Tests, which promised a close contest. But it turned out to be a one-sided affair, as Australia began dominating from the third Test onwards. As the series progressed, the home team exposed the visitor's recklessness and lack of discipline in all departments. Lloyd's team hadn't given much thought to the conditions they would encounter in Australia, including the hard and bouncy pitches, and failed to adjust accordingly. *Wisden* (1977) noted that Lloyd's captaincy was also well below par on most occasions.

As the series progressed, he increasingly became defensive. Lloyd had been the captain in India the previous year when the Windies won narrowly by the odd Test match in five. He had also drawn a three-match series without any wins in Pakistan before leading the West Indies to victory in the World Cup. So, Lloyd was under real pressure as a captain in Australia and did not find it easy. When the strain was greatest, Lloyd's own batting suffered several times.

In many ways, Lloyd's attitude was similar to that of Sobers. Lloyd also believed that his professionals would work it out for themselves. But in that series, his highly talented batters failed him. Much of the time, they threw their wickets away after having made good starts.

Adventurous stroke-making has always been how the Windies *like* to play, instead of the head-down, hard grind of a long inning. It is an *attitude* best explained by the Caribbean islands' easy-going living, merriment, *Calypso-style* music and playing sports purely for fun.

There were a few good innings: Fredericks and Lloyd (169 and 149, respectively, in the second Test, at Perth), Rowe and Kallicharran (107 and 101, respectively, in the first Test, at Brisbane). Viv Richards also did well in the last two Tests (101 in the fifth Test in Adelaide, followed by 50 and 98 in the sixth at the MCG). Still, the batters didn't do themselves justice. Gordon Greenidge, who came to Australia as an exciting young batter, struggled badly before being dropped, forcing Viv Richards to open with Roy Fredericks in the final two tests.

Australia's winning margin of 5-1 was huge. The defeated Windies felt humiliated. Man for man, the Windies were as talented as Australia. However, the difference lay in their response to pressure (*Wisden* 1977). Several West Indian bowlers performed poorly, including Holding (10 wickets at 61) and Boyce (9 wickets at 40). Only Roberts, with 22 wickets at 26, proved his worth.

In contrast, for Australia, Lillee took 27 wickets at 26, Thomson 29 wickets at 27 and Gilmour 20 wickets at 20. Gibbs, a faithful servant of the West Indies, took 16 wickets at 40, but critics said he should have received more support from his captain (*Wisden* 1977). Nevertheless, Gibbs broke Fred Trueman's record Test wicket haul of 307 to go ahead in the all-time wicket-takers list.

* * *

Greg Chappell had a purple patch, scoring 702 runs at 117 in the six Tests with two centuries. Redpath hit three centuries, scoring 575 runs at 52. Ian Chappell (449 at 45 with two centuries) and Turner (439 at 37) also scored heavily for Australia. Most pundits pointed out that while Greg had a tremendous first series as captain, the presence of brother Ian had the most significant influence on the team's success.

Greg benefitted from the side's cohesion in Ian's presence beside him in the slips. Greg is at the top of anyone's list for elegant batsmanship in post-war Australian cricket. But people knew he didn't have the same flair for leadership as his brother.

As the West Indies were humiliated and Australians rejoiced, the summer produced some great cricket. It was also the first 'million-dollar series' as the six Tests drew large crowds and a total box office of over $1.1 million (Hutchinson and Ross 1997: 425).

Viv Richards (426 at 39) was the only one who left Australia a better player than when he arrived. As the tour progressed, Viv worked out his problems independently. Opening the innings in later tour matches and the last two Tests, he found the added responsibility some help to concentrate harder. After the tour, history knows how Viv, *'Master Blaster'*, developed quickly as one of the world's all-time great batters.

Pakistan Tour Down Under (1976-77)

Doug played in all three Tests against Pakistan, who visited Australia in the summer under Mushtaq Mohammad. I listened to the commentaries on *Radio Australia*, which was ABC Radio's overseas broadcast. These were short-wave transmissions beamed to a vast region, all across South and South-East Asia and the South Pacific.

Mushtaq, a fearless cricketer, transformed Pakistan into a fighting outfit, a legacy that the country's most influential cricketer – Imran Khan, later inherited. In this series, apart from the flamboyant Imran, Australia saw for the first time one of the most talented of Pakistani soldiers, a streetfighter from Karachi, the 20-year-old Javed Miandad.

The Pakistanis arrived in Australia with one of the best batting teams in Test cricket. By the time they left, the team had Imran, a fast bowler who proved himself to be one of the world's finest (Wilkins 1978). In the third Test at the SCG, the handsome Imran, a poster boy in his youthful days, bowled brilliantly in both innings, leading to a Pakistan win after they had lost the second Test at the MCG.

Lillee's persistent jibes that 'Pakistan pacemen were not good enough' riled the visitors. Mushtaq's astute leadership, the batting of Asif, Zaheer, Majid and Sadiq, and the wily bowling skills of Sarfraz, combined with Imran's pace, ensured a fiercely fought but thrilling series (Hutchinson and Ross 1997: 428). The success in Sydney infused Pakistan with self-belief. They also unearthed a genuine fast bowler in Imran, a necessity for any great team (Shafqat 2011).

Most important was the shift in mindset and a belief that they could win in Australia. As Australia was swept away in just over three days in the Sydney Test, the harsh realisation dawned on them that the team was vulnerable again without Ian Chappell, Redpath, Edwards, Mallett and

Jenner (Wilkins 1978), as in the previous decade.

Thomson got injured in the first Test and didn't play again in the series. Although Walker bowled as cleverly in the last two Tests as the replacement, without Thomson's venom, Australia's new-ball attack was never as dangerous despite Lillee's tireless efforts.

* * *

In the first Test (24-29 December 1976), Pakistan won the toss and batted on an even-paced wicket at the Adelaide Oval. But they could only score 272. Zaheer (85) showed his class; Imran (48) and Sarfraz (29) made late-order runs. Others made good starts but succumbed.

Disaster struck early for Australia when Thomson, having dismissed Majid and Mushtaq in his first eight overs (2/34), ran towards square leg from his bowling mark attempting to catch Zaheer and collided with Alan Turner. Thomson dislocated the collarbone of his right shoulder and was out of the series. Kerry O'Keeffe took 3/42.

The Australian reply (454) was built around centuries by Ian Davies (105s with 14 fours and a six) and Doug's 107. Doug was subdued, hitting only nine fours. Pakistanis were upset by Doug's refusal to walk early on the third day when he was 35 (Wilkins 1978). Doug played at a ball from Altaf; the umpire rejected the appeal for a catch at the wicket, and he carried on for his 13th century in 58 Tests. McCosker (65) and Greg Chappell (52) scored well for the home side, while Mushtaq (4/58) and Miandad (3/85) took the bulk of the wickets.

Without Thomson's menace, Pakistan scored 466. Zaheer (101) made his third century in 21 Tests. Majid (47) and Mushtaq (37) also batted well. Asif Iqbal made a superb 152* in just four and a half hours with 14 fours. Asif found resolute partners in Miandad (54) and Qasim (4), with whom he shared a record 10th wicket stand of 87. Lillee strained a thigh but valiantly bowled 48 overs, taking 5/163. A foot infection kept Gilmour out. O'Keeffe bowled 53 overs, taking 3/166.

Australia needed to score 285 runs on the final day. While Chappell (70) and Doug (51) were there, the win was within their grasp. Qasim's guile slowed the run rate, and when the final 15 overs began, Marsh and Cosier had to score only 56 runs to win. To the outrage of the spectators, they didn't go for the runs. Finishing at 6-261, Australia was 24 runs short. The crowd booed Marsh and Cosier off the ground (Hutchinson and Ross 1997: 428), an incident rarely seen in Australia.

* * *

Australia won the second Test at the MCG (1-6 January 1977) by 348 runs as Lillee wreaked havoc, taking 10/135 for the match. Walker replaced Thomson. Pakistan brought back Sadiq Mohammad for Mudassar Nazar. Also, it replaced Sarfraz Nawaz, who had strained his left thigh, with Asif Masood. On a placid pitch, Lillee applied his remarkable will to win the task at hand (Wilkins 1978).

Australia won the toss and batted after a rain delay. But Pakistan squandered the new ball, and Davis and Turner registered a first-wicket stand of 134. Greg Chappell (121) made his 13th century in 42 Tests. Chappell shared a record fifth-wicket stand of 171 with Cosier (168 with 20 fours. Chappell declared the innings at 8-517 midway through day two. The spinner Qasim was Pakistan's best bowler with 4/111.

Majid (76) and Sadiq (105) emulated the Australian openers with a century stand. Zaheer scored a classy 90, and Asif made 35. Lillee (6/82) bowled with hostility. I recall that some of Lillee's venom was directed at umpire Tom Brooks for warning him about excessive bouncers and then for bowling his over too slowly.

Pakistan was 2-266 by lunch on the third day but imploded soon after. O'Keeffe dismissed Sadiq after an inning of five hours. Then Lillee took the new ball, and his additional pace gained him another five wickets for 30 runs in seven overs. The last eight wickets fell for 63 runs. Pakistan conceded a lead of 184 runs.

Davis (88) and McCosker (105) built on Lillee's efforts with a second-wicket stand of 176. Chappell (67) lashed out before declaring with the score 8-315. It left Pakistan to get 500 runs to win. Doug faced only three balls and was bowled by Imran for a duck. Imran took 5/122. In the second inning, Pakistan was bowled out for 151. Lillee (4/53) and O'Keeffe (4/38) troubled them. Only Zaheer (58), Majid (35) and Imran (28) resisted, but Australia won easily on the fifth day.

The Pakistanis were bitter about Lillee hurling abuse at their batters, many of whom were seasoned English county professionals. Lillee's secret weapon was the relentless cries of *'Lill-ee, Lill-ee'* emanating from Bay 13 at the MCG. He gave the home crowd what they wanted. Greg Chappell even encouraged Lillee to be as hostile as possible towards the opponents. The umpires did nothing to curb the bowler.

The Pakistan team manager, Colonel Shuja-Ud-Din, railed against the home team, saying, *'Lillee should keep his trap shut'*. *'My boys have been to the best Universities; half of your lads are illiterate'*. He also accused Greg and Lillee of waging a psychological war against the visitors in newspaper columns they wrote while the series was on. The practice of players writing stuff while in the middle of a Test series was frowned upon even by the senior commentators and journalists.

* * *

In the third Test at the SCG (14-18 January 1977), Pakistan won by eight wickets, thus squaring the series 1:1. Sarfraz returned to lead their attack, along with Imran, who was, by this time, bowling fast. Greg Chappell batted after winning the toss. Sarfraz and Imran made use of the humidity and swung the ball around. Chappell's decision to bat was proven wrong as four wickets fell for 38 runs, including Doug being caught behind for just two runs off Imran.

Chappell (28) and Cosier (50) then had a determined stand of 62, after which a flurry of wickets fell, triggered by Imran, who bowled with speed and persistence. Australia collapsed to 9-198 by the end of day one. Gilmour (32), Lillee (14), and Walker (34*) defied Pakistan grimly and allowed the home side a modest score of 211.

Pakistan batted brightly at first but wobbled at 4-111. The debutant Haroon Rashid (57), Asif (120) and Miandad (64) helped Pakistan to a score of 360 and a substantial lead of 149. Walker (4/112), Gilmour (3/81) and Lillee (3/114) took the wickets. Asif's century pulled his team into a winning position. The umpires frequently warned Lillee for bowling bouncers at unrecognised batters, to no avail.

Trailing by 149 runs, the Australians displayed poor application again and collapsed to 9-180 as Imran's pace and Sarfraz's accuracy unsettled them. The umpires also warned Imran for bowling too many bouncers. There was much bitterness in the contest. At one stage, I recall that Marsh gestured at Imran with his bat after a series of bouncers in the final session. Imran smelled blood and was fired up.

Marsh top-scored with 41 before being run out. Doug made 38 before he was caught behind by Wasim Bari off Imran. Imran finished with 6/63 off 19.7 overs and a bag of 12/165 in the Test. Pakistan needed only 32 runs for its first and richly deserved Test win in Australia. They won by eight wickets. It was a match in which Imran Khan, an all-time great bowler and future Pakistan captain, showed the world what he could do for Pakistan cricket.

* * *

The Pakistan journalist Saad Shafqat (2011) said that Pakistan cricket's rise in modern times can be traced back to this landmark win in 1977. It was triggered by the brilliance of Imran, who 'transformed from medium pace to fast and lethal'. When the series began, Imran had not yet developed into the legendary warrior he later became.

The handsome Imran, from a wealthy family in Lahore, captained Oxford University. After making his Test debut in 1971, he had only been an intermittent presence in the team. The SCG Test was only his 10th Test, and up to that time, he had a modest record of 25 wickets at 43 before the metamorphosis to become a giant in world cricket.

Bruised after a fight with their cricket board and stung by the harsh reception in Australia, Pakistan was determined to make an impact. In Mushtaq, they had the right leader to do so. The Test win at the SCG transformed and altered the course of the country's cricket history.

Reports said that the tour almost didn't happen. A month before, Pakistan's top players (all except Intikhab) had confronted the cricket board chief, the dictatorial Abdul Kardar, demanding better salaries. Controversy erupted on a dramatic scale and was resolved only by government intervention. Asif Iqbal later said: 'Kardar made us feel small for demanding better pay when all we wanted was more dignity, which was important for the future of Pakistan cricket' (Shafqat 2011).

Intikhab, a top-tier spinner, came on the tour but didn't play in any Tests as Mushtaq, Miandad, and Qasim played the spinners' roles. Wilkins (1978) noted that Intikhab remained a pleasant but sad figure on the outer because he refused to stand by the seniors in the dispute over payments. But on tour, Intikhab backed the team to the hilt.

Doug fires in New Zealand (1976-77)

The Kiwis hosted a two-Test series in 1976-77. Glenn Turner captained the hosts, while Greg Chappell led the Australians. The bat prevailed in the first Test, which was drawn, but Australia won the second by ten wickets after Lillee's match figures of 11/123. The series highlight was Doug's highest score in Test cricket, scoring 250 in the first Test. The Australians won the series 1-0.

* * *

Doug was in vintage form in the drawn first Test in Christchurch (18-23 February 1977). He made 250, surpassing his highest score of 242 against the Windies in 1968-69. It was Doug's 14th Test century and his highest three-figure innings in Tests. He took 390 minutes to score the runs with exhilarating pulls, cuts and drives. Doug's inning rescued Australia from a precarious 6-208 as they scored 552. Gilmour showed his all-around talents and hit his first Test century (101) in a record partnership of 217 with Doug for the seventh wicket.

It was a slow wicket on which the Kiwi bowlers, led by the Hadlee brothers, toiled. There were many fielding lapses from New Zealand, and Doug capitalised on some hard chances he gave, which were not taken. The Kiwi batters fought back well, replying with 357. Burgess (66) and Hedley Howarth (61) batted well, while O'Keeffe troubled the Kiwis with his leg spin, wheeling away 28 overs, taking 5/101.

Batting a second time, McCosker was 77*. and Doug, 20*, when Greg declared at 4-154. The hosts saved the match, scoring 8-293 while chasing 350. The former captain, Congdon, remained unbeaten at the end (107*). For Australia, Walker took a match-bag of 7/131 in 51 overs. In contrast, Lillee's results were poor (4/189 in 49 overs).

* * *

In the second Test, at Eden Park in Auckland (25 February-1 March 1977), Greg Chappell sent the Kiwis into bat on a grassy pitch. They were bowled out for 229, with Lillee taking 5/51. The Australians scored 377. McCosker (84), Chappell (58) and Gilmour (64) did the bulk of the scoring. This time, there was no Walters magic; Doug was out for only 16 (Hutchinson and Ross 1997: 430).

A rampant Lillee routed the Kiwis in the second inning for 175, taking 6/72. They were 5 for 31 at one stage as Lillee crashed through the top order. For the hosts, Richard Hadlee's all-around capabilities were on display (44 and 81), but the Kiwis lost by 10 wickets.

Doug topped the Australian batting averages, scoring 286 at 143, including the monumental 250. The Trans-Tasman series was played in good spirits this time, erasing the 1974 memories of the ugly clashes between the two sides. The bright cricket drew record crowds. The visitors were appreciated for being competitive.

The Australian players also received more money ($2340 each) for a month's work, which was considerably more than anyone ever received up to that time. This was due to a sponsorship deal with Benson & Hedges cigarette manufacturers. It was estimated that such pay allowed cricketers to earn about $30,000 per year playing cricket.

In the Tests against Pakistan only a few months before, the players received a base fee of $400 per Test plus $75 for expenses and a bonus of $275 for each Test. A $750 per Test payment would have been a pittance by today's standards. Nevertheless, the pay increases vindicated the battles Ian Chappell had earlier fought with the ACB over the pay for cricketers (Hutchinson and Ross 1997: 428).

* * *

Ronan O'Connell (2018) explained that cricket broadcasting in Australia went through its greatest-ever change in 1956 with the advent of TV. The ABC swiftly began live TV cricket coverage, with the first Shield match broadcast in November 1956. The first Test match shown on Australian TV (Black & White) was a women's Ashes match played in Melbourne in February 1958. Men's Tests followed later that year. TV coverage made the ABC the 'home of Australian cricket', and the national broadcaster's popularity grew steadily through the 1960s and '70s as more and more Australian households began to own TVs.

However, in the mid-1970s, the Australian TV industry suffered from lacking Australian content. The commercial networks depended on buying cheaper packages from the USA and the UK rather than commissioning Australian content.

The advent of colour TV in 1975 markedly improved sport as a TV spectacle to attract viewers, who could then be lured by advertisements for various products. However, cricket officials initially thought that live coverage of games on TV could severely drop revenue at the gates, a premise that was disproven.

The battle for commercial TV to show cricket began in March 1976 with Australia's Channel Nine Network owner, Kerry Packer, making offers to the ACB for exclusive rights to show the games with new technologies and wider coverage than ABC TV could show.

The ACB, who received Packer's first offer for the rights for $120,000, declined the offer. Packer spent many years trying to get the TV rights for cricket but had been continually rebuffed by the ACB, which incensed him. Packer's personality would not take a refusal lightly, and as an entrepreneur, he saw that cricket was money.

While the confused ACB was dragging its feet, doubling the offer to $236,000, in February 1977, Packer secured exclusive TV rights from the Test & County Cricket Board (TCCB) in England to show the forthcoming Ashes Tests on his commercial channel.

A TV war broke out, beginning the 'new era' of commercial TV taking over Test cricket coverage. Packer's counter-punch, World Series Cricket, sponsored by the Channel Nine TV Network, turned the world of cricket upside down. People were dismayed about what might be in store for Test cricket. Many commentators in Britain and Australia were also unsure about how cricket might be impacted by the war over commercial rights. ABC TV's effective monopoly on cricket ended with the arrival of WSC and Channel Nine winning the war.

It was evident that Packer used his wealth and influence to create a rival cricket product that he could market for profit. As cricket was so popular, it offered the opportunity to rake in millions of dollars in advertising revenue. Packer knew he was on to a winner. He also recruited three of the most influential figures he could persuade – Benaud to lead the commentary team, Ian Chappell and Greig as 'recruiters'. These were stokes of a genius from a master strategist.

The Centenary Test (March 1977)

Frank Tyson (1977), described by Arlott as a person 'With the mind of a scholar and an experienced Test cricketer, admirably equipped to write the Ashes history', authored the ACB's official publication of The Centenary Test. Tyson called it a momentous event, bringing hundreds of former players from both sides: 'One instinctively felt that the game was concerned with people – ex-Test players, current players and spectators alike – gathering together to honour a hundred years of human and cricketing achievements'.

A brief digression is warranted here to ponder the significance of the celebrated centenary of Test cricket. The first Australia v. England Test match, played in Melbourne on 15 March 1877, started a rivalry that has become part of the world's cricket history. Gordon Ross (1976), writing for *Wisden*, noted, 'The rivalry survived the ravages of one World War, and then another, to stand the passage of time, unchallenged in national affection in both countries'.

The 1876-77 tour was the fourth by an English team. The first-ever tour to Australia was in 1861-62 by a team led by H. H. Stephenson of Surrey, who obliged a request from a Melbourne catering firm (Spiers & Pond) that 'he would collect a team and go to Australia with an idea of pioneering cricket of international standard in that country'. Ross (1976) noted: 'It was all the more surprising that sponsorship took another hundred years to play a major role in cricket'.

The success of the 1861-62 tour stimulated cricket in the Colony. It resulted in many cricket clubs being formed in Victoria, NSW and South Australia. The second historical tour occurred in 1863-64, an English team led by George Parr. This was followed by perhaps the most important tour, 1873-74, a team led by W. G. Grace. After the tour, Grace wrote, 'cricket in Australia had improved wonderfully and was still improving; some very useful cricketers had been seen'.

In between, an Aboriginal Australian team toured England in 1868. This was 10 years before the first white tour. The team played 47 matches across various counties and minor teams (14 wins, 14 losses and 19 draws) Pollard, 1995: 6-8). Mullagh, a key player, impressed even W.G. with his 'all-round ability' (Hutchinson and Ross 1997: 26). Sadly, tour reports showed that *racism* was on display as *'cricket was supposed to have a humanising and civilising effect'* on the visitors.

The fourth English tour was in the winter of 1876-77 when twelve professional cricketers under James Lillywhite of Sussex arrived in Australia (Pollard 1995: 18-20). The first official Test, which Australia won by 45 runs, took place in Melbourne on 15 March 1877. England insisted on a second 'Test', granted and played on 31 March 1877 (Pollard 1992: 20-35). This time, England won by four wickets. Still, the Australian public accused England of kidding in the first match to obtain another game and gate revenues.

* * *

The 100th birthday of Ashes Test cricket was indeed the greatest cricketing event up to that time. The public rated the match as one of the greatest of the 20th Century. Played in Melbourne at the MCG from 12-17 March 1977, the Test received massive support from the Australian Federal government and various State governments.

It was also well supported by the hospitality and airline industries and Benson & Hedges, the official cricket sponsor. More than 61,000 people came to the MCG on day one. They watched a great spectacle, an opening ceremony, which celebrated the event's significance. It was a festival and reunion, such as cricket had never known.

The crowd was introduced to the 'honoured guests' – some eighteen former Test captains from either side. They also saw a galaxy of 200-odd former Test players, the oldest present being the Australian – Jack Ryder, 87, who died less than a month after the event. Percy Fender, 84, was the senior-most English cricketer who attended (Tyson 1977).

The England captains present were Bob Wyatt, 'Gubby' Allen, Norman Yardley, Freddie Brown, Len Hutton, Peter May, Ted Dexter, Mike Smith, Colin Cowdrey, Tom Graveney and Mike Denness. The Australian captains present were Don Bradman, Lindsay Hassett, Ian Johnson, Neil Harvey, Richie Benaud, Bob Simpson, Bill Lawry and Ian Chappell (Frith 1997: 304).

Many past players had been flown in with sponsorship funding and support from the Hilton Hotel chain. Bands from Australia's defence forces played *God Save the Queen* as the Australian and English flags unfurled from their masts at the top of the scoreboard. I was thrilled, listening to loud applause and cheers from the crowd, which resounded around the giant stadium.

Amazingly, the result was the same as in the inaugural Test, with Australia winning by 45 runs. I listened to the commentaries as the incredible drama unfolded. Many thought the contest would be over within three days because both teams collapsed in their first innings due to nervousness at the beginning. But what a dramatic Test it turned out to be? Both teams fought fiercely over five days when the nerves settled, making it an epic match. The ending fitted the 100-year Tests celebration, although England was thoroughly disappointed.

The Test has been dubbed Randall's Match. It deserves to be so-called because of the monumental second-inning knock of 174 by England's Derek Randall. His inning lit up the historical encounter. The perpetually moving, cheeky, but likeable Nottinghamshire batter is an unusual cricketer, both in appearance and demeanour, like a court jester in many ways. He is famous for fidgeting and on-field antics.

Derek was also a brilliant fielder in the covers or anywhere else on a cricket field. On that day in March 1977, Randall, batting at No. 3, put up a grand performance in front of the great galaxy of dignitaries, and on the final day, in front of Royalty – Her Majesty the Queen of England and Australia. It was indeed Randall's proudest moment in life.

* * *

Greig won the toss made with a gold commemorative medallion and put Australia in. His decision paid off as Australia collapsed to be all out for 138. The batting failed miserably under some steady bowling by Old (3/39), Underwood (3/16), John Lever (2/38) and Willis (2/33) and good fielding. The Australian opener, McCosker, suffered a broken jaw as he tried to hook a rising ball from Willis, which deflected off his bat, onto the face, and then fell on the stumps.

Greg Chappell made a patient 40; he batted for five hours. Greg also had a partnership of 51 with Marsh (28), doubling the score from 5-51 (when Doug fell) to 102 in the miserable collapse. Chappell was the ninth man out, bowled by Underwood as he lashed out. It was Underwood's 250th Test wicket; he ended up with 3/16 off 11.6 overs.

Doug scored four runs before being caught off a misjudged hook off a rising ball from Willis. The bumper was way outside his off stump and moving away when Doug hooked. The ball went straight up in the air to be caught by a jubilant Greig fielding at second slip. A 'bad shot' was how the commentator described it.

After the Australian innings folded up, England batted for an hour to be 1-29 at the end of an incredible day of slow scoring under bright sunlight and a good pitch. It was clear to everyone that the players felt utterly overawed by the celebratory occasion, playing in front of the large gathering of legendary stars of the past.

Resuming on day two, England crashed out to be 95 all out within two and a half hours. A fired-up Lillee (6/26 in 24.3 overs) and Walker (4/54 off 15 overs) were too much for England's batters. The partisan crowd roared and chanted '*Lill-ee, Lill-ee*' as he ran into bowl, the loud noise revibrating across the ground.

A huge banner gave a message to inspire Lillee: '*We All Luv Ya Dennis*', and he rewarded them with his decisive bowling. When Lillee intimidated the English batters, bowling with four slips, two gullies and the keeper behind, ready to catch anything, Arlott's excited and unmistakable voice described the scene colourfully:

> *Lillee setting a field of immense hostility... seagulls on the top of the stands looking on as vultures recruited for him. The crowd with sun and beer doing their work, appealing for quite significant non-events.*

It was one of the lowest Test scores that England had made against Australia and a huge embarrassment. The visiting greats were dismayed at the overawed team's lack of application. Tony Greig top-scored with 18. Only three other batters entered double-figures as England crashed from 2-30 to 95 in only 35.3 overs.

* * *

The second innings from both sides were a complete contrast and real Test cricket as their nerves appeared to settle down. With more than three and a half days to go, Australia needed a big score and a long inning to allow the wicket to wear and make life difficult for England chasing a big target. They started off well, cheered on by a vast crowd. Ian Davis (68) opened with O'Keeffe as McCosker was injured. But Australia was soon in trouble again at 3-53. For some minutes, it looked as if the inning might go the same way as the first.

Doug's experience settled things at this crucial stage. He needed a bit of luck at 16. Willis dropped him in the gully. At the end of day two, Doug and Davis had put on a half-century partnership, and Australia's lead was 147. Batting sensibly, Doug dominated a 79-run stand with Davis and steadied the inning.

Doug's inning included classic on-drives, straight drives, hooks and cuts, and all trademark shots that would have pleased the great assembly of batters watching. The inning delighted me as I held my breath, listening. When Doug was caught behind by Knott off Greig for 66, he had added 55 for the fifth wicket with the debutant, the left-handed David Hookes, and Australia had reached 5-187. By this time, the lead was well over 200, which allowed the 21-year-old South Australian debutant Hookes to become adventurous.

Hookes took to assault, striking five successive fours off Tony Greig's fastish off-spin, creating a sensation. It was a highlight of the Australian second inning, admired by the greats who had seen such ferocious counter-attacks previously. Hookes took his score from 36 to 56 with the five boundary hits, receiving a standing ovation from the crowd. But he was out immediately after, caught brilliantly at short-leg by a diving Fletcher off Underwood.

The commentators said, 'A new batting champion has arrived'. Someone needed to score more, with a score of 5-244, when Hookes departed. With a lead of 287, Marsh continued the assault, swinging the game Australia's way. When the eighth wicket fell at 353, the injured McCosker reappeared unexpectedly, his face tightly bound with bandages, which held his jaw together. This bravado was greatly appreciated by the cheering crowd. McCosker made some crucial runs, and the incident also made the Test memorable, even today.

The crowd recognised his courage further as McCosker batted in a cap – the helmet was not used in cricket until the following year. McCosker was 17*, Marsh 95* and Australia led by 430 by day three, with the next day a rest day. McCosker was out for 25 the next morning, but Lillee made 25, and when Chappell declared at 9-419, Marsh was 110*. Australia's lead was 463. Marsh was the first Australian wicket-keeper to hit a century in a Test, a record at the time.

* * *

Common sense returned to the Test match as England chased an improbable 464 to win. Batting with purpose, they ended the fourth day at 2-191 with Derek Randall 87* after four hours of batting. Brearley (43) had an 85-run partnership with Randall, who batted brilliantly, cutting, pulling, hooking and driving effortlessly. With England's fight back, following Australia's impressive second inning, at the end of day four, everyone was relieved that this was Test cricket at its best, contested by two evenly-matched teams.

England still needed 272 to win on the final day with eight wickets. Randall and Amiss (64) continued their third-wicket partnership from overnight. At lunch on the final day, with the score at 2-267, it looked as if England could pull off an unlikely victory. Lillee had a heavy workload by this time, as Gilmour was injured. Randall and Amiss put on 166. Fletcher fell for just one. When Greig joined Randall, the score was 4-290, and a victory for England was still on the cards.

More drama followed as Randall continued his assault, scoring more than half of England's runs. With the score at 4-324, he edged a Greg Chappell leg-cutter, and Marsh tumbled to hold the catch. Umpire Tom Brooks upheld the appeal, and Randall started walking back for 161. As the crowd applauded, Marsh told the umpire that the catch wasn't clean. Randall was recalled. Considering the state of the match, it was sportsmanship seldom witnessed in history, befitting the significance of the historic occasion.

With his score at 174 and England at 5-346, Randall fell to a diving catch at short leg by Cosier off O'Keeffe. He had batted a marathon of 448 minutes, faced 337 balls and hit 21 fours. Randall's great inning brought England close to what might have been a historic win.

The century made him the 14th English player to score a century in his first Test against Australia. Randall was in elite company in this regard. Others on the list who hit centuries in their first Tests against Australia included Grace, the three great Indian Princes who played for England – Ranjitsinhji, Duleepsinhji and Nawab of Pataudi Snr. – along with Herbert Sutcliffe, Maurice Leyland, Len Hutton, Denis Compton and Bill Edrich.

The Queen was present when England went into tea at 5-354, needing another 109 to win. Nothing appeared impossible as long as Greig and Knott were at the crease. But a victory looked improbable when Greig fell for 41, also caught by Cosier off O'Keeffe. The players were presented to the Queen at the break, and observers wrote that the occasion might have affected Greig's concentration.

Knott's fighting inning (42) ended when he was trapped lbw by Lillee in the second of the mandatory 15 overs in the final hour. It was also the end of England's second inning, with the score at 417. They were short by 45 runs – precisely the same winning margin as in the first-ever Test in 1877, one hundred years ago.

Incredibly, history had repeated itself! Lillee was hailed for a superhuman effort. He tirelessly bowled 34.4 overs in the second inning, taking 5/139 for a match haul of 11 wickets. O'Keeffe bowled 33 overs, taking 3/109. Fittingly, Lillee was presented with a cup – a replica of the one given in 1877 to the best bowler in the first Test.

Derek Randall won the Benson & Hedges *Man of the Match* award of $1500 and a gold medallion deservedly, ahead of Lillee and Marsh. Lillee, suffering from a back injury (a re-opening of the spinal stress fracture), dropped a bombshell on the morning of the final day of the Test by declaring himself unfit for the forthcoming tour to England.

* * *

Derek Randall, ever the crowd-pleaser, is known as *'Arkle'*, after the Irish thoroughbred racehorse who won many races in the 1960s to become a national treasure in Ireland. Everyone admired Randall for his on-field antics, including the celebratory cartwheeling, habitual eccentricities and brilliant fielding. He made a name for himself, sprinting after a ball across the ground, lightning-fast throws and direct hits at the stumps from cover.

Randall's antics during the Centenary Test are also well-known. While accepting the Man of the Match award, he barely said anything except to thank everyone. But he didn't forget to thank Lillee for hitting him on the head!. In the first innings, acknowledging a great bouncer, Randall doffed his cap, bowing to Lillee. He was heard jokingly saying: *'No point in hitting me there, mate; there's nothing in it'*. The very next ball, he was caught behind for only four.

In another instance, in the second inning, approaching his 150, Randall was hit by a vicious Lillee bouncer. He tottered and lost his cap, which nearly fell on his wicket. He went down but did a backwards somersault. England feared the worst. But the animated batter was on his feet quickly, eager to carry on the battle. After looking slightly rattled, he rubbed his head vigorously for a few minutes and continued without treatment. In the days when helmets were not available, even viewing the film footage makes one uneasy about how dangerous this might have been.

The Centenary Test was the 225th Test between the rivals. At its conclusion, the results tally in the Ashes battles stood at 88 Tests won by Australia, 71 won by England, and 66 drawn. Many cricket fans still talk about the hugely exciting Test at the MCG and the spectacle on the ground, which was bathed in brilliant sunshine every day.

The presence of all the cricketing dignitaries, the Australian Prime Minister, State Premiers, and the attendance of the Queen on the final day made it a truly remarkable event. While I wasn't there physically, I can attest to the same incredible shared feeling I got while listening to ABC Radio. These memories still linger more than four decades later.

Greg Chappell's Aussies - Routed in the Jubilee Series (1977)

Following their triumph in the Centenary Test, the Australians arrived in England to play a series dubbed 'The Jubilee Test Series, 1977'. They were without the injured Lillee. Greg Chappell's team was dubbed by the English press 'as the most hopeless team despatched to England by Australia in 30 years'. Events proved this to be the case. Chappell's team was routed by a more professional English outfit that played better at home in a dismally wet summer (Phillipson 1978).

I listened to the BBC broadcasts of each match and hoped for better performances from the Aussies as the series unfolded. Australia lost a great deal of prestige built during the Ian Chappell era. They only won five of the 22 tour games in the dismal tour. The Australian team was transitioning, particularly after Ian's retirement. Lillee's absence also weakened the bowling. Something else was also brewing in the background, which was the reason for the spate of poor performances.

The news about the formation of a 'rebel' organization by the Channel Nine TV owner and Media Mogul – Kerry Packer- broke out five weeks before the Test series. As negotiations with administrators broke, Packer threatened to organize his World Series Cricket (WSC) circus and Supertests by signing up elite players from different countries.

Secretively, his leading recruiter was the England captain – Greig. The Australian team was already in England when the news broke out. Ross (1978) reported what the manager, Maddocks, said:

> *I do not envisage the present development having a detrimental effect on this tour. But if any of the players play for a side contrary to the jurisdiction of the Australian Board, they will place their careers in jeopardy.*

The way this news came out with implications for the players utterly unsettled the team. The cause of the initial rift was the likelihood that while Australian players faced a ban, England players who had signed up continued to be regarded as open for selection to play in future Test cricket (Haigh 1993). At a meeting on 26 July 1977, just before the third Test, the ICC took a tough stand and said that any player in the Packer circus would be ineligible to play any Tests under its patronage.

This grim news hung over the touring party, affecting their performances. Two months earlier, in May 1977, the UK Cricket Council had already stripped Greig of his captaincy for his association with the WSC circus. The selectors chose Mike Brearley of Middlesex as England's next captain. Brearley, a renowned psychologist, became one of England's most successful captains in the modern era.

* * *

The enigmatic Boycott ended his self-imposed exile, in which he missed a possible 30 Test matches and made himself available to play for England again. His inclusion in the team wasn't popular as many former players considered Boycott's behaviour 'traitorous' at worst or 'unconscionably petulant' at best. Ever the dour Yorkshireman, Boycott ignored such noises and stated that he was available for consideration as captain, a generous offer that the selectors ignored.

Making his second debut in the third Test at Trent Bridge, Boycott answered his critics with scores of 107 and 80*. This was his 98th first-class hundred. He scored his 99th century in a county match against Warwickshire between the third and fourth Tests. In the fourth Test, Boycott reached the milestone of a hundred centuries. He scored a monumental 191, setting a record as the first man to achieve this remarkable feat in a Test.

* * *

The first Test played at Lord's (16-21 June 1977) was called the Jubilee Test match in honour of Queen Elizabeth's 25 years on the throne. It ended in a disappointing draw due to bad weather. Playing conditions were murky, cold and dark on four days, even in mid-June. More than 101,000 people attended the match and paid record receipts for any cricket match staged in Britain of more than £220,000.

Batting first, England made only 216 in the first inning as Thomson (4/41) and Walker (3/66) broke through. They owed everything to Woolmer (79) and Randall (53), who withstood the pressure from the Australian attack of Thomson and Len Pascoe.

Disciplined batting by Greg Chappell (66), Craig Sergeant (81, on debut) and Doug (53) helped Australia reach 296 and lead by 80 runs. Under dark clouds, batting wasn't easy. Chappell batted for three hours before he hit a four. Craig Sergeant, on debut, made a painful start to his career. He took 40 minutes to open his account. Bob Willis swept through the tail, taking 7/78 in 30 overs.

England had to do better in the second dig, which they did. Brearley (49) and Woolmer (120) wiped off the deficit with a second wicket stand of 132. Woolmer's solidity thwarted the Australians. Greig made an attacking 91, getting the score up to 305.

Australia needed 226 to win but lost wickets regularly in the chase. Hookes cracked a belligerent 50, but Doug fell to Underwood for 10. The Australians only scored less than four runs an over as they perceived a risk of losing the match. As a result, Rod Marsh accepted the umpires' offer of poor light to end the game in a draw.

* * *

England won the second Test (Old Trafford, 7-12 July 1977) by nine wickets. Doug (88) scored top in Australia's first inning of 297. This was his highest Test score in England. Greg Chappell (44), Marsh (36), and Ian Davis (34) batted well, while John Lever took 3/60. Woolmer (137), Randall (79) and Greig (76) helped England reach 437 and lead by 140 runs. Thomson bowled 38 overs (3/73); Walker bowled an incredible 54 overs, taking 3/131. The two spinners, Ray Bright (3/69) and O'Keeffe (1/114), also toiled for little reward.

Australia's second inning was a failure apart from Greg Chappell's masterful century (112) before Underwood bowled him. Underwood gave a virtuoso show of spin bowling, taking 6/66. Doug failed in the second inning, scoring only 10, and Australia was all out for 218. England needed only 78 and won easily (1-82). Brearley led the way with 44, registering England's first home Test victory against any country in 14 matches (Frith 1997: 307).

* * *

The third Test at Trent Bridge, Nottingham (28 July-2 August 1977) marked the second debut of Geoff Boycott and the Test debut of one of England's greatest all-rounders, Ian Terrence Botham. Botham's debut was outstanding, as England secured its first Test win over Australia at this ground since 1930.

Australia managed only 243 in the first inning. McCosker (51), O'Keeffe (48*) and Davis (33) were the leading scorers. Botham took 5/48 in 20 overs, announcing to the world the arrival of a great swing-bowler. He moved the ball prodigiously and had Doug caught by Hendrick in the slips for just 11.

England replied by scoring 364, with a slow century from Boycott (107 in seven hours) and Knott smashing his way to 135 in five hours. When Knott joined Boycott, England tottered at 5-82 but recovered with their 215-run partnership. McCosker dropped Knott at 87, a critical error (Frith 1997: 308). In a much-talked-about runout, Randall, at 13, sacrificed his wicket after a poor call from Boycott. Boycott was upset, but the incident made him even more determined not to give his wicket away. Len Pascoe (3/80) and Thomson (3/103) bowled with venom but couldn't stop Boycott and Knott from staging a recovery.

Trailing by 121 runs, Australia scored 309 in the second inning. I recall how McCosker occupied the crease for over seven hours for his 107. Hookes made a patient 42 in three hours; O'Keeffe, 21* in two hours; Robinson, 34 in 95 minutes, as the tourists tried to build a defendable total. Doug batted well but was out for 28, caught off a mistimed drive by Randall off Greig.

Bob Willis was again the lead striker for England, taking 5/88. Rod Marsh recorded two ducks in his 50th Test match. England lost only three wickets, scoring 189 and winning by seven wickets. Boycott was 80*, and Brearley was 81. Returning to Test cricket, Boycott's batting was the point of difference between the two teams.

* * *

The fourth Test at Headingley (11-15 August 1977) was memorable for Boycott as he made his 100th first-class century, the only player to do so in a Test match. Gates were shut on the first two days as his supporters poured in. Brearley won the toss; England batted first, reaching 4-252 at the end of the first day, with Boycott on 110*.

Thomson, Walker and Pascoe really tested him. But with patience and skill, Boycott passed the test with flying colours. He was the last man out, batting for ten hours for his second-best Test score (191). England's total was 436, with help from Knott (57), Greig (43) and Graham Roope (34). Thomson took 4/114 and Len Pasco 4/91.

Australia's batting was quickly ruined. Mike Hendrick of Derbyshire got movement off the pitch, rattling the tourists (4/41 in 16 overs). Doug fell to Botham, caught by Hendrick in the gully for just four. McCosker (27) was run out from a brilliant piece of fielding by Randall, a swoop and a direct hit at the non-striker end when the batter backed up too far. Australia crumbled for 103 as Botham ran through the tail, taking his first five-wicket haul (5/21 in just 11 overs).

Brearley enforced the follow-on. When day three ended in rain, Australia was 4-120. Greg Chappell (29*) batted long while others fell around him. Doug made only 15. More rain interrupted play, but the weather gods did not save Australia on this occasion. Chappell fell for 36 on day four to hasten the defeat. The tail wagged as Marsh (63) lashed out. Hendrick (4/54) and Willis (3/32) wrecked the batting. Australia made only 248, losing the match by an inning and 85 runs.

Randall took a spectacular catch to end the game at deep mid-off when Marsh slogged Hendrick. Ever the jester, he cartwheeled in sheer pleasure as Australia surrendered the Ashes. Knott passed 250 Test dismissals. The beleaguered visitors were down 3-0. The home side had captured the Ashes at The Oval in 1926, the year of the Queen's birth; then again in 1953, the year of her *Coronation*, and now, for the first time ever, at Headingley, in the year of her *jubilee* (Frith 1997: 309).

* * *

The fifth Test at The Oval (25-30 August) was drawn. Rain washed out the first day. By this time, the Australian team was deeply affected by the imminent split in the game due to the WSC debacle that hovered over the series. The Australian cricketers who had signed up with the Packer outfit feared they would soon become 'outlaws'.

As it happened, this was the case for the next two years. Australia dropped Davis and Robinson and introduced the promising young star and future Australian captain Kim Hughes. They also recalled Craig Sergeant to open the innings with McCosker. Pascoe lost his place to the fast-medium bowler Mick Malone, who made his Test debut.

Chappell won the toss and put England in. They struggled to reach 214, as Malone took 5/63. Thomson's 4/87 included his 100th Test wicket. Australia replied with 385 and showed resolve, especially from Hookes (85), Walker (78*), Marsh (57), Malone (46) and Chappell (39).

Kim Hughes fell for one, batting for an agonizing 30 minutes to get off the mark. Doug failed, making only four before Willis (5/102) bowled him. It was his last Test inning in England. England trailed by 171 runs. They were 2-57 when the play was called off due to bad light. Boycott (25*) scored his 5000th Test run before play was abandoned.

Following the stellar performances in the debut series, Ian Botham became a nemesis for Australia. He was knighted in 2007 and given the honour of a *Lordship* in the House of Lords in 2020 [38]. Boycott played in only three Tests but topped the batting (442 at 147). He was a divisive figure and a flawed genius. Still, Doug and I admire him as a 'perfectionist' and sheer willpower. Doug said he learned a few things from 'Boycs' about how to bat in England [39].

Australians were outplayed in all the matches. The star batter, Greg Chappell, only scored 371 runs at 41, while Hookes was the only other to average more than 30 (283 at 31). Doug's aggregate, only 223 runs at 25, was his lowest in a Test series. The seniors failed, except for McCosker's century in the third Test. The newcomers (Craig Serjeant, Ian Davis, Richie Robinson and Kim Hughes) mostly failed. The team's batting failures were epitomised by Gary Cosier, who lost form and never played Test cricket again.

---

38 Lord Ian Botham became England's captain in 1979 before quitting in 1980, bringing Brearley back again as England's captain. How Botham then went on to 'steal' an Ashes series (1980-81) from under the noses of Kim Hughes' Australians is part of cricket's legendary folklore. Botham is one of the greatest all-rounders in the world. He took 383 wickets at an average of 28; scored 5200 runs at 35.5 with 14 centuries, and took 120 catches, in 102 Test matches.

39 Boycott was awarded a knighthood in 2019. One of the greatest opening batters in cricket, he scored 8114 runs at 47.7 with 22 centuries, in 108 Tests.

In Packer's Shadow

I listened to the BBC broadcasts of all the Tests and was puzzled by Australia's dismal performances. But I soon realised what affected the team. Cricket was a distraction as I wrote my final exams in August 1977. The dark clouds of the Packer circus and its secrecy hovered over the players. Mistrust and disunity greatly affected the team morale.

In March 1977, only a few people knew of Packer's scheme to launch a rebel series of international matches that could be shown on Channel Nine TV. Greig had been sworn to secrecy and recruited players for the venture. While people were oblivious to the secretive machinations, Greig led the touring team to play the Centenary Test in Melbourne in March 1977. His name became anathema for a few years among all cricket lovers due to his involvement with Packer.

Delivering *'The Spirit of Cricket'* Cowdrey Lecture on 27 June 2012, at Lord's, in the same year he died, Greig said that when he joined WSC cricket, he had 'no regrets, nor did he have any doubt that he was doing the right thing'. Greig injected much-needed dynamism into England's cricket. Mike Selvey (2012) explained that Greig's massive influence was felt in both county and Test cricket.

Boycott's book *The Corridor of Certainty* (2014: 124-130) explains Greig's secret involvement as Packer's recruitment agent and how he fell out with Greig and the Court case in the UK, which decided in favour of WSC. However, Boycott also unequivocally believed that: 'Instead of destroying cricket, Packer's venture improved the lives of cricketers and the appeal of cricket, more broadly as a global sport'.

In Packer's shadow, 'Official cricket' won some minor victories. Packer couldn't use the terms 'Test Matches' or call his teams 'Australia'. The 'official' cricket rules also could not be used as they were copyrighted by the MCC. So, the five-day matches were called 'Supertests' and played between The WSC Australian XI' and the WSC World XI. Richie Benaud wrote a new set of rules for the games.

As WSC cricket was shut out of the traditional cricket venues, Packer hired football parks and other grounds in the big cities and dropped 'pre-prepared pitches' into place using cranes and helicopters. The 'drop-in' pitches were grown in hothouses outside the venues and then placed in holes, carefully dug up to the correct size. Without these and other inventions, WSC wouldn't have been successful.

CHAPTER 13

The Last Stand

Everything must come to an end, whether good or bad. The end of a cricketer's cricketing life can also be abrupt. Doug's wasn't quite so abrupt, but he knew it was on the cards, particularly after The Kerry Packer World Series cricket debacle upset cricket's cosmology.

Doug played 75 tests and scored 15 centuries in his career, with a career-best 250 against New Zealand in 1976. He played at the elite level when Australian cricket was transformed from something modest to a position of the world's best and the team to beat.

The Test batting average of 48.2 places him among the top of Australia's batters, a remarkable achievement. An entertainer to the bone, we can only speculate how many more runs he would have scored had his early career not been interrupted in 1966-68 for two years in National Service and if he hadn't missed the 1975-76 series against the West Indies.

The third interruption, after the WSC (1977-79), was also a setback for his Test career. Doug missed selection for the 1979-80 summer when the Windies and England toured Australia and played three Tests each.

Doug's Last Century - against Kiwis, 1980-81 Summer

In the summer of 1980-81, Doug made a superb 186 for NSW against South Australia in a Shield game in Sydney, which resulted in him being re-instated in the Australian team to play the two visiting teams – New Zealand and India. So, following the three years of WSC cricket, Doug was returning to Test cricket after a lapse of four years.

In the disastrous Australian 1978-79 summer of cricket, Mike Brearley's visiting England team thrashed Graham Yallop's weakened Australian team without top-tier players. Yallop (1979), in his *Lambs to the Slaughter* book, described how dreadful cricket was in that period when he tried his best to build a competitive team. The defeat by a 5-1 margin expedited a truce between Packer's rebels and the ACB.

The series against England was followed by another lacklustre two-match Test series in March 1979, when Mushtaq's Pakistanis visited Australia and held the series 1-all. Australians were captained first by Yallop in the first Test at the MCG (10-15 March 1979), which they lost by 71 runs as Sarfraz took an incredible seven wickets for only one run in the Australian second inning.

Yallop injured himself in a State match, which led to Kim Hughes taking over as captain for the second Test at the WACA in Perth (24-29 March 1979). Playing only his 11th Test, Hughes became the first Western Australian to lead the national team. Australia won the match by seven wickets to square a hard-fought series, but not before two controversial dismissals. Listening to the broadcasts, I recall how nasty the Australians were as they feared defeat.

Sikandar Bhatt, the Pakistani No. 10, was dismissed by Alan Hurst doing a Mankad. Pakistanis reciprocated. In the second inning, when Andrew Hilditch picked up the ball in a friendly way and handed it back to Sarfraz, the bowler appealed for 'handling the ball'. The umpire, Tony Crafter, gave Hilditch out. Both dismissals were within the game's laws but went against the 'spirit of cricket'.

* * *

A day after the series against Pakistan ended, on 30 May 1979, Bob Parish, the ACB Chairman, announced the end of the *Cricket War*, offering a truce to Kerry Packer. The ACB granted Packer the rights to promote cricket for the next 10 years and broadcast cricket on PBL's Channel Nine TV for three years. No WSC player was to be penalised for having been part of Packer's circus for the past two years. The ACB, which was to receive $1.5 million per year, also agreed to coloured clothing for one-day matches and day/night clashes as 'new' innovations to be adopted. Everyone heaved a sigh of relief.

As Doug said, the greatest beneficiaries of the WSC debacle were the players whose salaries would never return to the low payments of the pre-1977 era. Interestingly, the WSC Australians, who were on tour in the Caribbean when the truce was called, had no input into the negotiations. Some players feared discrimination from the ACB in the coming years. But this didn't happen.

However, the ACB opted to not select the WSC-contracted players for the tours of England for the 1979 World Cup (9-23 June 1979) and a subsequent two-month tour to India for six Tests later in the year. I followed these events closely, listening to broadcasts from both England and India. Both tours were led by Kim Hughes. Although the team performed creditably, they lost 2-Nil to the Indians led by Gavaskar. Back in Australia, the team's performances were called 'sub-standard'. Quickly, Greg Chappell was re-instated at the helm.

The ACB also requested India to defer its planned tour for 1980, paving the way for the Windies, newly crowned 1979 Second World Cup winners, to visit Australia and England. Except for a few players (Yallop, Hughes, Border and Hogg), the Australian team lacked quality in all departments. It was evident in the 1980-81 summer the selectors sought to strengthen the middle order after the awful summer of cricket in the previous season. They recalled Doug, but when Doug returned to the side, he was 35 years old in the summer of 1980-81.

* * *

Australia's 1980-81 summer included Doug's last six Test matches. Three of the Tests were against the Kiwis, touring under Geoff Howarth. The final three Tests were against Gavaskar's Indians. The visiting teams also played an ODI tournament between the Tests.

The Kiwis were without Glenn Turner, who couldn't be persuaded to make the visit. But the team had some accomplished batters, Howarth himself, John Wright, Bruce Edgar, John Parker and Mark Burgess, wicket-keeper Ian Smith, and all-rounders – Richard Hadlee and Lance Cairns, and John Bracewell, the off-spinner. Several Kiwi players had English County experience, which gave them the toughness and confidence to do well in Australia (Blofeld 1982).

Under Greg Chappell, the 'new look' Australian team had Graeme Wood and John Dyson as openers. Hughes, Border and Doug were back in the middle order. Marsh continued as the wicket-keeper; Lillee was still the spearhead of the attack, sharing the new ball with Pascoe. Jim Higgs, a right-arm leg-spinner, came in as the leading spinner. The out-of-form Jeff Thomson wasn't selected.

* * *

The first Test against the Kiwis was at the Gabba in Brisbane (28-30 November 1980). Australia won easily by 10 wickets within three days. New Zealand went to Brisbane for the first Test with little match practice because of the rain during the first weeks of the tour. Geoff Lawson, a right-arm paceman from NSW, made his Test debut.

Put into bat on a seaming, grassy pitch, Kiwis fought hard to score 225, with Howarth (85) and Burgess (52) batting cautiously, steadying the ship. Higgs took 4/59, while the pace of Pascoe (3/41) and Lillee (2/36) troubled the New Zealand batters.

The Australians ground out 305 and a lead of 80. It was a subdued response from the home team. Wood batted for over five hours for his 111. Greg (35) and Border (36) made valuable runs. On his return to Test cricket, Doug batted for over an hour but scored only 17 with two fours before edging Lance Cairns into his stumps. Cairns took 5/87 in 39 overs, and Richard Hadlee bowled 37 overs, taking 3/83.

When the Kiwis batted a second time, they were blown away by Lillee (6/53 in 15 overs). Pascoe and Lawson took two wickets each. After just 22 overs, the Kiwis were 7-61. But some brave hitting by Richard Hadlee (51*) helped them reach 142. Wood and Dyson scored the 63 runs Australia needed for victory in just over an hour.

* * *

Australia won again within three days in the second Test at the WACA, in Perth (12-14 December 1980), this time by eight wickets to take the series. Again, Kiwis capitulated to pace. Unusually, Australia omitted Lawson after just one Test and brought back Rodney Hogg. Kiwis were without Howarth, who injured his hand fielding in the match against NSW a week earlier. Mark Burgess captained the visitors.

Greg Chappell again won the toss and put New Zealand in on a pitch favouring the seam bowlers. The Kiwis lost four wickets before lunch on the first day. A fighting fifth-wicket stand between Coney (71) and Burgess (43) was worth 88, but New Zealand could only manage 196. Lillee was again relentless, taking 5/63 in 24 overs.

When Australia batted, the Kiwi seamers found movement off the pitch helpful. Australia was in trouble at 5-68. At No. 6, Doug (55) then combined with Marsh for a rescue act, adding 88. Doug's crucial inning lasted over two hours and included eight fours, while Marsh slammed 91 with eight fours and a six, helping Australia to reach 265. Trailing by 69, the Kiwis faltered to be all out for 121. Australia scored the required 53 runs to win by eight wickets.

In making 55 in the match, Doug passed 5000 runs in Test cricket. He was only the fifth player at the time to achieve the milestone. The others before him were Bradman (6996 in 52 Tests, 80 innings), Harvey (6149 in 79 Tests, 137 innings), Lawry (5234 in 75 Tests, 123 innings) and Ian Chappell (5345 in 75 Tests, 136 innings).

* * *

The third Test was a drawn match at the MCG in Melbourne (26-30 December 1980). The once-famous MCG pitch was in a terrible state at this stage with wildly inconsistent bounce, which saw balls pass through as grubbers or rear dangerously high. Bill Lawry, a Victorian to boot, harshly said, 'I wouldn't even take a dog for a walk out there' (Hutchinson and Ross 1997: 472).

The poor condition of the pitch was due to the damage caused by Australian Rules Football matches played on the grounds during winter and relentless cricket during the summer. Greg Chappell said that ACB should move Tests away from the MCG until the pitch was improved.

Geoff Howarth was back as captain for the Kiwis. He won the toss and put Australia in on an uneven pitch. Subdued knocks by Chappell (42 in over two hours), Hughes (51 in two and a half hours) and Border (45 in three hours) held the top-order batting together.

But it was Doug's 15th Test century that allowed Australia to reach 321. This was his first century since he made 250 at Christchurch in 1976-77. Doug batted for 276 minutes and hit only six fours, but not before drama and controversy. They were 9/261 when the last man, Jim Higgs, joined Doug, who was on 61.

Doug was on 77 when Higgs gloved a Lance Cairns lifter to the keeper Warren Lees. As the Kiwis celebrated and the players went off the field, the umpire Robin Bailhache indicated he had called a 'no-ball'. As Doug inquired, 'What was that for?' Bailhache explained that they were testing an experimental law that fast bowlers could not bowl short-pitched intimidatory deliveries to tail-enders (Mallett 2008: 297).

The Kiwis fumed at Bailhache. Incredibly, no one had explained the new rule being tested to the captains before the series. Benefitting from the 'life' given, Higgs batted on for another hour, scoring just 6*. Doug moved quickly from 77 to 107 off 206 balls in 276 minutes with six fours (Harte and Whimpress 2008: 624). Hadlee (3/89) and Coney (3/) were the main wicket-takers.

New Zealand then struggled to reach 317. Howarth (65), Parker (56), Burgess (49), and Coney (55*) fought hard on a rain-affected day three to not lose the match. Hogg (3/60). Higgs (3/87) and Pascoe (3/75) took most of the wickets as Lillee went wicketless.

Australia then fell over in the second inning to be all out for 188 on the final day. The collapse was caused by Richard Hadlee's inspired bowling (6/57 in 27 overs). Only Greg Chappell batted resolutely (78) before being bowled by Hadlee. Doug was run out for only two. The Kiwis needed 193 to win but played out the time (6-128) to end the match in a draw. Australia ended up winning the series 2-Nil.

* * *

Blofeld (1982) reported that the relentless pace of Lillee, Pascoe, and Hogg was too much for the New Zealanders. Although badly beaten in the first two, the team wasn't as poor a side as the scores suggested. Edgar and Wright developed into a stubborn opening partnership as the series progressed. However, Howarth, Burgess, Parker and Coney failed to do themselves justice with the bat.

By and large, Howarth emerged from the tour with credit as a wise captain who handled matters well during the tour. Richard Hadlee emerged with considerable credit from the tour, taking 19 wickets at 19 in the three Tests and winning the Player of the Series award. He was always accurate despite lacking support from the other end.

Doug scored 185 runs (at 45), including that century (107) in the third Test. Although Lillee troubled the Kiwis with his swing and lift, he wasn't the fastest bowler in the country anymore. Rodney Hogg, even more hostile, took that mantle during the series. Lillee still took 16 wickets in the three Tests at 15. In the second Test, he also passed Lindwall's tally of 228 Test wickets in 61 Tests. Lillee was only 19 short of Benaud's 248 wickets (in 63 Tests), the Australian record then.

* * *

The 1980-81 summer was marred by one of the most talked about, ugly incidents in Test cricket history. Trevor Chappell's 'underarm ball' controversy rocked the cricket world. The incident happened in the third ODI final between Australia and New Zealand on 1 February 1981 at the MCG. The ODI series was tied 1-1 at that stage, the Kiwis having won the first match and Australia the second.

In the third ODI, batting first, Australia scored 4-265 in their 50 overs. Greg Chappell (90), Graeme Wood (72), and Martin Kent (33) did the bulk of the scoring, and at the end, Doug was just six*. When the Kiwis batted, an opening stand of 85 between John Wright and Bruce Edgar kept the chase alive. Edgar went on to make 102*.

The unsavoury incident came when the Kiwis only needed a six to tie off the match from the last ball. At this point, Greg approached Trevor and asked how he was at bowling underarms. Trevor replied: 'I don't know. Why?'. Greg said: 'Well, you're just about to find out'. Rod Marsh was heard to say, 'No, Mate'. Bill Lawry was aghast in the commentary box and shouted: 'They are going to bowl an underarm. How disappointing is that?'. Ian Chappell was also heard yelling at the back of the commentary box: 'Greg, you can't do that!'.

The two umpires were informed. They didn't object because the law banning underarm bowling, recently installed in the English cricket law book, had not yet been embraced by the Australian Board. The batters were also informed; they looked stunned. Brian McKechnie was to face the ball and asked the umpires, 'Are you joking?'.

Trevor just rolled the last delivery along the pitch to McKechnie, who blocked it. McKechnie, a powerfully built former 'All-Blacks' Rugby player, made no attempt to smack it before he threw the bat away in disgust. Images of Trevor Chappell rolling the ball along the pitch as if he were playing bowls and a furious McKechnie lobbing away his bat have been shown countless times on TV worldwide. The crowd booed non-stop for many minutes.

The incident made a blot on Australia's legendary Test history. Trevor Chappell later admitted that he 'thought the underarm delivery was a pretty good idea at the time', even though 'it wasn't in the spirit of the game'. Greg Chappell said he was unaware of how badly his decision would go down until he walked off. One little girl ran beside him, tugged on his sleeve, and said, 'You cheated' (Williamson 2011).

Absolutely scathing in his criticism, Keith Miller didn't hide his disgust: 'Yesterday One-day cricket died, and Greg Chappell should be buried with it'. Ian Chappell had said, 'Fair dinkum, Greg. How much pride do you sacrifice to win $35,000?' Sir Don responded, 'I am very disappointed at Australia's win-at-all-costs attitude'.

In summing up the day's play for Channel Nine TV, Benaud decried Greg's poor decision, saying it was the 'most disgraceful and one of the worst things he had ever seen in a cricket match'. Benaud added: 'A captain got it wrong, and it should never happen again in cricket' and said that he wouldn't accept the excuses given – too much cricket and players being tired of tightly crammed matches.

Even the Prime Ministers of the two countries denounced the act. Australia's PM, Malcolm Fraser, said that Chappell had 'made a serious mistake, contrary to the spirit of the game'. New Zealand's PM, Robert Muldoon, went ballistic. In an address to the Parliament, he called the underarm delivery 'the most disgusting incident in the history of cricket', adding, 'It was an act of true cowardice'. He also said, 'It was appropriate that the Australians were dressed in yellow', referring to the yellow-coloured clothes Australians wore in ODI matches.

Greg Chappell appeared contrite to some extent and apologized to the public the following day. After the massive public outcry, he issued a statement, which someone else read. Greg Chappell did not face the media as he was at 'A friend's house' (Dennis Lillee) (Hutchinson and Ross 1997: 475). Chappell's statement said:

I have always played cricket within the rules of the game. I took a decision yesterday, which, whilst within the laws of cricket, within the cool light of the day, I recognize as not being within the spirit of the game. The decision was made whilst I was under pressure and in the heat of the moment. I regret the decision. It is something I would not do again.

Deploring Chappell's action, Phil Ridings, the chairman of the ACB, said that the Board 'advised him of their strong feelings on the matter and of his responsibility as Australia's captain to uphold the spirit of the game at all times. Writing in the March edition of the 1981 *Wisden Cricket Monthly*, David Frith said:

Shock waves touched all corners of the cricket world and beyond. Political cartoonists adapted the Chappells' derelict act for their drawings. Newspapers found it sufficiently profound to script it into their leaders -- one of them headed 'Unfair dinkum.

However reluctantly, the lesson must be accepted that nothing can no longer be left to 'the spirit of the law'. We live in an age when the sharper individuals in our midst are devoted to exploiting loopholes for financial gain.

The Kiwi Press roundly condemned Greg Chappell's action. It later emerged that Greg was in the process of mentally imploding. 'I wasn't mentally fit to captain Australia', he told ABC in 2004. 'I was mentally wrung out, I was physically wrung out, and I was fed up with the whole system... and it was a cry for help'. The excuse sounded hollow.

I doubt whether Greg Chappell ever recovered the prestige he had in Australian cricket after this incident. Two days after the incident, he was booed all the way to the middle when he walked out to bat in the fourth match of the tournament. But he won some crowd back with a match-winning 87 to secure a 3-1 series win for Australia.

The ICC amended the Laws of Cricket, making underarm deliveries illegal in ODIs as they were 'Not within the spirit of the game'. *Law 24 – Mode of Delivery* now says, 'Underarm bowling shall not be permitted except by special agreement before the match'. Williamson (2011) also noted that, accidentally, the two Chappells did more for cricket in New Zealand than anyone else as the interest in cricket rebounded. The public got so involved in the aftermath to support the resurgent Kiwis.

Doug's last Test Matches, vs Sunil Gavaskar's India, 1981

Under Sunil Gavaskar, the Indian team visited Australia for a three-Test series after the Kiwi tour ended. This was the last Test series featuring Doug. Gavaskar had regained the captaincy he lost to Venkataraghavan in the 1979 Indian tour to England.

Despite being an all-time great opener and the first man to go past Sir Don's batting record of 29 Test centuries (in 52 Tests) in his 95th Test and scoring more than 10,000 Test runs (125 Tests; 34 centuries at 51), Gavaskar was a controversial figure in India.

Under Gavaskar, India fought hard and squared the series 1-1. Beating Australia at home hadn't been easy for India. But it was the start of an unhappy reign for Gavaskar. Sunil managed only 118 runs at 19.7 in the three Tests against Australia. Still, he had an impact in Australia for a notorious walk-off incident in the third Test.

* * *

The first Test in 1981 against the touring Indians was played at the SCG (2-4 January 1981). Given the moisture on the ground and the pitch, Gavaskar ill-advisedly chose to bat first and was caught behind by Marsh off Lillee for a duck in the first over itself. India was routed for a mere 201 by Lillee (4/86) and Len Pascoe (4/61).

Several Indian players got reasonable starts but did not carry on. Only Sandeep Patil, a tall, well-built, middle-order batter, made a handsome 65, driving with great power against anything overpitched. Hooking a bumper from Pascoe, Patil, with no protective headgear, was struck a vicious blow over the ear and had to retire.

Kapil got help off the pitch when Australia batted. He quickly removed the Australian openers, Wood and Dyson, but Chappell (204) and Hughes (27) recovered the inning. After playing Test cricket for 10 years, Greg Chappell hadn't played against India. He graced the occasion with a masterly double century, hitting 27 fours. Batting at No. 6, Doug scored 67 in two and a half hours, with six fours, proving he was still capable of middle-order runs. Doug's 172-run partnership with Chappell doubled the score, and Australia reached 406.

Kapil bowled 36 overs tirelessly for his 5/97. The left-arm fast bowler, Karsan Ghavri, also excelled with 5/109, bowling 30 overs. On day three, India again collapsed for the same score as in the first inning (201), to be defeated by an inning and four runs. Lillee (3/79) and Higgs (4/45) were the wreckers. Chauhan (36), Vengsakar (34), and Kirmani (43*) resisted no to avail.

* * *

The second Test at the Adelaide Oval (23-27 January 1981) produced two brilliant innings, the best of the series. In Australia's first innings, Kim Hughes touched great heights, scoring 213 in 383 minutes with 21 fours. That India didn't fall hopelessly behind Australia's first inning of 528 was due to an equally aggressive 174, scored off only 240 balls by Sandeep Patil (one six and 22 fours).

Expecting the pitch to help them, India sent Australia in after winning the toss. But the home team weathered the spirited bowling of Kapil and Ghavri. At the end of the first day, Australia was 3-319, including a brilliant 125 by Wood (one six and 10 fours).

However, Hughes' 213 eclipsed others. In the total of 528, Greg (36) and Border (57) made valuable runs. Doug made only 20, hitting a six in the process, but holed out to the off-spinner (4/143 off 42 overs). Yadav and the left-armer Dilip Doshi (3/146 off 48 overs) tested the Australians with their flight and guile (Rutnagur 1982).

India fought back with an opening stand of 77 between Gavaskar (23) and Chauhan (97), thwarting the hostile attack of Lillee, Pascoe and Hogg. Still, wickets tumbled before Sandeep Patil entered the fray. After surviving a dropped catch off Yardley when he was only two, Patil (174) attacked with a dazzling array of strokes. His dominant inning helped India to reach 419, but 109 runs behind. Yashpal Sharma (47) played bravely, and his stand with Patil yielded 147 runs for the sixth wicket. As India was dismissed early, Lillee (4/80) and Yardley (2/90) took the bowling honours on day four.

With the ball turning, Doshi opened the bowling with Kapil and troubled the Australians in their second inning. Doshi prevented the home side from galloping away and adding to their lead of 109. After batting for over four hours, Australia was 4-165 at the close of the fourth day's play. Greg (52) and Hughes (53) were both subdued.

Doug made 33*. Batting cautiously for two hours, Doug hit only a single four. Chappell declared with the score at 7-253, hoping to bowl India out in the remaining time (four hours and twenty minutes) on the final day. However, the declaration came a bit too late to force a result.

India began the 'back-to-the-wall' fight to stave off the defeat badly. They were 5-93 at tea after just two hours. However, determined defence by Yashpal Sharma (13 in 169 minutes, facing 157 balls) and Kirmani (14 in 79 minutes, facing 81 balls) allowed India to escape.

After his monumental defiance, Yashpal controversially fell lbw to Yardley in the seventh over of the final 15 overs, and India was on the ropes.

Sidharth Monga (2011) recorded how Yadav and Ghavri then stepped up and kept India alive in the series after Yashpal and Kirmani exited. The pair defied Australia, batting out 10 overs in a ninth-wicket stand in the final 30 minutes of play. Ghavri played out 39 deliveries for seven n.o. Yadav blocked 28 deliveries without scoring.

The Australian press called Yadav's zero* 'the most valuable zero of all time'. The final score was 8-135 when the match ended as a draw. India had batted out 75 overs under intense pressure and received praise for their determination.

* * *

India made an astonishing comeback in the third and final Test of the summer (MCG, Melbourne, 7-11 February 1981), winning by 59 runs in a match that is remembered for many things, including the 'Gavaskar-Lillee' confrontation. India's victory was due to a super-human bowling effort by Kapil Dev who tore through Australia on the final morning, taking 5/28. Kapil had been injured with a thigh muscle strain and had needed a runner when he batted in India's second inning. He came in as the fourth change bowler of the final day but then bowled unchanged 16.4 overs as he performed a miracle.

But Kapil's effort wasn't the only significant thing that happened. There was an accomplished century from Viswanath (114, made in four and a half hours, with 11 fours) in the first inning and some resolute batting from the Indians, especially in the second inning on an uneven MCG pitch. The Test is also remembered for the fine show of courage by Shivlal Yadav, a gritty tail-ender.

In those days, when physiotherapists and doctors weren't available, Yadav took seven painkiller injections into his broken toe to score 20 runs in India's first inning. He then bowled 32 overs in Australia's first inning when India didn't have the services of two of its key bowlers (Doshi and Kapil) due to injuries. In an interview (Monga 2011), Yadav described how Pascoe first hit him on the helmet, then shoulder, forearm, ribs, thigh and then fractured the toe with a yorker.

Viswanath was heading towards his century and batting at the other end. He told Yadav to not remove the shoe, knowing that the sight of swelling might psyche Yadav up. Viswanath said, 'Don't worry about it, and bat till I am there', which is what Yadav did, even without asking for a runner. The pair added a crucial 40 runs for the ninth wicket before Vishy's rescue act ended with his score at 114. Ultimately, Yadav remained 20* as India was bowled out for 237.

The Australians replied with 419, passing the 400 mark for the third successive Test, batting well into day three; with a run rate of only 2.7 per over, it was slow going. Greg Chappell (76 in four hours) and Border (124 in five hours, hitting 12 fours) grafted for runs, stabilizing the inning. Doug chipped in with 78, taking three and a half hours to score those runs. He put on 131 for the fifth wicket with Border.

The Indian bowlers toiled on the unresponsive MCG pitch, and the Australians also struggled for runs. Doshi, the left-arm spinner, bowled 52 overs for his 3/109; Ghavri bowled 39 overs, taking 2/102; Yadav bowled 32 overs, hobbling on his injured foot, wearing size 11 boots, and took 2/100. The home team's healthy lead was 182 runs.

In the second innings, Gavaskar led a fight back with Chauhan and reduced Australia's lead by 108 by the end of day three. On the fourth morning, they added another 57 in 85 minutes before Gavaskar's contentious dismissal by Lillee. Gavaskar (70) had batted 226 minutes, and the Indian score was 1-165 when he left. It quickly became 2-176 as Chauhan (85), disturbed by the 'walk-out' incident, also fell to Lillee. However, Vengsarkar (41), Viswanath (30) and Patil (36) rebuilt the innings. India was 6-296 at one stage, but the lower order collazpsed. Lillee took 4/102 off 32 overs.

In the Test, Sunil Gavaskar was incensed by an lbw decision against him by Australian umpire Rex Whitehead, standing in just his third Test. Gavaskar was sure the ball had got an inside edge before hitting the pad and protested by standing his ground. TV replays were not available those days. Therefore, it is hard for anyone to come to a firm conclusion about who was right or wrong.

As the umpire was unmoved, the score was 165 and Gavaskar (70) was trudging off when 'something snapped', he said, because of the barrage of sledging that he and Sharma had been copping as they were wiping off the first-inning deficit of 182. Things got ugly with Lillee sledging the India captain. Gavaskar responded by storming off towards the dressing room, ordering Chetan Chauhan to follow him.

Only the intervention on the boundary's edge by the team manager, Wing Commander Shahid Durrani and his assistant, venerable cricketer – Bapu Nadkarni, stopped the 'walking off'. They acted quickly, pulled rank and persuaded Chauhan to return to the middle by pointing out in no uncertain terms what the consequences would be if he didn't return.

Vengsakar quickly joined the muddled Chauhan to resume the Indian innings. Unsettled by the incident, Chauhan didn't last long and was dismissed soon for a valiant 85 caught in the covers by Yardley off Lillee. So, averting a debacle, the Test continued.

Australia needed to make only 160 to win. However, the 'fired-up' Indians, particularly Kapil (5/28 in 16 overs bowling unchanged), routed the Australians to win by 59 runs. Ghavri (2/10 in eight overs) and Doshi (2/33 in 22 overs) also significantly contributed to India's victory. In Doug's last Test innings, he was unbeaten on 18.

Australia was shockingly dismissed for 83, one of its lowest scores at home. Although India won the match deservingly, Samyal (2022) reported that the Australian Press was quite unkind, suggesting that the Indian captain was *Sunny by nickname but not by disposition*!

Rutnagur's report (1982) indicated that Kapil followed Lillee's lead, bowled straight, and kept to a length. The uneven pitch did the rest. As Doug remained 18*, Marsh, Yardley, and Lillee were all bowled, as the ball repeatedly kept low. The match was over in just over two hours on the final day, humbling the home side, lacking determination.

The win squared the series 1-all and proved that India wasn't a pushover anymore. It was a remarkable end to a sensational match, not only for Australia's collapse in the second innings against an Indian attack that was handicapped by injuries. India had also come very near to forfeiting the match on day four when Gavaskar walked off when the LBW decision went against him, and he was insulted by Lillee.

* * *

Dennis Lillee broke through the 250-wicket mark in the Melbourne Test, setting up a new Australian bowling record. The controversial lbw against Gavaskar was his 248th wicket, equalling Benaud's record. Twenty minutes later, he had Chauhan caught at cover as his 249th wicket, thus becoming the highest Test wicket-taker for Australia.

Lillee wasn't the tearaway fast bowler of the early 1970s. Still, he operated within his physical limitations, relying more on length and movement. Many accounts indicate that Indians also saw the typical behaviour of *Dennis The Menace* in the summer. None of the venom Lillee showed towards opponents had dimmed in any way. He was still aggressive but was the most successful of the home team's attack, bowling 148 overs in three Tests against India, taking 21 wickets at 21.

Dicky Rutnagur (1982) reported that although Australia topped the 400 runs mark in each of the three Tests, their batting often looked vulnerable. Their 406 in the first Test was founded on Greg Chappell's 204, the highest by an Australian against India. It was surpassed in the second Test by Kim

Hughes (213) when Wood also made 125. Allan Border's 124 was at the core of Australia's first inning in the final Test.

However, Rutnagur (1982) also said that the Indians were at pains to dislodge Doug, who had a reputation for plundering runs off them [Doug's record against India was 10 Tests, 756 runs at 63]. But Doug didn't entirely dominate the Indian bowling in this final series. His highest score was 78 in the final Test. Doug finished the series with two not-outs, scoring 216 runs at 72. In this final series of his career, Doug bowled only nine overs but didn't take a wicket.

* * *

The Australian squad felt the strain of playing so many Test matches, without rest days, in just over two months, along with the ODIs. As early as in that 1980-81 summer, there were signs that too many ODIs were a strain on Test cricket. Too much international cricket also limited Test players from playing in Sheffield Shield matches, to the detriment of the much-heralded competition.

The 1980-81 summer also resulted in advertising revenue losses for TV channels as several Tests ended within three or four days. This was an outcome of the inability of the visiting teams to seriously test the Australians at home. Of the six Tests played in the summer, Australia battered the visitors and won three within three days. Also, the crowds attending the matches were down, averaging only about 47,000 for each Test, which caused concern for the cricket administrators.

* * *

In that final summer, Doug's scores against India were 67 at the SCG, 20 and 33* in Adelaide and 78 and 18 not out at the MCG for a total of 216 at 72. His final first-class knock for NSW was against Tasmania at the SCG. He scored 55. It was 7 March 1981: the last of his 258 first-class matches. When the team to tour England for the Ashes was selected in 1981, Doug's name was missing from the list. His Test career was effectively over, and he decided to retire.

Mallett recalled that Doug was quite disappointed to miss the 1981 tour of England. The main reason was that he had a point to prove – how to bat in England and had picked up some clues from Geoff Boycott. There is no doubt in my mind Doug's presence in the middle order would have stabilized the team. His close friendship with Marsh and Lillee, in particular, would have at least restrained the two seniors from unsettling Hughes's captaincy efforts.

CHAPTER 14

Once a Champion, Always a Champion

Cricket in Australia underwent many changes in the post-Bradman ("The Invincibles") era. The 1950s were modest in cricketing terms, but from that emerged Benaud's Australians, in the early 1960s, who fought hard but fairly. Bob Simpson, taking over in 1963, steered the team well during a re-building stage. Doug emerged from rural NSW as a precocious young cricketer in the 1960s and broke into Test cricket in 1965.

As has been done in Australian cricket many times, the young 19-year-old was thrown into the pool's deep end to fail or succeed entirely. Talented, as he was. Doug had no trouble fitting into an Australian team that looked for runs and believed in a policy of playing bright cricket and forcing the pace of Tests towards getting a result instead of dull draws.

Phil Wilkins, a cricket writer, cited by Mallett (2008: 205), described Doug as '*Once a Champion, Always a Champion*' in an article for the *Sydney Morning Herald* in December 1972. It is quite an apt portrayal.

After the horrors of the England tour in 1972, some critics called for Doug's head. His answer was a brilliant 159 against Western Australia, immediately bringing him back to the Test side. Doug, then, had a long stint as a critical member of Ian Chappell's team until the Packer debacle interrupted his Test career for a second time.

'Batters Must Hit the Ball Again'

The great English batter of the 1950s, Denis Compton (1968), writing in *Wisden*, lamented: 'Unenterprising cricket played by England in both county cricket and Tests was killing the game's enjoyment and the spectacle'. He insisted that the 'safety-first outlook and not hitting the ball when the opportunity arises has bedevilled English professional cricket far too long and must stop'.

Compton said that the attitude of most of the English batters was to play back to all the deliveries on a line with the stumps and wait for the loose ball to punish (á la Trevor Bailey, the 'barnacle'). Arguing against this, Compton encouraged English batters to leave the crease and attack simply by 'hitting the ball' just like Caribbean cricketers did. He probably thought of Headley, Constantine, the three Ws and Sobers when he wrote this. All were peerless stroke-makers who mesmerized cricket with their audacious batting and batsmanship.

Perhaps Compton also referred to others, such as Bradman, whom he had seen before, and other batting stars of his era, Miller, Harvey and O'Neill, who preferred to attack the bowling instead of waiting for a loose ball. I believe Doug has the same attitude towards batting. These great batters took risks but set benchmarks for batting and entertaining the public. Cardus was impressed by them all. In their day, they were all great artists, pure and simply matchwinners [40].

I also recall that famous exchange between Sobers and Lillee. When sledged by the irrepressible Lillee, Sobers once said: 'Well, you've got the ball, I've got the bat, let's see how it goes'. We all know who won that skirmish. Doug and Garry wouldn't be intimated by any fast bowler. They trusted their hand-eye coordination and instincts and would commit to stroke-making, just like Grace, Trumper, Hobbs, Bradman, Headley, Constantine, Miller, and Compton did.

'Play to Win and Entertain - the Australian Way'

Australians generally play for results in Tests more so than other countries. Over decades, they have been admired for this quality. It is one of the greatest legacies of Australian cricket. Meticulous planning, cricketers' physical fitness, and brilliant fielding are the other most significant contributions Australians have made to the global game.

After becoming captain, Benaud first instilled in the team the need to win every game, even against the odds. The policy of playing competitive cricket continued under Simpson's tenure (1963-68 and again in 1977-79). However, the dour Lawry's captaincy (1965-71) was during a re-building stage and slightly marred with dreary cricket.

---

40 Denis Compton played Test cricket from 1938 to 1956 and was a National icon. At just 19 years when he first played Test cricket, he was one of England's youngest Test players and the first *Superstar* 'brand', marketed by popular magazines, TV and billboards (Liew 2018; *Wisden* 2019a). Like Keith Miller, after the War, Compton's exuberant batting became a symbol of Britain's national renewal. Single-handedly, he ensured that cricket returned to its pre-war place in the Nation's affections. Only Ian Botham, decades later, has ever come remotely close to matching this National icon status.

Ian Chappell, who took over from Lawry in the middle of the Ashes Series loss in 1970-71, took the policy of always looking for a win to its peak. Ian is well remembered for being as combative as anyone in the history of cricket and admired by his fellow players for standing up to his responsibility concerning players and robustly engaging with the administrators for better pay contracts and playing conditions. History knows that he succeeded. By his own admission to Jack Eagan (1987: 204-205), Ian said he was lucky to have a group of highly combative players with him. His words were: 'Not just Lillee, Thomson and Marsh, who were very competitive guys, but the quieter ones who didn't show too much emotion on the field, like Walters and Redpath, were also highly competitive in their quiet way'.

Ian has said that it was easy for him to mould them together to become a winning team because they were a good bunch of blokes who got on well with each other. The fact that most of the 'good blokes' liked a drink also made it easy for them to bind together socially.

My interviews revealed that both Ian and Doug were firm believers in the entertainment element of cricket. Both had been influenced by Keith Miller's attitude to cricket and brilliance, and they agreed that Miller's audacious form of cricket cost him the national team's captaincy. Miller's global popularity was also a likely reason why he wasn't considered suitable to captain Australia. Australia was essentially an insecure nation in the 1950s. Bradman's influence on cricket in the 1950s and '60s was also largely unchallenged because of his stature.

Once Ian Chappell took over, he encouraged his teams to approach the game 'not as a picnic in the park'. With their imposing personalities, Simpson and Ian carried forward the ethos of 'playing to win' much more so than Lawry, a dour campaigner and a conservative personality (Eagan 1987; Hutchinson and Ross 1997).

While the English, in particular, didn't quite force the game's pace in the 1960s and '70s, there was a sense of urgency in most Tests that Simpson and Chappell presided over, which contrasted with Lawry's approach. In speaking to Doug and Ian, I also understood that they wanted to 'move things along a bit' when they played under Lawry.

Defensive Cricket - A 'No-No"

Bradman once complained about negative bowling. Compton (1968) recalled a famous confrontation in the middle between Norman Yardley, England's captain, and Bradman during the Test match at Nottingham in 1948. In those days, the new ball was taken after 55 overs. In that encounter, Bradman faced an entire over of medium pace from Yardley, a Yorkshireman, without once offering a stroke as the balls were wide down the leg side. At the end of the over, Bradman approached Yardley and said: 'If we are all going to continue playing cricket this way, we might as well give up the game'.

Yardley was so embarrassed that he responded positively. He changed his negative attitude, and the rest of the series was played at the right tempo. However, England lost to *Bradman's Invincibles* 5-nil.

Countless articles refer to how dreary cricket was in the 1950s and '60s due to the cautious attitudes of English captains. Even the teams under illustrious cricketers like Hutton, May and Dexter stood accused of 'killing the game'. Losing to the empire's former colonies was anathema to them. Defeat in cricket was seen as an unacceptable weakness. The English press also presented cricket as a 'war between nations'.

'*Leg theory*' (packing the legside field and bowling outside the leg stump to curb scoring) has been around for a long time and was used by even Grace (Cardus 1949a, b). The *Bodyline* bowling, as in the series in 1932-33 (p. 143), is a form of 'fast leg theory' with the added intimidation factor used to restrain batters from scoring runs. Trevor Bailey used the 'negative leg theory' in the fourth Test at Headingley (23-28 July 1953) and famously saved the Test. Australia needed 177 to win in 115 minutes on the final day, but Bailey took a long run-up and bowled outside the leg stump without any slips. Australians fell short by 30 runs (4-147 at the end) in a thrilling Test (ABC 2006).

In more recent times, in 2001, there was a nasty incident of Ashley Giles, the English spinner continually bowling wide down the leg stump to curtail the Indian star Sachin Tendulkar. When Tendulkar objected, it led to an ugly exchange between him, Giles and the captain, Nasser Hussain. The frustrated Tendulkar got stumped for the first time in his career. However, he won the battle by averaging 76 in the three Tests, as India won the series 1-0 (Tendulkar 2014: 128).

* * *

As early as the 1960s, all cricket-playing countries realised that cricket wouldn't survive without public support, attractive cricket, and changes in the format of the games. It also became clear that 'dead' and grassless pitches, especially in the Caribbean, Pakistan and India, contributed to the 'dull draws' in the 1950s and '60s. As a result, the Australian captains, in particular, appealed for good wickets in all countries to play on and better playing conditions.

Team spirit, cohesion, and solidarity among the players in a team were also crucial to the Australians' ability to play positive cricket. It is another legacy I would credit to them. Doug was undoubtedly fortunate to play most of his cricket under Simpson, Lawry and Ian, who, in unison, hailed the tremendous contributions Doug made to the team's harmony and 'spirit'. In contrast to bickering and in-fighting, which tarnishes the team spirit in some countries, Australians have always been exceptional in how they play as a team.

In his *Captain's Story*, Simpson (1966) recalled the agreement with Mike Smith in 1965 and a joint effort to play the Tests to get results and not dull draws. Simpson also recalled that Australians generally targeted getting 300 runs in a day. Ian Chappell, as captain, insisted that 300-330 runs per day are a minimum in 90 overs per day. Such a score, he said, 'sets the pace of a Test match towards a result'.

Entertainment has been paramount in Doug's mind since his debut century. While being his own man, plundering runs and enjoying it was his nature. Doug was never one to block for hours and stay at the wicket for long; he looked to force the pace all the time or get out, much like what Ian did throughout his career. They both despised negative cricket because they knew it wasn't what the spectators paid for and believed that cricket wouldn't survive without public support.

Between the Simpson-Chappell eras, the dour Bill Lawry often took a safety-first attitude to secure a series (Hutchinson and Ross 1997: 377). Lawry explained that he frequently curbed attacking play because of the brittleness of the batting that followed him. It fed into his becoming an insecure captain. Lawry wasn't convinced that he had a great team. Still, others didn't see Lawry's risk-averse approach as broadly helpful to cricket, which needed public support.

However, not just the English team but also other teams have played defensive cricket at times so they wouldn't lose a Test. Several incidents that have riled me come to mind. One incident I recall well was in 2019 in the Boxing Day Test between Australia and New Zealand at the MCG (26-29 December).

At one stage, Neil Wagner, the Kiwi left-arm paceman, set up the wicket-keeper (B. J. Watling) to stand down the leg side and bowled way outside the leg stump of Matthew Wade. The batter protested, leading to a heated exchange with the bowler. Still, the umpire didn't intervene (Wu 2019) when they should have. Under the ICC rules, umpires can nowadays call wides if they believe a bowler to be 'bowling down the leg side as a negative tactic'.

Andrew Wu (2019) noted that the rule is rarely applied. However, Australia was on the receiving end during India's second innings in the previous year's Boxing Day Test (MCG, 26-30 Dec 2018). The umpire,

Marais Erasmus, called a 'wide' when he realised the deliberate action of Tim Paine, the Australian captain and wicket-keeper, to stand way down the leg side to Pat Cummins. Paine's ploy was to prevent Rishabh Pant from scoring a single and keep Ravindra Jadeja on strike for the first ball of the next over. Not that Jadeja couldn't handle himself. The tactic backfired. As Paine protested, Erasmus told him it was unfair play, as the rule book states.

Erasmus added (Wu 2019): 'It didn't matter whether it was the first such delivery as the wicket-keeper had set up for it.... If he (Cummins) had bowled a ball down the leg and then you (Paine) had then dived, I wouldn't have deemed it a deliberate ploy'.

It is disturbing for cricket fans to see that the battles between Australia and New Zealand have become confrontational again in recent times. This is despite the calming influence of Kane Williamson, New Zealand's globally respected captain. In 2019, Andrew McGlashan wrote that the Australian captain, Tim Paine, set the tone for some ugly conflicts between the rivals across the Tasman Sea, remarking: 'It's going to be a bit of bodyline this series'. He thought that short-ball tactics from Wagner and Starc were 'great theatre' [41].

* * *

I don't doubt that Doug and several others benefitted from being in Ian Chappell's team, which rose to the top of the cricketing world in that crucial period in the early-to-mid '70s. Ian has often said, 'He wouldn't want to tour without Doug' because Doug is such an 'Ice-breaker on hard tours and a real match-winner'. In the chinwag I had with Ian on the 6th of May, 2023, at Newport, NSW, he gave forthright answers to my questions. Sharp as a razor-blade, hard as nails, Ian is never short of an opinion of cricket and its personalities.

In that sense, Ian is much like Fingleton, Miller, O'Reilly and McGilvray. He gives praise when the actions of players or officials deserve acclaim but does not hold his punches when he sees a disservice to cricket. As a much-respected commentator of more than 40 years, Ian has contributed enormously to constructive ideas on the evolving canvas of global cricket [42].

As Sheahan (1979) explained in his article – *Ian Chappell: The Man and the Myth*, Chappell's name is better known in Australia than many other

---

[41] Tim Paine's poor judgements and leadership came under scrutiny and criticism several times as the Australian team's reputation got further tarnished during his brief tenure as captain. Paine was an accidental captain, after the regular captain, Steve Smith stepped down following the *Sandpaper* debacle in South Africa, in 2018.

[42] Ian Chappell played his last Test for Australia in 1980 (3rd Test, MCG, 1-6 February), and retired with 5345 runs at 42 in 75 matches. He hit 14 centuries, took 20 wickets, held 105 catches in Tests and captained Australia in 30 Tests.

Australian legends. Doug agreed that Ian introduced *The Cutting Edge* to Australian cricket. Even those who don't like him much cannot deny Ian's positive impact on Australian cricket.

Praising Ian as a friend for life, Lloyd (1980) said that Ian was 'aggressive but always fair' in the field. Sobers (2002) said the same thing. They both admired Ian's toughness and razor-sharp cricket brain. Sobers had known Ian well since the early 60s when he played Shield cricket in South Australia. An injury to Sobers allowed Ian to play his first game for the State. Ian has the highest praise for Sobers, who was already a great cricketer then, being a mentor when he was 'nothing much' but just a young cricketer.

* * *

Arlott described Ian as 'a cricketer of effect rather than the graces'. Chappell characterized and defined Australian cricket resurgence for many years. However, there are also no fence-sitters where 'Chappelli' is concerned; people either admire his cricketing skills and philosophy or dislike him for his coarse behaviour, swearing and on-field arrogance.

Having played with him in the late 1960s and early 1970s, Sheahan (1979) and Doug agree that Ian can sometimes be mean, and his limitless confidence often spills over as arrogance both on and off the field. Still, importantly, Doug, Paul, Ian, and many other players of that era respect each other immensely and have remained personal friends.

Chappell resurrected his team in the early '70s like Brearley did in England a few years later in the late '70s. They were both great captains but with one very significant difference; Brearley was a professional psychoanalyst and a scholar, while Ian wasn't. Nonetheless, both knew fear and doubt lead to low confidence and render competence useless.

They both believed that a confident player or team would try out new things, feel better, and, in the process, accomplish more. Players like Doug, Sheahan, and others benefitted from the psychological premise that *'confidence begets confidence.'*

* * *

Chappell's impetuous nature was best illustrated by his compulsive hooking, displayed even towards the end of his career. Sometimes, he got out trying to hook every bouncer he received, but he quickly curbed hooking because it cost his wicket more than he liked. Yet his single-focused resolve was to not give an inch to a bowler trying to intimidate him by bowling at the body or bouncing. Ian's personality does not accept defeat easily. How to face the bouncer was a test of someone's character as far as Ian was concerned.

Ian is the grandson of Victor Richardson, a no-nonsense Australian captain of the past, albeit only briefly [43]. Ian's father, Martin, was a well-known first-grade cricketer in South Australia, which meant Ian came from good cricketing stock. Les Favell, an attacking Test batter, coached him. Influenced by such people, Ian developed a disposition that didn't allow him to be subservient to anyone, and indeed not to Bradman and Co., with whom he clashed several times (Haigh 2009; Sexton 2017; Kalra 2016; *Wisden* 2020a,b; Craddock 2022).

Ian was also one of Kerry Packer's key soldiers in Australia for the WSC circus. He led the Australian XI in the Super Test series in the Caribbean. In 1979, he got into serious trouble for striking a WSC official in Guyana, who was reluctant to permit play after thousands of spectators had been allowed into the Bourda Grounds.

The official infuriated Ian, but the litigation that followed the incident didn't make Packer happy. In a recent article, Krish Singh (2022) argued that the '*ugly Australian*' tag attached to Ian's team was invalid. The team played hard but fairly and respected opponents who were as talented as they were but had no time for wimps.

'Doug – One of the Best Runners and Fielders in the Game'

Ian's views of Doug as a team player, tour companion and friend are well-known. Ian explained in my interview how good Doug was at running between the wickets. He described a tour match against Northern Districts in New Zealand, played at Hamilton, in 1974, when Doug hit a century in a session without hitting a single boundary.

> *Another thing that people forget about Doug is that he was a great runner between leads. He got a hundred in a session on the biggest ground we played on in New Zealand in Hamilton...We made a big score; we got 500 in the day.*
>
> *But Doug got 100 in that third session and hit only one four. What I mean is that if a guy hits 100 in a session, you'd think it'll have a lot of fours. Doug hit one, but he hit a number of twos because they had all the fields on the boundary.*
>
> *And Doug would go just boom, boom, boom. He just kept hitting them firmly enough that he could run two, so he kept the strike...that's how good Doug was – if it was his day. He could manipulate the field and who was running with him. You never felt in any danger because his running between wickets was excellent. People often overlooked that.*

---

43 Victor Richardson, an attacking batter and a brilliant fielder, played 19 Tests, and won four of his five tests as captain (in South Africa in 1935-36).

Doug's account (Mallett 2008: 224) corrected Ian's recollections. Doug said that he actually didn't hit a boundary in that whole inning but RAN a four: 'The grass in the outfield was so long that it was impossible to hit the ball along the ground for a boundary'.

Doug recalled that he was always very good at running, even as a kid. His teammates have also said what a brilliant judge of a run Doug was and his exceptional running between the wickets. As Mallett said, a hundred in a session of first-class cricket without one single boundary might even be a World Record of some kind.

'Every Team Needs a Dressing-Room Pest - Doug Was One'

Ian Chappell often said he hated to tour without Doug because 'Every team needs a dressing-room pest who keeps the team loose in times of great tension'. Ian recently mused (2020) about Doug being such an asset to his teams in the 1970s, as follows:

> *Successful cricketers require the obligatory talent and determination to prosper at the highest level, along with the odd slice of luck. However, in a team, there's another ingredient that teams may find helpful in an era of extra tension: the 'dressing-room pest'.*
>
> *The guy who, despite all the pressure that builds during a five-day contest, still retains the ingenuity to drive his teammates to distraction with a series of practical jokes. Oh, and it also helps if that same guy can hold up his end of the bargain on the field; it's better that his teammates are laughing with him and not at him. I had the good fortune to play with such a cricketer for most of my career: Kevin Douglas Walters...*

Doug got the nickname Freddie early in his career. Mallett (2008: 40) explained that Redpath first called him Freddie. Redpath's view was that Doug's hair bobbed up and down as he ran into bowl, much like the way 'fiery' Fred Trueman's hair moved up and down.

As Ian Chappell said in introducing Doug's first book, 'Boy, we had a good time while still managing to play good cricket!'. Rest and relaxation are vital parts of being a good cricketer. For sporting relaxation, Doug was well-known as a card player and a smoker. But he wasn't a music fan, unlike a few other cricketing greats (for example, Viv Richards, Curtley Ambrose, Dwayne Bravo and Brett Lee).

'Cards, Smokes, Beers and Cheers'

Rothmans' cricket sponsorship began in the early 1960s, and Doug worked for them for many years. As Mallett (2008) said, Doug smokes no more but still enjoys a drink and a laugh. Stories of his pranks are a part of Australia's cricketing lore. Ian noted that Doug routinely puffed on more than 50 cigarettes, closer to 100, during his playing days.

It didn't matter whether he scored a hundred or a duck. Doug would return to the dressing room, remove his baggy green cap and gloves and light up a cigarette. Later on in life, in 2009, he gave up on cigarettes and overcame the habit, which he says was 'one of his greatest achievements'. He once said, 'For a large part of my life, I was down to 50 cigarettes a day. I climbed up a bit higher than 50 on most occasions. I am still alive and feel better for giving up smoking' He later estimated that he might have smoked 785,300 cigarettes in his life!

As Chappell wrote (2009), on the South African tour, in an old dressing room with wooden floors, Mallett preferred to walk around in socks to avoid splinters on the floor. But Doug used to throw cigarette butts in Mallett's path, making the 'clumsy off-spinner do military two-steps to avoid treading on the fag end of a lighted Rothmans'. Doug's antics made everyone but Mallett roll about in laughter.

This and many other episodes, recorded in many books (Walters 1988; Chappell et al. 1989; Marsh and Walters 1992), describe how Doug became a master of pulling childish, schoolboy pranks. Chappell said they eased up tensions in the dressing room, although sometimes the pranks made other players call him a 'pest'.

Stories about Doug's love of card games are also plentiful and well narrated by Mallett. Yarns about Doug's humour are also legendary. On one occasion, that famous humour apparently backfired. Doug had to undergo a fitness test a few days before the Brisbane Test against the Sobers-led West Indies in November 1968. He had strained a hamstring in a lead-up match for NSW, but as it was only a slight strain, he was confident he'd be alright with the big game.

Doug spent at least three hours on the track, batting, bowling and fielding for the fitness test. When a doctor approached him after training and asked how things were going, he felt really good. Still, he made the fatal mistake of saying, 'Well, so long as I don't have to open the bowling for Australia. I'll be right for the Test match'.

The old doctor smiled, and the next thing Doug heard was that the doctor had declared him 'not fit enough to open the bowling' and did not pass him fit to play. As a result, Doug missed the first Test but scored a *Bradmanesque* 699 runs at 116 in the remaining four Tests he played in the series, including 242 and 103 in the final Test.

Doug used to be a late sleeper. On one occasion, in the first Test against the West Indies in the 1973 tour (see p. 170), Terry Jenner and Doug went to the 'Rothman's Ball' the day before the second last day and drank too much. Doug woke up at 10:40 am in his hotel room and was late to arrive at the ground, which was 12 km away. They were bowling the third over when Doug walked onto the field.

Ian Chappell reprimanded him for oversleeping, stood him at the third-man fielding position all day, and made him change ends around the ground, from third man to fine leg, after every over. Doug found a somewhat surprising way to avoid getting tired. Out of nowhere, he borrowed a spectator's bike to ride from third man to fine leg after every over. This left his teammates in splits and his captain speechless. Doug confirmed that this happened only once; he had borrowed the bike from a young fan who was watching.

The *'Surprise Breakfast'* story is another well-known yarn about Doug and his close friend, the late Brian Taber (Walters 1988: 32-34). Towards the end of the 1970 South African tour, the Australian team had been away for six months and thrashed in the Tests 4-nil but still had two tour matches. 'Tabsy' was Doug's roommate for the whole tour and had been taking turns ordering what they called *Surprise Breakfasts*. At 8 am on the morning of the second-last tour game, after just getting home from celebrating the Test losses, there was a tap on the door. A waiter brought Brian Taber's *Surprise Breakfast*: six bottles of beer, which the pair happily downed.

After getting dressed and going downstairs, the two mates saw that the bloke at the bar was just about to roll up the shutters. Brian poked his head under and said, 'Two beers, please, mate' as Doug pointed out: 'Tabsy – play starts in an hour'. Taber responded, 'No worries', he 'had a car, he knew the way, and we'd be sweet'. Agreeing that the beer tasted good, Doug said, 'Two more of those please, mate'. Below is how Doug narrated the story:

> *Two minutes to start of play, we walked through the dressing-room door. And there's Lawry with his pads on, so I knew we'd won the toss. I was batting No. 5 or No. 6 in those days, so I looked at Brian, wiped my brow and said, "Well, thank goodness for that. At least I can have a bit of a breather". Brian just looked at me, shrugged his shoulders, and said, "Doesn't worry me, mate, I'm 12th Man!"*

Then I copped another surprise when Bill told me to pad up and bat No. 3. It started sounding like a conspiracy! I asked Stacky to keep his head down (I didn't have to tell Bill), but five minutes later, I heard just what I didn't want to hear: a cheer from the crowd. Stacky was out.

So there I was, out in the middle, trying to focus on Mike Procter, who's at the top of his mark. I'm wondering what I'll say to Taber when I get hold of him next. But his "Surprise Breakfast" was perhaps something I should've tried a lot more often because I went on to score my only hundred of that whole South African tour.

When I interviewed Doug, I learned there isn't much braggadocio when he speaks. He is witty and razor-sharp but quietly spoken. He is a genuinely modest cricketer and a human being. He is also a great punter. Betting on horses, a favourite pastime, continues to this date. Doug believes cricket gave him a good life despite strains, family pressures, and career highs and lows. Doug agrees with Viv Richards (1991: 215), who commented on how risky it is for sportsmen 'even when one is at the top of the world':

Sportsmen are used to life being something of a gamble. It is a gamble from day one. Statistically, it is a crazy career, and the chances of success are minute. It is a gamble all the way. Nobody knows how far your talent will stretch, least of all yourself...and the line between success and failure is terrifyingly small...At the back of every successful sportsman's mind is that big question mark – 'What will I do when this is all over?'

Helping Others and Cricket Development

A narrow-minded view within the ICC is that the 'top-tier', 'superior' Test-playing countries with higher cricket standards should more often play each other. With the fledgling nations vying for Test status, there has been pressure to establish a second tier, although this hasn't happened. In 2005, when Bangladesh was beaten by England within three days in their first-ever Test match, Benaud (SMH 2005) called it shambles and asked for 'our game's governing body, the ICC must make a firm decision to kick Bangladesh out of the top level cricket'.

Benaud said that Bangladesh and Zimbabwe should play only against A-Teams and minor sides, such as state teams, from the other eight Test countries and against each other. Not everyone agreed with Benaud on this issue, but he wasn't seriously challenged.

Benaud's misgivings on the emerging country were echoed by others like Shane Warne and Kim Hughes (ESPN Cricinfo 2005), who said they worried about the mediocre cricket standards in countries like Bangladesh and Zimbabwe [I noted that Sri Lanka wasn't mentioned]. All believed that the poor standards distort cricket records due to unmatched opponents playing against each other.

This pessimism ignored the evolutionary premise behind even the established teams: *All teams had to have a beginning somewhere!* The history of Test cricket shows that even for established teams like New Zealand and the West Indies, success in Test cricket came relatively slowly [44].

The perception in cricket's current order has always been that countries coming up the ladder (*minnows*) need to prove themselves beyond doubt with more wins. In emerging countries, issues have also been raised around sub-standard infrastructure and playing conditions (i.e., pitches, practice nets and dressing room facilities, stadia and spectator amenities). In some host countries, touring teams often raise concerns about hotels, food, transport, player safety, spectator numbers and behaviour, along with the usually chaotic management of games. Some of these issues are indeed justifiable and need fixing.

I might add to these issues of concern list corruption, mal-administration and nepotism in the way cricketers are selected and how the game is managed in countries like Sri Lanka, Bangladesh, Zimbabwe and even in more established cricketing countries like the West Indies, India and Pakistan. Indeed, no country can claim to be entirely free of political interference or media influence in how cricket is played and administered. However, despite shambolic tour schedules and poorly handled tours, socio-political issues like corruption in a country may not directly affect the conduct of a game. Nevertheless, such problems profoundly affect those societies, and cricket is often not immune to that exposure.

* * *

When some emerging cricketing nations and 'developing' countries wanted ICC recognition and a *seat at the table*, they underwent repeated refusals over extended periods. The delays in admitting those countries to the elite

---

44 Bangladesh, given Test status in 2000, had only won one Test in 37 they played in their first five years (against Zimbabwe). New Zealand was admitted to Test Cricket in 1930 with their first Test against England. But they took 45 attempts and 26 years for their second win (in 1956, against the Windies). On the other hand, the Windies, admitted to Test rank in 1928, took only seven years to record their first Test win (against England, in 1935) and waited another 18 years for their second win (against India). Clearly, Kiwis were admitted to Test cricket so early because it was a former British colony.

club were always stated as a question of *standards of cricket*, which must be maintained. With my unrelenting interest in the game, I witnessed the agonies and ecstasies of Sri Lanka's efforts to be recognized as a country worthy of Test status over at least fifteen years. That story, agonizing as it is for Sri Lankan fans to read about, is well-published (Roberts and James 1998; Wijesinghe 2008; Brookes 2022). Life at the Test level was quite a struggle for the Sri Lankans, whose early years contained more lows than highs. Despite some world-class performers, successes for the island were rare and sweet in those days.

The *myopic* view of inferior cricket in the fledgling nations vying to obtain the Test status can only be explained by the 'refusal by the old guard to accept the evolutionary character of cricket', a fundamental tenet in any sport. Kampmark (2008) said, 'It defied the logic of promoting and spreading the game'. Quicker admission to the Test status would have hugely benefited countries like Sri Lanka, Bangladesh and Zimbabwe. It could have also attracted a much bigger global audience to cricket in the 1970s.

I agree with Kampmark's view that cricket authorities in developed countries should be more sensitive to the complex problems in those emerging cricketing countries, such as social and political issues, race, and economic situations. Walter Hadlee (1982), Chairman of the New Zealand Cricket Board, four decades ago argued that:

The ICC represents the cricketers of the world. Its future can only be threatened if members allow themselves to be involved in politics rather than cricket. To be a truly effective body, it must encourage the game's development wherever it is played. It must be aware of the problems of member countries but always believe that sporting contacts, especially through cricket, can be the catalyst in resolving such problems.

Thankfully, the ICC has undergone many changes in the past two decades. It is now better represented by a host of nations, with no one having veto power. As Chappell (1992: 41) said, 'Cricket needs to be run by competent people who comprise a global body, which has the overriding aim of serving the best interests of the game, rather than the playing of petty politics'.

Kampmark (2008) said that a lack of cricket infrastructure or efficient administration shouldn't be used to brand the fledgling cricket nations as *inferior*, as they are genuinely 'developing countries' socially, economically and politically. Everyone knows these countries also have uniquely talented cricketers. Instead of discouraging, an international body, like the ICC, should support those countries generously to improve those inadequate facilities and structures.

Listening to cricket over decades, I am used to hearing that apart from the Ashes', no other contest mattered. The 'Ashes' is a great contest, but this is not a literal truth. Over the past few decades, seemingly mediocre teams have beaten the so-called superior teams.

Some contests have also been nail-biters. Billions of people nowadays watch cricket, beamed by numerous TV channels. As a result, the interest among cricket fans in the contests for the honour of winning the Frank Worrell Trophy, Border-Gavaskar Trophy or the Chappell-Hadlee Trophy can rival the interest in the Ashes [45].

* * *

In Year 2000, Doug and a few others went to Sri Lanka. The trip was sponsored by the national carrier – Sri Lankan Airlines. The organisers expected to get some help to augment the school cricket system and improve the game's standard. The visiting cricketers were asked to evaluate the available talent of Sri Lanka's younger crop.

The island's cricketers developed through the school system and an annual National Schools Competition. The best of the gifted youngsters then joined the senior clubs. While the system continually threw up talented cricketers, authorities thought the process could be expedited with the help of former Test players.

The contingent from Australia comprised Doug, Geoff Lawson and Peter Philpott. Barry Knight and Peter Roebuck were also part of the contingent from England. Bandula De Silva (2000), a one-time Secretary to the Board of Control for Sri Lanka cricket, reported that Doug was highly impressed with Sri Lanka's progress in cricket at that time. The assignment picked up 65 young cricketers for further coaching. Doug's words at a press conference were:

---

45 The *Frank Worrell Trophy* is awarded to the winner of the West Indies-Australia Test series. It was first awarded at the end of the 1960-61 series in Australia, the first Test of which was a tie. It was Bradman who commissioned a former Test cricketer and jeweller, Ernie McCormick, to create a perpetual trophy following the tie. The design incorporated a ball used in the tied Test.

Between 1947 and 1996, the Indian team played against Australia in 50 Test matches. In 1996, the competition was named the *Border-Gavaskar Trophy*, honoring the legends – Allan Border of Australia and Sunil Gavaskar of India.

The *Chappell–Hadlee Trophy* is a *One Day International* cricket series between Australia and New Zealand, named after the legendary cricketing families from the two countries: the Chappell brothers (Australia), and Walter Hadlee and his three sons (Barry, Dayle and Sir Richard) of New Zealand.

I first came to Sri Lanka way back in 1969. I was a member of the Australian Team on its way to tour India. The talent I saw 30 years ago was pretty good, but when I came back here after three decades with my colleagues, I found that Sri Lanka has done remarkably well in unearthing talent again.

The giant strides made in both forms of the game are amazing...You won the World Cup in 1996, beating us again in Colombo after we won the 1999 World Cup. That is some achievement. Your recent record in the Test arena is equally impressive, beating England, Australia, Zimbabwe and Pakistan in series wins during the last year.

The ICC recognized the growth and interest in cricket and strong performances in giving the Test status to Afghanistan and Ireland in 2018, taking the number of countries with full ICC Membership status to 12. With more than 100 Associate Members now (ICC 2024), the expansion of cricket in the world is assured. Australia and England are fortunate to continue to be the dominant teams in the world, with India hot on their heels and already claiming a far more powerful say in global cricket. Pakistan and New Zealand have also come up in their cricket standards, while the once mighty West Indies are in the doldrums.

Kampmark (2008) rightly noted that 'the greatness of sporting teams moves in cycles of triumph and decay' best illustrated by the decay of the Windies. The global game is poorer for the decline of West Indies cricket, as everyone knows.

Recently, there have been many instances of the easy-beat *minnows* handing out crushing defeats to the elite teams. The rise of cricket in countries like Sri Lanka and Bangladesh is seen as a threat to the status enjoyed by the top teams. This fear has reduced the contests between the established and emerging countries, curbing developments in the latter.

The absurd argument that 'if you removed Zimbabwe and Bangladesh from the main circuit of Test cricket, it would cut down the players' workload by 10%' is not supported by the West Indies, India, Pakistan and Sri Lanka. This means that ways to reduce player workloads need to be found elsewhere. Fledgling cricket nations shouldn't be blamed for too much cricket and its declining quality. As I explore in the next chapter, *the game has changed so much* in the last 50 years since Doug played at the elite level.

* * *

Doug believes that the structures Australia have in place now are substantial and must be maintained to keep the Australian standard of cricket high. The only way to develop cricket is to keep the standard of junior competitions high with good wickets, umpires and coaches.

These standards should then extend from club cricket to grade and state levels. Even though these may seem like a drain on finances, Doug believes that cricket officials interested in developing players for the future will have to support such activities with funds from the elite tournaments. Up-and-coming, outstanding players must be scouted, hand-picked and helped, if necessary, with cricket scholarships.

For several years, the *Cricket Academy* in Australia, initiated in 1987, was at the forefront of developing young cricketers into high-quality and classy players [46]. Its impact was so high that other countries emulated the model within a few years, with a high degree of success. Australian coaches are also often sought by these institutes, as they are regarded as strict in training youngsters.

However, unlike in the sub-continent, many schools in Australia have eliminated cricket from the sports choices mainly because of the time involved in matches and the sun protection factor. Still, Doug believes there is still sufficient interest in kids who love cricket for some to develop as outstanding players. The money in cricket also helps the better ones to stay focused.

World Series Cricket and its Aftermath

As documented in Doug's books and by Mallett (2008: 203, 223), cricketers were so poorly paid in the 1950s, 60s and 70s when they played at the elite level. They all worked at their own occupation and played cricket by taking leave and time off from their employers. Some married cricketers found it impossible to balance the travel and demands of season-long cricket while attending to a home front.

Since the late 1960s, Ian Chappell led the fight for better payments for players. As a result, by the mid-1970s, Ian wasn't popular with the ACB. Players today do very well with sponsorships and endorsements. They can receive payments for many things – from wearing jackets and sunglasses to training shoes. But that wasn't the case in the mid-1970s. Doug said that hopeless wages were always on his mind while playing cricket and deeply disturbed his family life as a young, married man.

---

46 The *Australian Cricket Academy* was initially located in Adelaide. In 2004, it moved to Brisbane. The Academy was a joint initiative of the *Australian Institute of Sports* (AIS) and the ACB. Many outstanding Australian players graduated from the Academy during the past three decades.

The most revolutionary period of cricket history – Packer's WSC – changed all that. Packer initially signed up 66 top cricket players, including many of the world's biggest stars, to play for his tournaments for an *Australian XI*, the *West Indies XI* or the *World XI*.

The new inventions of multiple cameras, coloured clothing, and floodlights ensured the success of commercial TV showing cricket to a global audience. Until the WSC revolution, cricket coverage was the domain of public broadcasters – ABC, BBC, and Doordarshan (India). Packer capitalized on the colossal market potential of cricket and then shared the spoils. In this venture, he won the support of players who were not paid enough to make a living from cricket.

Many people who supported Packer's views agreed that the cricket boards could not utilize the advantages of colour TV, increasing viewer audiences of sports events and the commercial potential of cricket (Haigh 1993). Ultimately, the weight of Packer's money squashed the ACB into submission. Some previous Packer opponents also 'turned' seduced by the opportunities presented by the razzmatazz.

O'Connell (2018) noted that Channel Nine revolutionized the TV coverage of cricket in Australia by increasing the number of cameras used on each ground to view the action from varied angles. Elaborate graphics also enhanced the coverage. Replacing the ABC before them, Channel Nine became Australia's home of cricket, with Benaud, Lawry, Stackpole and Trueman at the helm of the microphones.

Building on their fame, the quartet described the TV spectacle convincingly. After two years, *'Benaud's Boys'* became six with the newly retired players Ian Chappell and Tony Greig. Their star power allowed Channel Nine TV to maintain a stranglehold on cricket in Australia. Suffice it to say that Packer changed cricket's cosmology. His TV innovations allowed cricket to be seen by millions who had previously enjoyed cricket only by listening to the radio or seeing a match. Due to the intense cricket played, elite players also needed to be fitter than ever. Top-tier players in all countries have become well-paid professionals, mainly through TV rights; broadcasters now have a considerable say in the game's running.

Ian Chappell (2022) was a staunch backer of the WSC because he believed that cricket's true potential had not been realised as a spectator sport. As Ian was criticised for his WSC involvement in recruiting many elite cricketers, Lloyd (1980) jumped to his defence, saying that the WSC provided much-needed financial security for the West Indian cricketers, who were always poorly paid. Lloyd had personally seen the plight of several former greats of the past following their exit from first-class cricket.

The WSC paid the Australian players $30,000 per season with all expenses, a figure Doug said 'most cricketers never imagined possible'. Doug's initial sign-on fee for WSC for three seasons of cricket was a mere $25,000. But it was still five times higher than he had earned playing cricket in the previous 12 months.

As a result, it was easy for Doug to sign up for Packer's circus, which only lasted two seasons (1978 and 1979) before it folded up. Doug's retirement fund more than doubled due to the fees he received for the six 'unofficial' Tests he played for WSC. The fund suddenly totalled more than what he had accumulated for the 69 Tests he had played previously up to that time.

Doug said he received £180 for each Test (equivalent to Aus $360) from the first Test onwards. He said those were the standard fees from the 1930s onwards and hadn't changed for a long time. Those amounts were peanuts by today's standards. Nowadays, the elite Australian players are 'contracted' for amounts ranging from about $300,000 to over $900,000 per year. The top contract earners usually make more than $3 million a year with tour payments and match fees.

Today's players should thank Ian and his colleagues for securing a better deal from the ACB. Instead of annual 'contracts', Doug favours higher match fees and a superannuation scheme that would benefit players in retirement. But he said that a contract provides security for players, allowing them time to be fit and ready to play at short notice without worrying about jobs.

Match fees have increased dramatically, from a meagre Aus $360 per Test to a fee as high as $20,000. This increase has been recently suggested for all countries by the ICC, including Australia and England, to 'save Test cricket and stop the luring of the best players by T20 tournaments' (Conn 2024). Apart from more money to the players and the ACB, Packer's influence brought in other positives. To get the best out of the players and a grand spectacle on TV, Packer urged players to play hard and keep the spectators and TV audiences entertained. While investing vast money in the venture, he didn't put up with anyone slacking or the contests to be friendly affairs.

McGilvray (1985, p. 119) noted several severe repercussions from the WSC debacle. These included the deceit of the operation, which eroded the trust among long-standing friends. Many international cricketers were banned from playing for their countries. It led to several 'rebel tours' to South Africa, which hadn't been admitted back into Test cricket then. The aftermath of the WSC also pushed Australian cricket a long way back [47].

---

47 When Packer's Australians were banned, Australian cricket suffered greatly. Simpson, at the age of 42, was persuaded to make a comeback after being out of Test

In his book *The Game is Not The Same*, McGilvray opened (pp. 11-12) with what he called 'the most unpleasant and terrible confrontation between two Australian cricketers'. Alan said that he had never witnessed anything like that in a lifetime of travelling with cricketers. The violent crossfire of abuse and counter-abuse occurred between Kim Hughes, still the captain in 1983, and Rod Marsh, who had been overlooked for the captaincy. Alan's decision to highlight this incident at the beginning of a book is a sad indictment of Australian cricket.

Marsh was the popular choice of the hardcore players who survived the Greg Chappell era of the late 1970s and the debacle of WSC cricket. But he wasn't the selectors' choice, as they looked to the future. Marsh couldn't accept that, and with his teammate and friend, Lillee, in particular, bore a huge grudge and directed their dislike at Hughes, the post-Packer era's batting star. The story of this rift between senior players and the back-stabbing of the captain – one of their own from Perth, completely destabilized Australian cricket [48].

Due to the conflicts between senior players, McGilvray (1985) deeply lamented the sorry state of Australian cricket in the immediate post-Packer era. He said that in the past when disagreements arose about captaincy or other decisions by the selectors, those differences of opinion were amicably resolved with dignity without causing a full-blown crisis. Alan was also highly critical of the ACB and the selectors for not helping Hughes by intervening in the dispute they created.

---

cricket for 10 years. His weakened side to the West Indies was battered and beaten in the 1977-78 series.

48 Christian Ryan's book on *Golden Boy* (Kim Hughes) is a sad account of this incident and the period, which is well captured in the book's sub-title: *'The bad old days of Australian cricket'*.
   Alan McGilvray's book (1985) also dedicates the penultimate chapter to further analyse and describe *'The Hughes Affair'* (pp. 179-184). Alan categorically says that Kim Hughes was not a good captaincy material compared with other notable Australian captains. Alan criticised Hughes for blaming the media for his demise as a captain and said that Hughes made matters worse for himself by not making the attempt to smooth things out with the senior players.

CHAPTER 15

Different Countries, Different People, The Pleasure is The Same

Although international cricket has had a glittering history, the game has also seen its reputation and integrity severely tested at times. The sport's finest moments are, of course, the aspects we would prefer to remember. But both distasteful and shocking episodes have regularly threatened to damage the game's fabric throughout history.

These extend from racial abuse of non-white cricketers, match-fixing, ball tampering and other forms of cheating, on-field tantrums and unworthy player behaviours to betting and drug scandals, as well as political protests. It would be fair to say that the cricket world has almost endured it all, and more will come with time!

Wither Orthodox Cricket?

Doug played an orthodox form of cricket, even when dancing down the wicket to spinners, pulling or hooking the pacemen on the back foot. He has often been described as 'audacious' and always looking to score. No one remembers Doug getting bogged down. Bowlers like Underwood, Illingworth, Snow and Willis knew Doug wouldn't hang around without scoring too long and would take some risk. They exploited this tendency. Nonetheless, Doug thrashed them all in full flow, executing classical strokes flawlessly. Essentially a backfoot player, Doug favoured the cut, hook and pull more than driving.

When I watched film footage of his batting, especially that inning in Perth in 1974, Doug reminded me of the greatest striker of the ball – Gilbert *Croucher* Jessop. An Englishman who played international cricket between 1894 and 1914, Jessop is widely acclaimed as an astonishing *box-office attraction* (Ryder 1975) in those early decades of cricket. Jessop's 1902 ferocious attack of short-pitched Australian bowling is often the benchmark for big-hitting and risk-taking that can turn a match around (Thomson 1968; Smith 1996: 19-27).

In a fierce attack, the *power-hitter* – Jessop – scored 104 in 75 minutes, facing only 76 balls; it was the fastest Test century in history up to that time. This was at the Oval, in the fifth Test (11-13 August 1902). He wasn't a tall man; he crouched low when he batted and, from this position, sprang up. James (1963: 98) reminded how Jessop, playing for Gloucestershire on 28 June 1990, hammered 157 in one hour against the touring Windies at Bristol grounds. Called *The human catapult*, the energy of Jessop's shots was 'like a catapult released', and the ball travelled far, often out of the ground.

The *London Times* said: 'As long as cricket lasts, Mr. Jessop's great performance will be remembered' as it is 'one of the most outstanding Test innings that any batsman has ever played'.

Cardus devoted a chapter in his book *Days In The Sun* (1924: 155-158), describing 'An innings of Jessop was invariably a cyclone of batsmanship'. He debunked the argument that Jessop's methods, 'to take a ball from a foot or so outside the off and deposit it in the heart of crowd at the on-side boundary', was unscientific.

On Lawry's Australians bowling too much short stuff in the 1968 series, Cardus (1968: 7) said, 'Jessop would have cut them to ribbons'. Jessop's batting reminds me of Doug's hook for the last ball of that Bob Willis short-ball in Perth, making the fabulous century in one session. Like Jessop, Doug wasn't slogging when he cut the English attack to ribbons in that inning. It was a calculated assault by a master batter. A metaphor would be the methodical *slaying of a dragon*. Doug made the powerful English attack look like schoolboys.

Wisden chose Gilbert Jessop as one of the five Cricketers of the Year for the 1898 issue and wrote of him, 'We have never before produced a batter of quite the same stamp. We have had harder hitters, but perhaps never one who could in twenty minutes or half an hour, so entirely change the game's fortunes' (Ryder 1975).

Much the same can be said of how Doug played. Doug changed the course of a game several times within 30 minutes or an hour of attacking batting. He didn't play those silly *switch-hits* against spinners. Nor did he play with ramps and other new inventions. But, on a good day, the mastery at the crease would see no bowler stop him from scoring. All great batters share this attribute.

Doug was also not into too much coaching, which Cardus (1949b: 254) identified as the bane of English cricket: 'In England, the natural ability of a player to drive and cut is ruined by too much coaching by unimaginative professionals'. In contrast, 'Australians allow players with natural abilities to express themselves', Cardus lamented.

* * *

Thanks to the shorter-format games, many players have changed their styles and adopted a more aggressive attitude to batting, even in Test cricket. I recall Ian Chappell often saying that any batting side, batting a full day, should be targeting 300 or well above that. Ian and Doug played a very orthodox form of cricket when they batted. They looked to score at every opportunity, every ball, with hard running and skilful placement. Attack was their way of subduing opponents. They targeted a score well above 300 in a day, placing the pressure back on the opponents even without the *slash-and-bang Bazball* cricket [49].

Like many great batters of the past, Doug and Ian also had certain qualities, such as personifying class, freedom, and elegance, which are often missing in modern batters. In the opinion of most writers, the *Three Ws* were the epitome of these qualities.

In some ways, *Bazball* can also be seen in that light. The coach (Brendon McCullum) and the captain (Ben Stokes) are also working on a form of cricket that is breath-taking to watch, bringing out results and galvanising players to do their utmost in tight situations. An underlying principle of *Bazball* is for individuals to believe in themselves and be given the freedom to achieve their best.

Racial Abuse in Cricket - A Tactic of the 'Weak'

As explained by Ian Chappell, his first experience of racist banter was in South Africa in the 1966-67 tour in which the Australians under Simpson were thrashed 3-1 by the home side led by Peter van der Merwe. The apartheid system deeply segregated South African society.

In the second Test (2-5 January 1967, Cape Town), which Australia won by six wickets, the Springboks abused the 'coloured' player in the visiting team. Ian said that Grahame Thomas, who had a part-Aboriginal, part-American-Indian lineage, was sledged as he was caught by Tiger Lance off Eddie Barlow after making a defiant 50: 'Why don't you pick Garry Sobers?

---

49   '*Bazball*' is a term coined by ESPN Cricinfo UK Editor Andrew Miller on an episode of the *Switch Hit* podcast. It was developed after the appointments of the New Zealander – Brendon McCullum (whose nickname is *Baz*) as Test head coach and Ben Stokes as Test captain in the England team.

The *Bazball* mindset emphasizes taking positive decisions in attack and defense, whether batting, bowling or fielding. Many of these skills were first developed in playing ODI and T-20 cricket. With a mix of fast scoring and unorthodox stroke play, the style of play is now increasingly on display in Tests as well.

Then you will have a team full of blacks!'. Sensibly, Thomas walked away without any quarrel. Australians scored 542, which was their highest in the series. It frustrated the hosts.

* * *

Ian explained that he would not tolerate any form of racial abuse. He threatened his team that if he ever heard a comment with the prefix 'black' attached to it, there would be trouble: 'You don't call someone a lucky white bastard. So, why include the word 'black' in any outburst?'

Ian Chappell has reported that he had never heard of racial abuse from his team. Still, after his retirement, he heard Viv Richards complain about racial abuse by the Australians under Greg Chappell. When Ian quizzed Viv about this, he later clarified that it was just a single player and the matter had been sorted.

Viv Richards has been quite outspoken about racism. One must listen when someone like him writes it in a book. Richards said (1991: 75) that 'there was too much racism in cricket. The racists are people who derive a perverse kind of pride, a 'white supremacist' attitude that comes through as 'non-whites have no right to be competing with them on the same stage'. This deep-rooted view is a relic from the colonial era and manifests everywhere in the British Empire.

It is based on the myth of the *superiority* of the European 'whites'. The 'whites' might have been superior (due to guns, ships, steam engines and the Industrial Revolution), but this was in a past era. *Superiority* does not last forever, not in any sport. *Slavery* was interwoven into this narrative as cheap labour was required to establish the colonies, and enslaved people were obtained from Africa. This is how racism in cricket began. Doug and I *abhor racism in all forms of expression.*

In cricket, the warped view held by some people for a long time was that 'only Englishmen can really play'. This myth was quickly debunked as Caribbean players of 'slave stock' made such a massive impact on cricket. Cricketers from both India and Ceylon had the same effect. The 'White' rulers couldn't believe that the 'natives' would beat them at their own game. Regarding the way the West Indians play, the view was, 'Oh, you only have to bowl outside the off stump, and they hit across the line; they can never play properly in England'. Viv said (1991: 75) that those still holding such notions 'are fatally weak'.

In Richards' book, a chapter titled *'Fear and Loathing in Australia'* gives us a sense of what it was like to face the Lillee-Thomson barrage in 1975: 'All the bullying by shouting, snarling, glaring…any method of intimidation that a fast bowler can think of is all an attempt to unsettle the mind of a batter and dent that all-important confidence'. Richards (1991: 73) said the Windies came up against *'extreme savagery and racism'* in that series. History knows that Lloyd responded to the 'savagery' the Windies faced by developing the pace batteries that dominated world cricket for the next two decades.

* * *

In 1976, the newly appointed England captain Tony Greig said his team would make the West Indies *grovel*. Irked by newspaper articles on the tourists' strength, Greig let rip in a BBC's *Sportsnight* interview before the first Test: 'I'm not sure they're as good as everyone thinks', he said. 'These guys, if they get on top, are magnificent cricketers. But if they're down, they grovel, and I intend, with the help of Closey [Brian Close] and a few others, to make them grovel'.

The British press initially thought the comments showed the bravado of the new captain but soon realised it was folly(Williamson 2007). 'It stirred us', Richards said (1991: 96-98); it was quite deliberate and not just an off-the-cuff remark. The word grovel is associated with slavery, and the South African-born Greig was familiar with the word in South Africa, used to put down the subjugated black population.

The fatal error handed the Windies the ammunition they needed to fire up. Michael Holding blew them away in the first inning of the third Test (8-13 July 1976) for 71 runs, taking five wickets for just 17 runs in a frighteningly fast spell (Holding and Cozier 1993). He earned the nickname *Whispering* Death from Dickie Bird (1997: 350), who said:

> He [Holding] *walked back many a mile, turned, and then set off on his flowing run, faster and faster, until he exploded into action beside me and released a delivery as quickly as anything I had seen. I was frightened to death just standing there watching as it rocketed towards the England captain. Greig's bat was still on its way down as the leg and middle stumps went cartwheeling past the startled wicket-keeper. It was an absolutely magnificent yorker, and Greig never saw it...It was* 'death delivered to the batter in a whisper'.

Simon Lister's article (2015), *'When Death Whispered'*, explained the impact of the Windies' fast bowlers in this *'Fiery Series'*. Greig was targeted for special treatment and was bowled five times in the Tests, three times by Holding and once each by Roberts and Daniel. In avenging the abuse, Lloyd's team hammered England into submission. Viv Richards scored a ton of runs (829 runs at 118), playing in only four Tests (he was injured and didn't play in the second Test).

Viv's aggregate included a mammoth 291 in the fifth Test at The Oval, 232 in the first Test at Trent Bridge, and 135 in the third Test at Manchester. Gordon Greenidge (592 with three centuries) and Roy Fredericks (517 with two centuries) weren't far off either. Wasn't that enough for firing up an opponent? That's why Benaud once cautioned the Australians – 'One needs to be careful about who you hurl abuse to'. Actions, no doubt, have consequences [50].

Beaten by a margin of 3-0 and humiliated, Greig lasted only nine months more as captain and joined the Packer circus as its chief recruiter. Three decades later, talking about it, Greig said: 'Anyone who suggests it was my South African background that was behind my comment and put any racist tone to this thing just doesn't know me'.

When he became a TV presenter, Greig changed his persona when he realised that racism has no place in the world. Globalization, multiculturalism and other forces that defined the last five decades left no room for people to be racist in the way they were in past eras [51].

The English press castigated the Windies for excessively attacking England's batters with bouncers and express deliveries (Williamson 2015c). Jonathan Agnew wrote: 'A 45-year-old man [Brian Close] up against a lithe, magnificent young fast bowler, bowling at his very fastest. He had no helmet, chest pad, or arm guard and a little thin towel tucked over his right thigh to prevent the bruising'. The story is quite well-known in cricket history. Helmets for protection came in 1977, coinciding with the WSC circus.

* * *

Racism in cricket is simply unacceptable, as bad player behaviour, match-fixing and other scourges which threaten our noble game. Boards of Control of cricket in all countries say that they deplore all forms of racism but do very little about it. The Boards and match referees wriggle out of most

---

50   Richards' 829 has been exceeded only four times -- Bradman 905 against England (1930). Hammond, 905 for England in Australia (1928-29); Mark Taylor, 839 for Australia vs. England (1989) and Harvey, 834 for Australia in South Africa (1952-53). Walcott (827 in 1955 vs. Australia) and Sobers (824 in 1957-58 vs. Pakistan) come next (ESPN Cricinfo 2024d).

51   Greig passed away on 29 December 2012. He had lung cancer and died of a heart attack at the age of 66. Greig was one of the most transformative forces in cricket (Frith 2012; Selvey, 2012). He quickly corrected the mistake of often acting like he was better than others. Tony's style at the microphone became an institution on TV. His televised pitch inspections, poking at the pitch with his car keys, at the beginning of a Test match, amused millions of cricket lovers. His insightful post-match comments were much loved by people. Once, when Tendulkar was batting, he assured his viewers that *'God Is Batting'*!

incidents, much to the dismay of cricket fans, saying, 'It is really up to individual players and umpires'.

Often, the onus of adjusting falls on the target! 'Coloured' players are told to *grow a thicker skin*, not take much notice of insults or cope with racism differently. Sociologists Karen Farquharson and Tim Marjoribanks (2006) highlighted that racism incidents are reported poorly in Australia. The target is often blamed for inflating the issue. The victim is even accused of drawing attention to themselves! Only a few cricketers have spoken out about racism in cricket and have won compensation for their suffering. Most try to ignore it and live with it.

In January 2002, Muttiah Muralitharan, the greatest wicket-taker in the world, vowed never to return to Australia for cricket because of the racial abuse hurled at him for his bowling action for which he had been officially cleared. The Australian media and commentators did little to condemn such outrageous crowd behaviour.

In January 2003, in a well-publicized rant, Darren Lehmann called the Sri Lankans *Black C***s* after being run out by Russel Arnold in an ODI. The team defended him stoutly, saying it was *Out of character* and *In the heat of the moment*. On the other hand, the Lankans were criticised for being over-sensitive (Gemmell 2008: 24).

In this despicable incident, Lehmann, who later became Australia's coach, was punished by match referee Clive Lloyd after the outburst. Returning to the dressing room fuming after he was run out, his frenzied scream at the visitors: *C****, C****, fucking black C*****, was heard by others. The Sri Lankans lodged an official complaint with Lloyd. Lehmann quickly apologised to the visitors (Lamb 2003).

Having received the apology, Davnell Whatmore, the Sri Lankan coach who first reported the slur (Mitchell 2003), asked Lloyd to be lenient. Whatmore's plea saved Lehmann from a certain match ban. Instead, Lloyd scolded Lehmann under a breach of Level 3.4 of the ICC Code of Conduct. He also warned the Australian team of the seriousness of the offence. Level 3.4 of the Code reads: 'Using language or gestures that offends, insults, humiliates, intimidates, threatens, disparages or vilifies another person on the basis of that person's race, religion, colour, descent or national or ethnic origin'.

* * *

The pattern of abusive sledging of opponents has been a blight on Australian cricket for decades. It began in the 1980s and continued through the 1990s, well into the new millennium. The abuse has been well-directed towards not just 'coloured' teams but also others like South Africa and New Zealand, with predominantly 'white' teams. In the 2005-06 summer, in the first Test at Perth, South Africans were racially abused by the Australian crowds. Makhaya Ntini, Ashwell Prince, Garnett Kruger and Shaun Pollock were taunted as *kaffirs* or *kaffir-lovers*. This prompted Ali Bacher, the chief executive, to call for life bans for the offenders. South Africans were similarly abused in the second Test (MCG) and the third Test (SCG), which led to a formal complaint to the ICC (ESPN Cricinfo 2006; Gemmell 2008: 24).

Sledging – 'A Curse of the Modern Game"

Sport reflects elements of any society in which it evolves. At any one time, it represents society's good, bad and ugly elements. While all Australian crowds may not abuse their opponents, it is not too far-fetched to suggest that the impolite behaviour of the Australian team itself prompts abusive crowd responses in Australia.

More than 25 years ago, Frank Tyson, the much-respected former England paceman and journalist, called out the Australians in particular for sledging under the veil of gamesmanship. In a hard-hitting article in *The Cricketer* (1997: 9), Tyson called 'Sledging – the Curse of the modern game'. He said that the frequency of sledging in cricket showed a severe erosion of player behaviour standards at all levels. Tyson pointedly spoke about the Australian teams in the 1990s, led by Allan Border (1984-94; 93 Tests) and Mark Taylor (1994-99, 50 Tests).

Tyson wanted the players indulging in this ugly practice to be severely penalised. Fortunately, in every international team, only a few unsavoury individuals sledge. The worst sledging has resulted in retaliation, considerable animosity, and long-standing feuds between some players. Bill O'Reilly (1979), another vocal critic of sledging, said:

> *In Australian vernacular, sledging is a term "minted" to describe the unethical, distasteful and ugly practice of talking at the opponent in an abusive way with the singular aim of helping him to lose his concentration.*

Writing his newspaper column in the *Sydney Morning Herald*, O'Reilly (1979) railed against the dreadful standards of behaviour between the rival teams led by Yallop and Brearley. As 'sledging' had become a norm, 'Cricket suffered immeasurably'. In his view, 'it was a wonder how on-field insults have not led to off-the-field skirmishes as the offended players try to square accounts'. He wanted the team captains to do more and umpires to be given more powers to eradicate sledging from cricket. But his advice went unheeded by the authorities.

Cricket fans worldwide should make the right call to call sledging' for what it is: a curse to be eradicated. But it will continue as long as the contests are fierce and the rewards are incredibly good. The saddest part is that, by all accounts, especially in Australia and England, sledging is now rampant even in school cricket, encouraged by professional coaches. Kids are told, 'It's part of the game; toughen up; don't be a wimp and grow a thicker skin'! [52]

Australians were not alone in using racial abuse against their opponents. Imran Khan's book (1988: 117) gave a specific example of Bob Willis calling Viv Richards a *Black bastard* in a Test match at Old Trafford in 1984. Richards didn't forget as he exacted revenge on Willis in that match and the rest of the series. Both Richards and Greenidge have said that the racial abuse the West Indians received in 1975-76 in Australia were both distressing and transformative.

Daniel Harris (2016) noted what Greenidge said: 'Being bombarded by comments and behaviour, well, I had encountered some ignorance before, but this was different, very, very different...it degraded me and downgraded me a great deal'. While the Australian authorities did little to curtail this behaviour, the Windies said to themselves, *Never again*!.

The result of the humiliation of the normally fun-loving Caribbean cricketer was that it led Lloyd to bring together the most fearsome-ever pace attack in the world to intimidate opposing teams. Lloyd's teams often operated with four pacemen, *hunting as a pack*, picked from Roberts, Garner, Croft, Daniel, Marshall and Sylvester Clarke. They devastated opposing batting line-ups in the late 1970s and early '80s.

Later, other speed merchants, Patrick Patterson, Ian Bishop, Courtney Walsh and Curtley Ambrose, repeated the same dose their previous comrades gave. Mike Selvey (2010) observed that until then, fast bowlers hunted in pairs, such as the well-known pairings of Larwood-Voce, Lindwall-Miller, Trueman-Statham and Hall-Griffith combinations. Cricket changed its course due to the insults that Lloyd's team endured in Australia [53].

---

52 One of the most hilarious sledges on record is the exchange between Marsh and Botham on one occasion: *'How's your wife and my kids?'* asked Marsh from behind the stumps. *'The wife's fine'*, replied Mr. Botham, *'But the kids are retarded'*! Marsh shut his mouth up quickly.

53 The West Indian fast bowlers were world class players as shown by their statistics: Roberts (1974-1983) 47 Tests, 202 wickets at 25.6; Holding (1975-1987) 60 Tests, 249 wickets at 23.7; Garner (1977-1987) 58 Tests, 259 wickets at 20.9; Croft (1977-1982) 125 wickets at 23.30; Marshall (1978-1991) 81 Tests, 376 wickets at 20.9; Walsh (1984-2001) 519 wickets at 24.4; Ambrose (1988-2000) 98 Tests, 405 wickets at 20.9.

* * *

Doug said the word sledging wasn't around in the 1960s when he first started playing first-class cricket. It arose at Huck Finn's home in Adelaide as the outcome of a friendly swearing contest. Huck Finn was the president of the Glenelg Cricket Club, the club for which the Chappells played. He organized drinks at home every time the NSW team visited and played against South Australia.

On this occasion (sometime in the late 1960s), as the chatter around drinks progressed in the evening, a challenge was made about who could be the best swearer. According to Doug, the NSW nominee (Geoff Davies, a player from Randwick, NSW) went head-to-head with the Glenelg Club's opening batter.

John Benaud, the NSW captain, had described Davies as *subtle as a sledgehammer* for on-field swearing. The NSW player won the contest and became 'King Sledge'. Unfortunately, the term took over from *'gamesmanship'* almost overnight and began to be used everywhere (Walters and Waugh 1999: 206).

Bill Brown, a great Australian player of the 1930s who played alongside Sir Don, said he wanted all forms of sledging to stop. As reported (ESPN Cricinfo 2002), Brown had once asked Bradman about sledging and what he would do. Bradman responded, 'I would give them one warning, and if they didn't stop it, they wouldn't be in the side anymore'. However, Bradman didn't have to take such action against any player because no one crossed the line then.

* * *

A player insulting another during a game is expected to make the latter angry, becoming unbalanced. In cricket, it might bring about a batter's downfall due to a rash shot or a bowler losing control and bowling badly. Benign forms of 'sledging' existed for as long as cricket was played; the great W.G. used to chirp at batters; it was considered a part of *gamesmanship*. Fred Trueman, a great fast bowler, was a master at sledging, but his worst was simple swearing and growling at the batter.

Nowadays, sledging involves profanity, lewd comments, witty put-downs and incessant cursing of the batter. Sledges are loud enough to be heard by the batter but not the umpire. A bristling fast bowler, frustrated by lack of success, would often question the legitimacy of a batter's birth. Bowlers and fielders frequently ask how the batter's wife, sister or mother spent the previous night.

Excuses aside, captains and umpires have failed miserably in curbing this offensive behaviour. Therefore, they are responsible for harming the game we love so much. All cricket fans know harsh words are exchanged between rival players when things become frustrating. These are soon forgiven by the players, if not entirely forgotten.

Ian and Doug have repeatedly said that sharing a beer with your opponents at the end of a gruelling day of contest is the time to iron out any differences with goodwill. They both believe that what is said should be left on the field without players carrying on with grudges. While they didn't mind a bit of on-field banter and needling, they don't recommend youngsters resorting to personal insults and abuse.

* * *

In his *Wisden* Editorial, Preston (1973b) noted that the Local Umpires Association in Australia had complained to the ABC about players' behaviour in a Sheffield Shield match between NSW and Western Australia in Sydney. The report complained of foul language and bowlers badgering the batters, which 'has been a growing trend in the last six or eight years, and young players are "aping" better-known players'. Those were early times in the discourse.

The *sledgers* believe the target should be strong enough to withstand the pressure and not be over-sensitive to slurs. I recall the Sri Lankan captain, Arjuna Ranatunga, complaining about constant insults hurled at him and his players by the Australians. The umpires took no action. Allan Border, the Australian captain, said: 'Grow up, you babies'!

Some notable Indians (e.g., Saurav Ganguly, Virendra Sehwag, M. S. Dhoni) also think that cricket would be 'Dull without sledging' but the chatter 'Shouldn't cross a line and be left on the field'. Emma John (2021) recently reported what Virat Kohli, the Indian great, said: 'These days, we take it well and give it back even better'.

So, although Australians may have mastered it, most teams appear to indulge in some form of 'on-field banter'. Several wicket-keepers – England's Alec Stewart, Australia's Ian Healey and Brad Haddin, and the Sri Lankan Kumar Sangakkara – have often been in the spotlight for endless and needless chirping aimed at distracting the batters.

Media reports show that sledging controversies involving the Australians intensified from the Allan Border era (1985-94), past Mark Taylor's reign (1994-1999), into Steve Waugh's captaincy tenure (2000-03). Responding to the growing crisis, in 2003, the ACB issued a stern warning to its players. The Australian coach, John Buchanan, also warned his team to 'cut down sledging if they want their achievements to gain respect' (BBC 2003a; b).

The ICC responded by developing a *Code of Conduct* (Law 42) to rein in the players' bad behaviour on-field.

Player Behaviour - The Bad and The Ugly

In a notorious sledging controversy in 2008 (*Monkeygate* Affair), when India played Australia in the SCG New Year's Test, Harbhajan Singh, the Indian off-spinner, called Andrew Symonds a *monkey*. Mike Procter, the match referee, fined Harbhajan Singh $3000 when Ricky Ponting, the Australian captain, charged him. But racial abuse charges were dropped, and a three-match ban was overturned on appeal.

Harbhajan said that the Australians insulted him for wearing his Sikh turban: 'You have testicles on your head'. Now, I think that's an unacceptable and serious insult. The ignorant Australians touched a nerve by trespassing on Harbhajan's religion.

In the *Sydney Morning Herald* (2008), Roebuck (2008) denounced the Australians for the continuous 'baiting' of Harbhajan and sledging. He also asked Ponting, Gilchrist, and Hayden to be sacked for bringing the game to disrepute. Roebuck's words were scathing:

> *In the past few days, Ponting has presided over a performance that dragged the game into the pits. He turned a group of professional cricketers into a pack of wild dogs...If Cricket Australia cares a fig for the tattered reputation of our national team in our national sport, it will not for a moment longer tolerate the arrogant and abrasive conduct seen from the captain and his senior players over the past few days.*
>
> *Beyond comparison, it was the ugliest performance by an Australian side in 20 years. The only surprising part is that the Indians have not packed their bags and gone home. There is no justice for them in this country, nor in any manners.*

Another ugly incident occurred in the 2013-14 Ashes whitewash in the Brisbane Test watched on TV by millions of fans. In the incident, Michael Clarke – the Australian captain (2011-15), snarled at Jimmy Anderson, the English paceman and No. 11, '*Get ready for a f*** broken arm*'. It was alleged that Anderson had been riling the team's top fast bowler, Mitchell Johnson, whose fierce pace decided the series' fate. Clarke was fined part of his match fee for the unacceptable behaviour, but sledging continued unabated (ESPN Cricinfo 2013a).

Tim Lane (2017), one of the current broadcasters, wrote that 'Australia's Sledging Culture Needs to be Addressed'. He noted that despite constant reminders, there were far too many on-field incidents involving Australians in the Steve Smith-led team. Smith maintained, 'It should be the umpire's and match referee's job to determine what is acceptable regarding sledging'. His view has little support among the cricket-loving Australian public.

Disputing Smith's view, Tim Lane said: 'As the Laws of Cricket state, the major responsibility for ensuring the spirit of fair play rests with the captains'. In *The Cricket Monthly*, Jarred Kimber (2019) said: 'Sledging and other distasteful tactics have ruined the image of Australian cricket' across the cricketing world, giving them back 'The *'Ugly Australian'* tag. Australia's obsession with 'winning at all costs' was why this tactic was used to unsettle the opponents.

Sub-continental teams, particularly in the 1970s and 80s, were not used to sledging. Many Indian, Pakistani and Sri Lankan cricketers attest to being rudely shocked by the experience when they first encountered it in the late 1970s and throughout the 1980s.

Given that the sub-continent has always welcomed the high-ranking teams visiting to play any number of matches, the mocking insults and profanity greatly upset them. These cricketers didn't know what to do, as they were brought up to play with different values. Unfortunately, the story is often written differently in the Australian media, as if players in other countries also sledged as much as Australia did. This claim, frequently heard on radio and TV, is entirely untrue.

* * *

In Sri Lanka, we consider goodwill, sportsmanship, and camaraderie crucial tenets of cricket or any other sport. Bad player behaviour was unheard of in Sri Lanka until recently. As a game played over many days, cricket offers plenty of opportunities and subtle ways of unfairly gaining an advantage. These bits of *gamesmanship* included time-wasting, batters doing too much 'farming' on the pitch or taking too long adjusting their equipment, negative bowling, altering the ball, rubbing it with dirt (*á la* Michael Atherton) or the accidental, head-high beamer by a frustrated paceman.

Sometimes, it could be a fielder sneakily relocating from cover to mid-off, a deep square leg moving finer, or the non-striker dragging his bat beyond the crease before the bowler delivers the ball. Nowadays, cheating includes more extreme ball tampering methods to make it swing more, match-fixing, spot-fixing and illegal betting. Rules have been tightened to eliminate such cheating. Still, these scourges are part of the reason for the decline in the popularity of modern-day cricket.

Although rare, bad player behaviour includes tense exchanges among individuals on the same side. An ugly example of this was the paceman Rodney Hogg taking a swing in blind anger at his own captain, Kim Hughes. The incident occurred in a match against Trinidad when the Australians were touring in 1984. An image of raw anger adorns the Front Matter in Christian Ryan's book (2009) *Golden Boy*, a story of the travails of Hughes [54]. Despite the evidence, Hogg's absurd claim was '*A photograph telling a lie*' (Ryan 2009: 328).

The incident showed the bad blood between Hughes and Hogg, which exploded on that day in front of thousands of spectators [55]. Hogg's unpleasant behaviour had long been ignored in Australia as they searched for a paceman to replace Lillee and Thomson. Hogg loomed as the next pace weapon in 1978 when the weakened Australian team under Yallop was beaten by Brearley's England 5-1.

* * *

Rarely, minor clashes between an umpire and a frustrated player or captain may occur. The famous class between Mike Gatting and the Pakistan umpire Shakoor Rana happened in a Test in 1987. Rana, the square leg umpire, saw Gatting move a fielder with a wave of his hands just when the bowler delivered and ruled 'dead ball'.

Gatting objected furiously with some swear words and finger-waving. Rana accused the English captain of using foul language. He refused to continue as the umpire, stopping the game. Gatting and the England team apologised, after which the game continued. All such instances can be attributed to the moment's heat, not planned actions. These differ from gamesmanship and trickery in which relentless chatter and appeals aim to disturb the batter's concentration.

Gamesmanship also took the form of Tony Greig, standing so close to the bat

---

54 The tough time the young Test captain, Kim Hughes had, stabbed by his own teammates, is one of the saddest stories in cricket annals. After he quit the captaincy in 1985, Hughes became an alcoholic for years before recovery. He still volunteers talks in Perth at various forums on how to overcome the challenges, stresses and strains of life.

55 In a stop-over tour in Sri Lanka, in an unofficial Test (P. Sara Stadium, Colombo, 7 May 1981), Hughes clashed with Hogg. Frustrated by his inability to break up a stand between Roy Dias and Ranjan Madugalle, Hogg marked a cross between his eyes and nearly decapitated Madugalle with a beamer. Hughes admonished Hogg: '*That's not on, Rodney*'.
Unsettled by the beamer, Madugalle snicked the furious next delivery to Steve Rixon and was out for 25 (Ryan 2009: 18). Hogg also cursed at the crowd near the Sri Lankan Presidential enclosure: which earned him a stern warning (*The Canberra Times* 1981).

at a silly point that he could touch the batter with his outstretched hand and prattling to distract the batter. Many such incidents occurred in the 1977 series in India, which England won 3-1 against Bedi's side. Brettig and Gollapudi (2012) reported how Greig defended his action, saying, 'Fielding up close to the bat isn't just about pulling off blinding catches and taking blows to the body, but applying pressure, and getting a batter to play differently'.

The English team also admitted to ball-tampering with 'Vaseline' (John Lever), although this went unpunished. Greig was also reported for repeatedly stomping on the ball to get it back into shape in the Madras Test. These incidents were poorly handled by the Indian umpires and tarnished England's reputation immensely. Greig's side came under criticism for clowning and juvenile antics of attempted humour (mainly by Randall) that the Indians were unfamiliar with.

* * *

Cantankerous on-field swearing directed at players was rife in the 1970s and exploded in the 1980s. Australians were often accused of extreme hostility towards all weaker opponents. The English umpire 'Dickie' Bird (1997) said that umpires tolerated swearing and other forms of *gamesmanship* because they were technically within the rules of the game. Still, he agreed that umpires could do more to intervene when a team attempts to impose unfair pressure on opponents.

Bird often chose a non-confrontational approach – a quiet word to the offending player or his captain – on or off the field. He disliked 'adding fuel to the fire of a tense situation'.

Stories of unacceptable player behaviour towards umpires are also plentiful. Lloyd's West Indies was involved in some of the worst offences on record in 1980 on a tour to New Zealand. The visitors lost for the first time to the Kiwis 1-nil. This was just after Lloyd's team had crushed the Australians 2-nil in a three-Test series. Lloyd's resurgent team had *avenged* the humiliation they had suffered at the hands of Greg Chappell's Australians in 1975.

Backed by powerful batters and bowlers, the West Indies were on the way to becoming cricket's world champions, a position they occupied for the next 15 years. Even without Vivian Richards, who had gone home with a strained back, the Windies juggernaut was poised to crush the Kiwis.

The tourists were upset about what they called *farcical arrangements* in New Zealand. The team had to carry their kits to the bus and were housed in cramped motels rather than five-star hotels. They didn't like the food on the grounds, 'usually, only sausage and beans'. The first Test at Dunedin (8-13 February 1980) saw the home team stun the Windies with a one-wicket win (Brittenden 1981). But the game would forever be remembered for how badly the Windies behaved over umpiring decisions. On day three, with the Kiwis needing only 104 to win, the tourists were frustrated as a few decisions went against them.

Holding sent through a ripper with the score at 2-28, which he thought John Parker edged to the keeper Murray, but the umpire was unmoved. An enraged Holding walked to the striker's end and let fly a kick, knocking the stumps out of the ground. The photograph of the kick is one of the most spectacular ever taken in cricket history. It epitomized player misconduct. There was still far worse to come.

At Christchurch, in the second Test (22-27 February 1980), one of the most deplorable acts in Test cricket occurred. Colin Croft, the Windies paceman, pretending to lose his run-up, ran into the umpire Fred Goodall, nearly knocking the umpire off his feet. After being no-balled in the previous delivery, Croft flicked off the bails as he returned to his mark. It wasn't an *'on the heat-of-the-moment'* incident.

Croft continually argued with the umpires as he was no-balled for overstepping and wide bouncers. It was the height of discourtesy when Goodall, wanting on two occasions to speak to Lloyd about Croft's swearing, had to walk all the way to the captain, standing deep in the slips. Lloyd made no attempt to meet the umpire or restrain his bowler.

Incensed by some decisions against them, after the incident, the Windies refused to take the field after tea on the third day, saying they wouldn't continue unless umpire Goodall was removed. They were finally swayed to continue after some delay. That evening, there was a likelihood of the tour being abandoned. After lengthy negotiations with the NZ Board of Control, the match and the rest of the tour continued. The Board insisted that Croft shouldn't play in the third Test at Auckland, but as a compromise, he was allowed to play.

Lloyd expressed some remorse after returning home, admitting that his team was tired, but said that the atrocious umpiring was too much to withstand on the back of a challenging tour of Australia. The incidents led to significant ICC rule changes regarding player behaviour and stricter penalties. Reporting for *Wisden*, Brittenden (1981) observed that the Windies were 'badly led and managed and were the author of their own misfortunes'. This wasn't very pleasant for a side considered the best in the world and the strongest since the 1948 Australians. It was extraordinary that the Kiwis, held in scant regard by the Windies, actually deserved their narrow victory. They played better cricket and played as a team, whereas the visitors 'sulked and whined'.

* * *

In a book paying tribute to Doug Walters, a thorough 'gentleman', examining too much bad player behaviour is not necessary. But because it is such a critical issue in cricket, I give below a few examples that exemplify what is not cricket in the way we were brought up to believe. Incidents of bat-throwing and breaking things in the dressing rooms are plentiful in Test cricket. Mallett's book refers to several. Marsh, Snow, and Greg Chappell have done it in heated battles. But they shouldn't have, and some paid penalties by being fined.

Lillee's kick aimed at the Pakistan captain, Miandad, is undoubtedly at the top of my list of bad behaviour, not least because it was racially motivated. The *Wisden Cricketers' Almanack* described it as 'one of the most undignified incidents in Test history'. It tarnished our great game.

It happened at the WACA in Perth on 16 November 1981 during the Pakistan tour's first Test (13-17 November). Miandad was still under 23 years old when he took over the captaincy from Asif a year or so earlier. I was totally shattered in England when the BBC reported this undignified dust-up. I have looked at it many times on film footage. A die-hard Australian fan, my cricketing world suddenly collapsed around me with this incident.

It would be a long bow to draw if one were to call Lillee a racist. He was probably not so. Ian and Doug regard him as a highly competitive player. The unchecked hostility towards any opponent, however, was based on Lillee's thinking that it would bring him better rewards than *being genteel. What a shame that such a great bowler needed this extra weapon?*

In the second inning, on 16 November 1981, Pakistan faced an impossible 543 to win but was putting up a fight. Two young men, Miandad and Mudassar Nazar, were building a partnership. Miandad turned Lillee behind square for a single, and in completing an easy run, he collided with the bowler. Lillee sidestepped to block Miandad's path as he ran between the wickets before aiming a kick at Miandad.

Never one to turn the other cheek, the Pakistan captain exploded, wielding his bat above his head before the umpire intervened. Eyewitnesses said Lillee purposely moved into the batter's path. Miandad claimed that Lillee 'pushed him out of the way'; Lillee's version has Miandad abusing him as he approached and Lillee replying in kind but does not mention any contact (Williamson 2010) [56].

The media were in no doubt where the blame lay. Simpson wrote that it

---

56 The *Lillee-Miandad* dust up, swiftly condemned by the commentators, can be viewed on YouTube (https://www.youtube.com/watch?v=yIHN52fA7r0).

was 'the most disgraceful thing I have seen on a cricket field'. In the Sydney *Sunday Telegraph*, Miller added that Lillee 'should be suspended for the rest of the season', and Ian Chappell said that Lillee's actions were those of 'a spoiled, angry child' (Williamson 2010). But what followed off the pitch rubbed salt in the wound.

By the following day, Greg's team rallied around Lillee and condemned Miandad at an inquiry. The truth got lost a bit in that inquiry. Incensed about it, the Pakistanis nearly abandoned the tour. Instead of a severe reprimand, Lillee received a paltry fine of $200 and a two-ODI match suspension.

Even the umpires, Tony Crafter and Mel Johnson, appealed to the ACB for a more significant penalty for Lillee (Mossop 1981). 'Star players' get away with misdeeds most of the time; that's always the case in any sport, and Lillee was a hero for the public. I am willing to bet that Lillee would never have kicked a white cricketer or even an English-speaking West Indian.

The implausible allegation against Miandad was that he was the 'provocateur' as he chirped away in *Urdu*, his native language. Speaking to himself was Miandad's way of motivating himself. Everyone felt that this appalling incident came about due to Lillee's frustration of not being able to dismiss the Karachi 'street fighter'.

A lack of respect for opponents contributed to the incident. McGilvray said Lillee should have been suspended for his disgraceful behaviour. In his book (McGilvray 1985: 128), Alan recorded how Lillee went on the warpath a week or two later when their paths crossed in Adelaide and launched into a tirade of abuse and noted this abuse as 'one of the great regrets of his [Alan's] life in cricket'.

Ball-tampering, Betting, Bribery and Match-Fixing

Ball tampering has been going on for a long time, although I had not heard much about it when I was a kid. When Greig was captain, the 'Vaseline' episode involving John Lever in the Madras Test in India (1977) exposed that 'greasy substances' had been used in the past. There were also admissions from Botham and Imran about 'bottle tops' being used to scuff the ball's surface in County cricket in the 1970s. These alerted the cricket world that ball-tampering was rife.

Australian cricket's integrity was forever tainted in the notorious *Sandpapergate Affair* in South Africa when ball-tampering was discovered. In March 2018, during the third Test at Newlands (Cape Town), Cameron Bancroft, the Australian opening batter, was caught by TV cameras trying to rough up the ball with sandpaper hidden in his underwear. Captain Steve Smith and vice-captain David Warner were found to be involved, and all three players received exceptional sanctions from Cricket Australia.

Although the coach, Lehmann, was found not to have been involved, he quit his role. The scandal led to Steve Smith being replaced by Tim Paine as Australia's captain in all formats before Aaron Finch took over from Paine in ODIs and T20Is.

Doug is adamant that the Australian teams of the past 'took pride in their honesty and integrity'. Historical facts bear out this truth. Unfortunately, the affair in South Africa has re-kindled the baseline of how Australians are viewed by the rest of the cricketing world. The *'win-at-all-cost'* attitude, which never entirely disappeared, backed by big money, caused the *Sandpapergate* scandal. No more needs to be said on this topic except perhaps read below the astute observations of Sharda Ugra (2018), a senior editor for ESPN Cricinfo:

> *Throughout its colourful and rich history, Australian cricket has offered us some of the game's most magnificent qualities: competitiveness, daring, energy and positivity. For the better part of the last two decades, they were the gold standard for the game.*
>
> *Yet, slowly, during the same period, so many major series featuring the Aussies have begun to produce an overheated, eventually absurd subplot in which they usually claim to be the victims while often being deliberate and even skilful agent provocateurs.*

Betting against one's team must also be rated as a high-level offence as bad player behaviour. Much has been written about the alleged Lillee-Marsh betting scandal in that disastrous Ashes tour in 1981. Kim Hughes' sad story (Ryan 2009) describes how Marsh and Lillee's lack of support for the young captain affected the 1981 touring party. Even today, 40-plus years later, a shiver runs through my body when I recall how badly Hughes was treated by the senior pair.

One of the most shameful incidents in that ill-fated tour was Marsh and Lillee betting against their team. This outrage occurred in the third Test when England was teetering towards an innings defeat at tea on the fourth day, despite a miraculous Ian Botham century (149*) (Steen 2001). The alleged story is that the two players found the Ladbroke's 500/1 odds on an England victory irresistible.

Betting against their own team, Lillee and Marsh put £10 and £5 bets, respectively, on England winning. They netted a jackpot of £7500 between them as Bob Willis (8/43) tore through Australia's batting.

Dismissing the visitors for 111, England won by 16 runs. Lesser players would have been sent home immediately. The Australian press treated it like a joke, saying that there was no evidence to suggest that the pair sacrificed the match to make a personal gain. The culprits escaped with slight reprimands. However, watching the events unfold in the U.K., my view was that it was a case of utter disrespect for their captain, pure and simple. Both hated Hughes so much.

* * *

Bribery and match-fixing have plagued cricket since the game became a money-spinner. Doug said that in the 1950s and 60s, there was little incentive for match-fixing and not much betting. As well documented in cricket history, the *Hansie Cronje Affair* opened cricket's dark underbelly and permanently damaged its reputation.

In 2000, the South African captain, Hansie Cronje and three teammates (Nicky Boje, Herschelle Gibbs and Pieter Strydom) were charged by the New Delhi police for match-fixing during the one-day series against India (Kremmer and Ray 2022). The charges were 'Cheating, fraud and criminal conspiracy related to match-fixing and betting'. Cronje was banned for life in 2000. In 2002, he died at the age of 32 in a plane crash (The Guardian 2000; ESPN Cricinfo 2013b).

One of the longest and most comprehensive inquiries in cricket history was conducted in Pakistan into bribery and match-fixing that had been going on in the 1990s involving a raft of Pakistan cricketers and others, as well as bookmakers from Pakistan and India. The commission, led by Justice Malik Muhammad Qayyum, explained in their final report (ESPN Cricinfo Pakistan 2009) how deep bribery and match-fixing were. They called it 'an international threat to cricket'.

Australian cricket's integrity was damaged by Shane Warne and Mark Waugh being involved in a betting scandal in 1994-95. *The Age* (1998) later reported that four years earlier, in 1994, the ACB kept a cover on the matter but penalised the players for passing information on pitch conditions and team changes to an Indian bookmaker.

On the way to Pakistan in 1994, the Australians made a short trip to Sri Lanka for the Singer Cup. Here, the bookmaker, 'John', approached the two cricketers in a hotel room and asked questions about the pitch and weather conditions and the teams in return for payment. Waugh received $6000 and Warne $5000. Both players said they didn't give information about the team's lineup or tactics. Waugh said they gave mundane information, 'the same as in any pre-match media interview'. Waugh was fined Aus $10,000 and Warne $8000, but the pair were cleared of match-fixing allegations (ESPN Cricinfo 1998).

In the Pakistan tour, the betting scandal erupted. It involved Salim Malik, a Pakistan captain. Malik had been exposed by the *Herald* and *The Age* in 1995 for offering Shane Warne and Tim May $US200,000 to bowl poorly on the last day of the 1994 Karachi Test and Mark Waugh the same amount to perform poorly during a one-day international (Hopps 2000; ESPN Cricinfo 2000). Malik's bribery offers to several players *"to throw matches"* were brought to light first by the Pakistani wicket-keeper Rashid Latif.

Blowing the whistle, Latif also implicated Pakistan cricket officials in match-fixing. Qayyum's length inquiry took evidence from several Australians. The Commission found Malik to be the main instigator of match-fixing. It banned him from cricket for life for corruption (overturned in 2008). Malik was also the first cricketer to be jailed. Many Pakistan players, including the famous fast-bowling pair Wasim Akram and Waqar Younis, were also implicated in match-fixing and have been censured and fined (ESPN Cricinfo Pakistan 2009).

In 2000, Mohammad Azharuddin, a former Indian captain, was also condemned for match-fixing. During India's tour of South Africa in 2000, a series that Sourav Ganguly's team won by 3-2, Azharuddin scored only 112 runs at 28. Azharuddin was found guilty in the scandal that erupted after the series and banned for life, a decision overturned in 2012 due to lack of evidence.

Ganguly asserted that 'No Code of Conduct can prevent betting and match-fixing and only the honesty of cricketers can prevent the game from losing its character. At the end of the day, cricketers have to be honest' (ESPN Cricinfo 2000).

The cancer of betting and match-fixing ran deep in the 1990s, as revealed in many such incidents. Corruption in sports exists because people can make significant profits by betting on the result of a match that can be fixed. In writing for Cricinfo, John Polack (2000) provides a detailed account of the most notable and alleged incidents.

England captain Adam Hollioake disclosed he was offered bribes in the 1997 Champions' Cup. The South African umpire Rudi Koertzen revealed he was approached in 1999 by a bookie to fix the Singapore International Challenge final. The England all-rounder Chris Lewis said he was approached by the Indian sports promoter, Ashim Khetrapal, and offered

£300,000 to influence players to perform poorly during the home Test series then underway against New Zealand.

All countries are now committed to a 'zero-tolerance' approach to bribery and corruption. In 2000, the ICC's *Anti-Corruption Unit* was strengthened with an *Integrity Division* and Country panels to receive complaints and conduct investigations.

Countries must enforce strict vigilance on betting, player behaviour, and discipline. The obligations of players, officials and others involved in cricket are now clearly stated in the ICC *Code of Conduct* (ICC 2017, revised in 2020). Upholding the *Code* is expected to help cricket-playing countries eradicate corruption of a game by the match 'fixers'.

Partisan Crowds and Rioting

Hero-worshipping of your team by ecstatic crowds happens all over the world. Sometimes, heightened emotions lead to people not accepting what's going on in the middle and starting riots. Test cricket has often witnessed these instances, especially in the West Indies and India. Raucous crowds frequently insult the opposition. No single individual takes responsibility. The *Barmy Army* of English supporters is a fine example of relentlessly mocking the opponents.

The Australian crowds also return the favour, and sometimes, the behaviour of both groups in the Ashes battles can be dreadful to watch. Individual player misconduct incidents are now commonplace in almost all top-tier Test-playing countries. Doug and I believe these elements are harmful to cricket. Misbehaving players and baiting opponents, seen by large masses on TV, cheapen the game and down-market the sport in the long run, driving people away from the sport.

There are many accounts in cricket literature alluding to Australian crowds being described as *Ockers*. The word is applied to aggressively boorish Australian males. The dictionaries describe *Ockerism* as stereotypically Australian in speech, manner, and way of life for many average Australian males. However, I find that the exact same ocker bloke can also be an honest, laid-back, fun-loving larrikin.

The term could just as well be applied to a naughty young person or mature male who is a bit rowdy but one who disregards social norms or political conventions. Boycott, who suffered at their hands (1979: 183), said: 'It is a way of life for many young and older Australians – a hard term to define, but it also means enjoying a reputation for being a bit brash and hard and also basic and unsophisticated'.

Everyone can hear a great deal of swearing and shouting by excited crowds. Some may even break ground rules. However, calling the noisy Australian crowds, such as those who barracked Lillee and Thomson on their heyday, a 'bunch of rowdy ockers' is not valid. Still, it is a shame that genuine cricket fans suffer because of abusive crowds.

The English came under heavy fire whenever they visited Australia. Notable Australian columnists warned touring teams 'not to expect much goodwill down under' and 'should be ready for tough cricket, and not a lot of sympathy' in Australia. The British *Daily Mail*'s renowned journalist, Ian Wooldrige, once reported that T-shirts slogged in Perth depicted the slogan: *Keep Australia Beautiful: Kill A Pom A Day*. Such unwelcome insults horrify cricket fans like me. We now know that the 'gentlemen's game' is truly over.

During the 1980 England tour of Australia, the ODI matches were marred by atrocious crowd behaviour. Brearley sparked a row by saying that he feared for the lives of his boundary fielders as pieces of metal were thrown at them: 'Somebody could get killed out there'.

Underwood was struck by a large block of ice, and Botham was repeatedly targeted. Bob Taylor, the 12th man carrying drinks, had metal staples fired at him. While admitting that that were some rowdy elements, Chappell said, 'That was only the beer-talking lot…Brearley must have been playing on a different ground' because, as far as the players are concerned, the 'Australian crowds are all right'.

On Media and Pressures of Cricket

McGilvray (1985, 1987) always reminded broadcasters and journalists of their duty to report on cricket and its personalities as accurately as possible. Alan despaired about the quality of reporting throughout the 1980s and 90s as commercialization took hold. Viv Richards (1991: 212) swiped at the notorious English tabloid press:

> *Cricket journalists should also look at better ways of reporting the game, analyzing batting and bowling performances in greater depth, and going beyond radio and TV's instant coverage. 'Muck-raking' and relentlessly sneaking into players' private lives does no good to any sport.*

The English press has always been quite unkind to Australians, and the Australian media has also returned fire in recent decades. Nowadays, there is hardly any objective reporting because stories must be catchy and sensational to draw readers in. Cricketers and other sportspeople have always been cannon fodder to the media as some enjoy celebrity status. Many reporters 'sneak around' touring parties and players and then come up with sensational stories.

It is a classic method by which great cricketers, at the top of their sporting prowess, can be mentally destabilised. [Ian Botham, Shane Warne and Viv Richards all have had their dose of scandals]. However, Doug never attracted much media attention except when he plundered runs off bowlers. The media has been kind to him because he was a simple cricketer who communicated his enjoyment of cricket to everyone by doing things his way. Doug loved cricket so much that he gave us pleasure, and he did that without the help of modern-day 'super-coaches', physiotherapists and shiny-suited media advisors.

Is there Too Much Cricket?

Calling cricket a professional 21st-century (sporting) behemoth, Tanya Aldred (2016) said:

> *Cricket is no longer the sleepy creature that stretched out across the Commonwealth until the 1970s. Today's game is slobberingly greedy. It has riches beyond its wildest dreams yet exists in a closed world of vast inequality. It is on a constant merry-go-round of self-justification and selling, selling, selling.*
>
> *It needs sponsors to survive, and to justify the sponsors, gives its name to clothing, cars, bats, drinks, insurance, supermarkets, banks, and beer, until little by little, hashtag by hashtag, fragments of [Cricket's] soul leach away.*

Before World War I, there were only three or four Tests per year; only England, Australia and South Africa (1889) were then Test-playing countries. Between the two Wars, three other countries joined the Test rank (West Indies, 1928; New Zealand, 1930; and India, 1932), and the number of Tests played in a year grew to about eight. After the end of World War II, this number more than doubled; about 17 Tests were played in a year up to 1976, as Pakistan also got Test status in 1952. In the 1990s, about 20-25 Tests were played yearly, increasing to about 36-37 after 2010 in the new millennium [57].

A lot of cricket is played these days. Test cricket and other forms of international cricket are proliferating out of control. One season dovetails into the next without respite. The calendar is so crowded that most top-tier countries struggle to schedule tournaments and tours.

In 2022, England's captain Ben Stokes called on authorities to: 'stop treating players like 'cars' that can just be 'filled up" and used and then ready to be fuelled up repeatedly'. Stokes lamented that the crammed schedules of Test cricket, ODIs, and T20 cricket give players no respite. Stokes said: 'It leads to him and other elite players having to choose one form or another and giving up some formats'.

Without a doubt, the more cricket is played, the better it is for the game, but only if the 'product' is of the highest quality. The public wants to see the best players at the peak of their careers perform and play as much as they can. Individuals have to make judgements on playing and resting their bodies as much as possible to prolong their playing careers. While Jimmy Anderson and Stuart Broad are good examples of longevity in cricket, they are rare. Anderson, at the age of nearly 42, retired in July 2024. Broad retired in 2023 at 37. Both played so long by picking white-ball cricket over other formats [58].

Cricket is now attractive to a vast following. Night cricket and pink balls have ensured a whole new audience, with thousands of women and girls joining the boys and men. The lure is no longer enjoyment but big money, especially in the shorter formats. *Big Bash* (BBL), IPL and other T20s extravaganzas have significantly improved batting and bowling, unbelievable fielding and players' physical fitness.

Doug said that he never felt there was too much cricket in those days. He severely criticises players complaining about the arduous nature of tours and workloads (Mallett 2008: 306-312).

All the Test countries are supposed to be playing the same amount of Test cricket, but this never happens. The globally popular ODIs and T20 cricket mean that cricketers play an enormous amount of cricket and must invest time and energy to remain in peak fitness and form.

---

57   In a research article, Nicholls et al. (2023) stated that between 2000 and 2020, the top eight teams played 724 Tests (average of 36-37 Tests per year). In 2023, the ICC shows 37 Tests played between the top-tier countries.

58   Stuart Broad retired after the final Ashes Test in June 2023 with a record of 607 wickets at 27.6 and 3662 runs in 167 Tests. James Anderson took 704 wickets (in 188 Tests at 26.5) and retired after the Lord's Test (10-14 July 2024).

Doug agrees with what Sobers said (2002: 386) that life at the top of one's game can be relatively short, and these days, cricketers are paid so well to fulfil their obligations, which is really *paid work*. Only a few have made it past mid-thirties or thereabouts into the forties and still get automatically picked. Those who survive for long are rare and exceptional individuals, given the enormous mental and physical pressures under which they perform at the elite level.

CHAPTER 16

The Game Has Changed

In 1978, as he retired from being an administrator of Australian cricket after 30 years, Bradman lamented the sharp decline in cricket standards: 'Cricket occupies a unique place because of the great character-building qualities inherent in the game. Cricket has come a long way since then'.

Sadly, although cricket's popularity has increased, it can hardly be recognized as the game of yesteryear. The entertainment value, however, has increased. In the past, Test cricket was painfully slow but endured by its fans. It was bright at times, dull at other times, but appreciated by supporters as a tussle between worthy opponents. In contrast, nowadays, Test cricket is no longer played 'softly-softly' by gentlemen pushing and prodding; instead, it is now fiercely competitive, with the opponents going at each other hammer-and-tongs.

Doug agrees that today's game lacks basic good manners and sportsmanship. Years ago, a fast bowler swearing at an umpire for a decision turned down was unheard of. No batter gesticulated angrily or glared at an umpire when given out. No fielder would even think of insulting a rival batter in the field.

Today, fielders appeal without reason at every opportunity. The ploy is to get the batter out by hook or crook. The Game Has Changed, indeed! How appropriate is the title of McGilvray's 1987 book?

'Winning Isn't Everything'

Simon Taufel, a respected Australian umpire, delivering the Cowdrey *Spirit of Cricket* Memorial Lecture in 2013, clarified some of the common phrases that appear in cricket discourses: 'It's just not cricket' relates to fairness; 'A gentleman's game' refers to honour and respect amongst competitors and doing the right thing when it is required and 'Spirit of Cricket' relates to applying a high moral standard and integrity when playing – not engaging in cheating or taking undue advantage of someone else's misfortune.

In the past, when the phrase 'It isn't cricket' was used in criticising anything unfair in a cricket match, it meant that cricketers shouldn't stoop to do anything low. Way back in 1966, the *Wisden* Editor (Preston 1966). referred to the tarnishing of the game's public image by dubious tactics, such as 'chucking', the excessive use of bumpers, claiming catches when the ball hadn't carried to the fielder, and a batter not walking when he knew he was clearly out. These problems arise when Test cricket is played like *warfare* instead of an enjoyable sport.

Even in the early days, the call went out for the leading players to portray everything that is best in the game to secure its future and public support. Both Australia and England, as the pre-eminent cricketing nations, have been poor losers, which takes much of the fun out of cricket. Both countries do not readily accept the possibility of defeat by the emerging Test-playing countries. This partly explains their long-standing, on-field nastiness towards other nations.

* * *

Jarrod Kimber (2019) pointed out that open hostility and racial taunts aimed at disorienting the opponents by some players gave Australian teams a bad name. In this era of social media, outside Australia, the Australian team may not feel warmly welcomed in other countries, which is a shame. Individual players may still be respected for their skills. But many exchanges I've had with cricket fans indicate that the Australian team, as a whole, is just tolerated by other nations without being admired as they once were. Many ardent Australian fans have also dumped the team because of the culture of bad behaviour.

Stories of greats like Vivian Richards and Brian Lara getting upset about the insults thrown at them attest to the dark period of Australian cricket. As I recall, the 'damn the opposition, come what may' attitude came to the fore around the re-building of the Australian side under *'Captain 'Grumpy'* Allan Border. Border's uncompromising approach was anchored by Simpson, the coach, and there are stories that both took some players to task for being too *friendly* with the opponents.

While Border presided over the initial period, the hostility towards opponents continued, without exception, under all of the Test captains who followed him. Sadly, while Alan McGilvray (1985; 1987), Peter Roebuck (2008), Jarrod Kimber (2019), Tim Lane (2017) and others openly lamented, the ACB did very little to redress the issue.

Apart from a few muted comments, others in the media appear to find ways to describe this awful culture as somehow acceptable as all part of a fiercely contested sport. I regret that the mighty Australians, who were so well respected in the past, lost their way during the past three decades. The legacy of those dark years will plague Australian cricket for some more time.

However, most people will agree that Steve Smith, the captain of Australia until 2018, and the current captain, Pat Cummins, have done much to repair the bad Aussie image. For this effort, these two gallant cricketers must be congratulated and respected. Their personalities appear devoid of overt nastiness towards opponents.

I think winning is vital in any sport, but it is not everything. Doug agrees with me on this issue. *How you win is even more important than winning itself.* To become memorable in the public's eye, you must win in a fair contest. It would help to respect your opponents as combatants, proudly representing their countries. They ought not to be insulted. An unbending attitude to win by any means is synonymous with Australian cricket. This matter hasn't been dealt with effectively in Australia because of the forces of commercialisation of cricket, which is a multimillion-dollar business.

Most commentators, except a few, fear that criticizing Australian cricketers in any form might alienate the public. Most stick to a strict code of avoiding comments that might upset their media masters.

'Cricket-in-a-Hurry' - Fast-format Cricket

Ian Chappell said, 'The WSC insurrection was all over pay and conditions', which must be correct from the players' viewpoints. But everyone knows Packer only wanted to market cricket via TV and use advertising to make plenty of money. As it turned out, he did. At the same, he saw the opportunity to popularize the game, which he loved. We all agree that it was the 50-over game that eventually prospered.

Cricket today is dominated by *Cricket-in-a-hurry* formats. While Test cricket is not in decline, it has to compete with ODIs and T20s for attention. Test cricket is still loved because of its traditions. The ODI game is all about 'bums on seats' and money, but it gives the spectators a result of the contest within a few hours.

Getting a result suits the fast lifestyles of the new millennium. Doug calls it '*instant gratification*' and states that the shorter game will always be one of chance, in which both teams have an equal opportunity to win. Arguably, it is a devalued enterprise rather than a forum for developing talent in cricket.

Doug agrees that the shorter formats are not as sophisticated as the five-day game. Still, there is nothing wrong with spectators' liking for ODIs and getting a result. We believe it will finally be Test cricket that will determine the best cricket team in the world. ODIs, however intoxicating they might be, may never replace Test cricket. Generally, most of the boisterous crowd that turns up for instant gratification of short-format cricket are not genuine cricket lovers. I think life would be intolerable without the longer format of Test cricket.

Doug remembers times when huge crowds attended Test cricket, such as in Calcutta, India, which regularly boasted more than 50,000 spectators daily. In most South Asian cricketing countries, crowds have since diminished to 20-30,000 per day. It is also a fact that most people nowadays don't have the time to sit through a five-day Test. Cricket must also compete with faster-moving sports like soccer, baseball, Australian Rules Football and rugby.

Too much traffic on the road, too many people, and too many distractions (e.g., the internet) are other factors that prevent spectators from crowding the cricket grounds. The excellent TV coverage of Test cricket is also a crucial factor. Many thousands prefer to watch live TV pictures beamed on TV because they are so good these days. From an armchair, one can feel *present* on the ground without missing any unfolding action of the spectacle. In fact, often, one could see, via live-action on TV, many little things that you would not see quite so clearly while watching from a seat on the ground.

* * *

With short-format cricket and live TV, billboards and smartphone adverts, much money is made from the advertising bonanza it offers. Huge masses adhere to cricket, rugby and football as if the sports were personal religions. Tapping into such crowds means vast amounts of money for companies. The lure of money trumps everything else.

Nowadays, advertisements between overs urge you to buy a particular beer brand or a soft drink. At the same time, your favourite batter leans into a classic drive, which you will miss. But advertising pays the players more money than anything else, without which many would leave cricket for greener pastures.

The razzmatazz of short-format games often appear vulgar, acting like an addictive opiate. For those in it to make money, such as the *Indian Premier League* (IPL), T20 cricket is a gold mine. Players are bought and sold in auctions, like 'goods and services' as the franchise owners wish. *It is almost obscene!*

The commercial benefits of the spectacle are so great that T20s are now vigorously promoted in the Middle East, North America, Malaysia and Hong Kong. A few decades ago, these countries had no organised cricket. Much to the detriment of cricket in their respective countries, these lucrative competitions lure many overseas players as 'hired guns' propping up the teams to attract bigger crowds.

Hundreds of new stadiums have been built in different countries, and the schedules are filled with T20 games. The cricket boards have healthier bank balances worldwide, taking their cut. There are many instances in recent times, in all countries, where the number of Test matches scheduled in a season has been reduced simply to 'fit-in' limited overs tournaments. Cricket's orthodoxy has indeed been changed by the 'slap-and-dash' allure of the shorter format cricket.

Field restrictions, power plays and other rules make this format exciting. T20 cricket has also allowed skilled batters to develop new techniques. The traditionalists, such as the good Dr. W. G. Grace, would decry strokes, such as the *ramp*, the *scoop* or the *helicopter* [59], which did not exist as cricket strokes until recently.

Switch-hit is also very common now, where the batter changes hands and flicks the ball over the slip's cordon [60]. While all these unorthodox shots are re-writing the coaching manuals, the bowlers have also developed exceptional skills, particularly with slower deliveries and fastish leg- and off-cutters to thwart scoring.

The shorter game has lifted players' fielding skills and fitness to another plane. Nowadays, fans constantly see fantastic catches and mind-boggling fielding displays on TV. Despite the above, Doug and others have frequently cautioned players seeking short-term, lucrative contracts that they risk burnout or injury as the calendar gets crowded. Too much cricket is never good, not for the individuals who could get tired and injured, nor for the countries or cricket boards who have to manage tournaments, people and global sports.

* * *

Although he is naturally a traditionalist, Doug is in favour of moving with the times and new ideas (e.g., heavier bats, which allow more sixers to be hit down the ground) and rules (such as a free hit for a no-ball). Such ideas

---

59 The *Ramp* was invented by Sri Lanka's opener T.M. Dilshan in a T20 World Cup game against Australia in 2009. It was dubbed '*Dilscoop*' for a while and is now a common stroke whereby the batter crouches down, positioning under the ball before flaying it over the keeper or fine leg to the boundary. The 'helicopter' is a speciality of India's Suryakumar Yadav, a high impact batter.

60 *Switch-hits* (Reverse sweep) were rarely employed in the past. I have two classic pictures from the past of Ken Barrington and Mushtaq Mohammad reverse sweeping. The stroke is now used by most elite players. It was Kevin Pietersen who popularized it in 2006 by switch-hitting and scything Sri Lanka's Muttiah Muralitharan's off-breaks repeatedly to the cover boundary.

do not change the basics of the game itself nor diminish its dignity, but they entertain the spectators.

Money for every six that is hit is an embellishment that makes tournaments more entertaining. Fast-format cricket has indeed had a positive effect on Test cricket as players have developed skills that can be applied across both formats. Cricket can remain viable as a sport only if crowds turn up. Given this, Doug has long advocated making cricket more interesting with 'small changes' to draw crowds and 'positive and attacking leadership' (Walters and Waugh, 1999, p. 238).

Viv Richards (1990, p. 201) was of the view that because cricket is such a mental game, it is pretty stressful to 'constantly change from the deep concentration needed over five days to the quick-fire business of the one-day game; it puts the cricketer under horrendous pressure'. It is an interesting viewpoint from one of the most successful short-format cricketers. However, there is no evidence of anyone listening.

Richards said that under imaginative management, five-day Tests must never lose their position as the ultimate showcase of cricketing talent. Doug and Ian unanimously believe cricket benefits from a few different playing formats to satisfy customer needs. Chappell (2023) recently said that professional cricketers must be able to adjust according to the needs of the various formats.

Umpires' Decisions Not So Final Anymore

In cricket, the umpire used to be much revered. But the erosion of standards in the 1980s and '90s saw umpires coming under enormous pressure and being challenged by players. Off the field, umpires were an easy target for maligning by the press when they got some decisions wrong. Skilled umpires with integrity have become critical nowadays, as earnings from game winnings are so high. They need to be fit and firm and know all the rules. Bad umpiring decisions spoil the joy of a great match. Alertness, efficiency, and integrity are essential qualities of a good umpire who must also ensure that the game flows and is not interrupted by players' misconduct or rule violations.

I recall that sub-continental players initially mooted the idea of neutral umpires. Leading proponents were the two Pakistani captains, Asif Iqbal and Imran Khan. They were fully supported by India's captains, The Nawab of Pataudi and Sunil Gavaskar, in the mid-1980s.

These cricketing giants were sick of hearing their countries being accused of partisan and *nationalistic* umpires, who gave them a '*home advantage*'. Imran masterminded the first step towards quelling the accusation that had dogged home umpiring by inviting two Indian umpires – V. K. Ramaswamy and Piloo Reporter to stand in the second Test Pakistan played against the Windies in Lahore (7-9 November 1986). He furthered the idea by inviting John Hampshire and John Holder (both from England) to be the umpires for the Pakistan home series against India in 1989-90 (Rajesh 2011).

The ICC soon realised it was the way forward, but implementing it took another six years. One neutral umpire per Test was appointed experimentally in 1992, and the system was adopted two years later. The progression to two neutrals was made in 2002, starting with India's tour of the West Indies. As a result, umpires became the most travelled members of the cricket community and were no longer charged with partisanship. But the irony was that home teams fared better since introducing a neutral umpire, with a win-loss ratio of 1.6:1 compared to 1.4:1 before.

As cricket fans, we know that neutral umpires will not lead to Tests free of disputed decisions. Umpires are also like players; they make mistakes. History shows that serious mistakes, even a single bad one, can decide the fate of a Test match and a Test series. While no umpire is perfect, some are better than others. Runouts have always been difficult for umpires since there is a flurry of activity with the wicket and the crease. Bat-pad catches, stumpings, and no-balls are also difficult unless the umpires are super-sharp.

Instances of umpiring mistakes have been recorded since cricket's beginning (Bird 1997). What neutral umpires do, however, is to remove the doubt that umpires from any country may be biased towards the home team. When Doug played, there were no neutral umpires. But Doug and I agree that neutral umpires are good in cricket. However, what is even more important is to ensure that umpires also achieve an acceptable global standard. In my view, the number of mistakes an umpire makes must be considered to keep them in an 'elite' group.

* * *

Since the *Bodyline series* and the *Griffith affair*, intimidatory bowling has been difficult for umpires. Whether or not someone is bowling at the body of a batter with a deliberate intention to cause bodily harm [as Griffith was accused of by O'Neill, Lawry and Simpson] is hard for an umpire to determine. Larwood said: 'I never bowled to injure a man in my life. Frighten them, intimidate them, yes'.

When Snow bowled bumper after bumper in the 1970-71 Ashes series, he attracted severe displeasure from the Australian press and crowds. The umpires sometimes warned Snow, to which both the bowler and the captain objected strongly. A few years later, when Lillee and Thomson fired their missiles at the beleaguered Englishmen, causing many injuries, the umpires couldn't do much except warn against too many short-pitched deliveries.

Intimidatory fast bowling was a hallmark of the much-feared West Indies *mean machines* of the late 70s, throughout the 80s, under Lloyd and Richards, and extended into Richie Richardson's tenure as captain in the mid-90s. The vicious *throat ball* was a Courtney Walsh speciality, delivered from a height of nearly seven feet. All West Indian fast bowlers were supreme in their craft. They did intimidate. Batters were fearful of them. Can anyone prove that they intended no bodily harm?

McGilvray (1985: 85) observed that, as a whole, English umpires were a lot better than Australian umpires because they had so much more experience. More even light, less glare, less heat and less pressure were also factors, as Alan suggested. The Australian umpires often had far less experience because much less cricket was played on the continent. Doug confirmed that appeal by players en masse was not a prevalent practice in the early decades when he played. However, it became an unsavoury addition to the game in the 1980s and is practised nowadays by all international teams. The umpires, those days, were much stricter than now and did not appreciate the tactic. Film footage proves that even fast bowlers like Snow, Willis, McKenzie, Procter, Griffith and Hall didn't appeal much unless they were convinced that a batter was out.

* * *

Sobers (2002: 344) said, 'Modern technology, aggressive player behaviour and appealing have changed umpires' lives', which is 'No longer a friendly, pleasant way to earn a living or pass the time'. These days, wildly inaccurate appeals by close-in fielders are common. One can see fielders running in from deep positions to congratulate a bowler even before a decision has been made. High fives galore as fielders glare at the batter and put pressure on the poor umpire!

Doug and I lament that the *gentleman's game* has changed so much that good manners play no part in the game anymore. It is a shame that the fierce competitiveness and the *winner-takes-all* mentality eroded camaraderie in player interactions. We believe that umpires should do more to control the game and players who misbehave.

Rules must be tightened to impose heavier fines for unacceptable conduct. Presently, the penalties in the ICC rule book are too lenient as deterrents. Most match referees also tend to find the easiest way out by dishing out lenient penalties when dealing with such issues.

Many umpires dread the TV replays as it can lead to a reversal of their original decision. Fielders often claim catches when they know the ball hasn't been carried. Few players walk when they get a touch behind the wicket. On this aspect, Doug and I disagree with Ian Chappell, who maintains that a batter needn't walk if he has nicked it but leave that decision to the umpire. Sobers (2002: 350) said that Chappell is wrong on this issue that a batter should '*walk off*' if he knows he is out and 'make the umpire's job easier'.

The umpires' job is a nightmare these days with TV cameras everywhere. The belated inclusion of a third umpire is a welcome development, particularly for run-outs, stumpings, faint tickles to the keeper, slip catches, which may not carry to a fielder, boundary hits and sliding stops. These instances are hard for an umpire to see clearly. The number of cheating incidents has grown steadily in recent times. The criticism of umpires has also sadly grown in the past few decades.

There is a view that the new technologies help umpires get most of their decisions right. However, there is also a view that the *Decision Review System* (DRS), which nowadays involves *Hawkeye*, *Spider Cam*, *Hot Spot*, and *Snick-O-Meter* technologies, have made the umpires' job quite tricky. Nevertheless, the emphasis must be on reducing errors and correcting most decisions[61]. Umpires and technology wizards must work together to improve these helpful tools for cricket.

The third umpire idea was first suggested in 1982 by Mahinda Wijesinghe, a Sri Lankan journalist and ardent cricket fan. Wijesinghe's pioneering idea (2008: 115-116) was to have a third umpire watching the TV monitors and action replays. He proposed the development of facilities to have replays and the third umpire to have direct walkie-talkie communication with the two on-field umpires. The idea was initially unsupported when presented at the ICC meeting in July 1984 but subsequently gained acceptance. The

---

61   *Hawkeye* is a computer system first used in 2001 to show the path of a cricket ball. It is used to confirm the decisions, especially LBWs. The *Spidercam* enables TV cameras to move both vertically and horizontally over the playing field.
The hot spot technology is used to review whether the bat has touched the ball. If there is contact, the heat generated is indicated by a change to that area of the bat. Hot Spot uses two infra-red cameras positioned at either end of the ground. These cameras measure heat from friction generated by a collision, such as ball on pad, ball on bat, ball on ground or ball on glove.
Invented by the English computer scientist Allan Plaskett, the *Snick-O-Meter* is a sensitive microphone located in one of the stumps. It can pick up the sound when the ball nicks the bat. It is only used to show TV audiences if the ball actually hit the bat. The umpires are still to get the benefit of hearing snicks.

system for on-field umpires to refer a decision to a TV umpire or off-field umpire, as part of a DRS, was first used in Tests in 1992 [62].

The Future of Cricket

McGilvray (1987) acknowledged that 'change is inevitable as time progresses and societies evolve'. But, he said that 'not all of the changes in cricket have been pleasant'. Alan constantly reminded the Australian listeners that the rituals of the game are not sacrosanct, nor should the coaching manuals be. His words were:

> *Approaches to the game and attitudes need to change with time. However, while sponsors and spectators are critical elements of any sport, the 'gentle' game must resist the 'greed and selfishness that come with money and commercialization.*

As for reasons for the decline in standards and etiquette, Alan's view was that international players were under much less pressure those days because they played much less cricket in a calendar year. Also, public scrutiny, media interest and commercial pressures were much less intense. McGilvray was a lone voice in stating explicitly that there should have been no room for such unacceptable behaviour and that the Australian selectors at that time failed in their duties. They should have sorted out the acrimony between the senior players.

Alan was in no doubt that given the seriousness of the indiscretions of Marsh and Lillee during the Ashes tour in 1981, they should have been dropped. If the selectors were genuine, they could have given more room and time for Kim Hughes to build a more cohesive team.

The Board hesitated because of cricket's horror period during the WSC crisis. Also, officials have always heeded the cries of the more boisterous part of the Australian public, who wanted success in cricket *at any cost*. Despite their brashness, these elite players delivered what the Australian public desperately wanted [63].

---

62 Sachin Tendulkar became the first ever cricketer to be adjudged run out by a third umpire (Karl Liebenberg) in a Test between India and South Africa. It was a game-changing moment in cricket as it was the first time technology played a role in dismissing a cricketer. It was 14 November 1992.

63 Roebuck's 1984 article is an eye-opener of the ugliness of the *Kim Hughes affair* where the 'Blue-eyed' shining knight, chosen by the selectors as a response to the WSC debacle, was *killed* by his own mistakes and teammates.

Studying in the UK then, I witnessed Marsh and Lillee's awful relationship with their young captain. The senior pair's disrespect for Hughes was blatantly evident in the monumental *Botham's Series* 1981. The internal conflict was the primary reason for Australia's defeat in the series. Reading Christian Ryan's book – *Golden Boy* (2006) is still a gut-wrenching experience for me. Other journalists and cricket observers agree with my view (Malcolm 2009; Smyth 2011).

I've often thought that if Doug had been on that 1981 Ashes tour, he might have been a stabilizing factor. More than likely, the young captain would have benefitted from Doug's maturity and closeness to Marsh and Lillee. Opinions on this testosterone-filled era of Australian cricket are still divided. Three decades later, Sengupta (2015) reminds us of how differently the players and the observers interpreted the ugly incidents within the team in those days.

* * *

Just like the unacceptable behaviour towards opponents by a few Australian players was challenged by commentators like McGilvray and Roebuck, the public should abhor cheating. Doug fully agrees. His laid-back personality was focused almost entirely on enjoying the game while entertaining the crowds and the fellowship of the cricket fraternity. McGilvray went one step further, wishing that 'cricket should remain a humble and noble sport, to be played with the grace and splendour it inspired for generations of cricketers and spectators'.

The limited-overs game evolved because of perceived boredom with Test cricket. T20 grew on the back of supposed stagnation in 50-overs cricket. Doug and Ian support the T20 format mainly because its intensity and player development skills have helped build all aspects of the game. They decry the 'dehumanising' of opponents that landed some notable Australian players and even the teams in trouble.

However, Doug and Ian appreciate the camaraderie among players that the T20 formats have built by bringing together established and new players from different countries. There is no time for slack running, fielding, batting or bowling in the shorter formats. Nor is there time for racism, rudeness and petty gamesmanship.

I believe the friendships developed among players since IPL have contributed to moderating the usual aggression Australian players show towards their opponents. The constant vigilance of TV cameras and heightened expectations of codes of conduct in the field also may have contributed to the positive developments in player behaviour. International cricket is much healthier nowadays, despite the occasional glitches. Thankfully, the days when an opponent would call Sri Lankan cricketers *'Black C****'* are well behind us! This nasty behaviour of Australians tarnished cricket's rich history. Still, it was vital for me that *Doug epitomized quite the opposite.*

However, cricket is unsure about T10 formats and other shortened versions. The game's future needs thoughtful consideration. Decisions are required on how many playing formats are best for international cricket to ensure that the game evolves progressively.

A positive promotion of the game should be done hand in hand with the players, including women's cricket. Most believe an *International Players' Association* should be essential to cricket's future. The administrators never imagined the enormous power they conceded to the players when they unleashed the incredibly lucrative T20 format.

* * *

Cricket, nowadays, is also often embroiled in various scandals. There are diverse stresses on cricketers, umpires and cricket officials in the Test-playing countries. Despite these strains and setbacks, I have no doubt that Test cricket will endure. Some of its oldest traditions have waned, lost or eroded. Cricketers are now paid mind-boggling amounts of money in Test cricket and the short-format tournaments, thanks to the benchmark put down by the mega-rich IPL.

The *sledgers* still rant and rave, and *match-fixers* prowl around team hotels and match venues, bringing the game to disrepute. Nevertheless, I am thankful that Test cricket continues as a grand spectacle when played in the right spirits by individuals who enjoy sportsmanship.

As mentioned earlier, cricket's journey towards international competitions and eventually Test cricket originated early in the 18th Century (1843-44). Cricket then weathered two brutal World Wars in the 20th Century and slowly developed into a formidable sport. It also faced huge controversies, such as the *Bodyline War* (1932-33), the *D'Oliveira Affair* (1968), South Africa's expulsion from the international sports arena in the late 1960s, and the WSC revolution during 1977-78.

Cricket has also endured distasteful incidents of unacceptable player behaviour, extensive corruption, match-fixing and racism. Despite these obstacles, apart from a few rule changes, cricket, as it is played today, has remained much the same as it was 140-odd years ago. Therefore, Doug and I are confident that *cricket will survive.*

CHAPTER 17

An 'Artist' to the Core

Success in sports involves performing in front of audiences. The most successful sportspeople are usually very good at the art of elevating their performance levels in the big arena. This ensures that their achievements and records will be long remembered within that sport.

To achieve a memorable name, one must have the essential ingredients – natural talent, well-attuned skills, discipline and commitment. However, the flip side of sports is that once they retire from the field, unless one is 'someone special', most individual players are seldom remembered in sports.

It is a shame that Doug is not well remembered as an Australian Cricket great. Memories are disappearing fast in this era of smartphones. I have had many conversations with people much younger than me, telling them that 'Doug Walters was my favourite cricketer of all time'. Many have looked at me with blank expressions.

I ask myself – How can Australian cricket fans forget someone who played the game as elegantly as Doug Walters? If he had played today on some of the flat tracks and small boundaries they play on today and using one of the heavy bats they now use, Doug would have easily averaged about 60.

A 'Rare Organism'' in Cricket

In Beyond A Boundary, James (1963: 196) wrote, 'Cricket is as art; it is not a bastard or a poor relation, but a full member of the [Art] community'. He emphasized: 'Cricket is first and foremost, a dramatic spectacle that belongs with the theatre, ballet, opera and dance...All games are dramatic'. Can anyone argue with these eloquent views?

> *To many thousands of people, a great batter is a man who makes a lot of runs. Not to me. A really great batter (there are not many) is to me as strange a human being as a man seven feet tall or a man I once heard of who could not read but spoke six languages.*

Praising Headley and Bradman, James (1963: 139-141) wrote: 'Every great batter is a special organism; it must be so, for they are very rare; as rare as great violinists'. James added: 'Neither failed in a single Test series; they were so good at batting on any wicket and condition'.

In a tribute to Sobers, written for *The Cricketer* (1969/70), James lamented that the knives were out for Sobers, blamed for losing two series and an indifferent attitude in captaining the team in Australia. Defending Sobers, James reminded the cricket world that this *genius* was precisely the same as Headley and Bradman, *a rare organism* who could show the cricket world *'what a man can do'*.

> *One of the fundamentals of cricket, which is as true today as it has been for the past 140-odd years of Test cricket, is that, over a period, good batters will make plenty of runs. Great batters will make vast quantities, while good bowlers will take wickets a plenty, great bowlers will take hundreds and hundreds.*

James' expressive descriptions of hard-to-find great batters and their impacts on the game also fit Doug Walters. Doug was quick on his feet, like all great batters. He saw the ball early off the bowler's hand. Fast reflexes, muscular forearms and strong wrists allowed him to place the ball precisely wherever he wanted. Quick scoring was his method, not allowing any bowler to dictate to him for too long. Doug was never a defensive player unless the circumstances demanded it.

Colleagues say that Doug had exceptional hand-eye coordination, stamina, and endurance. He didn't do a lot of training, nor did he take net practices too seriously. Batting, bowling and fielding were all natural to Doug. Doing everything with an individual style, Doug was a *rare organism*, an entertainer to boot, with unique talents.

Ian Chappell said he had never seen anyone better than Doug who could play off-spin bowling. Plenty of film footage shows that Doug was never dull; he could drive well on the off-side or on-side, the late-cut, square-cut, the pull, sweep or hook, just the array of strokes a master batter would have. In his prime, Doug was mentally and physically fit and strong, which made him a great cricketer. With all the highs and lows, ebbs and flows, Australia was fortunate to have him in that remarkable era since he broke into the Test arena in 1965.

* * *

Mallett (2008: 239-249), who knew Doug closely as a teammate and personal friend, had no doubt that – on his day, Doug compared well with Bradman. In Chapter 11 – *A Touch of Bradman*, Mallett wrote:

> *In many ways, [Doug] was like Bradman. They had similar upbringings. Both were country lads. And there was a naïve and likeable boyishness about them that captured the hearts of a nation, The Don in the 1930s and Doug in the 1960s. On most days, Bradman could destroy an attack, and Doug, in his day, could also tear an attack to shreds, very much in the same ruthless Bradman vein...To me, Dougie's Perth epic drew him closer to being 'Another Bradman' than any other batter of my time.*

One of the articles I loved as a kid was in the *Sport & Pastime* (15 June 1968) by Jack Fingleton, whose relationship with Bradman wasn't always friendly. Praising Bradman's batting, Fingleton wrote: 'Every bowler, every fielder, every spectator in Don's heyday sensed that he was using not a bat so much as an axe dipping with the bowler's blood and agony'. To be compared with the Don is an honour for anyone.

Ian Chappell reminded me that 'Doug had done the 'batting "hat-trick", a century in a session three times'. The hundred before lunch against the World XI at the MCG (1971), a hurricane ton against the Windies in Port-of-Spain between lunch and tea (1973) and thrashing England in Perth (1974), hitting a hundred between tea and stumps.

'A Bloke's Bloke'

It is easy to agree with Mallett's following observations (2008: 2):

> *As a Test player, Doug was a hero to thousands of admirers. Yet, his image of himself never changed—he was an uncomplicated bloke who was one of the mob. What endeared him to his fans was his matter-of-fact, down-to-earth attitude to life, which remains unchanged.*
>
> *With Doug, there are no pretensions: he is a bloke's bloke who lives life to the full, and throughout his cricket career, Doug loved a beer, a smoke, a bet and a bat, not necessarily in that order.*

In a recent article, Ian Chappell (2020) repeated that he would hate to tour in an Australian side that didn't include Doug, not least because of Doug's 'match-winning batting and the freakish ability to break a partnership'. It was also because 'Every team needs one, a dressing-room pest who keeps the team loose in times of great tension'.

According to Chappell, 'Doug's impish humour, dressing room antics and pranks 'contributed greatly to team spirit, morale and enjoyable time'. Ian told me about how Doug used smoking and card playing to relax between innings or during breaks when he was batting. Ian reckoned that Doug got through about 100 cigarettes per day.

As I've discussed in the book, Doug Walters is *someone special*, not ever forgotten by his fans for the enjoyment he brought to the game. Often, cricketers have uneasy relationships with the media. But, one wouldn't find any unkind words about this exceptional cricketer, even when he had a bad game. The media has been kind to Doug, which I think is because of his pleasant demeanour.

The Australian public loves him because he is a 'cool guy, essentially one of them, a quintessential Aussie bloke, relaxed, carefree, cheerful, without pretence'. As I have experienced, there isn't a single bone of racism in Doug's body. He enjoys everyone's company. Cricket didn't teach him that. *He was born that way.* Doug never offended anyone. He only offended the hapless bowlers by 'belting the hell out of some of the greatest bowlers to have drawn breath' (Mallett 2008: 3).

Doug is satisfied with how it all worked out in his career and life. His teammates, the press and the man in the street loved him. He was a bloke who liked a drink like they did; he enjoyed a smoke, as they did, and played the game as much as they might play. Doug has often been described as one who: 'Gets to the game, has a quiet smoke, goes out and hits a quick-fire hundred, then sits in the calm of the dressing room, reaches for a cold beer and lights up a cigarette'.

Journalist Norman Tasker, the bloke who rang the Walters' household with the news of Doug's selection in the NSW team, says:

> *Doug was a supreme talent as a cricketer. A very natural talent. I once worked with him on a coaching series in The Sun, aimed at kids, somewhere about 1969. That experience gave me the impression that Doug didn't know what he did at the crease. He just hit the bloody ball.*

I think Norman hit upon Doug's batting secret. He simply hit the ball like many of the great batters before him. Doug reigned supreme on true pitches where the ball came at a consistent height. However, on the sluggish tracks of England, where the ball darted off the seam most of the time, Doug struggled a bit. Failing in the Tests in England for a fourth successive time upset Doug for a while.

The way Doug played his cricket is inseparable from his laid-back persona. His personal qualities enhanced his cricket, as he played to please the spectators while enjoying the game. Doug also had common sense and was competitive. He motivated the team through his individual and high-impact performances, as proven by his batting records. Doug was a genuine *asset* to any captain of any team.

Doug is a personality that I would call *a true Australian cricketing legend*. The term *legend* has been used a great deal in cricket, and some who do not deserve to be of legendary status also enjoy the limelight while it lasts. Just think of a host of Australian cricketers who brought the game to disrepute. They may be legends for some people, but not for genuine cricket fans like me. People should not be immortalised for disgraceful conduct that has often gone unpunished.

David Warner, a serial offender (English 2013), is not the only one to disgrace Australian cricket. Doug Walters, in contrast, has been showered with much adulation by the public for being a decent man. I have never met anyone in my life who has a different opinion of Doug. In contrast, I have met plenty of fans who do not particularly admire some Australian players for their rude and boorish on-field behaviours.

* * *

Doug's retirement was seen by some as premature in 1980-81. The world of cricket had been turned upside down by Packer's WSC. Doug's performances in the WSC tournaments were indifferent, with nothing outstanding to show. However, on his return to Test cricket, against New Zealand and India, Doug made 397 runs at 56.7 with a sparkling 107 against the Kiwis. Despite this return to form, he didn't make the touring team to England in 1981, led by Kim Hughes.

This non-selection hurt Doug as he considered himself to be with considerable batting and bowling experience under English conditions. The English players and press also respected Doug immensely and were probably puzzled by his non-inclusion. Doug's Test career was over after he missed the tour. He did play for NSW State in the 1980-81 season and club cricket for Cumberland Cricket Club in 1981-82 before hanging his boots up. Doug also worked as a Channel Nine cricket commentator in the 1987-88 season.

Honours: Hall of Fame and Others

The *Australian Cricket Hall of Fame* (2022) was first proposed by the Melbourne Cricket Club in 1995 and opened a year later. All inductees must have retired from international cricket for at least five years to be eligible for selection. Ten players were inaugurally inducted into the *Hall of Fame* in 1996. They were Fred Spofforth, John Blackham, Victor Trumper, Clarrie Grimmett, Bill Ponsford, Don Bradman, Bill O'Reilly, Keith Miller, Ray Lindwall and Dennis Lillee.

In 2000, former Australian captains Warwick Armstrong, Neil Harvey and Allan Border were inducted into the *Hall of Fame*. Since then, the following great cricketers have been inducted:

Bill Woodfull and Arthur Morris (2001), Stan McCabe and Greg Chappell (2002), Lindsay Hassett and Ian Chappell (2003), Hugh Trumble and Alan Davidson (2004), Clem Hill and Rod Marsh (2005), Monty Noble and Bob Simpson (2006), Charles Macartney and Richie Benaud (2007), George Giffen and Ian Healy (2008), Steve Waugh (2009), Bill Lawry and Graham McKenzie (2010).

In 2011, Doug was inducted into the *Hall of Fame* at the *Allan Border Medal Ceremonies*. The former Australian captain, Mark Taylor, was also honoured at the same event. Altogether, there are now 44 cricket legends recognized by this honour. This recognition is possibly the most significant honour their peers can bestow on a cricketer.

Doug deserved to be recognized for his bountiful contributions earlier, perhaps along with his former teammates, notably Simpson, Lawry, McKenzie and Ian Chappell, from the list. These giants played in an era different from how cricket was played in the 1980s, 90s and later decades. But I am happy Doug was recognised, belatedly but correctly; it is always better late than never. It is good that some people remembered to nominate the great cricketer.

* * *

The *Doug Walters Stand* at the SCG was so named in 1985. It was, however, demolished in 2007. Construction of the new $70 million Hill Grandstand commenced in February 2007. It replaced the old *Doug Walters Stand* and *The Hill* area. Doug was disappointed but got over it quickly. He is philosophical about it as it shows how market-oriented cricket and other sports are. Sentiments become secondary when there is money to be made via stadium expansion. Safety concerns for large numbers of spectators, better public facilities, and modernization have also been factors in the changes made.

On 14 June 1975, Doug Walters was appointed *Member of the British Empire* (MBE, The Order of the British Empire – Member (Civil) for services to cricket. As recently as in June 2022, Doug Walters received another accolade, as he was appointed *Member of the Order of Australia* (OA) in the 2022 Queen's Birthday Honours for 'Significant service to cricket at the elite levels'.

A Place in History: Among Australia's Leading Run Scorers

The hallmark of a great batter is his ability to score runs in all types of wickets and conditions. It is impossible to judge the greatness of a batter simply by looking at the mass of runs scored over a relatively long career. Therefore, comparing Doug with other greats in career statistics is just an academic exercise.

Sometimes, statistics are a hollow representation of the delight and joy a batter gave to the game. Nevertheless, *statistics measure a batter's calibre*. Doug fares very favourably in elite company, as shown in the summary statistics Table below.

The Top 25 Australian Test Run-Scorers - Averages

	Player	Span (Matches/Inns)	Nos	Runs	HS	Ave	100s	50s
1	D. Bradman	1928-48 (52/80)	10	6996	334	99.9	29	13
2	S.P.D. Smith	2010-23 (99/175)	22	9113	239	59.6	32	37
3	G. Chappell	1970-84 (87/151)	19	7110	247*	53.9	24	31
4	R.T. Ponting	1995-12 (168/287)	29	13,378	257	51.9	41	62
5	M.E. Hussey	2005-13 (79/137)	16	6235	195	51.5	19	29
6	S.R. Waugh	1985-04 (168/260)	46	10,927	200	51.1	32	50
7	M. Hayden	1994-09 (103/184)	14	8625	380	50.7	30	29
8	A.R. Border	1978-94 (156/265)	44	11,174	205	50.6	27	63
9	M.J. Clarke	2004-15 (115/198)	22	8643	329*	49.1	28	27
10	R.N. Harvey	1948-63 (79/137_	10	6149	205	48.4	21	24
11	K.D. Walters	1965-81 (74/125)	14	5357	250	48.3	15	33

	Player	Span (Matches/Inns)	Nos	Runs	HS	Ave	100s	50s
12	A. Gilchrist	1999-08 (96/137)	20	5570	204*	47.6	17	26
13	W.M. Lawry	1961-71 (67/123)	12	5234	210	47.2	13	27
14	B. Simpson	1957-78 (62/111)	7	4869	311	46.8	10	27
15	J.L. Langer	1993-07 (105/182)	12	7696	250	45.3	23	30
16	D.A. Warner	2011-23 (106/193)	8	8338	335*	45.1	25	35
17	D.C. Boon	1984-96 (107/190)	20	7422	200	43.75	21	32
18	M.A. Taylor	1989-99 (104/186)	13	7525	334*	43.5	19	40
19	M.J. Slater	1993-01 (74/131)	7	5312	219	42.8	14	21
20	I. Chappell	1964-80 (75/136)	10	5345	196	42.4	14	26
21	M.E. Waugh	1991-02 (128/209)	17	8029	153*	41.8	20	47

Source: *ESPN Cricinfo (2024e)*

This brief analysis reveals the most updated data on the top 21 Australian batters and their performances. Only Don Bradman features in the Table of the pre-World War II cricketers. One reason is the number of Tests played in the early days, which was very low. It is also essential to recall that the lack of international cricket during 1939-46 (World War II) affected many Australians [64]. Many greats, like Bradman, Miller, Hassett and others, lost many of their peak cricketing years during the war years (Hutchinson and Ross 1997: 250-258).

Batters of earlier eras had to contend with pitches that were not well prepared or covered against rain. The competitiveness of the contests also changed with time as monetary stakes began to rule the game. Whether a player was well-paid or had to worry constantly about losing a job would have also affected their mental state and physical fitness.

Any judgment on the batting greatness of players must consider the era in which they played. Playing conditions were vastly different when Don Bradman played compared with subsequent eras. In the past, a batter's performance was affected by the nature of pitches and other factors,

---

[64] International cricket resumed less than a fortnight after the war ended, and the Germans surrendered in May 1945. A series of five Tests were played by the Australian Services team against England between May and August named the *'Victory Tests'* (Pollard 1995: 97-99). Bradman did not play in this series as he wasn't in England.

including his status as a paid professional and the game's rules. All of the above changed with time. One can only imagine the number of runs Bradman might have scored if he had played another 20 to 30 Test matches during those years that were lost to the war [65].

The number of matches played within a year also changed markedly as more cricket was played in recent decades. This meant that players had to be supremely fit throughout the year and needed to be in 'form' to play a lot of cricket across varied conditions and be ready for travel worldwide. History shows that such factors have significantly impacted the performances of many cricketers.

A batting average above 48 in 74 Tests (125 innings) puts Doug among the best-of-the-best Australian batters. It is the record of an accomplished cricketer whose supply might be better judged from the stability he brought to the middle-order that produced 5,357 runs with 15 centuries at a strike rate of 49. Words of praise have also come many times from McGilvray (1987: 63). who knew Doug very well:

Doug Walters played Test cricket for 15 years and finished with an average of nearly 44 [Corrected to 48]. But that didn't measure his impact. There was almost a national rebellion when he was omitted from the Australian team that toured England in 1981 after a season of handy scores. Such was his appeal. Doug Walters was one young fellow who thrived as a youth. And he kept thriving, mainly because he never let that youth go, no matter how old he was.

Doug will be best remembered not for the number of runs he made but for how he scored and the delight he gave to the public. As Ian Chappell re-iterated in the interview with me:

Doug could turn a match around in a short time – through batting, bowling or fielding. He not only won games, but he also created many instances from which the team could push for a victory.

---

65 In the Victory Tests, in 1945, immediately after the War, Lindsay Hasset (a warrant officer) captained Australia, while Wally Hammond captained a star-studded England team. The series ended 2-2 and was singularly a great triumph for cricket (Williamson 2015a; Military History 2013; Holland 2020), which resumed in earnest shortly thereafter. Responding to the sense of the euphoria of victory, both captains eschewed the traditionally safety-first approach of pre-war cricket. The result was some spectacular cricket. Sadly, by the time the real business of the 'Ashes resumed 16 months later, attritional cricket returned.

Records show that Doug wasn't at his best on England's grassy and seaming wickets. In four tours of England (1968, 1972, 1975 and 1977), Doug played 18 Tests, scored 81 and 86 in his first game in 1968 at Old Trafford, and another 88 at the same venue in 1977.

But he only averaged 25.68, with no hundreds and just six half-centuries in 30 innings in 16 other Tests. This performance contrasts with Doug's career average of 48.26 in 75 Tests (125 innings). Doug appears to thrive on fast and bouncy tracks. Given this, he would have averaged well over 50 had England's slow-turning tracks been more receptive to his dominant stroke play.

While Doug never got a Test hundred in England and South Africa, in every other Test-playing country worldwide, at that time, he made hundreds and averaged 56.24. In South Africa and England, Doug only hit centuries in tour matches. Under *'Highs and Lows'*, Chapter 1 of *The Entertainers*, Doug said that the English captains worked out his flaws facing the seaming ball under English conditions. Nevertheless, he still insisted that if he had converted those three 80-run knocks into hundreds, the story of his career might have been different.

Also a decent partnership-breaker, Doug ended his Test career with 49 wickets, just one short of 50 wickets-5,000 run double. As Ian said, 'Doug would often deliver breakthroughs at crucial junctures in a match, when his team needed him the most'.

His achievements have come in all sorts of wickets and countries. Nevertheless, some journalists have unkindly criticised Doug for the lack of success in England, ascribing it to an 'inability to cope with the seaming ball on grassy pitches, etc.' Doug dismisses such views as all nonsense. He brushed off the failures in his typical way and carried on as if nothing had happened.

Final Words - Doug Walters' Traits

Mark Nicholas (2020) once asked Bradman: 'Is there a secret to batting?' Bradman answered: 'Concentration, first and foremost, then courage, character, footwork and speed, of hand and eye'. Mark said when he asked Viv Richards the same question, the answer was: 'Keep it simple, head still, watch the ball. Fellas these days want to over-complicate batting. Come forward at the face of the man who challenges you, show him who's boss, then spring back if you must'.

Doug displayed all those attributes: The ability to concentrate, footwork, great hand-eye-coordination, keeping it simple, and the talent and confidence to take it up to the bowler, no matter what.

One of cricket's greatest pleasures is to look back and savour. Cricket, by its very nature, leaves impressions that are enduring. The great matches, the great innings, the great feats of courage, the great men. These seem to stick in mind as with no other sport.

That was Alan McGilvray, in the preface of his second book (1987: 7-8). I agree with Alan that: 'Cricket's rich heritage should not be lost'. Memories of great individuals need to be kept alive simply because of the enjoyment they gave, which was a profound service to human societies at different times and eras.

Doug wrote in his book *The Entertainers* (1999: 253-255): 'Time waits for no one. It passes all too quickly'. He also said, 'People are seldom happy with their salaries in all walks of life, but playing for one's country is such an honour that he would have happily played for Australia even if they were not paid for it'.

As this book – *My Sentimental Journey* – ends, I am reminded that cricketers may come and go. But I can say without contradiction that the ones who are cherished most by the fans are those who played the *'gentlemen's game'* holding its highest ideals. The 'nasties' – especially those who sullied the game's reputation fall by the wayside. I stand firm on this issue for the sake of cricket.

Overt nastiness and bad player behaviour crept into the game as cricket was *commodified and sold* as a spectacle, along with greed and fame, which took hold of a few players. Cricket and other sports are essential in any society – for inspiration, relaxation and enjoyment. Sports are also linked to how people interact. Those who didn't uphold high standards harmed the game.

Sport is not about winning alone. It is mainly about participation and sharing in the joys or despair. Winning is just a temporary bonus for the individual participant or a team. *Isn't that what we teach our kids?* At least, sports psychology, which is a well-developed field nowadays, says so. We must remind ourselves that cricket is not played in a vacuum. Ethical conduct is part of its attraction, as tens of thousands of people sit through a Test match over several days. In a long, drawn-out sport, there is plenty of time to reflect on how we behave towards each other and ponder our other social obligations.

* * *

Sport is nowadays a giant public spectacle. As a result, sportspeople have a *social contract* to uphold, a moral and philosophical undertaking and an obligation to society. The seemingly abstract concept of a 'social contract' extends to players and everyone involved in the sport, such as managers, coaches, ground staff, administrators, media men, advertisers, sponsors, fans, and even the selectors and betting agencies.

In cricket, it is neither a matter of the scoreboard nor the number of runs scored or wickets one takes. It is how one conducts oneself in the glorious game we love. This applies both on and off the field.

Another way I see it is athletes of all sports, including people like Doug, are *surrogates* for fans like me who cannot actually participate for lack of talent but who identify strongly with players that their destiny, fate, and security are bound up together. While I don't expect any *surrogate* to uphold all of my personal virtues, it is pleasing to conclude, after a critical analysis of Doug's life, that we share many ideals of what a good sportsperson should be.

With such a sentimental connection to a great cricketer, my book should reveal what a cricket-mad fan feels about players and *'heroes' who went to battle on the cricket field on his behalf*. Doug is unrepentant about how his career panned out and unaffected by 'glory and fame'. Those, too, are virtues I share with him.

The 'social contract' and personal and collective obligations are no longer nebulous concepts. Those who misbehaved 'crossed the line'. Those who 'fixed' matches, took prohibited substances, bet against their own team and abused the opponents using racist language broke their social contract to varying degrees.

Others who tampered so blatantly with the ball, viciously kicked the wickets and crashed into umpires broke the rules of cricket. Their stains blotted forever cricket's proud history book. In simple terms, these villains of cricket let their fans and their respective countries down through callousness, greed, personal insecurity and self-interest.

Sadly, the controversial individuals who misbehaved in cricket are remembered only for those stains rather than their performances. They were probably never taught that *esteem, honour, dignity, respect, pride, status, rage, and masculinity* must be balanced with a sensible life approach. Some sports education for cricketers, including psychology, would have reduced the misdemeanours blighting the game.

* * *

Doug has repeatedly said that cricket owes him nothing. He proudly represented his country and has been amply rewarded for his efforts. Not everyone gets to do something they love, like playing cricket, receiving the honour of representing their country, travelling the world with an elite team and earning a comfortable living as a professional sportsman.

Like hundreds of others, Doug has been fortunate, although he remains essentially the humble man he always was.

Unlike some of his peers, Doug's career has never been blemished by ugly verbal skirmishes with opponents, umpires, or other distasteful actions. He respected the bowlers who were trying to get him out.

Broadly, I think while Doug brought unbridled joy to thousands of his admirers, he underachieved as a captain. He could have been a good captain of NSW, although he never wanted the cut-and-thrust of captaincy and everything that goes with it. But, after my meticulous research for this book, I am surprised that the selectors did not make him vice-captain to Ian Chappell in the Test team at the height of his cricketing powers. Given the fraught relationship Ian had with the selectors, he probably never got a chance to suggest this.

If Doug had been *almost the perfect team player*, would he not have been a great asset to the captain? Doug was as astute as any top-tier cricketer because he learned how to win a game from a young age. He also knew that in a 'team sport' like cricket, a player must play the role expected of him to be successful. A vice-captain role might have made him even more successful in Ian Chappell's Australian team.

I am sure if Doug had tried harder and taken fewer risks in his attacking batting style, he might have scored a few thousand more runs and centuries than he made. Doug has often said that it was impossible to be successful in scoring runs all the time. But a great batter must be able to thrill the spectators when it comes off.

His teammates attest that fear of failure did not deter Doug. He is grateful to his father and other senior players for not being too critical when he was a kid and whenever he failed to make a substantial score. This allowed him to develop a full range of strokes without any inhibitions, including some risky shots, which became his trademark.

Doug maintains that success in cricket requires one to remain humble. One must also adhere to the general rules that determine success in life. Generosity and humility are trade-mark Doug Walters traits, which he learnt growing up as part of a hard-working family in the bush. While Doug displayed super confidence at the crease, those who played with or against him attest that Doug was never arrogant. That's why he was so much liked by his peers, including his opponents.

* * *

Doug's success in cricket is based on his easy-going personality, cricket knowledge and personal traits of humility, self-belief and intelligence.

He also had the mental capacity to absorb pressure and the discipline to manage it. When in top form, Doug was a fearless stroke-maker, much like Bradman, Sobers and Viv Richards.

Those who saw Doug's batting say that when he was 'on song', no one left the seat, fearing they might miss some dazzling strokes. His teammates have no hesitation in describing the elegance at the crease and the beauty of classical batsmanship that Doug displayed. To say that *'They don't make cricketers like that anymore'* may sometimes be seen as condescending, but it is appropriate for Doug. He will also be remembered as one who captured the essence of cricket and its enjoyment without ever becoming its slave.

Doug served Australia well with passion and commitment whenever given a chance. He performed as a very high-impact player for more than a decade. At the same time, he never forgot that cricket was just a sporting contest. In the end, a laugh and entertainment mattered.

I didn't have it in me to become a cricketer beyond softball cricket, nor did I chase such a career. The joy I got from cricket and the lasting recollections of the imagery came from the commentators' voices and the words of the great cricket writers. In my extensive research for the book, I found the final word that should be said on behalf of all cricket fans like me. I thank Sunil Gavaskar, the great Indian captain and batter, for those words in his MCC Spirit of Cricket *Cowdrey Lecture*, 2003.

> *Let me end by repeating part of what Sir Don Bradman said about the game. We are all custodians of the game, and it will prosper if we can leave it better than we found it. It is something that we must all endeavour to do – and it is achievable if we work sincerely towards it. I am confident that we can do it, and when – and not if – we do it, Colin, sitting up there with the gods, will smile and say, "Well done, chaps – that's the spirit".*

In my opinion, cricket fans are also custodians of the game; they love the game so much, not just the players. Cricket, in all formats, is for the young and old, haves and the have-nots, and those from myriad backgrounds, with cricketing talents and not so. It is a game that can sometimes be frustrating, as we all have witnessed from time to time.

Most importantly, pleasure from cricket, either by watching or listening, comes from players like Doug, who adorned the game with their skill and style. Many thousands of fans and I have been fortunate to experience those joys and pleasures.

Doug was undoubtedly a trustworthy custodian of cricket and the spirit in which it should be played – *hard but fair*. Standards must be upheld, preserved and even improved as past giants endeavoured to do in cricket's history. Doug stands head and shoulders above those who didn't do so in the past or make no attempt even today. That's why Doug enjoys a special place in Australian cricket history.

* * *

Reminiscing, as I have done, has been a productive exercise because of what these great cricketers represented. They drew thousands, if not millions, of people together as cultural icons. Their sheer hard work and natural talents place them among some of humanity's greatest sportspeople. The game also grows and develops, learning from this history, as all other human endeavours do.

More than five decades ago, the prolific cricket author A. A. Thomson (1968) reminded us how applicable the world-famous phrase '*It was the best of times, it was the worst of times*' is to cricket. The great novelist Charles Dickens wrote these words as the opening sentence of his memorable book, *A Tale of Two Cities*. Cricket, too, is greatly affected by the period in which matches are or were played.

No age or decade is immune from the forces operating, especially in a long, drawn-out game like cricket. Needless to say, Doug played at the *best of times and some of the worst of times*, but the operating forces didn't change the man. He continues living as he always did, never to be forgotten (I hope my book helps!). No recriminations. No fuss.

Being Doug Walters, he continues in his own distinctive manner, enjoying cricket, golf and the friendship of former mates and fans, beer, yarns and all. Although he gets riled when the Australian team fails, he doesn't take the game or anything else in life too seriously.

It has been a great honour for me to be his friend, much more so than I ever imagined as a kid back in 1965. Completing this book has also been a wonderful personal experience, and I am grateful to Doug, Caroline and his family for being part of it.

APPENDIX

Doug Walters - Playing Records

First Class Career - Batting

Matches	Innings	NO	Runs	HS	Fifties	Hundreds	Average
258	426	57	16,180	253	81	45	43.84

NSW vs South Australia, Adelaide, 1964-65; (Debut: 1962-63, NSW vs Queensland, Sydney)

First Class Career - Bowling

Caught	Balls	Maidens	Runs	Wickets	Best	Average	5/Innings
149	13,251	304	6,782	190	7/63#	35.69	6

NSW vs. South Australia, Adelaide, 1964-65

Sheffield Shield Career - Batting

Matches	Innings	NO	Runs	HS	Fifties	Hundreds	Average
91	157	16	5,602	253#	24	16	39.73

NSW vs South Australia, Adelaide, 1964-65; Debut: 1962-63, NSW v Queensland, Sydney

Sheffield Shield Career - Fielding and Bowling

Caught	Balls	Maidens	Runs	Wickets	Best	Average	5/Innings
49	7,688	190	3,609	110	7/63#	32.81	4

NSW vs South Australia, Adelaide, 1964-65

Test Career - Batting

Matches	Innings	NO	Runs	HS	Fifties	Hundreds	Average
74	125	14	5,357	250#	33	15	48.26

Australia vs New Zealand, Christchurch, 1976-77; Debut: 1965-66, Australia v England)

Test Career - Fielding and Bowling

Caught	Balls	Maidens	Runs	Wickets	Best	Average	5/Innings
43	3,295	79	1,425	49	5/66#	29.08	1

Australia vs West Indies, Georgetown, 1972-73

ODIs - Batting

Matches	Innings	NO	Runs	HS	Fifties	Hundreds	Average
28	24	6	513	59#	2	-	28.50

Australia vs Sri Lanka, The Oval, 1975; Debut: 1970-71, Australia v England

ODIs - Bowling

Caught	Balls	Maidens	Runs	Wickets	Best	Average	5/Innings
10	314	3	273	4	2/24#	68.25	-

Australia vs England, Birmingham, 1972

Domestic Limited Overs - Batting

Matches	Innings	NO	Runs	HS	Fifties	Hundreds	Average
13	11	3	340	71#	4	-	42.50

NSW vs Victoria, Melbourne, 1972-73; Debut: 1970-71, NSW v Queensland

Domestic Limited Overs - Bowling

Caught	Balls	Maidens	Runs	Wickets	Best	Average	5/Innings
4	596	7	405	16	3/33#	25.31	-

NSW vs Victoria, Melbourne, 1980-81

Performance Analysis by Batting Position

Position	Inns	NO	100s	50s	0s	HS	Runs	Average
4	29	3	4	10	2	112	1313	50.50
5	49	4	5	14	1	242	2134	47.42
6	45	6	6	9	1	250	1869	47.92
7	2	1	0	0	0	23	41	41.00
Overall	125	14	15	33	4	250	5357	48.26

BIBLIOGRAPHY AND REFERENCES

Books, Articles and CD

ABC (1976). Bradman to Chappell. 2nd Edition. The Australian Broadcasting Commission, Sydney, p. 160.

ABC (2006). History of Australian Cricket. The Australian Broadcasting Commission, Sydney, A Set of Six CDs containing Film Footage and Interviews with former great cricketers from Australia and overseas.

Agnew, J. (Ed.) (2013). Cricket: An Anthology. Harper Collins, London, p. 510.

Allison, L. (1980). Batter and Bowler: The Key Relation of Victorian England. Journal of Sport History, 7(2): 5-20 (http://www.jstor.org/stable/43610351).

Arlott, J. (1979). John Arlott's Book of Cricketers. Angus & Robertson Publishers, London. 180.

Bailey, T. (1978). 'Sunny Breeding Ground for Cricketing Greats'. The Sportstar (India). 16 Dec., p. 16.

Benaud, R. (1998). Anything But...An Autobiography. Hodder & Stoughton, London. p. 278.

Benaud, R. (2005). My Spin on Cricket. Hodder & Stoughton, London. p. 293.

Bennett, J. et al. (1982). A Photo Album: The ABC from 1932 to 1982. Australian Broadcasting Commission. p. 113.

Bird, D. (1997). My Autobiography. Hodder & Stoughton, London, p. 479.

Boycott, G. (1979). Put To The Test. Arthur Barker Ltd., London. p. 200.

Boycott, G. (2014). The Corridor Of Certainty: My Life Beyond Cricket. Simon & Schuster U.K., p. 278.

Bradman, D. 1950. Farewell To Cricket. Harper Collins, Sydney, Australia, p. 316.

Brearley, M. (2013a). Keynote Address. "What do they know of cricket who only cricket know?". C.L.R. James's Beyond A Boundary. 50th Anniversary Conference, University of Glasgow, UK, 10-11 May 2013.

Brearley, M. (2013b). Socrates and C. L. R. James. In: Featherstone, David et al. (Eds.), Marxism, Colonialism and Cricket: C.L.R. James's Beyond A Boundary. Chapter 23, pp. 223-239. Duke University Press, Durham and London.

Brookes, N. (2022). An Island's Eleven: The Story of Sri Lankan Cricket. The History Press, p. 535.

Browning, M. (1998). 'That's Out! Yeesss. Got 'Im!'. Australian Cricket. February 1998. pp. 18-20.

Cardus, N. (1935). Batting and Batsmanship. In: Moult, T. (Ed.) Bat and Ball. Chapter 2 (pp. 41-47). Magna Books, U.K.

Cardus, N. (1949a). Days In The Sun: A Cricketer's Book. Rupert Hart-Davis, London. p. 187 [The original book was written and published in 1924]

Cardus, N. (1949b). Good Days. Rupert Hart-Davis, London. p. 260 [The original book was written and published in 1934].

Chappell, I. (1992). Chappelli: *The Cutting Edge*. Swan Publishing, Nedlands, WA, p. 184.

Chappell, I., Robertson, A. and Rigby, P. (1989). *The Best of Chappelli*. Swan Publishing, Byron Bay, NSW, p. 160.

Chapman, A.P.F. (1935). Cricket Tours Abroad. In: Moult, T. (Ed.) Bat and Ball. Chapter 9 (pp. 123-131). Magna Books, U.K.

Clarke, J. (1966). With England in Australia: the M.C.C. tour 1965-66. Stanley Paul Publishers, London, p. 192.

Davidson, A. (1963). Fifteen Paces. Marlin Books, Victoria, p. 190.

Edwards, R. (1977a). Masters of Cricket No. 8: Doug Walters. Lords' World of Cricket Monthly, Jan. 1977. pp. 20-22.

Edwards, R. (1977b). Masters of Cricket No. 18: Bob Simpson. Lords' World of Cricket Monthly, Nov. 1977, 5(11): p. 10-13.

Eagan, J. (1987). The Story of Cricket in Australia. Australian Broadcasting Corporation (ABC Books), Crows Nest, NSW, p. 234.

Farquharson, K. and Marjoribanks, T. (2006). Representing Australia: race, the media and cricket. Journal of Sociology, 42(1): 25-41 (https://www.researchgate.net/publication/249673962).

Fay, S. and Kynaston, D. (2018). Arlott, Swanton and the Soul of English Cricket. Bloomsbury Publishing. p. 400.

Ferriday, P. and Wilson, D. (Eds.) (2013). Masterly Batting: 100 Great Test Centuries. Von Krumm Publishers, Great Britain [Kindle version available for purchase].

Fingleton, J. (1947). Cricket Crisis. Cassel and Company Ltd., London, p. 313.

Fingleton, J. (1961). The Greatest Test of All'. Collins, London, p. 103.

Frith, D. (1997). Australia Vs. England – A Pictorial History of Every Test Match Since 1877, 9th Edition. Richard Smart Publishing, Sydney, p. 384.

Frith, D. (1982). To Test Cricket: A New Son, Safely Delivered. *The Cricketer*, April, 3(11): 26-29.

Gemmell, J. (2008). All White Mate? Cricket and Race in Oz. Cricket, Race and the 2007 World Cup. Routledge, London, pp. 23-38 ⚹.

Gemmell, J. and Majumdar, B. (Eds.) (2008). Cricket, Race and the 2007 World Cup. Routledge, p. 192 [66].

Gibbs, B. (1979). 'Doug Walters – The Dungog Dasher'. Cricketer, Vol. 7(2), November 1979, pp. 8-9-12.

Haigh, G. (1993). The Cricket War – the Inside Story of Kerry Packer's World Series Cricket, Text Publishing. p. 398.

Haigh, G. (1997). Australian Cricket Anecdotes. Oxford University Press. p. 288.

Haigh, G. (2006). The Summer Game. Australian Broadcasting Corp. (ABC Books), Sydney, p. 342.

Harte, C. and Whimpress, B. (2008). The Penguin History of Australian Cricket. Revised Edition. Penguin Books, London, U.K. p. 862.

Holding, M. and Cozier, T. (1993). Whispering Death. Andre Deutsch, London. p. 225.

Hutchinson, G. and Ross, J. (1997). 200 Seasons of Australian Cricket. Pan Macmillan Australia. Sydney, p. 640.

James, C. L. R. (1963). Beyond A Boundary. Hutchinson Publishing, London. p. 269.

James, C. L. R. (1969/70). 'Sobers – A Rare Organism in Danger'. *The Cricketer*. Winter Annual, Vol. 50 (12): 11.

Kampmark, B. (2008). A Matter of Necessity: The Minnow and World Cricket Gemmell, Jon and Majumdar, Boria (Eds.) Cricket, Race and the 2007 World Cup. Routledge, London, pp. 172-184 ⚹.

Khan, I. (1988). All Round View. Chatto and Windus Ltd., London, UK., p. 255.

Lawry, B. (1966). Bill Lawry – His Own Story: Run-Digger (Ed. Phil Tressider). Souvenir Press, London, UK. p. 128.:

Lloyd, C. (1980). Living for Cricket. Stanley Paul & Co. Ltd., p. 185.

Mallett, A. (2005). Chappelli Speaks Out. Allen & Unwin. Crows Nest, p. 264.

---

66 ⚹ Jon Gemmell and Boria Majumdar (Eds.) book on *Cricket, Race and the 2007 World Cup* was first published in 2007 in the journal: *Sport in Society – Cultures, Commerce, Media, Politics*, Volume 10 Issue 1.

Mallett, A. (2008). One of a Kind: The Doug Walters Story. Allen & Unwin, Crows Nest, p. 331.
Mallett, A. (2009). Thommo Speaks Out: The Authorised Biography of Jeff Thomson. Allen & Unwin. Crows Nest, p. 296.
Manley, M. (1988). A History of West Indies Cricket. André Deutsch Ltd., London, p. 575.
Marsh, R. and Walters, D. (1992). Two for the Road. Swan Publishing, Nedlands, WA.
MCC (1987). Lord's: The Official Pictorial Souvenir. Marylebone Cricket Club. English Life Publications, Derby. p. 24.
McGilvray, A. (1985). The Game Is Not The Same [As told to Norman Tusker], Australian Broadcasting Corporation (ABC Books), Crows Nest, NSW, p. 188.
McGilvray, A. (1987). *The Game Goes On* [As told to Norman Tusker], Australian Broadcasting Corporation (ABC Books), Crows Nest, NSW, p. 220.
Moss, P. (1968). 'There is £38,000 to Win: As Cash rises to boost pleas for brighter cricket'. *The Cricketer* (UK), 12 July, pp. 2-3.
Nicholls, S. et al. (2023). The Challenge in Test Cricket Performance Following the Introduction of T20 Cricket: Implications for Tactical Strategy. Sports Innovation Journal, 1: 1-16 (https://www.researchgate.net/publication/368191232).
Oborne, P. (2014). Wounded Tiger: A History of Cricket in Pakistan. Simon & Schuster, London, p. 592.
Perera, S. (2000). "Cricket, with a Plot": Nationalism, Cricket and Diasporic Identities. Journal of Australian Studies and Australian Cultural History. Special Joint Issue, 65: 14-26.
Perry, R. (2000) Captain Australia. A History of Celebrated Captains of Australian Test Cricket. Random House Australia. p. 393.
Phillipson, N. (1978). The Jubilee Test Series 1977: England vs. Australia. Pelham Books, London. p. 80.
Piesse, K. (2013a). Century No. 16: Doug Walters -242. In: Ferriday, P. and Wilson, D. (Eds.) Masterly Batting: 100 Great Test Centuries. Von Krumm Publishers, U.K.
Piesse, K. (2013b). Century No. 17: Doug Walters – 104. In: Ferriday, P. and Wilson, D. (Eds.) Masterly Batting: 100 Great Test Centuries. Von Krumm Publishers, U.K.
Pollard, J. (Ed.) (1968). Cricket The Australian Way. Newnes Books, The Hamlyn Publishing Co., Middlesex. p. 197.
Pollard, J. (1992). The Complete Illustrated History of Australian Cricket. Penguin Books Australia Ltd., Ringwood, Victoria, Australia. p. 843.
Pollard, J. (1995). A Complete Record of Australian Cricket Tours – Home and Away. Australian Broadcasting Corp. (ABC Books), Sydney, NSW. p. 293.
Rajan, A. (2011). Twirlymen: The Unlikely History of Cricket's Greatest Spin Bowlers. Yellow Jersey Press, p. 400.
Richards, V. (1991). Hitting Across the Line. Pan McMillan Australia, Sydney. p. 288.
Rippon, A. (1982). Classic Moments of The Ashes. J. M. Dent Pty Ltd., Melbourne & Sydney. p. 160.
Roberts, M. and Alfred, J. (Eds.) (2008). Crosscurrents, Walla Walla Press, Sydney, p. 168.
Roberts, M. (1998a). 'Controversies: The SL Cricket Team's 1995/96 Tour of Australia'. In: Michael Roberts and Alfred James (Eds.) Crosscurrents, Walla Walla Press, Sydney, pp. 112–123.
Roberts, M. (1998b). 'Fundamentalism in Cricket: Crucifying Muralitharan'. In: Michael Roberts and Alfred James (Eds.) Crosscurrents, Walla Walla Press, Sydney, pp. 124–125.
Roberts, M. (1998c). 'Avoiding Lanka: Australia and the World Cup'. In: Michael Roberts and Alfred James (Eds.) Crosscurrents, Walla Walla Press, Sydney, pp. 131–142.
Roberts, M. (2008). 'Landmarks and Threads in the Cricketing Universe of Sri Lanka'. Gemmell, Jon and Majumdar, Boria (Eds.) Cricket, Race and the 2007 World Cup. Routledge, London & New York, pp. 110-132.

Ryan, C. (2009). Golden Boy: Kim Hughes and the Bad Old Days of Australian Cricket. Allen & Unwin, p. 438.

Sandiford, K. A. P. (1982). Cricket and the Victorians: A Historiographical Essay. Historical Reflections, 9(3): 421–36 (http://www.jstor.org/stable/41298796).

Sexton, M. (2017). Chappell's Last Stand. Affirm Press, Melbourne, p. 232.

Sheahan, P. (1979). Ian Chappell – The Man Behind the Myth. Cricketer, Vol. 7(2), November 1979, pp. 25-27.

Simpson, B. (1966). Captain's Story. Marlin Books, 30-32, Cremorne Street, Victoria, 3121. p. 173.

Smith, R. (1996). Great Days in Test Cricket. Australian Broadcasting Corporation (ABC Books), Sydney, p. 231.

Sobers, G. (2002). Garry Sobers: My Autobiography. Headline Book Publishing, London, p. 471.

Stevenson, M. (1978). Illy: A Biography of Ray Illingworth. Midas Books, Tunbridge Wells, Kent, U.K. p. 135.

Tendulkar, S. (2014). Playing It My Way: My Autobiography. Hodder & Stoughton, U.K. p. 351.

Thomson, A.A. (166). 'Cricketers of My Time: G.L. Jessop, The Most Furious of All Hitters'. *The Cricketer*, December, 47(17): 10-11.

Tyson, F. (1975). Test of Nerves: Test Series 1974-75 Australia versus England. Manark Pty Ltd., p. 256.

Tyson, F. (1977). The Centenary Test. The Australian Cricket Board Publication, p. 63.

Tyson, F. (1997). 'Sledging' – Curse of the Modern Game. *The Cricketer*, July 1997. pp. 8-9.

Wagg, S. (2008). 'To Be an Englishman': Nation, Ethnicity and English Cricket in the Global Age. Gemmell, Jon and Majumdar, Boria (Eds.) Cricket, Race and the 2007 World Cup. Routledge, London, pp. 1-22.

Walters, D. (1971). Looking For Runs. Pelham Books, London, p. 175.

Walters, D. (1988). One for the Road. Swan Publishing, Milsons Point, NSW.

Walters, D. & Waugh, M. (1999). The Entertainers. Random House Australia. Milsons Point, NSW. p. 270.

Warner, P. F. (1935). Some Personalities of the Game. In: Moult, T. (Ed.) Bat and Ball. Chapter 2 (pp. 175-183). Magna Books, U.K.

Wells, B. (1969). 'The Strength behind Sobers' Calm'. *The Cricketer* (UK), 5 September, p. 25.

Willis, R. (1982). A Spark in the Ashes. *The Cricketer*, August 1982. p. 31.

Woodcock, J. (1968a). 'It's First Blood to the Australians'. *The Cricketer* (UK), 28 June, pp. 14-15.

Woodcock, J. (1968b). 'Frustration: That's the Word for 200th Test'. *The Cricketer* (UK), 12 July, pp. 2-3.

Yallop, G. (1979). Lambs to the Slaughter. Outback Press, Melbourne, Victoria. p. 175.

Other Sources - Internet Articles and Websites

ACB (2000). Australian Cricket Board – ACB announces 2000-2001 contracted players list (https://www.espncricinfo.com/story/acb-announces-2000-2001-contracted-players-list-90680).

Aldred, T. (2016). 'The Waste of Cricket'. ESPN Cricinfo: The Cricket Monthly, (https://www.thecricketmonthly.com/story/999431/tanya-aldred-on-cricket-s-impact-on-the-environment).

Arlott, J. (1975). 'Cricket's Most Versatile Performer: Sir Garfield Sobers'. *Wisden* Almanack (https://www.espncricinfo.com/*Wisden*almanack/content/story/152526.html).

Ashdown, J. (2016). 'All out at Lord's: streaker Michael Angelow paints memorable Ashes scene'. The Guardian. 6 Aug. (https://www.theguardian.com/sport/2016/aug/02/lords-streaker-michael-angelow-ashes-1975).

Australian Cricket Hall of Fame (2022). https://www.mcg.org.au/the-stadium/mcg-history/cricket/Australian-cricket-hall-of-fame.

Bagchi, R. (2013). '20 Great Ashes Moments – No 15 David Steele 1975'. The Guardian, 17 June (https://www.theguardian.com/sport/blog/2013/jun/17/ashes-20-great-moments-david-steele).

BBC (2003a). BBC Cricket: 'Aussie Board Raps Players'. 13 May (http://news.bbc.co.uk/sport1/hi/cricket/wi_v_aus_2003/3022973.stm).

BBC (2003b). BBC Cricket: 'Buchanan Issues Warning'. 15 July (http://news.bbc.co.uk/sport1/hi/cricket/3066811.stm).

Bailey, T. (1973). 'Keeper of the Ashes: Ray Illingworth, C.B.E.' *Wisden* Almanack (https://www.espncricinfo.com/*Wisden*almanack/content/story/152468.html).

Becca, T. (2010. 'Lean, Mean, Pace Machines'. ESPN Cricinfo, 12 July (https://www.espncricinfo.com/story/west-indies-all-time-xi-fast-bowling-shortlist-466820).

Blofeld, H. (1970). West Indies in Australia, 1968-69. *Wisden* Almanack Archives (https://www.espncricinfo.com/*Wisden*almanack/content/story/152424.html).

Blofeld, H. (1974). Australia in West Indies, 1972-73. *Wisden* Almanack, 15 April (https://www.espncricinfo.com/story/australia-in-west-indies-1972-73-152519).

Brettig, D. (2021). 'Australian Spin Great Ashley Mallett dies'. 29 Oct., Sydney Morning Herald (https://www.smh.com.au/sport/cricket/australian-spin-great-ashley-Mallettt-dies-20211029-p594hs.html).

Brettig, D. and Gollapudi, N. (2012). 'You need to change the way the batter plays'. ESPN Cricinfo. 9 Feb. (https://www.espncricinfo.com/story/tony-greig-mark-waugh-and-brian-close-on-fielding-close-in-552553).

Brittenden, R.T. (1981). The West Indians in New Zealand, 1979-80. *Wisden* Almanack Archives (https://www.espncricinfo.com/*Wisden*almanack/content/story/153587.html).

Cardus, N. (1968a). 'Jessop would have cut them to Ribbons'. *The Cricketer*, 9 August. p. 9.

Cardus, N. (1968b). 'The Modern Golden Age. From 1948 to 1968'. *Wisden* Almanack Archives (https://www.espncricinfo.com/*Wisden*almanack/content/story/152385.html).

Chappell, I. (2009). 'Talking on the Field Doesn't Make You Tough'. Interviewed by Simon Lister, 13 August, ESPN Cricinfo (https://www.espncricinfo.com/story/talking-on-the-field-doesn-t-make-you-tough-419169).

Chappell, I. (2011). 'Keith Miller was my sporting idol, a war hero, a sharp thinker and the best captain Australia never had'. Sydney Morning Herald, 26 Oct. (https://www.smh.com.au/sport/cricket/keith-miller-20111025-1mi2s.html).

Chappell, I. (2015). Match That Changed My Life: 'Captain Hook'. The Cricket Monthly, ESPN Cricinfo, June 2015 (https://www.thecricketmonthly.com/story/871281/ian-chappell-on-the-match-that-changed-his-life).

Chappell, I. (2016). 'That Eccentric Summer of '75'. ESPN Cricinfo. 7 Aug. (https://www.espncricinfo.com/story/ian-chappell-recalls-the-eccentric-english-summer-of-1975-1043261).

Chappell, I. (2019). Jeff Thomson: 'The most lethal bowler I've seen'. *Wisden* Almanack. 16 Aug. (https://*Wisden*.com/almanack/jeff-thomson-leathal-pacer-almanack-ian-chappell).

Chappell, I. (2020). 'Every Cricket Team needs a Dressing-room Pest'. ESPN Cricinfo. 5 July (https://www.espncricinfo.com/story/every-cricket-team-needs-a-dressing-room-pest-1226204).

Chappell, I. (2021). 'Ashley Mallett, my Courageous, Brilliant teammate! Mid-Day, 2 Nov. (https://www.mid-day.com/sports/cricket/article/ashley-Mallettt-my-courageous-brilliant-teammate-23199160).

Chappell, I. (2022). 'We need a Debate on Cricket's future, and we needed it Yesterday'. ESPN Cricinfo. 31 July (https://www.espncricinfo.com/story/ian-chappell-we-need-a-debate-on-cricket).

Chappell, I. (2023). 'Is it already too late to sort out the balance of cricket's formats?'. ESPN Cricinfo, 23 August (https://www.espncricinfo.com/story/ian-chappell-is-it-already-too-late-to-sort-out-the-balance-of-cricket-s-formats-1373672).

Compton, D. (1968). 'Batters Must Hit the Ball Again'. *Wisden* Almanack. (https://www.espncricinfo.com/*Wisden*almanack/content/story/152380.html).

Conn, M. (2024). 'Australia, England lobby ICC for increased payments to help save Test cricket'. Sydney Morning Herald, 14 March (https://www.smh.com.au/sport/cricket/australia-england-lobby-icc-for-increased-payments-to-help-save-test-cricket-20240313-p5fc4j.html).

Cozier, T. (2015). 'Ninety years of Everton Weekes'. ESPN Cricinfo, 26 Feb. (https://www.espncricinfo.com/story/tony-cozier-ninety-years-of-everton-weekes-839157).

Craddock, R. (2022). Cricket Legends – Interview of Ian Chappell, 3 May (https://www.youtube.com/watch?v=g43Jgi3d4T4).

Crutcher, M. (2002). 'No sledging as Bill Brown turns 90'. ESPN Cricinfo. 31 July (https://www.espncricinfo.com/story/no-sledging-as-bill-brown-turns-90-117274).

Cricket Australia (2023). Our History (https://www.cricketaustralia.com.au/about/our-history).

De Silva, B. (2000). Sri Lanka's young outstation talent impresses Doug Walters'. ESPN Cricinfo. 20 Apr. (https://www.espncricinfo.com/story/sri-lanka-s-young-outstation-talent-impresses-doug-walters-84482).

De Silva, A. C. (2012). Clive Inman – world record for fastest 50 in 8 minutes! Sunday Observer (Sri Lanka). 27 May (http://archives.sundayobserver.lk/2012/05/27/spo11.asp).

English, P. (2013). 'David Warner's behaviour exposes a worrying lack of Australia leadership'. The Guardian, 16 June (https://www.theguardian.com/sport/2013/jun/15/david-warner-australia-lack-of-leadership).

ESPN Cricinfo (1967). Essay: 'Some dates in Indian Cricket History'. 15 Apr. (https://www.espncricinfo.com/story/some-dates-in-indian-cricket-history-152361).

ESPN Cricinfo (1977). West Indies in Australia, 1975-76 (https://www.espncricinfo.com/*Wisden*almanack/content/story/153010.html).

ESPN Cricinfo (1995). 'Fred Bennett Dies'. 27 Jan. (https://www.espncricinfo.com/story/bennett-dies-27jan95-71902).

ESPN Cricinfo (1998). 'Waugh, Warne speak on bookies scandal: 9 December 1998' (https://www.espncricinfo.com/story/waugh-warne-speak-on-bookies-scandal-9-december-1998-75165).

ESPN Cricinfo (2000). 'How the match-fixing drama unfolded'. 13 Nov. (https://www.espncricinfo.com/story/how-the-match-fixing-drama-unfolded-part-10-91958).

ESPN Cricinfo (2005). 'Warne and Hughes Call for Bangladesh Dumping'. 31 May (https://www.espncricinfo.com/story/warne-and-hughes-call-for-bangladesh-dumping-210188).

ESPN Cricinfo (2006). 'South Africa complain of more Racial Abuse'. (https://www.espncricinfo.com/story/south-africa-complain-of-more-racial-abuse-231664).

ESPN Cricinfo (2009). World XI in Australia, Nov 1971/Feb 1972 (http://static.espncricinfo.com/db/ARCHIVE/1970S/1971-72/WORLD-XI_IN_AUS/).

ESPN Cricinfo (2010). 'Lawry and McKenzie gain places in Hall of Fame'. 14 February (https://www.espncricinfo.com/story/lawry-and-mckenzie-gain-places-in-hall-of-fame-448134).

ESPN Cricinfo (2011). Match of My Life: Glenn Turner-Beating Big Brother. 18 July (https://www.espncricinfo.com/story/2000-tests-glenn-turner-on-new-zealand-s-first-test-win-over-australia-in-1974-523639).

ESPN Cricinfo (2013a). 'Clarke fined by ICC over Anderson sledge'. 25 Nov. (https://www.espncricinfo.com/story/clarke-fined-by-icc-over-anderson-sledge-692367).

ESPN Cricinfo (2013b). 'The Cronje chronicles'. 22 July (https://www.espncricinfo.com/story/a-timeline-of-the-hansie-cronje-match-fixing-scandal-654219).

ESPN Cricinfo (2024a). Records for Test Matches: Hundred in each inning of a match (https://www.espncricinfo.com/records/hundred-in-each-innings-of-a-match-282951).

ESPN Cricinfo (2024b). Records for Test Matches: Carrying bat through a completed innings (https://www.espncricinfo.com/records/carrying-bat-through-a-completed-innings-283149).

ESPN Cricinfo (2024c). Records for Test Matches: Longest Careers (https://www.espncricinfo.com/records/longest-careers-283451).

ESPN Cricinfo (2024d). Records for Test Matches: Most Runs in a Series (https://www.espncricinfo.com/records/most-runs-in-a-series-282849).

ESPN Cricinfo (2024e). Cricket Records for Australia in Test matches (https://www.espncricinfo.com/records/team/batting-most-runs-career/australia-2/test-matches-1).

ESPN Cricinfo Pakistan (2009). Justice Qayyum's Report (https://i.imgci.com/link_to_database/NATIONAL/PAK/NEWS/qayyumreport/qayyum_report.html).

Frith, D. (2010). 'Hero, headliner, heartthrob' ESPN Cricinfo, 17 Oct (https://www.espncricinfo.com/story/david-frith-on-keith-miller-482217).

Frith, D. (2012). Tony Greig – Obituary, 31 Dec. (https://www.theguardian.com/sport/2012/dec/30/tony-greig).

Frith, D. (2015). Richie Benaud – Obituary, 10 April (https://www.theguardian.com/sport/2015/apr/10/richie-benaud-obituary).

Gavaskar, S. (2003). Spirit of Cricket – The Colin Cowdrey Lecture, Lord's, 29 July, ESPN Cricinfo (https://www.espncricinfo.com/story/the-colin-cowdrey-lecture-by-sunil-gavaskar-129197).

Hadlee, W. (1982). 'The escalating effects of politics on cricket'. *Wisden* Almanack Archives. 28 Nov. (https://www.espncricinfo.com/*Wisden*almanack/content/story/152205.html).

Harris, D. (2016). 'When Gordon Greenidge unleashed hell on Australia'. The Guardian, 8 Jan. (https://www.theguardian.com/sport/blog/2016/jan/08/west-indian-epic-when-gordon-greenidge-unleashed-hell-on-australia).

Hartman, R. (2005). 'When They Were Kings'. ESPN Cricinfo, 29 Dec. (https://www.espncricinfo.com/story/when-they-were-kings-231051).

Hayter, R. (2019). 'Keith Miller: Anything but dull'. *Wisden*. 28 Nov. (https://*Wisden*.com/almanack/keith-miller-australia-all-rounder-anything-but-dull-almanack).

Holland, J. (2020). 'How the 1945 Victory Tests rekindled cricket's competitive spark'. *Wisden*, 19 Nov. (https://*Wisden*.com/stories/how-the-1945-victory-tests-rekindled-crickets-competitive-spark).

Hopps, D. (2000). 'Malik banned for life as Pakistan blows the whistle'. The Guardian, 25 May (https://www.theguardian.com/sport/2000/may/25/cricket).

ICC (2017). The ICC Code of Ethics. p. 25 [updated, Nov. 2020] (https://www.icc-cricket.com/about/integrity/ethics/code-of-ethics).

ICC (2023). History: 1909 – 1963 – Imperial Cricket Conference (https://www.icc-cricket.com/about/the-icc/history-of-icc/1909-1963).

ICC (2024). Members (https://www.icc-cricket.com/about/members).

James, S. (2013). 'How Beyond A Boundary broke down the barriers of Race, Class and the Empire'. The Guardian. 3 Apr. (https://www.theguardian.com/commentisfree/2013/apr/02/beyond-a-boundary-broke-cricket-barriers).

John, E. (2021). 'Chirp war: India also win escalating swearing contest with England'. The Guardian, 17 Aug. (https://www.theguardian.com/sport/2021/Aug/16/chirp-war-india-also-win-escalating-swearing-contest-with-england).

Kalra, G. (2016). Interview: Ian Chappell. The Cricket Monthly, 3 Sep. (https://www.thecricketmonthly.com/story/1052513/ia).

Kimber, J. (2019). 'The Ugly Australian: The Evolution of a Cricket Species'. The Cricket Monthly, ESPN Cricinfo, 25 Apr. (https://www.thecricketmonthly.com/story/1181098/t).

Laha, S. (2022). 'India's 'Sunny' days'. Hindustan Times (https://www.hindustantimes.com/75th-independence-day/cricket/india-s-sunny-days).

Lamb, S. (2003). 'Lehmann charged under ICC's Code of Conduct'. ESPN Cricinfo, 16 Jan. (https://www.espncricinfo.com/story/lehmann-charged-under-icc-s-code-of-conduct-127873).

Lane, T. (2017). 'Australia's Sledging Culture Needs to be Addressed'. Sydney Morning Herald, 9 Dec. (https://www.smh.com.au/sport/cricket/australias-sledging-culture-needs-to-be-addressed-20171209-h01quw.html).

Liew, J. (2018). 'The Denis Compton legacy: The first superstar of cricket's television age', *Wisden*, 23 May (https://*Wisden*.com/stories/features/the-legacy-of-denis-compton).

Lister, S. (2016). 'When Death Whispered'. ESPN The Cricket Monthly, Jan. 2016 (https://www.thecricketmonthly.com/story/953181/simon-lister-on-michael-holding-s-14-wickets-at-the-oval-1976).

Malcolm, A. (2009). 'Burnished and tarnished: Kim Hughes could have been a hero but fell short. Christian Ryan has the story'. ESPN Cricinfo. 8 March (https://www.espncricinfo.com/story/burnished-and-tarnished-393637).

Mallett, A. (2005). 'Do you want to press charges against a Mr. Jeff Thomson?'. ESPN Cricinfo. 9 Feb. (https://www.espncricinfo.com/story/ashley-Mallett-on-jeff-thomson-s-fearsome-spell-against-sri-lanka-at-the-1975-world-cup-826971).

Mallett, A. (2014). 'The swashbuckling flight lieutenant'. ESPN Cricinfo, 3 Nov. (https://www.espncricinfo.com/story/ashley-Mallett-on-keith-miller-the-swashbuckling-flight-lieutenant-794473).

Marks, V. (2015). Obituary: 'Brian Close- funny, generous, a wee bit mad and awesomely brave'. The Guardian. 15 Sep. (https://www.theguardian.com/sport/blog/2015/sep/14/brian-close-dies-somerset-yorkshire-botham-richards-vic-marks).

Mason, P. (2021). Ray Illingworth Obituary. The Guardian, 21 Dec. (https://www.theguardian.com/sport/2021/dec/26/raymond-illingworth-obituary).

McGlashan, A. (2019). 'It's going to be a bit of bodyline this series' – Tim Paine. ESPN Cricinfo, 15 Dec. (https://www.espncricinfo.com/story/it-s-going-to-be-a-bit-of-bodyline-this-series-tim-paine-1210182).

Melford, M. (1969). 'The D'Oliveira Case: Cancellation of South African Tour, 1969'. *Wisden* Almanack Archives (https://www.espncricinfo.com/*Wisden*almanack/content/story/152399.html).

Military History (2013). 'War Culture: Cricket in WWII'. Military History, 20 Dec. (https://www.military-history.org/feature/war-culture-cricket-in-wwii.htm).

Mitchell, K. (2003). 'Darren's Disgrace'. The Guardian, 19 Jan. (https://www.theguardian.com/sport/2003/jan/19/cricket.comment).

Monga, S. (2011). 'Shivlal Yadav returns to familiar battleground'. ESPN Cricinfo, 24 Dec. (https://www.espncricinfo.com/story/shivlal-yadav-returns-to-familiar-battleground-546793).

Moorehouse, G. (1998). 'W.G. Grace: 150 Years On'. ESPN Cricinfo, 15 April (https://www.espncricinfo.com/story/w-g-grace-150-years-on-151913).

Mossop, B. (1981). 'Umpires Appeal Lillee Case'. Sydney Morning Herald. 18 Nov. page 62 (https://fairfaxmedia.newspapers.com/newspage/122729486/).

Nicholas, M. (2020). 'The King and I'. ESPN Cricinfo, The Cricket Monthly, 10 April (https://www.thecricketmonthly.com/story/1220406/the-king-and-i).

Nicholas, M. (2022). 'Cricket is changing, but not for the worse'. ESPN Cricinfo, 10 Oct. (https://www.espncricinfo.com/story/mark-nicholas-cricket-is-changing).

Nicholas, M. (2023). 'My Life through the Ashes: from *Deadly Derek* to Stoke's Boys'. ESPN Cricinfo, 12 June (https://www.espncricinfo.com/story/my-life-through-the-ashes-from-deadly-derek-through-warnie-to-stokes-boys-1381073).

O'Reilly, B. (1979). 'Sportsmanship given a terrible hiding'. The Sydney Morning Herald. 16 Feb. (https://news.google.com/newspapers?id=6Z9WAAAAIBAJ&dq=sledging&pg=2751,4288214).

Polack, J. (2000). A Definitive Overview of Cricket Match-Fixing, Betting and Corruption Allegations. ESPN Cricinfo, 10 May (https://www.espncricinfo.com/story/a-definitive-overview-of-cricket-match-fixing-betting-and-corruption-allegations-90877).

Preston, N. (1951). West Indies in England 1950. *Wisden* Almanack Archive (https://www.espncricinfo.com/*Wisden*almanack/content/story/155259.html).

Preston, N. (1969). Australians in England, 1968. *Wisden* Almanack Archive (https://www.espncricinfo.com/*Wisden*almanack/content/story/150223.html).

Preston, N. (1972). 'Spirit of Cricket'. Notes by the Editor. *Wisden* Almanac Archive (https://www.espncricinfo.com/*Wisden*almanack/content/story/152465.html).

Preston, N. (1973a). Australians in England, 1972. *Wisden* Almanack Archive (https://www.espncricinfo.com/*Wisden*almanack/content/story/152472.html).

Preston, N. (1973b). 'Serious decline in English batsmanship, 1973'. Notes by the Editor. *Wisden* Almanack Archive (https://www.espncricinfo.com/*Wisden*almanack/content/story/152471.html).

Preston, N. (1975). 'Home Alone'. Notes by the Editor. *Wisden* Almanack Archive (https://www.espncricinfo.com/*Wisden*almanack/content/story/154892.html).

Preston, N. (1976a). The Prudential World Cup Final, 1975: Australia v. West Indies. *Wisden* Almanack Archive (https://www.espncricinfo.com/*Wisden*-almanack/content/story/150279.html).

Preston, N. (1976b). The Australians in England, 1975. *Wisden* Almanack Archives.

O'Connell, R. (2018). 'From tapping coconuts with a pencil to 4K coverage: The history of cricket broadcasting in Australia'. The ROAR, 13 Oct.

Raghavan, K. N. (2018). 'Doug Walters – The Ultimate Cool Customer'. Onmanorama, 12 April.

Raghavan, K. N. (2022). 'Legacy of Indian Royalty in Cricket'. Onmanorama, 19 Sep.

Rajesh, K. (2011). Neutral Umpires, ESPN Cricinfo, 16 April.

Roebuck, P. (1984). 'Why the captain lay down and cried'. [First published in The Sunday Times, Dec. 1984].

Roebuck, P. (2007). 'The Aussie Way'. ESPN Cricinfo, 19 Dec.

Roebuck, P. (2008). 'Arrogant Ponting must be fired'. Sydney Morning Herald, 8 Jan.

Ross, G. (1976). 'The Greatest Centenary of them all!'. *Wisden* Almanack Archives.

Rutnagur, D. (1982). The Indians in Australia and New Zealand, 1980-81. *Wisden* Almanack Archives.

Ryder, R. (1975). 'Gilbert Jessop- the most exciting cricketer of them all'. *Wisden* Almanack Archives.

Sambandan, V. S. (2006). 'When Ceylon Ruled the Airwaves'. The Hindu. 1 January.

Samyal, S. K. (2022). 'Gavaskar riled by Aussies'. Hindustan Times (https://www.hindustantimes.com/75th-independence-day/cricket/gavaskar-riled-by-aussies).

Selvey, M. (2010). Turning Points: 'Lloyd's Pace Quartet'. ESPN Cricinfo, 25 July.
Selvey, M. (2012). 'Tony Greig – Showman, salesman, Charismatic Leader and Cricketing Great'. The Guardian. 31 Dec.
Selvey, M. (2013). 'Fifty years ago, the very first Gillette Cup changed cricket forever'. The Guardian. 1 May.
Sengupta, A. (2014). 'Commentators in Cricket History- 1: Alan McGilvray – Voice of the Game in Australia'. Cricket Country, 14 Sept.
Sengupta, A. (2015). 'Kim Hughes clashes against Lillee, Chappell and Marsh'. CricMASH, 15 Jan.
Sengupta, A. (2016). 'Bapu Nadkarni bowls 21.5 overs without conceding a run! Cricket Country, 8 Jan.
Shafqat, S. (2011). 'It All Began in Sydney'. ESPN Cricinfo, 17 Dec.).
Singh, K. (2022). 'Ian Chappell defied 'Ugly Australian' Myth'. The Print, 26 Sept.
SMH (2005). 'Bangladesh must go, says Benaud'. Sydney Morning Herald, 31 May.
Smyth, R. (2011). 'Kim Hughes: the golden boy whose career was a glorious kind of tragedy'. The Guardian, 14 Sept.
Sports Australia Hall of Fame. Keith Miller MBE, OA.
Sports Australia Hall of Fame. Doug Walters, MBE, OA.
Steen, R. (2001). '500-1: The day England defied the Odds'. The Guardian, 13 August.
Steen, R. (2014). 'How the World Cup came to be'. ESPN Cricinfo, 5 Nov.
Sunday Times, Sri Lanka (2002). Appreciations: Fitzroy De Mel: Cricketer and Actor, 24 March (https://www.sundaytimes.lk/020324/plus2.html#2LABEL4).
Sundaresan, P. N. (1971). Australians in Ceylon and India, 1969-70. *Wisden* Almanack Archives.
Taufel, S. (2013). Spirit of Cricket – The Colin Cowdrey Lecture, Lord's, 24 July. The Guardian, 25 July (https://www.theguardian.com/sport/2013/jul/24/simon-taufel-spirit-cricket).
The Age (1998). 'Warne, Mark Waugh took bookie's cash, 9 Dec. (https://www.theage.com.au/sport/cricket/warne-mark-waugh-took-bookies-cash-19981209-gdtz28.html).
The Age (2003). 'Howzat for style? Cleaning up cricket's bad-boy image'. 11 Oct.
The Ashes Bail (2019). Website: https://www.ashesbail.com.au/love-story.
The Canberra Times (1981). 'Hogg Bowls Himself into Trouble'. 10 May (https://trove.nla.gov.au/newspaper/article/125632967).
The Guardian (2000). 'The Scandal Breaks: The World Reacts'. 13 June (https://www.theguardian.com/sport/2000/jun/12/cricket9).
The Guardian (2012). From the Archive: 'D'Oliveira left out of England cricket tour of apartheid South Africa'. 29 Aug. 1968.
Tiruchelvam, N. (2013). 'When the Lankans won a 'Test' in India'. ESPN Cricinfo, 13 Aug.
Tuberville, Huw (2021). Ashes Chronicles–Part 6: Air Travel Spooks England in 1965/66 (https://www.thecricketer.com/Topics/ashes/ashes_chronicles_part_6_air_travel_spooks_england_1965_66_.html).
Ugra, S. (2015). Advance Australia Diverse. The Cricket Monthly. January.
Ugra, S. (2018). 'The problem with the Australian Line of Control'. ESPN Cricinfo, 8 March (https://www.espncricinfo.com/story/sharda-ugra-the-problem-with-the-australian-line-of-control-1139310).
Walters, D. (2022). Profile, Biography and Statistics. ESPN Cricinfo (https://www.espncricinfo.com/player/doug-walters-8151).
Wellings, E. M. (1967). M.C.C. Team in Australia and New Zealand, 1965-66. *Wisden* Almanack Archive.

Wellings, E. M. (1972). M.C.C. in Australia and New Zealand, 1970-71. *Wisden* Almanack Archive.
Wijesinghe, M. (2008). Sri Lanka Cricket – At The High Table. p. 123 [Book published by Mahinda Wijesinghe, Battaramulla, Sri Lanka).
Wilkins, P. (1972). 'Walters Answers His Critics With A Chanceless 159', Sydney Morning Herald, 6 Dec. (quoted by A. Mallett, 2008, p. 330).
Wilkins, P. (1974). Pakistan in Australia, 1972-73. *Wisden* Almanack Archive.
Wilkins, P. (1978). Pakistan in Australia, 1976-77. *Wisden* Almanack Archive.
Williamson, M. (2005a). ICC: A Brief History, ESPN Cricinfo, 18 May.
Williamson, M. (2005a). 'When people power sunk South Africa'. ESPN Cricinfo, 30 Sep.
Williamson, M. (2006). 'The sublime Sobers'. ESPN Cricinfo, 7 Oct.
Williamson, M. (2007). 'Who Is Grovelling Now'. ESPN Cricinfo, 18 May.
Williamson, M. (2010). 'One of the most undignified incidents in Test history'. ESPN Cricinfo, 10 Nov.
Williamson, M. (2011). 'Underhand, Underarm'. ESPN Cricinfo. 29 Jan.
Williamson, M. (2012). 'The Birth of a Nation'. ESPN Cricinfo. 24 March.
Williamson, M. (2013). 'Overexposed at Lord's'. ESPN Cricinfo. 20 July.
Williamson, M. (2014). 'Shell-shocked and Bloodied'. ESPN Cricinfo. 10 Oct.
Williamson, M. (2015a). 'A Victory for Cricket: Within days of World War II ending, England and Australia were meeting at Lord's'. ESPN Cricinfo. 1 May.
Williamson, M. (2015b). 'The fungus that floored the Aussies'. ESPN Cricinfo, 25 July.
Williamson, M. (2015c). 'Facing Holding with a little thin towel'. ESPN Cricinfo, 19 Sep.
Wisden (1965a). Australia in India and Pakistan, 1964-65 *Wisden* Almanack Archives.
Wisden (1965b). 'Neville Cardus: Thousands more enjoying the game through his writing'. *Wisden* Almanack Archive.
Wisden (1975a). New Zealand in Australia, 1973-74. *Wisden* Almanack Archives.
Wisden (1975b). Australia in New Zealand, 1973-74. *Wisden* Almanack Archives.
Wisden (1976). The Prudential World Cup, 1975 *Wisden* Almanack Archives.
Wisden (1977). West Indies in England, 1976). *Wisden* Almanack Archives.
Wisden (2018). 'The unrufflable Mike Denness: Ashes inferno, Kent's golden years and umpiring controversy'. *Wisden* Almanack Archives. 1 Dec.
Wisden (2019a). 'Denis Compton: Much more than a cricketer' – Almanack Tribute. *Wisden* Almanack Archives, 23 April.
Wisden (2019b). 'Keith Miller: The Golden Nugget'. *Wisden* Almanack Archives. 11 Oct.
Wisden (2020a). 'Ian Chappell: The players' player who turned Australia into legitimate winners'. *Wisden* Almanack Archives, 26 Sept.
Wisden (2020b). *Wisden* Cricketers of the Year. *Wisden* Almanack. 26 Jan.
Wooldridge, I. (2019). 'Garry Sobers: Cricketers of the Century Tribute'. *Wisden* Almanack, 28 July.
Wu, A. (2019). 'Australian camp questions legality of New Zealand's 'negative' bowling'. Sydney Morning Herald, 19 Dec.

INDEX

A

Abbas, Zaheer 59, 147, 149, 153, 164, 166, 168, 221, 222, 223
ABC 17, 20, 45, 47, 49, 63, 75, 76, 77, 78, 80, 81, 83, 84, 86, 115, 151, 155, 193, 210, 219, 227, 234, 248, 258, 272, 285, 330, 331, 332, 333
Aboriginal Australian team 228
Adelaide 2, 12, 22, 23, 35, 36, 84, 87, 88, 106, 109, 139, 142, 152, 153, 165, 166, 181, 190, 199, 218, 220, 222, 250, 254, 271, 284, 292, 328
Adelaide Oval 22, 35, 139, 152, 153, 165, 181, 199, 222, 250
Agnew, J. 56, 280, 330
Ahmad, Saeed 166
Akram, Wasim 295
Alaganan, Balu 117
Alam, Intikhab 147, 149, 151, 152, 153, 164, 165, 166, 167, 168, 169, 225
Aldred, Tanya 298, 333
Ali, Abid 118
Ali, Inshan 173, 175
Ali, Talat 165
Allan Border Medal Ceremonies 318
Allan, Peter 13, 14, 19, 22
Allen, David 20, 21, 25, 73
Allison, Lincoln 37, 330
Altaf, Salim 165, 167, 222
Amaranath, Lala 118
Ambrose, Curtley 218, 263, 283
Ames, Lesley 199
Amiss, Dennis 93, 192, 193, 197, 214, 232
Ananda College 52
Anandarajah, C. 52
Anderson, James 299
Angelow, M. 213, 333
apartheid 100, 112, 125, 131, 146, 277, 339
Arlott 31, 34, 39, 45, 46, 48, 49, 55, 56, 79, 82, 84, 86, 101, 102, 133, 213, 228, 231, 261, 330, 331, 333
Armstrong, W. 318
Arnold, Geoff 156, 161, 188, 193, 198, 200, 206, 211, 281
Ashdown, J. 213, 333
Ashes 2, 13, 16, 23, 25, 27, 32, 33, 4, 39, 61, 63, 64, 66, 72, 73, 74, 75, 77, 81, 85, 90, 92, 93, 94, 95, 96, 98, 99, 101, 132, 133, 134, 135, 142, 144, 145, 147, 154, 156, 159, 161, 163, 164, 170, 187, 188, 189, 190, 191, 192, 193, 198, 199, 200, 201, 210, 211, 213, 215, 218, 227, 228, 229, 234, 238, 239, 254, 257, 269, 286, 293, 296, 297, 299, 307, 310, 311, 321, 332, 333, 334, 338, 339, 340
Associate Members 72, 270
Association of Cricket Umpires (ACU) 47
Association of Cricket Umpires and Scorers in Sri Lanka (ACUSL) 47
Atherton 287
Auckland 186, 290
Australian Board of Control for International Cricket 77, 179
Australian Cricket Board, ACB 64, 77, 91, 112, 122, 123, 124, 130, 147, 152, 201, 226, 227, 228, 241, 242, 243, 245, 248, 271, 273, 274, 285, 292, 294, 302
Australian XI 142, 240, 262, 272

B

Bach 61
Bacher, Ali 126, 128, 130, 282
Bagchi, Rob 200, 210, 334
Baig, Abbas Ali 70, 118
Bailey, Trevor 26, 40, 56, 84, 135, 188, 256, 258, 330, 334
Bailhache, Robin 197, 245
Balakrishnan, C. 113
Bancroft, Cameron 292
Bangladesh 71, 72, 266, 267, 268, 270, 335, 339
Barbados 6, 40, 101, 114, 171
Barber, B. 17, 18, 19, 20, 22, 73, 92, 93
Bardsley, W. 183
Bari, W. 165, 224
Barlow, Eddie 125, 126, 127, 128, 129, 130, 277
Barmy Army 296
Barnes, Alan 201
Barnes, Sid 80
Barrington, K. 17, 18, 19, 20, 22, 23, 24, 39, 62, 63, 66, 73, 90, 93, 95, 210, 305
Basin Reserve in Wellington 183
batsmanship 58, 59, 60
Bazball 277
BBC 45, 58, 63, 78, 84, 86, 90, 92, 154, 202, 206, 210, 213, 216, 235, 240, 272, 279, 285, 291, 334
Becca, T. 218, 334
Bedi 64, 115, 118, 119, 120, 121, 122, 147, 151, 152, 153, 289
Bedser, A. 46, 210, 214
Beethoven 61
Benaud 1, 4, 5, 6, 8, 9, 10, 11, 12, 25, 26, 27, 28, 35, 46, 49, 63, 64, 75, 76, 77, 81, 89, 115, 129, 145, 190, 191, 228, 229, 232, 240, 246, 247, 253, 255, 256, 266, 267, 272, 280, 318, 330, 336, 339
Benaud, John 11, 151, 152, 167, 175, 284
Bennett, Fred 47, 113, 121, 123, 130, 330, 335
Bennett, Jack 80
Benson & Hedges 226, 229, 233
Beyond A Boundary 30, 43
Bhatt, Sikandar 242
Bhutto, Z.A. 169
Big Bash (BBL) 299
Bird 279, 289, 307, 330
Bishop, I. 218
Blackham, John 318
Bligh, Ivo 74, 75, 209
Blofeld 45, 56, 84, 86, 102, 103, 106, 110, 112, 170, 173, 174, 176, 177, 243, 245, 334
Bodyline 143, 163, 189, 258, 307, 312
Boje, Nicky 294
Bolus, B. 66
Bombay 51, 61, 67, 115

Bond, James 76
Boon, D.C. 320
Booth, B. 6, 7, 11, 14, 15, 18, 20, 22, 67, 77, 81
Borde, C. 66, 68, 88, 118, 122
Border 65, 243, 244, 245, 249, 250, 252, 254, 269, 282, 285, 302, 318, 319
Border-Gavaskar Trophy 269
Botham, I. 134, 209, 237, 238, 239, 256, 292, 297, 298, 311
Bothams Series 311
Bourda Grounds, Georgetown 174, 262
Boxing Day 197, 259
Boyce, Keith 173, 174, 175, 204, 205, 220
Boycott 2, 17, 18, 19, 20, 22, 29, 59, 73, 90, 94, 99, 135, 136, 137, 139, 140, 144, 147, 156, 163, 178, 188, 212, 236, 237, 238, 239, 240, 254, 296, 330
Brabourne Stadium 67, 115
Bracewell, John 243
Bradman, Don 1, 5, 8, 9, 10, 11, 13, 16, 17, 18, 20, 21, 26, 28, 29, 37, 42, 48, 49, 59, 60, 77, 80, 81, 84, 88, 89, 108, 110, 122, 123, 140, 142, 143, 147, 149, 150, 151, 178, 179, 183, 195, 202, 216, 229, 232, 244, 255, 256, 257, 258, 262, 269, 280, 284, 301, 314, 315, 318, 319, 320, 321, 322, 326, 330
Brearley 45, 232, 235, 236, 237, 238, 239, 241, 261, 282, 288, 297, 330
Brettig, D. 2, 289, 334
Brisbane 9, 12, 14, 16, 25, 27, 35, 36, 78, 81, 87, 104, 107, 110, 111, 136, 148, 165, 191, 193, 220, 243, 264, 271, 286
Bristol 276
British Empire 45, 278, 319
British Tobacco Company 77
Brittenden 290, 334
Broad, Stuart 299
Brookes, N. 51, 52, 54, 70, 207, 209, 268, 330
Brooks, R.S. 74
Brooks, T. 196, 223, 233
Brown, Bill 107, 284, 335
Brown, David 15, 16, 18, 19, 20, 21, 22, 73, 90, 91, 93, 96
Brown, Freddie 229
Browning, Mark 46, 330
Bryan Bomber Wells 111, 333
Buchanan, John 285

Buddhist 52
Burge, Peter 14, 15, 19, 22, 25, 28, 62, 67, 77
Burgess, Mark 226, 243, 244, 245, 246
Burgher Recreation Club (BRC) 52
Burke, J. 9
Butcher, Basil 33, 40, 102, 104, 105, 106

C

Cairns, Lance 243, 244, 245
Calcutta 67, 119, 304
Calcutta Cricket and Football Club 51
Calypso Style 220
Camacho, Steven 102, 104, 105
Cambridge Blue 69, 169
Captain Hook 334
Cardus, N. 29, 39, 42, 44, 49, 56, 57, 58, 59, 60, 61, 79, 84, 98, 158, 256, 258, 276, 330, 334, 340
Carew, J. 103, 104, 106, 108
Caribbean 31, 33, 34, 38, 40, 44, 49, 50, 51, 52, 65, 71, 80, 81, 83, 84, 90, 101, 165, 167, 169, 170, 192, 205, 219, 220, 256, 258, 262, 272, 278, 283
Cartwright, Tom 91, 100, 112
Catholic schools 53
Cavaliers 102
Centenary Test 228, 234, 240, 333
Ceylon 1, 13, 16, 17, 20, 24, 31, 32, 33, 35, 36, 37, 45, 47, 50, 51, 52, 53, 54, 58, 61, 62, 64, 67, 70, 71, 72, 73, 76, 77, 78, 79, 81, 84, 100, 112, 124, 164, 203, 206, 278, 338, 339
Ceylon Daily News 53, 64, 72, 76
Cfroft, C. 290
Chakrapani, V.M. 117
Chandrasekhar, Bhagwat 67, 68
Chanmugam, D. 207
Chanmugam, N. 113
Chanmugam, Neil 62
Channel Nine TV 145, 210, 227, 235, 240, 242, 247, 272
Chapman, A.P.F. 32, 330
Chappell, Greg 12, 64, 123, 135, 136, 142, 143, 147, 150, 152, 153, 155, 157, 159, 161, 162, 166, 167, 170, 171, 173, 174, 175, 176, 178, 180, 181, 182, 183, 186, 188, 191, 192, 193, 194, 195, 198, 200, 205, 207, 215, 219, 220, 222, 223, 224, 225, 226, 230, 233, 234, 236, 237, 238, 239, 243, 244, 245, 246, 247, 248, 249, 250, 252, 253, 274, 278, 289, 291, 292, 297, 318, 319
Chappell Hadlee 269
Chappell-Hadlee Trophy 269
Chappell, Ian v, vii, viii, 2, 12, 13, 18, 22, 23, 25, 28, 55, 56, 59, 65, 80, 85, 87, 90, 91, 92, 94, 95, 97, 103, 104, 106, 110, 113, 114, 117, 118, 120, 121, 122, 123, 125, 128, 129, 130, 131, 136, 138, 139, 140, 144, 145, 147, 148, 149, 151, 152, 153, 154, 155, 156, 157, 159, 162, 163, 164, 165, 166, 167, 169, 170, 171, 173, 174, 175, 176, 177, 178, 179, 180, 181, 183, 184, 187, 189, 191, 192, 193, 195, 196, 197, 198, 199, 200, 201, 206, 210, 211, 214, 215, 216, 220, 226, 228, 229, 235, 244, 246, 247, 248, 254, 255, 257, 259, 260, 261, 263, 265, 268, 271, 272, 277, 284, 292, 303, 306, 309, 314, 315, 316, 318, 320, 321, 325, 330, 333, 334, 337, 339, 340
Chappell, Trevor 247
Chauhan, C. 250, 252
Chegwyn 4, 5
Christchurch 184, 186, 225, 245, 290, 328
Christian schools 38
Clark, David 142
Clarke, J. 73, 330
Clarke, Lady Janet 74
Clarke, M.J. 286, 319, 336
Clarke, Sir William 75
Clarke, Sylvester 283
Close, Brian 133, 134, 190, 279, 280, 337
Colley, David 146, 155, 159
Collinge, Richard 184, 185
Colombo 17, 29, 31, 47, 50, 51, 52, 53, 58, 70, 72, 81, 97, 113, 164, 203, 209, 270, 288
Colombo Central Railway Station 31
Compton, D. 59, 233, 255, 256, 257, 326, 335, 337, 340
Coney, Jeremy 181, 182, 244, 245, 246

Congdon, Bevan 180, 182, 183, 184, 185, 186, 226
Conn, M. 273, 335
Connolly, A. 12, 14, 77, 89, 91, 92, 94, 95, 97, 105, 106, 107, 109, 116, 118, 120, 124, 126, 128, 138, 144, 145
Connolly, A., 112
Constantine, Learie 33, 37, 43, 44, 50, 59, 60, 256
Corling, Graham 62, 77
Cosier, G. 222, 223, 224, 233, 239
Cowdrey 93
Cowdrey, C. 19, 22, 23, 37, 46, 73, 90, 93, 94, 96, 97, 118, 133, 134, 136, 138, 139, 190, 191, 192, 193, 196, 197, 198, 199, 201, 211, 216, 229, 240, 301, 326, 336, 339
Cowper, B. 14, 15, 19, 21, 22, 23, 25, 28, 62, 67, 77, 87, 91, 92, 93, 94, 95, 96
Cozier, Tony 56, 84, 86, 202, 205, 279, 331
Craddock, Robert 262, 335
Crafter, Tony 242, 292
Craig, Ian 8, 10
Cricket Academy 271
Cricket Australia 286, 293, 335
Cricketer (Australia) 9
Cricket Hall of Fame 49, 145, 146, 318, 334
Croft, C. 218, 283, 290
Crutcher, M. 335
Cumberland Club 6
Cummins, Pat 260, 303
Cunis, B. 147

D

Daily News 73, 113
Davidson, A. 6, 9, 28, 46, 63, 76, 89, 107, 129, 318, 331
Davies, Geoff 284
Da Vinci 61
Davis, Charlie 102, 104, 105
Davis, Ian 184, 223, 231, 237, 239
Days In The Sun 56
Decision Review System (DRS) 309, 310
Dell, Tony 140, 180
De Mel, Fitzroy 47, 113, 339
Denness, M. 188, 198, 199, 200, 201, 206, 210, 211, 216, 229, 340
Derbyshire 155, 238
De Silva, A. C. 335

De Silva, Bandula 269, 335
De Silva, D.S. 207
Dexter, E.R. 46, 62, 63, 72, 75, 76, 77, 84, 94, 229, 258
Dias, Roy 288
Dickens 327
Dilscoop 305
Dilshan, T.M. 305
DOliveira Affair 112, 312
DOliveira, B. 91, 92, 93, 96, 99, 100, 136, 137, 139, 141, 144, 159, 161, 163, 337, 339
DOliveira, B., 92
Doordarshan 272
Doshi, D. 250, 251, 252, 253
Dowe, Uton 171
Duleepsinhji 233
Duncan, Ross 138, 139, 140
Dunedin 289
Dungog vii, viii, 1, 2, 3, 5, 6, 8, 10, 13, 26, 28, 331
Durani, Salim 68
Durrani, Shahid 252
Dutch origin (Burghers) 51
Dymock, Geoff 182, 183, 184, 200
Dyson, John 243, 244, 249, 250

E

Eagan, Jack 257, 331
Eastwood, Ken 140
Eden Park, Auckland 185, 226
Edgar, Bruce 243, 246
Edgbaston 93, 210, 211, 216
Edmonds, Phil 214
Edrich 18, 19, 20, 21, 23, 46, 59, 73, 90, 91, 94, 95, 96, 135, 136, 137, 139, 140, 141, 144, 156, 159, 160, 162, 163, 192, 193, 197, 198, 200, 211, 212, 214, 215
Edrich, Bill 233
Edwards, Reg viii, 7, 8, 11, 26, 27, 64, 99, 162, 175, 331
Edwards, Richard 103, 104, 106
Edwards, Ross 155, 156, 159, 161, 162, 163, 165, 167, 170, 191, 192, 194, 195, 197, 205, 211, 212, 213, 214, 215
Edwards, Wally 191
Einstein 61
Elliot, C. 210
Embury, John 209
Engineer, Farokh 70, 118, 119, 120, 121, 122, 147
English, P. 317, 335
Erasmus, M. 260

ESPN Cricinfo 51, 123, 145, 146, 147, 184, 186, 190, 191, 219, 267, 277, 280, 282, 284, 286, 293, 294, 295, 320, 333, 334, 335, 336, 337, 338, 339, 340

F

Farquharson, K. 281, 331
Favell, Les 262
Fay, Stephen 55, 84, 331
Fernando, Herbert I.K. 62
Fernando, R. 207
Ferriday, Patrick 331, 332
Fingleton 55, 56, 84, 98, 107, 123, 143, 260, 315, 331
Fisher, Barry 6
Fletcher, Keith 93, 94, 95, 136, 139, 195, 198, 199, 200, 209, 211, 214, 232
Forbes Burnham 170, 175
Foster, Maurice 171, 173, 175
Francis, Bruce 157, 159
Frank Worrell Trophy 101, 108, 269
Fraser, Malcolm 247
Freaker 213
Frederick, Norton 62
Fredericks, Roy 104, 106, 109, 171, 174, 175, 176, 220, 280
Fredericks, Roy, 102
Freeman, Eric 89, 94, 104, 105, 106, 108, 112, 120, 127, 128, 134
Freemantle Doctor 36, 149
Frith, D. 18, 49, 74, 75, 88, 137, 138, 196, 199, 209, 229, 237, 238, 248, 280, 331, 336
Fuard, Abu 62
Fusarium Test 159

G

Gabba 35, 78, 87, 107, 136, 148, 191, 218, 243
Galileo 61
Galle Face Hotel 113
Gandotra, A. 118
Ganguly, S. 285, 295
Garner, J. 218, 283
Gatting, Mike 288
Gavaskar, Sunil 59, 99, 147, 149, 152, 153, 178, 191, 243, 249, 250, 251, 252, 253, 269, 306, 326, 336, 338
Gemmell 281, 282, 331, 332, 333
George Parr 228
Ghavri, Karsan 249, 250, 251, 252, 253

Gibbs, Barry viii, 9, 331
Gibbs, Herschelle 294
Gibbs, Lance 33, 46, 102, 104, 105, 106, 108, 170, 171, 172, 173, 174, 175, 194, 220
Giffen, G. 318
Gifford, Norman 160
Gilchrist, Adam 195, 286, 320
Giles, A. 258
Gillet Cup 77
Gillette Cup tournament 205
Gilmour, G. 180, 181, 182, 186, 204, 206, 210, 214, 216, 220, 222, 224, 225, 226, 233
Glamorgan 22, 69
Gleeson 5, 90, 91, 92, 93, 95, 104, 105, 106, 108, 109, 112, 113, 115, 126, 127, 128, 137, 139, 140, 155
Glenelg Cricket Club 284
Globalization 280
Gloucestershire 43, 276
Goddard, T. 12, 128
Gollapudi, N. 289, 334
Gooch, Graham 209, 211, 212, 214
Goodall, Fred 290
Good Days 56
Goonasena, G. 37
Gower, David 209
Grace 37, 43, 44, 59, 61, 228, 233, 256, 258, 305, 337
Graveney, T. 84, 90, 94, 95, 96, 229
Greenidge, Gordon 220, 280, 283, 336
Greig 147, 149, 150, 151, 152, 153, 156, 157, 159, 162, 163, 188, 191, 192, 196, 197, 198, 200, 210, 211, 212, 214, 216, 228, 230, 231, 232, 233, 235, 237, 238, 240, 272, 279, 280, 289, 292, 336, 339
Griffith, Billy 24
Griffith, C. 40, 80, 81, 83, 102, 103, 104, 105, 106, 107, 108, 283, 307, 308
Grimleys 6
Grimmett, Clarrie 155, 318
Groucho Marks 212
Grout, W. 24, 28, 67, 108
Grundig 39, 46, 58, 63, 70, 78, 87, 90, 94, 157, 219
Gubby Allen 21, 142, 229
Guha, S. 118
Gunasekera, C.I. 62
Guyana 174, 177, 262

H

Hadlee, Dayle 181, 183, 184, 186
Hadlee, Richard 181, 182, 184, 226, 243, 244, 245, 246
Hadlee, Walter 268, 269, 336
Haigh, G. 17, 90, 112, 123, 125, 130, 146, 205, 207, 235, 262, 272, 331
Hall of Fame 49, 318, 335, 339
Hall, W. 6, 33, 40, 46, 102, 103, 105, 106, 108, 283, 308
Hamilton 187, 262
Hammet, Major A.W. 27
Hammond, Jeff 146, 155, 169, 171, 174, 176
Hammond, Walter 195, 212, 280, 321
Hampshire 322
Hampshire burr 55
Hampshire, John 139, 161, 214, 307
Haramanis 58
Harmer, Russell 164
Harris, Daniel 283
Hart-Davis, Rupert 330
Hartman, R. 131, 336
Harvey, N. 6, 9, 10, 14, 19, 28, 46, 63, 76, 84, 89, 145, 166, 216, 229, 244, 256, 280, 318, 319
Hassett, L. 12, 27, 84, 88, 179, 229, 318, 320, 321
Hawke, N. 12, 14, 19, 21, 22, 23, 62, 69, 77, 89, 91
Hawkeye 309
Hawkins, Stephen 61
Hayden, M. 195, 319
Hayter, R. 48, 49, 336
Headingley 63, 159, 206, 214, 215, 238, 258
Headley, G. 33, 37, 43, 44, 50, 59, 60, 256, 314
Healy, I. 318
Hendrick, M. 188, 193, 237, 238
Hendricks, J. 106, 108
Heyn, David 113, 164
Higgs, Jim 243, 245, 249
Higgs, Ken 15, 18, 19, 20, 73, 91, 93
Hilditch, A. 242
Hill, Clem 318
Hobbs, Jack 36, 56, 60, 256
Hogg, Rodney 246, 288
Holder, John 307
Holder, Vanburn 171, 204
Holding, M. 218, 220, 279, 283, 290, 331, 340
Holford, David 103, 104

Hollioake, A. 295
Hookes, D. 232, 236, 237, 239
hot spot 309
Howarth, Geoff 243, 244, 245, 246
Howarth, Hedley 226
Huck Finn 284
Hughes, Kim 114, 123, 239, 242, 250, 254, 267, 274, 288, 293, 310, 317, 333, 337, 339
Hunte, C. 33, 40
Hunter Valley of NSW 3
Hurst, A. 182, 242
Hussain, N. 258
Hussey, M.E. 319
Hutchinson and Ross 12, 49, 65, 67, 69, 76, 77, 81, 89, 93, 96, 107, 110, 117, 155, 159, 164, 168, 185, 197, 199, 221, 222, 226, 229, 245, 247, 257, 259, 320, 331
Hutton, L. 46, 48, 59, 133, 190, 210, 229, 233, 258
Hutton, R. 147

I

Ibadulla 69
ICC 71, 72, 107, 114, 164, 206, 208, 235, 248, 259, 266, 267, 268, 270, 273, 281, 282, 286, 290, 296, 299, 307, 308, 335, 336, 337, 340
ICC Code of Conduct 281, 296
Illingworth 2, 91, 93, 94, 95, 132, 133, 134, 135, 136, 137, 139, 140, 141, 142, 144, 154, 156, 158, 160, 161, 162, 163, 188, 275, 333, 334, 337
Imperial Cricket Conference (ICC) 71
India 27, 28, 30, 31, 33, 36, 37, 39, 40, 45, 46, 50, 51, 64, 66, 67, 68, 69, 70, 71, 72, 87, 88, 89, 107, 112, 114, 115, 116, 117, 118, 119, 120, 121, 122, 123, 124, 126, 133, 134, 146, 158, 177, 179, 188, 203, 209, 219, 241, 242, 243, 249, 250, 251, 252, 253, 254, 258, 259, 267, 269, 270, 272, 278, 286, 289, 292, 294, 295, 296, 298, 304, 306, 307, 317, 322, 330, 337, 339, 340
Indian Premier League (IPL) 124, 299, 304, 311, 312
Inman, Clive 37, 335
Insole, Doug 100

International Cricket Conference 71
International Cricket Council 72
Inverarity 95, 97, 104, 155, 156
Iqbal, Asif 69, 164, 167, 221, 222, 223, 224, 225, 291, 306
Irvine, Jock 134
Irvine, Lee 125, 126, 128, 130

J

Jadeja, Ravindra 260
Jaisimha, M.L. 88
Jamaica 50, 81, 114, 170, 175, 177
James, Alfred 332
James, C.L.R. 30, 31, 38, 41, 43, 44, 45, 50, 52, 54, 56, 58, 59, 111, 142, 276, 313, 314, 330, 331
James, Selma 31, 50, 336
Jardine, D. 133, 142, 143, 163
Jarman, B. 66, 67, 90, 91, 94, 95, 100, 106, 111
Jayasinghe, S. 37
Jenner, Terry 2, 135, 140, 141, 152, 167, 171, 174, 175, 192, 193, 196, 197, 199, 265
Jessop 29, 37, 39, 59, 60, 275, 276, 333, 334, 338
Johannesburg 124, 125, 127
John -bookmaker 294
John, Emma 285, 337
Johnson, Brian 45, 79, 84, 86
Johnson, Ian 9, 27, 49, 229
Johnson, Mel 292
Johnson, Mitchell 286
Jones, I.J. 19, 20, 21, 22, 73
Jordan, R. 134
Jubilee Test match 236
Julien, Bernard 204
Jumadeen, R. 175

K

Kaduru Bola 40
Kaduwa 58
Kallicharran, Alvin 171, 174, 175, 176, 220
Kalra, G. 262, 337
Kaluperuma, L. 207
Kalu-Suddhas 53
Kampmark, B. 268, 270, 331
Kandy 113
Kanhai, Rohan 33, 46, 102, 104, 105, 106, 109, 147, 148, 149, 170, 171, 174, 175, 176, 177, 204

Kapil 249, 250, 251, 253
Karachi 51, 69, 221, 292, 295
Kardar, Abdul Hafeez 169, 225
Kensington Oval, Bridgetown 171
Kent 32, 69, 91, 94, 155, 188, 199, 212, 340
Kent, Martin 246
Khan, Ayub 112
Khan, Imran 168, 221, 222, 223, 224, 283, 292, 306, 331
Khan, Majid 59, 69, 164, 166, 167, 168, 169, 221, 222, 223
Khetrapal, Ashim 295
Kimber, Jarrod 287, 302, 337
Kingston 177
Kipling 45
Kippax, A. 80
Kippax Lake 5
Kirby, Prudence 111
Kirmani 249, 250
Kline, L. 108
Knight, Barry 19, 20, 23, 62, 73, 93, 269
Knott 2, 90, 96, 136, 147, 157, 161, 163, 192, 194, 195, 197, 198, 199, 211, 212, 213, 214, 215, 232, 233, 237, 238
Koertzen, Rudy 295
Kohli, Virat 29, 285
Kripal Singh, A.G. 118
Kruger, Garnett 282
Kultur (cultured) 58
Kynaston, David 55, 84, 331

L

Laha, S. 337
Lahore 51, 225, 307
Laker, Jim 46, 84, 158, 189, 216
Lamb, S. 281, 337
Lancashire 20, 102, 170, 212
Lancaster Park, Christchurch 182, 183
Lance, T. 277
Lane, Tim 287, 302, 337
Langer, J.L. 320
Lara, B. 29, 195
Larter, D. 73
Larwood, H. 142
Latif, R. 295
Lawry, Bill 11, 12, 13, 14, 15, 16, 18, 19, 21, 22, 23, 24, 25, 28, 39, 59, 62, 66, 67, 68, 76, 77, 80, 81, 87, 89, 90, 91, 92, 93, 94, 95, 96, 97, 98, 103, 104, 105, 106, 107, 108, 109, 110, 112, 113, 114, 115, 116, 117, 118, 119, 120, 122, 123, 124, 125, 126, 127, 129, 130, 131, 134, 136, 137, 138, 139, 140, 143, 144, 145, 153, 154, 155, 179, 216, 229, 244, 246, 256, 257, 259, 265, 272, 276, 307, 318, 320, 331, 335
Laws of Cricket 72, 287
Lawson, Geoff 243, 244, 269
Lees, W. 245
Leeward Islands (Nevis) 171
Lehmann, Darren 293, 337
Leicestershire 37
Lentil (Lens esculenta) 41
Lever, John 230, 237, 289, 292
Lever, Peter 137, 139, 188, 193, 199, 200, 214
Lewis, Chris 295
Leyland, Maurice 233
Lieversz, Darrell 62
Liew, J. 256, 337
Lillee 39, 64, 85, 131, 135, 139, 141, 143, 146, 148, 149, 150, 152, 155, 156, 157, 158, 159, 160, 161, 162, 163, 164, 165, 166, 167, 168, 169, 171, 176, 177, 188, 189, 190, 191, 192, 194, 196, 197, 198, 199, 200, 201, 204, 205, 207, 210, 211, 212, 215, 216, 217, 218, 219, 220, 221, 222, 223, 224, 225, 226, 231, 232, 233, 234, 235, 243, 244, 245, 246, 247, 249, 250, 251, 252, 253, 254, 256, 257, 273, 274, 278, 288, 291, 292, 293, 297, 308, 310, 311, 318, 338, 339
Lillywhite, James 229
Lindsay, Denis 127, 128
Lindwall, Ray 27, 28, 46, 48, 59, 246, 283, 318
Lister, S. 123, 216, 279, 334, 337
Lloyd 29, 33, 59, 98, 102, 103, 104, 105, 106, 108, 109, 111, 147, 149, 154, 170, 173, 174, 175, 176, 177, 202, 204, 205, 217, 219, 220, 261, 272, 279, 281, 283, 289, 290, 308, 331, 339
Lloyd, David 193, 196, 197
Lock, Tony 2, 46, 156, 158, 189
London Evening Standard 17
London Times 159, 276
Looking for Runs 1, 2, 115, 124
Lords 36, 55, 71, 72, 75, 92, 157, 158, 177, 191, 199, 203, 211, 212, 213, 236, 240, 332, 333, 336, 339, 340
Lord, Thomas 36

Loxton, Sam 145, 166, 216
Luckhurst, Brian 135, 136, 137, 139, 141, 159, 163, 193, 196

M

Macartney, C. 318
M. A. Chidambaram Stadium 66
Mackay, Ken 63
Maddocks 235
Madras 51, 66, 121, 172, 289, 292
Madugalle, Ranjan 209, 288
Mailey, Arthur 190
Majumdar, Boria 331, 332, 333
Malay 51
Malcolm, A. 311, 337
Malik, S. 295
Mallett viii, 2, 3, 4, 5, 6, 13, 14, 15, 17, 18, 26, 27, 28, 46, 49, 96, 97, 99, 104, 105, 110, 112, 113, 115, 116, 117, 118, 119, 120, 121, 122, 123, 126, 127, 129, 130, 134, 137, 138, 139, 140, 152, 153, 155, 160, 161, 165, 166, 167, 169, 176, 178, 179, 181, 185, 186, 187, 189, 193, 194, 195, 196, 197, 198, 199, 200, 201, 206, 207, 208, 210, 211, 212, 213, 214, 215, 216, 218, 219, 245, 254, 255, 263, 264, 271, 291, 299, 314, 315, 331, 332, 334, 337, 340
Manjrekar, V. 67
Mankad 107, 242
Mankad, A. 115, 119
Mankad, V. 107
Manley, M. 38, 50, 151, 153, 170, 174, 175, 176, 332
Marjoribanks, T. 281, 331
Marks, Lyn 7
Marks, V. 134, 337
Marsh 64, 135, 136, 137, 138, 139, 143, 148, 149, 152, 155, 156, 157, 159, 162, 163, 165, 166, 170, 171, 175, 176, 182, 184, 185, 186, 192, 194, 197, 198, 199, 211, 214, 216, 222, 224, 230, 232, 233, 236, 237, 238, 239, 243, 244, 246, 249, 253, 254, 257, 273, 274, 291, 293, 310, 318, 332, 339
Marshall, M. 218, 283
Martin, Johnny 11, 62
Marylebone Cricket Club 32, 240, 332
Masood, Asif 147, 165, 223

Massie 146, 153, 155, 156, 157, 158, 165
Mayne, Laurie 127, 128
May, P. 46, 75, 84, 229, 258
May, Tim 295
MBE 206, 319, 339
MCC 7, 13, 24, 26, 32, 36, 43, 55, 72, 73, 75, 142, 143, 152, 188, 190, 240, 326, 332
McCabe, S. 8, 11, 318
McCormick, Ernie 269
McCosker 198, 200, 201, 207, 210, 211, 213, 214, 215, 216, 222, 223, 226, 230, 231, 232, 237, 238, 239
MCC Spirit of Cricket Cowdrey Lecture 190, 326
McCullum, Brendon 277
McDonald, C. 9
MCG 12, 16, 19, 23, 39, 87, 89, 104, 137, 138, 149, 166, 180, 197, 199, 201, 220, 221, 222, 223, 229, 234, 242, 244, 246, 251, 252, 254, 259, 282, 315
McGilvray 7, 9, 10, 25, 45, 46, 47, 55, 56, 78, 79, 80, 81, 82, 83, 84, 85, 86, 115, 123, 124, 125, 130, 135, 142, 144, 145, 146, 147, 150, 153, 158, 159, 160, 170, 173, 174, 176, 179, 191, 260, 273, 274, 292, 297, 301, 302, 308, 310, 311, 314, 321, 323, 332, 339
McGlashan, Andrew 260, 337
McGlew, Jackie 127
McKenzie 12, 14, 18, 19, 22, 23, 28, 66, 67, 68, 69, 77, 89, 90, 91, 95, 104, 105, 106, 109, 112, 113, 115, 118, 120, 124, 126, 127, 128, 134, 136, 137, 138, 145, 149, 155, 308, 318, 335
Meckiff, I. 108
Melbourne 23, 27, 35, 36, 39, 74, 75, 88, 104, 111, 118, 132, 137, 138, 147, 149, 151, 167, 168, 170, 197, 199, 201, 227, 228, 229, 240, 242, 244, 246, 251, 253, 260, 318, 329, 332, 333
Melbourne Cricket Grounds 39
Melford, M. 100, 337
Mendis, D. 207, 208
Miandad, Javed 59, 221, 222, 224, 225, 291, 292
Middlesex 32, 235, 332
Milburn, C. 93, 100
Military History 321, 337

Miller 9, 27, 28, 37, 44, 47, 48, 49, 50, 55, 59, 81, 82, 84, 109, 123, 130, 179, 247, 256, 257, 260, 277, 283, 318, 320, 334, 336, 339, 340
minnows 267, 270
Mitchell, K. 281, 337
Mohammad, H. 31, 37, 69
Mohammad, M. 164, 166, 167, 169, 221, 222, 242, 305
Mohammad, Sadiq 164, 166, 221, 223
Monga, Sidharth 251, 337
Montego Bay 177
Moorehouse, G. 44, 337
Morphy, Florence 75
Morris, Arthur 27, 183, 318
Morrison, John 181, 182, 183
Mossop, B. 292, 338
Moss, P. 92, 332
Moult, T. 32, 36, 43, 56, 330, 333
Mozart 61
Muldoon, Robert 247
Mullagh 229
Multiculturalism 280
Muralitharan, Muttiah 281, 305, 332
Murdoch, Rupert 16
Murray, Derryk 171, 290
Murray, John 73

N

Nadkarni, Bapu 66, 67, 68, 252, 339
Nairobi, Kenya 125
National Service Lottery 26
National Servicemen Duty 26
National Stadium 69
native Ceylonese 53
Nawaz, S. 167, 221, 222, 223, 224, 242
Nazar, Mudassar 223, 291
Neeley, Don 186
Newlands, Cape Town 126, 277, 292
Newton 61
New Zealand 10, 38, 71, 72, 114, 127, 131, 147, 169, 179, 180, 181, 182, 183, 184, 186, 201, 203, 225, 226, 241, 243, 244, 245, 246, 247, 248, 258, 259, 260, 262, 267, 268, 269, 270, 281, 289, 296, 298, 317, 322, 328, 334, 338, 339, 340
Nicholas, Mark 159, 190, 193, 322, 338

Nicholls 299, 332
Noble, Monty 80, 105, 318
Northamptonshire 93, 212
Northern Districts 187, 262
Nottinghamshire 37, 102, 111, 230
NSW Colts 2, 5, 9, 12
NSW Country XI 4
NSW State 2, 4, 5, 7, 10, 12, 83, 156
Ntini, Makhaya 282
Nurse, Seymour 33, 40, 102, 105, 108, 109
NZ Board of Control 290

O

Oborne, Peter 168, 169, 332
Ockerism 296
OConnell, Max 139
OConnell, Ronan 80, 227, 272, 338
ODI 177, 203, 210, 246, 247, 277, 281, 292, 297, 303
OKeeffe 135, 140, 165, 167, 174, 181, 182, 186, 222, 223, 226, 231, 233, 237
Old, C. 188, 196, 211, 214
Old Trafford 62, 63, 64, 90, 91, 93, 98, 156, 158, 237, 283, 322
One-Day Internationals 77
ONeill 6, 8, 9, 11, 17, 19, 26, 28, 62, 66, 67, 77, 81, 107, 256, 307, 326
Opatha, T. 207
Order of Australia 319
OReilly 5, 17, 28, 55, 56, 82, 84, 123, 179, 260, 282, 318, 338
Outschoorn, L. 37
Oxford University 225, 331

P

Packer 64, 65, 145, 210, 216, 227, 235, 239, 240, 241, 242, 255, 262, 272, 273, 274, 280, 303, 310, 312, 317, 331
Paine, T. 260, 293, 337
Pakistan 31, 33, 37, 51, 66, 69, 70, 71, 72, 112, 114, 133, 146, 147, 164, 165, 166, 167, 168, 169, 188, 203, 208, 219, 221, 222, 223, 224, 225, 226, 258, 267, 270, 280, 288, 291, 294, 295, 298, 307, 332, 336, 340
Panadura 1, 31, 36, 39, 41, 52, 78, 151
Panadura Sports Club 39

Pan, Shambhu 116
Pant, Rishabh 260
Parfitt, Peter 73, 160, 161
Parish, Bob 91, 242
Parker, John 181, 182, 243, 245, 246, 290
Parkinson 49
Parks, Jim 18, 19, 22, 23, 62, 73
Parramatta 5, 110
Pascoe, Len 236, 237, 238, 239, 243, 245, 249, 250, 251
Pataudi, Nawab of 31, 37, 66, 67, 68, 70, 88, 115, 118, 121, 122, 306
Pataudi, Nawab of Snr. 233
Patterson, P. 218
Perera, Suvendrini 52, 332
Perry, Roland 8, 12, 65, 76, 332
Perth ix, 2, 24, 35, 65, 73, 136, 137, 143, 148, 149, 156, 165, 178, 193, 195, 218, 220, 242, 244, 274, 275, 276, 282, 288, 291, 297, 315
Phillipson, N. 235, 332
Philpott, Peter 11, 18, 22, 269
Pieris, M. 207
Piesse, Ken 108, 109, 110, 186, 332
Pietersen, K. 305
Plaskett, Alan 309
Pocock, P. 92
Polack, John 295, 338
Pollard, J. 28, 75, 143, 229, 320, 332
Pollock, G. 12, 29, 59, 126, 127, 128, 130, 153
Pollock, P. 125, 126, 128, 130, 147, 150
Pollock, Shaun 282
Polonnowita, Anuruddha 62
Ponniah, M. 62
Ponsford, Bill 20, 318
Ponting, Ricky 286, 319, 338
Port-of-Spain 176, 315
Prasanna, Erapalli 115, 117, 118, 119, 120, 121, 122, 172
Preston, Norman 50, 90, 94, 97, 98, 141, 154, 155, 158, 161, 162, 163, 200, 204, 210, 211, 215, 216, 285, 302, 338
Prideaux, R. 94
Prince, Ashwell 282
Prior, W. 218
Procter, Mike 125, 126, 127, 128, 130, 147, 266, 286, 308
Prudential World Cup 202, 210, 338, 340

P. Saravanamuttu Stadium 62, 70, 209, 288
Puri, D. 116

Q

Qasim, I. 222, 223, 225
Qayyum, M.M. 294, 295, 296, 336
Queen Elizabeth 236
Queensland 5, 6, 9, 13, 66, 119, 138, 140, 146, 165, 182, 188, 218, 328, 329
Queens Park Oval 173, 175, 194

R

RAAF 27, 28, 49
Radio Australia 221
Radio Ceylon 58, 64
Radio France Internationale 78
Raghavan, K.N. 88, 338
Rajan, A. 189, 332
Ramaswamy, V.K. 307
Rana, Shakoor 288
Ranasinghe, Anura 207
Ranatunga, Arjuna 209, 285
Randall, D. 230, 233, 234, 236, 237, 238, 289
Randalls Match 230
Randwick 4, 199, 284
Ranjitsinhji 37, 61, 233
Rashid, Haroon 224
Redman, Caroline Joy 28
Redpath 14, 15, 77, 84, 89, 93, 94, 95, 97, 105, 106, 107, 109, 114, 115, 118, 121, 122, 126, 127, 128, 130, 131, 136, 137, 138, 140, 144, 155, 166, 167, 170, 171, 173, 174, 176, 183, 184, 186, 187, 191, 192, 197, 198, 199, 200, 220, 257, 263
Reid, Buddy 62
Reid, John 180
Renneberg, Dave 89
Reporter, Piloo 307
Rest of the World XI 102, 147
Richards, Barry 29, 59, 125, 126, 127, 128, 129, 147
Richardson, Richie 308
Richardson, V. 65, 80, 82, 85, 143, 261
Richards, Viv 29, 33, 59, 65, 134, 202, 204, 205, 220, 221, 266, 278, 279, 280, 283, 289, 297, 298, 302, 306, 308, 322, 332

Ridings, Phil
145, 166, 216, 248
Rigby, Paul 189
Rippon, A. 98, 332
Roberts, Andy
217, 218, 220, 279, 283
Roberts, Michael
51, 54, 70, 204, 268, 332
Robinson, Richie 239
Rodrigo, Lasantha 62
Roebuck 34, 55, 56, 217, 269, 286, 302, 310, 311, 338
Roope, Graham 215, 238
Ross, Gordon 228, 235, 338
Rothmans 6, 187, 264, 265
Rowan, Lou 136, 141
Rowe, Lawrence 171, 174, 220
Royal Australian Airforce (RAAF) 49
Run Digger (1966) 68
Russell, E. 73
Rutnagur, D. 250, 253, 254, 338
Ryan, Christian
274, 288, 293, 311, 333, 337
Ryder, Jack 13, 89, 216, 229
Ryder, R. 275, 276, 338

S

Sabina Park, Kingston 81, 170
Sambandan, V.S. 64, 338
Samyal, S.K. 253, 338
Sandiford, Keith A.P. 37, 333
Sandpaper 260
Sandpapergate 292
Sardesai, Dilip 68, 70, 118, 122
SCG viii, 4, 5, 6, 7, 12, 20, 22, 35, 39, 87, 89, 105, 108, 132, 137, 140, 165, 167, 168, 169, 181, 189, 198, 199, 221, 224, 225, 249, 254, 282, 286, 318
Selvey, Mike
77, 240, 280, 283, 339
Sengupta, Arunabha
66, 311, 339
Sergeant, Craig 236, 239
Setalvad, Anant 117
Sexton, Michael 262, 333
Shafqat, Saad
221, 224, 225, 339
Sharma, Y. 250
Sheahan 10, 11, 28, 87, 90, 91, 92, 93, 94, 95, 97, 98, 104, 105, 106, 107, 114, 117, 118, 120, 122, 127, 128, 129, 130, 144, 154, 155, 160, 162, 163, 166, 167, 260, 261, 333

Sheffield Shield 6, 7, 9, 10, 11, 13, 26, 101, 134, 156, 165, 201, 218, 219, 254, 261, 285, 328
Shell Petroleum 77
Shodan, D. 118
Shuja-Ud-Din 223
Simpson, Bob 6, 7, 10, 11, 12, 13, 14, 15, 16, 17, 18, 19, 20, 21, 22, 23, 24, 25, 26, 27, 28, 37, 59, 61, 62, 63, 64, 65, 66, 67, 68, 69, 76, 77, 80, 83, 87, 88, 89, 98, 127, 153, 178, 179, 183, 190, 229, 255, 256, 257, 259, 273, 277, 291, 302, 307, 318, 320, 331, 333
Singer Cup 294
Singh, Hanumant 67, 70, 118
Singh, Harbhajan 286
Singh, Krish 262, 339
Sinhala 53, 70
Sinhalese 40, 41, 51, 58
Sinhalese Sports Club (SSC) 52
Slater, M.J. 320
Smith, Ian 243
Smith, M.J.K. 7, 16, 17, 20, 21, 22, 24, 25, 72, 90, 133, 134, 158, 216, 229, 259
Smith, Rick
74, 135, 143, 275, 333
Smith, S.P.D.
260, 287, 293, 303, 319
Smyth, R. 311, 339
Snow 2, 90, 91, 94, 95, 96, 134, 135, 136, 137, 138, 139, 141, 144, 145, 147, 156, 158, 159, 160, 161, 188, 206, 211, 212, 214, 275, 291, 307, 308
Sobers 12, 29, 30, 33, 34, 37, 40, 46, 49, 59, 90, 99, 101, 102, 103, 104, 105, 106, 107, 108, 109, 111, 133, 146, 147, 148, 149, 150, 151, 152, 153, 170, 175, 177, 178, 219, 261, 264, 277, 280, 300, 308, 309, 314, 326, 331, 333, 340
Solkar, Eknath
118, 119, 120, 121
Solomon, Joe 108
South Africa 10, 12, 27, 48, 71, 72, 100, 112, 123, 124, 125, 126, 127, 128, 130, 131, 133, 134, 146, 147, 179, 217, 260, 262, 273, 277, 279, 280, 281, 292, 293, 295, 298, 312, 322, 335, 339, 340
South African Cricket Association 112, 130

South Australia 2, 7, 9, 101, 135, 153, 165, 218, 219, 228, 241, 261, 262, 284, 328
Spencer, Tom 213
Spirit of Cricket 143, 338
Spofforth, Fred 74, 318
Sport & Pastime 28, 30, 31, 36, 54, 66, 70, 87, 88, 315
Sri Lanka 30, 38, 40, 47, 51, 52, 54, 58, 70, 71, 72, 78, 90, 114, 125, 146, 151, 164, 203, 208, 209, 210, 267, 268, 269, 270, 287, 288, 294, 305, 329, 332, 335, 339
Sri Lanka, 112
Sri Lanka Broadcasting Corporation (SLBC) 206
Sri Sumangala College 52
Stackpole 22, 23, 25, 104, 105, 106, 114, 115, 116, 117, 118, 120, 122, 127, 129, 130, 136, 137, 139, 140, 142, 144, 145, 147, 148, 149, 152, 153, 156, 157, 159, 160, 162, 167, 170, 171, 173, 174, 176, 180, 181, 184, 187, 266, 272
Stainless Steel 216
Statham, B. 214
Steele, D.
212, 213, 214, 215, 334
Steen, Rob 204, 210, 293, 339
Stephenson, H.H. 228
Stevenson, Mike
135, 141, 142, 333
St. Johns Wood 36, 213
Stokes, Ben 195, 277, 299
Stollmeyer, Jeffrey 170
Strychnine tree 41
Strydom, Pieter 294
Subramanya, Venkataraman 88
Sundaresan, P.N.
115, 120, 122, 339
Super Cat 177
Surita, Pearson 46, 117
Surprise Breakfast 265
Surrey 36, 44, 96, 189, 228
Surti, R. 87, 88, 118
Sussex 32, 94, 210, 229
Sutcliffe, Bert 180
Sutcliffe, Herbert 233
Swanton, E.W. 55, 56, 84, 331
Sydney Cricket Ground viii, 35
Sydney Morning Herald 17, 165, 255, 282, 286, 334, 335, 337, 338, 339, 340
Symonds, Andrew 286

348

T

T20 273, 299, 304, 305, 311, 312, 332
Taber 108, 111, 116, 118, 129, 135, 144, 155, 265, 266
Tamil 31, 51, 52, 53, 64, 113
Tamil Tigers (LTTE) 52
Tamil Union 52
Tasker, Norman 6, 46, 83, 316
Taufel, S. 301, 339
Taylor, Bob 147, 209, 297
Taylor, Mark 65, 280, 282, 285, 295, 318, 320
Telligra 3, 101
Tendulkar, Sachin 29, 258, 280, 333
Tennekoon, A. 113, 114, 206, 208
Ten-Pound Poms 83
Test & County Cricket Board (TCCB) 160, 227
The Age 294, 295, 339
The Ashes Bail 75, 339
The Australian 12, 16, 28, 29, 49, 65, 69, 74, 83, 89, 152, 179, 185, 198, 210, 216, 222, 230, 235, 254, 271, 281, 296, 308, 316, 318, 330, 332, 333
The Ballad of the East and West 45
The Butterfly Effect 100
The Canberra Times 288, 339
The Cricketer 36, 54, 92, 111, 126, 282, 314, 331, 332, 333, 334
The English Flag 45
The Golden Nugget 48
The Guardian 50, 294, 333, 334, 335, 336, 337, 339
The Jubilee Test Series 234, 332
The Oval 36, 62, 70, 96, 113, 156, 164, 208, 209, 215, 216, 238, 280, 329
The Ramp 305
The Sportstar 40, 330
Thomas, G. 11, 21, 22, 81, 277
Thomson, A.A. 275, 327, 333
Thomson, Alan 134, 138, 139, 140
Thomson, Jeff 39, 64, 85, 164, 166, 167, 188, 189, 190, 191, 192, 193, 196, 197, 198, 200, 204, 205, 206, 207, 208, 210, 212, 215, 216, 217, 218, 219, 220, 222, 223, 236, 237, 238, 239, 243, 257, 278, 288, 297, 308, 332, 334, 337
Tiruchelvam, N. 70, 339
Tissera, M. 62, 70, 113, 114, 164, 208
Titmus 2, 3, 7, 14, 15, 16, 17, 18, 19, 20, 21, 22, 23, 25, 73, 172, 193, 194, 196, 198
Townsend, Norman 166
Trent Bridge 158, 162, 236, 237, 280
Trimborn, P. 128
Trinidad 114, 170, 172, 173, 175, 176, 194, 288
Trueman 46, 84, 214, 220, 263, 272, 283, 284
Trumble, H. 318
Trumper, V. 29, 37, 59, 60, 178, 195, 256, 318
Tuberville 24, 73, 339
Turner, Alan 207, 210, 211, 214, 222
Turner, Glenn 59, 180, 181, 182, 183, 184, 185, 186, 187, 205, 220, 225, 243, 335
Tyson, Frank 110, 149, 190, 201, 228, 282, 333

U

Ugly Australian 185, 287, 339
Ugra, S. 293, 339
UK Cricket Council 235
underarm ball 246
Underwood 2, 39, 91, 93, 94, 95, 97, 136, 137, 138, 144, 160, 161, 179, 193, 198, 199, 209, 214, 215, 230, 232, 236, 237, 275, 297
Utilitarian 59

V

Vaseline 289, 292
Vengsakar, D. 252
Venkataraghavan 70, 115, 116, 122, 249
Victoria 6, 89, 134, 137, 140, 182, 228, 329, 331, 333
Victorian era 43
Victory Tests 48, 320
Vietnam War 26, 28, 119, 190
Vievers, T. 19, 28, 62, 66, 67, 68, 77
Villiers, A.B. de 195
Viswanath 118, 120, 121, 251, 252
Viswanath, G. 59
Voice of America 78
Vorster, John 100

W

WACA 136, 137, 148, 193, 194, 197, 242, 244, 291
Wadekar, A. 88, 116, 119, 120, 121
Wade, Matthew 259
Wadsworth, Ken 181, 182
Wagg, S. viii, 333
Wagner, Neil 259
Walcott, Clyde 33, 40, 72
Walker, Max 166, 167, 168, 169, 171, 174, 175, 176, 180, 181, 182, 183, 184, 185, 186, 191, 192, 194, 198, 199, 200, 204, 206, 210, 211, 212, 214, 215, 216, 222, 223, 224, 226, 231, 236, 237, 238, 239
Walsh, C. 218, 283, 308
Walters, D. v, vii, viii, ix, 1, 2, 3, 6, 7, 8, 11, 12, 14, 16, 17, 21, 25, 26, 28, 42, 60, 61, 82, 85, 87, 88, 92, 94, 98, 105, 106, 108, 114, 115, 119, 124, 125, 155, 165, 172, 174, 178, 185, 186, 193, 194, 219, 226, 254, 257, 260, 263, 265, 284, 291, 306, 312, 313, 314, 316, 317, 318, 319, 320, 321, 322, 325, 327, 328, 331, 332, 333, 335, 338, 339, 340
Walters, May 3, 4
Walters, Ted 3
Wanderers Stadium 127
Ward, Alan 137
Ward, William 36
Warnapura, Bandula 207, 209
Warne 267, 294, 295, 298, 339
Warner, David 293, 317, 320, 335
Warner, Pelham 36, 43, 56, 333
Watkins, John 167
Watling, B.J. 259
Watson, Graeme 156
Waugh, Evelyn 44
Waugh, Mark 2, 4, 7, 284, 295, 306, 320, 333, 335, 339
Waugh, Steve 285, 318, 319
Wayne, John 76
Weeks, Everton 33, 40, 202
Wellings, E.M. 16, 20, 21, 22, 23, 24, 25, 138, 139, 339
Westaway, Col 6
Western Australia 2, 7, 35, 134, 136, 156, 165, 255, 285
Western Australian Cricket Association (WACA) 136
West Indies 29, 30, 33, 35, 38, 44, 50, 71, 72, 81, 83, 90, 99, 101, 102, 103, 104, 105, 106, 107, 108, 109, 110, 111, 114, 115

, 133, 167, 169, 170, 171, 174, 175, 176, 177, 183, 191, 202, 203, 204, 205, 206, 216, 217, 219, 220, 241, 242, 243, 258, 264, 265, 267, 269, 270, 272, 274, 279, 289, 296, 298, 307, 308, 322, 329, 332, 334, 335, 338, 340
Wettimuny, S. 114, 207, 208
Whatmore, Dav 281
Whispering Death 279, 331
whistlestop tour 73, 112
Whitehead, Rex 252
Whitlam, Gough 170
Wijesinghe, M. 268, 309, 340
Wilkins, Phil 165, 169, 221, 222, 223, 225, 255, 340
Willet, Elquemedo 171, 173
Williamson 71, 72, 146, 159, 188, 189, 192, 193, 201, 209, 213, 247, 248, 279, 280, 291, 292, 321, 340
Williamson, K. 260
Willis 137, 139, 142, 178, 188, 191, 194, 195, 196, 209, 230, 231, 236, 238, 239, 275, 276, 283, 294, 308
Wilson, D. 110, 331, 332
Wisden 16, 21, 25, 31, 36, 48, 54, 56, 66, 67, 90, 94, 97, 106, 112, 115, 122, 135, 139, 141, 154, 156, 162, 163, 169, 173, 179, 180, 181, 182, 183, 185, 186, 188, 200, 204, 206, 209, 210, 211, 215, 216, 217, 219, 220, 228, 245, 248, 255, 256, 262, 276, 285, 290, 291, 302, 333, 334, 335, 336, 337, 338, 339, 340
Wisden Cricketers Almanack 36
Wisden, John 36
Wood, Barry 161, 212
Woodcock, John 92, 96, 133, 333
Woodfull, William 80, 143
Wood, Graeme 243, 244, 246, 249, 250, 254
Wooldridge, Ian 17, 101, 150, 297, 340
Woolley, Frank 56
Woolloongabba 35
Woolmer, B. 212, 213, 214, 215, 236
Worcestershire 37, 183
World War I 298
World War II 9, 27, 48, 78, 298, 320, 340
Worrell, Frank 33, 35, 37, 40, 44, 50, 59, 101, 107, 177
Wright, John 243, 246
WSC 64, 65, 216, 227, 235, 239, 240, 241, 242, 262, 272, 273, 274, 280, 303, 310, 312, 317
Wu, A. 259, 340
Wyatt, B. 229

Y

Yadav, S. 250, 251, 252, 337
Yallop, G. 241, 243, 282, 288, 333
Yardley, B. 250, 253
Yardley, N. 229, 257
Yorkshire 38, 93, 133, 134, 188, 214
Younis, Waqar 295

Z

Zimbabwe 71, 72, 266, 267, 268, 270

www.ingramcontent.com/pod-product-compliance
Lightning Source LLC
Chambersburg PA
CBHW061733070526
44585CB00024B/2648